Sea Bed Mechanics

Ocean Engineering: A Wiley Series

EDITOR:
MICHAEL E. McCORMICK, Ph.D.
U.S. Naval Academy

ASSOCIATE EDITOR:
RAMESWAR BHATTACHARYYA, D. Ingr.
U.S. Naval Academy

Michael E. McCormick	Ocean Engineering Wave Mechanics
John B. Woodward	Marine Gas Turbines
H. O. Berteaux	Buoy Engineering
Clarence S. Clay and Herman Medwin	Acoustical Oceanography: Principles and Applications
F. W. Wheaton	Aquacultural Engineering
Robert M. Sorensen	Basic Coastal Engineering
Rameswar Bhattacharyya	Dynamics of Marine Vehicles
Jerome Williams	Introduction to Marine Pollution Control
Stephen C. Dexter	Handbook of Oceanographic Engineering Materials
John B. Woodward	Low Speed Marine Diesel
J. P. Hooft	Advanced Dynamics of Marine Structures
Owen F. Hughes	Ship Structural Design: A Rationally-Based, Computer-Aided, Optimization Approach
Sv. Aa. Harvald	Resistance and Propulsion of Ships
James F. Wilson	Dynamics of Offshore Structures
J. F. A. Sleath	Sea Bed Mechanics
Joseph M. Bishop	Applied Oceanography

SEA BED
MECHANICS

J. F. A. SLEATH

Cambridge University

A Wiley-Interscience Publication

JOHN WILEY & SONS

New York · Chichester · Brisbane · Toronto · Singapore

Library of Congress Cataloging in Publication Data:

Sleath, J. F. A. (John F. A.), 1939–
  Sea bed mechanics.

  (Ocean engineering, a Wiley series, 0275-8741)
  "A Wiley-Interscience publication."
  Includes index.
    1. Ocean bottom. 2. Ocean currents. 3. Ocean waves.
  4. Ocean engineering. I. Title. II. Series: Ocean
  engineering (John Wiley & Sons)
  GC87.S58 1984   551.46'08   84-2179
  ISBN 0-471-89091-X

SERIES PREFACE

Ocean engineering is both old and new. It is old in that man has concerned himself with special problems in the ocean for thousands of years. Shipbuilding, the prevention of beach erosion, and the construction of offshore structures are just a few of the specialties that have been developed by engineers over the ages. Until recently, however, these efforts tended to be restricted to specific areas. Within the past decade an attempt has been made to coordinate the activities of all technologists in ocean work, calling the entire field "ocean engineering." Here we have its newness.

Ocean Engineering: A Wiley Series has been created to introduce engineers and scientists to the various areas of ocean engineering. Books in this series are so written as to enable engineers and scientists to learn easily the fundamental principles and techniques of a specialty other than their own. The books can also serve as textbooks in advanced undergraduate and introductory graduate courses. The topics to be covered in this series include ocean engineering, wave mechanics, marine corrosion, coastal engineering, the dynamics of marine vehicles, offshore structures, and geotechnical or seafloor engineering. We think that this series fills a great need in the literature of ocean technology.

MICHAEL E. MCCORMICK, EDITOR
RAMESWAR BHATTACHARYYA, ASSOCIATE EDITOR

v

PREFACE

The aim of this book is to study various aspects of the flow near the sea bed: the currents that carry pollutants from one place to another, the dissipation of wave energy, the formation of ripples and dunes, the transport of sediment.

One of the first problems confronting anyone writing a book like this is the question of balance between steady flow and oscillatory flow effects. The sea bed is subjected to the action of both waves and currents but so much more is known about steady flows that it would be easy to devote the entire book to that alone. To avoid this temptation, each chapter except that on sediment properties is split into three parts: one deals with waves alone, one with currents alone, and one with the combined action of waves and currents. If this treatment seems to overemphasize the importance of wave effects, I can only plead that there are already many excellent books dealing with steady flows and their interaction with erodible beds.

A second problem is the interdisciplinary nature of this field. Engineers, geologists, geographers, oceanographers, and earth scientists all have an interest in various aspects of the topics discussed in this book. All have different requirements about the choice and presentation of these topics. Compromise thus is inevitable. I hope, however, that where subjects have been passed over rather quickly there are enough references to background work to allow the interested reader to study the problem in greater detail.

Finally, I should like to thank all authors, societies, institutions, and publishers who have so kindly given permission for the use of figures from their publications.

J. F. A. SLEATH

Cambridge
April 1984

CONTENTS

NOTATION

a orbital amplitude of fluid just outside the boundary layer at the bed

b wave number of gravity waves $(=2\pi/\lambda)$

c phase speed of gravity waves

c_g group velocity of gravity waves

C sediment concentration

$\bar{C}$ value of C averaged over one wave cycle

C_0 value of concentration at the bed

C_y value of concentration at height y above the bed

C_D drag coefficient

C_d drag coefficient in Morison equation

C_f friction factor for steady currents $(=2\tau_0/\rho\bar{U}^2)$

C_L lift coefficient

C_M inertia coefficient in Morison equation

d mean depth of water

d_1 depth of permeable bed

d_2 pipe diameter

d_3 depth of water beneath wave trough

d_b mean depth of water at breakers

D median grain size of the sediment

D_{65} grain size exceeded by 35% by weight of a sample of sediment

D_{90} grain size exceeded by 10% by weight of a sample of sediment

E wave energy

f	Darcy Weisbach friction factor $(=8\tau_0/\rho \bar{U}^2)$; value of f_w as $R\rightarrow\infty$.
f_w	wave friction factor $(=2\hat{\tau}_0/\rho U_\infty^2)$
f_0	vortex shedding frequency
g	acceleration due to gravity
G	shear modulus of elasticity of the bed
h	ripple height
H	wave height (significant wave height if the waves are irregular)
H_0	wave height in deep water
H_b	wave height at breaking
i	$(-1)^{1/2}$
k	wave number of the ripples $(=2\pi/L)$; coefficient of permeability
k_s	roughness length of the bed
K	specific permeability of the bed; Karman constant
l	mixing length of turbulent eddies
L	wave length of the ripples
n	porosity of the bed
p	pressure
P	rate of energy dissipation
$\bar{P}$	mean rate of energy dissipation
q_s	volumetric transport rate of sediment at a given instant
Q_s	time-mean volumetric transport rate of sediment
R	$U_\infty a/\nu$
R_θ	Reynolds number based on momentum thickness
sw	subscript indicating solitary wave
t	time
T	period of oscillation
u	horizontal component of velocity
$\bar{u}$	time-mean value of u
$\bar{u}_{mt}$	mass transport velocity in horizontal direction
u'	fluctuating component of u in a turbulent flow
u_0	value of u just outside oscillatory boundary layer at the bed
u_s	velocity of center of sphere or cylinder relative to fluid velocity at that point in the absence of the sphere or cylinder
$\bar{u}_s$	time-mean value of u_s
u_*	shear velocity at bed $\left[=(\tau_0/\rho)^{1/2}\right]$
$\hat{u}_*$	amplitude of u_*

$\bar{u}_*$	time-mean value of u_*
$\bar{U}$	mean value of u over a vertical
$\bar{U}_1$	value of u outside the boundary layer
U_∞	amplitude of u_0
U_0	amplitude of u_s
v	vertical component of velocity
$\bar{v}_{mt}$	mass transport velocity in vertical direction
v'	fluctuating component of v in a turbulent flow
$\bar{v}$	longshore current at distance x from the shore
V_0	amplitude of v at the bed
$\bar{V}$	mean longshore current
W	Fall velocity; immersed weight of grain of sediment
x, y	distances measured in the horizontal and vertical directions
y_1	thickness of boundary layer
y_0	constant in log-law velocity distribution
α	$(1+i)\beta$; angle between wave crests and shore; angle between current direction and wave crests
β	$(\omega/2v)^{1/2}$
γ	specific weight
δ	thickness of viscous sublayer
ε	eddy viscosity; diffusion coefficient
λ	length of gravity waves
λ_0	wave length in deep water
μ	dynamic viscosity
v	kinematic viscosity
v_1	viscosity of the bed
v_2	Poisson's ratio for the bed
ρ	fluid density
ρ_1	density of the bed
ρ_s	density of the sediment
σ	coefficient of surface tension
τ	shear stress
$\bar{\tau}$	time-mean value of τ
τ_0	shear stress on the bed
τ_c	critical value of τ_0 for initial motion
$\hat{\tau}_0$	amplitude of τ_0

$\bar{\tau}_0$	time-mean value of τ_0
τ_1	Reynolds stress
ψ	Shields parameter $(=\tau_0/(\rho_s-\rho)gD)$
ψ_c	critical value of ψ for initial motion
θ	beach or bed slope
ϕ	angle of repose of the sediment
ω	$2\pi/T$

Sea Bed Mechanics

BASIC WAVE
AND CURRENT THEORY

1.1. INTRODUCTION

The object of this book is to study various aspects of the sea bed boundary layer and the complex interaction between the motion of the fluid and the movement of the sediment making up the bed: the formation of ripples, the dissipation of energy, the transport of sediment. To do this we need to make use of standard results for the velocities and pressures in the fluid above. This chapter briefly summarizes these known results. For reasons of space and because these topics are already well covered in a large number of existing books the derivations and discussions are kept as brief as possible.

Waves Alone

The waves of greatest importance as far as the dynamics of the sea bed are concerned are the *gravity* waves formed by wind action on the water surface. In relatively deep water these *surface* waves are *progressive*. However, near a boundary, *standing* waves caused by reflection of incident progressive waves may be significant. *Edge* waves, both progressive and standing, may also be important near the coast. All of these waves are *periodic*: because they come

1

in groups or steady wave trains it is possible to identify a period of oscillation. In an ideal fluid the only nonperiodic wave of permanent form is the *solitary* wave. In deep water these waves, also called *tsunamis*, are mainly caused by movements of the earth's crust. Although they may produce considerable damage when they reach the coast, they are relatively infrequent. It might be thought that the theory of solitary waves would be of limited importance for the sea bed effects we are considering here. However, as periodic waves move into shallow water their profile becomes progressively more like that of solitary waves. Thus a study of solitary waves is relevant to the dynamics of the nearshore region.

The density of sea water varies by only a small amount from one point to another. The variation that does occur has a negligible effect on the dynamics of surface waves. However, density variations do have a very significant effect on *internal* waves. These waves are seldom of great importance as far as flow near the sea bed is concerned. Consequently, most of this chapter is concerned with surface waves and the study of internal waves is restricted to Section 1.8.

1.2.   WHICH WAVE THEORY?

Because the free-surface boundary condition is nonlinear, most of the available solutions for the velocities and pressures induced by wave action are based on approximations that are valid only over a restricted range of conditions. It is true that an exact solution of the governing equations has been obtained numerically, but this requires very significant computing resources. The various solutions currently available may be grouped as follows:

1. Small-amplitude theory. The first approximation is often referred to as "Airy waves" and higher approximations are usually called "Stokes waves."
2. Shallow-water theory. Included under this heading are "Cnoidal waves" and, as a special case, "solitary waves."
3. Rotational wave theory. The best known example is "Gerstner's" theory, which is also referred to as "trochoidal" theory.
4. Numerical methods. These include the exact solution of Cokelet and the nonexact but somewhat more manageable "stream function" and "vocoidal" theories of Dean and Swart.

The question of which wave theory to use often comes down to a choice between convenience and precision. Numerical solutions are laborious but for relatively steep waves give much better accuracy than other methods. On the other hand, where the wave height is not too large or where only a rough approximation is required small-amplitude or shallow-water theory usually is adequate. Rotational theories are rarely used.

Figure 1.1 shows how the phase speed of the waves varies with depth according to solitary wave theory, cnoidal wave theory, and first-order small-amplitude wave theory. Housley and Taylor (1957) suggested, on the basis of experiments in a wave channel, that the break even between first-order small-amplitude theory and cnoidal theory was given approximately by

$$\frac{H}{d} = 160 \left(\frac{d}{gT^2} \right) \tag{1.1}$$

Unfortunately, cnoidal wave theory is inconvenient to use. Consequently, many engineers prefer to restrict the choice to small-amplitude theory and solitary wave theory. According to Housley and Taylor, the break even between these two theories is approximately

$$\frac{H}{d} = 1600 \left(\frac{d}{gT^2} \right)^{5/4} \tag{1.2}$$

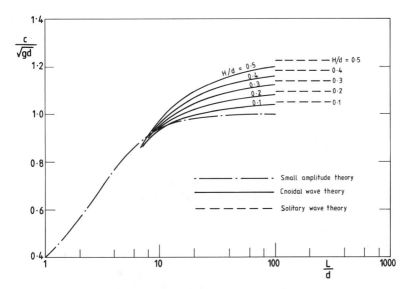

Figure 1.1. The way in which wave speed predicted by different wave theories varies with relative depth (after Housley and Taylor, 1957).

Equations (1.1) and (1.2) are based on measurements of the wave speed. Somewhat different break-even conditions are obtained for other variables. For example, Isaacson (1978) suggested on the basis of a comparison of the mass transport velocity near the bed that cnoidal theory was preferable to small-amplitude theory if

$$\frac{H}{d} > 350 \left(\frac{d}{gT^2}\right)^{3/2} \tag{1.3}$$

These equations are based on comparisons of the lowest order approximation in each case. They do not tell us anything about the relative merits of higher order solutions. Figure 1.2 shows suggested boundaries between the domains of applicability of the various theories. This figure is based on similar plots by Le Mehaute (1976) and Dean (1970) but has been updated to take account of the work by Cokelet (1977). Following Le Mehaute it is suggested that cnoidal theory is preferable to small-amplitude theory for

$$\frac{H\lambda^2}{d^3} > 26 \tag{1.4}$$

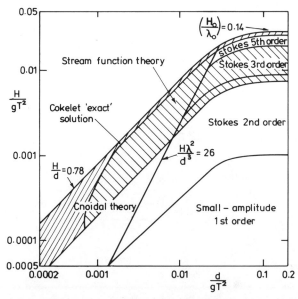

Figure 1.2. Limits of validity of various wave theories (after Dean, 1970, and Le Mehaute, 1976).

Dean (1970) showed that his stream-function theory gave better results than the small-amplitude and shallow-water theories in the shaded region in Fig. 1.2. However, Cokelet's "exact" solution is preferable in the immediate vicinity of the breaking limit and also in very shallow water as indicated. Even the modified version of stream function theory suggested by Chaplin (1980) is not capable of giving accurate results right up to the breaking limit.

1.3. SMALL-AMPLITUDE WAVE THEORY

We consider the case of a steady train of waves of constant height as shown schematically in Fig. 1.3. The bed is horizontal and impermeable and there is no superimposed mean current.

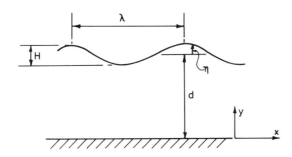

Figure 1.3. Definition sketch for progressive waves.

1.3.1. The Assumptions

The Flow Is Two–Dimensional

If only a single train of waves of constant height and period is being considered this approximation is usually well justified.

The Flow Is Incompressible:

$$\frac{\partial u}{\partial x}+\frac{\partial v}{\partial y}=0 \tag{1.5}$$

For surface waves in water compressibility is almost always entirely negligible.

The Flow Is Irrotational:

$$\frac{\partial u}{\partial y} - \frac{\partial v}{\partial x} = 0 \tag{1.6}$$

Apart from thin boundary layers at the bed and at the free surface, which are approximately a few millimeters thick, viscous effects are usually unimportant for waves alone and consequently the flow may be regarded as irrotational. This assumption would not be well-founded if there were a steady current since, under these circumstances, the vorticity may spread throughout the fluid. However, if the current is relatively weak, the assumption of irrotationality may still be a reasonable approximation.

The Wave Height Is Small Compared with both the Wave Length and the Water Depth

This condition is usually expressed as

$$\frac{H}{\lambda} \ll 1 \tag{1.7}$$

$$\frac{H\lambda^2}{d^3} \ll 1 \tag{1.8}$$

The reason for this restriction is that the nonlinear boundary condition at the free surface is approximated, using Taylor's theorem, by an equivalent condition at the mean water level. This approximation is only reasonable if (1.7) and (1.8) are both satisfied. The parameter $H\lambda^2/d^3$ is called the Ursell parameter.

1.3.2.   The Boundary Conditions

At the bed:

$$v = 0 \tag{1.9}$$

No condition is applied to the horizontal component of velocity u because the possibility of finite u has to be accepted, since the flow is assumed irrotational. In reality, the horizontal component of velocity falls from the value given by the irrotational solution to zero at the bed itself in a thin boundary layer.

At the free surface:

$$\frac{\partial \eta}{\partial t} = v - u \frac{\partial \eta}{dx} \qquad (1.10)$$

$$p = \text{const} \qquad (1.11)$$

In (1.10), η is the height of the free surface, at any given x, above the mean water level. Equation (1.10) expresses the condition that a fluid particle at the free surface remains there. Equation (1.11) is only true if the effects of surface tension may be neglected. This is a reasonable approximation in most situations of importance in engineering, since surface tension is only important for very short waves and periods (typically $\lambda < 0.07$ m and $T < 0.2$ s). Such short waves have little effect on the flow near the sea bed.

1.3.3. First-Order Solution

Combining (1.5) and (1.6) we see that the fluid velocities satisfy Laplace's equation. The first-order solution which satisfies the boundary conditions is

$$\phi = - \frac{\omega H \cosh by \sin(\omega t - bx)}{2b \sinh bd} \qquad (1.12)$$

Here y is measured vertically up from the sea bed. The velocity components are given in terms of the velocity potential ϕ as

$$u = \frac{\partial \phi}{\partial x} \qquad (1.13)$$

$$v = \frac{\partial \phi}{\partial y} \qquad (1.14)$$

The pressure is obtained from the unsteady Bernoulli equation as

$$p = \frac{\rho g H \cosh by \cos(\omega t - bx)}{2 \cosh bd} + \rho g(d - y) \qquad (1.15)$$

Laplace's equation is only a second-order differential equation, which means that only two boundary conditions can be satisfied. The fact that there are three boundary conditions imposes a relationship between wave period and length. This may be written as

$$c = \frac{\omega}{b} = \left(\frac{g}{b} \tanh bd\right)^{1/2} \tag{1.16}$$

If surface tension is taken into account, (1.16) becomes

$$c = \frac{\omega}{b} = \left[\left(\frac{g}{b} + \frac{\sigma b}{\rho}\right) \tanh bd\right]^{1/2} \tag{1.17}$$

Combining (1.12) and (1.13), we see that the horizontal component of velocity at the bed is

$$u_0 = U_\infty \cos(\omega t - bx) \tag{1.18}$$

where

$$U_\infty = \frac{\omega H}{2 \sinh bd} \tag{1.19}$$

Other quantities of interest which may be obtained from this first-order solution are

$$\text{kinetic energy per unit surface area} = \frac{\rho g H^2}{16} \tag{1.20}$$

$$\text{potential energy per unit surface area} = \frac{\rho g H^2}{16} \tag{1.21}$$

Consequently the total wave energy per unit area is

$$E = \frac{\rho g H^2}{8} \tag{1.22}$$

The group velocity, which is the speed at which the energy contained in a small group of waves is carried along, is

$$c_g = \frac{d\omega}{db} = \frac{c}{2}\left(1 + \frac{2bd}{\sinh 2bd}\right) \tag{1.23}$$

Offshore of the first line of breakers the energy dissipation of waves approaching the coast is very small. The flux of energy in the direction of wave propagation can therefore be assumed constant:

$$Ec_g = \text{const} \tag{1.24}$$

Using (1.22) and (1.23), and assuming that the wave period does not change with depth, we obtain

$$\frac{H^2}{b}\left(1 + \frac{2bd}{\sinh 2bd}\right) = \text{const} \tag{1.25}$$

In conjunction with (1.16), this expression allows the change in wave height with depth to be determined.

In addition to energy, waves also transport momentum. The components of the radiation stress, which may be thought of as the momentum flux per unit area due to the waves, obtained from the first-order solution are

$$S_{xx} = \frac{\rho g H^2}{8}\left(\frac{1}{2} + \frac{2bd}{\sinh 2bd}\right) \tag{1.26}$$

in the direction of wave propagation and

$$S_{zz} = \frac{\rho g H^2}{8}\left(\frac{bd}{\sinh 2bd}\right) \tag{1.27}$$

at right angles to the direction of wave propagation.

These expressions for radiation stress may be used to calculate the change in mean water level caused by the flux of momentum in the direction of wave propagation. Offshore of the breaker line waves advancing toward the coast produce a reduction in water level ("set-down") compared with that in deep water

$$\text{wave set-down offshore of breakers} = \frac{H^2 b}{8 \sinh 2bd} \tag{1.28}$$

In the surf zone, that is, between the first line of breakers and the shore, the wave height is quite well represented by

$$H = \alpha d \tag{1.29}$$

where α is a constant. Under these circumstances, there is a rise ("set-up") in mean water level. By taking the level in deep water as the datum it is found that

$$\text{wave set-up in surf zone} = \left(\frac{d_b - d}{1 + \dfrac{8}{3\alpha^2}}\right) - \frac{H_b^2 b}{8 \sinh 2bd_b} \quad (1.30)$$

1.3.4. Second-Order Solution

$$\phi = - \frac{3H^2\omega \cosh 2by \sin 2(\omega t - bx)}{32 \sinh^4 bd} \quad (1.31)$$

$$p = \frac{\rho g H^2 b}{8 \sinh 2bd}\left[\left(\frac{3 \cosh 2by}{\sinh^2 bd} - 1\right)\cos 2(\omega t - bx) + 1 - \cosh 2by\right] \quad (1.32)$$

1.3.5. Standing Waves

Standing waves may be thought of, at least as far as a first-order solution is concerned, as the sum of two progressive wave trains of equal wavelength and frequency traveling in opposite directions. Thus the first-order solution for the velocity potential is

$$\phi = - \frac{\omega H \cosh by}{2b \sinh bd}\sin(\omega t - bx) - \frac{\omega H \cosh by}{2b \sinh bd}\sin(\omega t + bx) \quad (1.33)$$

Therefore,

$$\phi = - \frac{\omega H' \cosh by}{2b \sinh bd}\sin \omega t \cos bx \quad (1.34)$$

where $H' = 2H$ is the crest-to-trough height of the standing waves, which is equal to twice that of the incident progressive waves.

The velocity components are still given by (1.13) and (1.14) so that the horizontal component of velocity at the bed is

$$u = U_\infty \sin \omega t \sin bx \quad (1.35)$$

where

$$U_\infty = \frac{\omega H'}{2 \sinh bd} \quad (1.36)$$

Similarly, the first-order solution for the pressure is

$$p = \frac{\rho g H' \cosh by}{2 \cosh bd} \cos \omega t \cos bx + \rho g(d-y) \tag{1.37}$$

1.4.   SHALLOW WATER THEORY

Once again, results will be quoted only for waves of constant height advancing in water of constant depth.

1.4.1.   The Assumptions

The first three assumptions are the same as for small-amplitude wave theory:

The flow is two-dimensional
The flow is incompressible
The flow is irrotational

Thus (1.5) and (1.6) still apply and the velocity components satisfy Laplace's equation. Only the last of the four assumptions is different:

The wavelength is very long compared with the water depth and the wave height is small compared with the depth

If conditions are only changing very slowly in the direction of wave propagation it would seem probable that the pressure variation would be hydrostatic. Although some investigators have taken this assumption as their starting point, it is clear from higher-order solutions that the pressure is only hydrostatic as a first approximation.

1.4.2.   The Boundary Conditions

The conditions to be satisfied at the bed and at the free surface are the same as those given by (1.9), (1.10) and (1.11).

1.4.3.   Cnoidal Waves

Once again the nonlinear boundary condition, (1.10), has to be solved by successive approximations using Taylor's theorem. The first-order solution for cnoidal waves gives the wave profile (measured vertically up from the

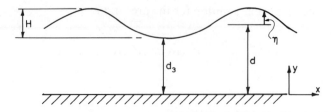

Figure 1.4. Definition sketch for cnoidal waves.

mean water level as shown in Fig. 1.4) as

$$\eta = d_3 - d + H \, \text{cn}^2 \left[2\bar{\bar{K}}(\bar{K}) \left(\frac{x}{\lambda} - \frac{t}{T} \right), \bar{K} \right]$$ (1.38)

where cn is one of the Jacobian elliptic functions (hence the name "cnoidal" for this type of wave), $\bar{\bar{K}}$ is the complete elliptic integral of the first kind, $E(\bar{K})$ is the complete elliptic integral of the second kind

$$\bar{K} = \left(\frac{H}{2d\bar{L} + d - d_3} \right)^{1/2}$$ (1.39)

$\bar{L}$ is given by

$$(2\bar{L}d + d - d_3)E(\bar{K}) = (2\bar{L}d + 2d - H - 2d_3)\bar{\bar{K}}(\bar{K})$$ (1.40)

and d_3 is the height of the wave troughs above the bed.

To a first approximation the pressure is hydrostatic

$$p = \rho g(\eta + d - y)$$ (1.41)

The horizontal component of velocity is

$$u = (gd)^{1/2} \left[-\frac{5}{4} + \frac{3d_3}{2d} - \frac{d_3^2}{4d^2} + \left(\frac{3H}{2d} - \frac{d_3 H}{2d^2} \right) \text{cn}^2(\gamma) \right.$$

$$- \frac{H^2}{4d^2} \text{cn}^4(\gamma) - 8H\bar{\bar{K}}^2(\bar{K}) \left(\frac{d}{3} - \frac{y^2}{2d} \right) \{ -\bar{K}^2 \, \text{sn}^2(\gamma)\text{cn}^2(\gamma)$$ (1.42)

$$\left. + \text{cn}^2(\gamma)\text{dn}^2(\gamma) - \text{sn}^2(\gamma)\text{dn}^2(\gamma) \}/\lambda^2 \right]$$

where

$$\gamma = \left[2\bar{\bar{K}}(\bar{K}) \left(\frac{x}{\lambda} - \frac{t}{T} \right), \ \bar{K} \right]$$

Equally unpleasant expressions are available for other quantities of interest (e.g., Wiegel, 1964). Although tables of elliptic functions are readily available, it is clear that most calculations involving cnoidal waves are likely to be laborious.

1.4.4. Solitary Waves

Solitary waves may be regarded as the limiting case of cnoidal waves for which the wavelength is infinite. Under these circumstances the solution, according to Boussinesq (1872), is

$$\eta = H \operatorname{sech}^2 \left[\left(\frac{3H}{4d^3} \right)^{1/2} (x - ct) \right] \tag{1.43}$$

$$u = \frac{c\eta}{d + \eta} \tag{1.44}$$

$$v = 0 \tag{1.45}$$

$$c = \left[gd \left(1 + \frac{H}{d} \right) \right]^{1/2} \tag{1.46}$$

$$p = \rho g (\eta + d - y) \tag{1.47}$$

$$\text{total potential energy per unit width} = 4\rho g \left(\frac{Hd}{3} \right)^{3/2} \tag{1.48}$$

total kinetic energy per unit width =

$$\frac{2\rho g d^2 (d + H)}{(3H/d)^{1/2}} \left[\frac{H}{d} - \frac{1}{2} \left(\frac{H}{d + H} \right)^{1/2} \ln \frac{(d + H)^{1/2} + H^{1/2}}{(d + H)^{1/2} - H^{1/2}} \right] \tag{1.49}$$

Here η is the height of the free surface above the still water in front of and behind the wave and d is the depth of this still water as shown in Fig. 1.5.

Boussinesq's solution has been shown by various investigators (e.g., Naheer, 1977) to be in close agreement with experimental measurements.

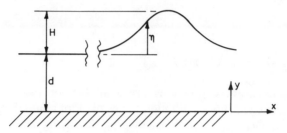

Figure 1.5.   Definition sketch for solitary waves.

1.5.   NUMERICAL SOLUTIONS

All the wave theories discussed so far have been approximate. For many engineering purposes, an approximation may be all that is needed. However, for waves near the breaking limit the prediction provided by the small-amplitude and shallow-water theories becomes very poor. If reasonably accurate results are required for near-breaking waves, it is necessary to make use of some form of numerical solution.

1.5.1.   Exact Solution

Cokelet (1977) obtained an exact numerical solution for the case of a steady train of irrotational waves in water of constant depth.

This solution shows the very interesting result that wave speed and many integral properties of waves do not increase steadily with wave steepness, but have maxima shortly before the limiting steepness is reached. However, Cokelet's work has two disadvantages. First, the numerical procedure is complex and is not readily adapted to engineering purposes. Second, although the solution is exact if the waves are assumed to be irrotational, all real waves show some effect of viscosity. Although these viscous effects are normally very small, they can have a significant influence on other factors, such as the point at which waves propagating over a horizontal bed will break. For this reason, the prediction of real waves may not be significantly better than that provided by one of the other, more convenient, numerical methods.

1.5.2.   Stream-Function Wave Theory

Of the wave theories used for design purposes, the theory formulated by Chappelear (1961) and Dean (1965) and extended by Dalrymple (1973), Chaplin (1980), and Rienecker and Fenton (1981) probably comes closest to providing an exact solution.

As in the small-amplitude and shallow-water wave theories, the flow is assumed to be two-dimensional, incompressible, irrotational, and periodic in x and t. Consequently the stream function ψ satisfies Laplace's equation and the general solution may be expressed as the Fourier series

$$\psi = \sum_{n=1}^{\infty} a_n \sinh nby \cos n(\omega t - bx) \qquad (1.50)$$

where $a_1, a_2, \ldots$, are constant coefficients.

The boundary conditions are the same as those given in Section 1.3.2. In principle, the problem is one of substituting (1.50) into the various boundary conditions and using the resulting equations to determine the coefficients a_1, a_2, and so on, and the wave number b, assuming the period and wave height are known. Of course, no computer can solve an infinite number of simultaneous equations and, consequently, the series represented by (1.50) has to be truncated at a finite number of terms. For this reason, the solution is not exact.

Dean (1974) has provided tables to facilitate the use of this method. Chaplin (1980) found that these tables contained errors which became progressively more important as the wave height approached its limiting value. However, for waves of less than 75% of the limiting height, the errors were negligible (typically less than 1% on wave height) except for waves in extremely shallow water.

1.5.3. Vocoidal Theory

This theory was put forward by Swart and Loubser (1978). As in the other theories, the wave motion is assumed to be two-dimensional, incompressible, and periodic in x and t. The condition of irrotationality is also approximately satisfied. The boundary conditions are the same as those set out in Section 1.3.2. The basic assumptions are that the free surface profile may be approximated by an expression of the form

$$\eta = H(\cos^2 bx)^p - \frac{H(1 - 16p + 128p^2)}{128(p^5 \pi)^{1/2}} \qquad (1.51)$$

and that the horizontal component of velocity is

$$u = \frac{c\eta Mb \cosh Mby}{\sinh Mb(d + \eta)} \qquad (1.52)$$

where

$$c = \left(\frac{g}{b} \tanh Nbd \right)^{1/2} \qquad (1.53)$$

The quantities P and N are constants but M is a function of x. Swart and Loubser obtain the function M explicitly in terms of the other variables but P and N have to be obtained by numerical solution of the various boundary conditions.

Swart and Loubser (1978) found close agreement between their theory and Dean's stream-function theory for values of H/d less than 0.78. They suggest that an advantage of their theory is that it can be used for values of H/d up to 1.3 or more. This is somewhat surprising since the exact solution of the equations on which vocoidal theory is based shows that, with the assumed boundary conditions, the value of H/d should not exceed 0.83. Larger values of H/d are found experimentally only when the bed is not horizontal or the waves are not steady (as assumed in the theory). The fact that vocoidal theory can be used with larger values of H/d is a further indication that the solution is only approximate. On the other hand, it may be useful to have a method for waves with values of H/d greater than 0.83 even if it is only approximate.

1.6. ROTATIONAL WAVE THEORY

Viscous effects are mainly confined to the boundary layers at the bed and at the free surface. For this reason, irrotational wave theory usually gives good agreement with experimental measurements. The assumption of irrotationality may not be justified under some circumstances, such as when there is a steady current superimposed on the wave motion. The difficulty with rotational theories is that the solution is dependent on the assumed distribution of vorticity, which varies from one experimental situation to another. In practice, rotational theories are rarely used and, for this reason, only one such theory is mentioned here.

1.6.1. Gerstner or Trochoidal Wave Theory

This theory was presented by Gerstner (1802) and was the first to deal with finite amplitude waves. It is an exact solution of the governing equations.

The assumptions are the same as those presented in Section 1.3.1 except that the flow is not assumed to be irrotational. The free surface boundary conditions are the same as those given by (1.10) and (1.11). Gerstner only considered waves in deep water.

The coordinates (X, Y) of a fluid particle are found to be given in terms of the mean position (x_0, y_0) of the particle during the course of a wave cycle by

$$X = x_0 + \frac{H}{2} e^{by_0} \sin(\omega t - bx_0) \tag{1.54}$$

$$Y = y_0 + \frac{H}{2} e^{by_0} \cos(\omega t - bx_0) \tag{1.55}$$

Here Y and y_0 are measured vertically up from the mean water level.

The pressure is

$$p = -\rho g y_0 + \frac{\rho g H}{4} e^{2by_0} \tag{1.56}$$

and the vorticity:

$$\Omega = \frac{2\omega H^2 b^2 e^{2by_0}}{(4 - H^2 b^2 e^{2by_0})} \tag{1.57}$$

Although the surface profile is in reasonable agreement with experimental measurements other features of this solution are unrealistic.

This theory was extended to include waves in water of finite depth by Gaillard (1904).

1.7.   EDGE WAVES

So far, we have been concerned with waves propagating either in water of constant depth or in water where the depth changed so slowly that it could be treated as if the depth were constant. However, when the bed slope is significant, another type of waves, called edge waves, is possible.

If we take the x-axis horizontal and perpendicular to the coast, the z-axis along the coast, and y-axis vertically upward from the mean water level, the first approximation to the velocity potential for edge waves on a uniform slope at angle θ to the horizontal is

$$\phi = A \left\{ e^{-b(x\cos\theta - y\sin\theta)} + \sum_{m=1}^{n} (-1)^m \prod_{r=1}^{m} \frac{\tan(n-r+1)\theta}{\tan(n+r)\theta} \right.$$
$$\left. \times \left[e^{-b(x\cos(2m-1)\theta + y\sin(2m-1)\theta)} + e^{-b(x\cos(2m+1)\theta - y\sin(2m+1)\theta)} \right] \right\} \cos(\omega t - bz) \tag{1.58}$$

where the constant A is related to the wave height H at the shoreline by the expression

$$H = \frac{A\omega}{g} \left[1 + \sum_{m=1}^{n} (-1)^m \prod_{r=1}^{m} \frac{2 \tan(n-r+1)\theta}{\tan(n+r)\theta} \right] \quad (1.59)$$

The integer n may take any of the values $0, 1, 2, \ldots$, subject to the condition

$$(2n+1)\theta \leqslant \frac{\pi}{2} \quad (1.60)$$

We see that the wave propagates parallel to the coast. At any fixed height y, the fluid particles move in circular orbits. The amplitude of the motion falls off exponentially with distance x from the coast. The fluid particle orbits are the same in a horizontal plane as those in a vertical plane of deep water progressive waves.

The speed at which the wave propagates is

$$c = \left[\frac{g}{b} \sin(2n+1)\theta \right]^{1/2} \quad (1.61)$$

The above results apply to progressive edge waves. The solution for standing edge waves may be obtained by superimposing the solutions for waves of equal height and period propagating in opposite directions.

Edge waves are frequently identified in records made near beaches at periods of around one minute.

1.8. INTERNAL WAVES

The change in density of sea water from one part of the globe to another does not exceed about 4%. This maximum change is mainly due to the enormous difference between the pressure at the surface of the sea and the pressure at depths of 10 km or so in the deepest parts of the ocean.

The density of sea water is also affected by the temperature and the salinity. Temperature varies from freezing point, 271 K for sea water, up to about 300 K. This temperature difference produces a variation in density of about 0.5%. The salinity ranges from about 0.034 to about 0.037 and produces density variations of approximately 0.2%.

Somewhat surprisingly, it is the relatively small change in density produced by salinity and temperature variations which determines the dynamics of internal waves rather than the much larger changes due to hydrostatic pressure.

One example of internal wave formation is at the boundary between two fluids of different density. For example, in many deep estuaries, fresh river water moves seaward above the heavier salt water. Waves may be produced at the interface (e.g., by the passage of a ship). If the density of the upper fluid is ρ_1 and the density of the lower fluid is ρ_2 and if each fluid is semi-infinite in its extent, it is found that the speed of these waves is given by

$$c = \frac{\omega}{b} = \left(\frac{g}{b} \frac{\rho_2 - \rho_1}{\rho_2 + \rho_1} \right)^{1/2} \tag{1.62}$$

From (1.16), the corresponding expression for surface waves when the depth d is infinite is

$$c = \frac{\omega}{b} = \left(\frac{g}{b} \right)^{1/2} \tag{1.63}$$

Surface waves may be thought of as internal waves at the interface between air and water. In this case $\rho_2 \gg \rho_1$ so that (1.62) reduces to (1.63) as expected.

If the densities of the two fluids are not too different, we see that the speed of propagation of internal waves at the interface is much less than that of surface waves of similar wavelength. Alternatively, for a given wavelength, the period of oscillation is much lower for internal waves.

Another example occurs where there is a continuous variation in density with depth. Changes in temperature and salinity initiated at the surface produce instabilities which thoroughly mix the fluid in the upper layer of the ocean. However, below this "well-mixed" layer, there is a sharp transition, called the thermocline, in which temperature drops steeply with increasing depth and there may also be some increase in salinity. Internal waves may be formed in this region of changing density in much the same way as they are formed at the sharp interface between two fluids of different density. The frequency of such waves is

$$\omega = N \cos \theta \tag{1.64}$$

where θ is the angle between the direction of fluid oscillation and the vertical and N is the Vaisala-Brunt frequency which is given to a good approximation by

$$N = \left(-\frac{g}{\rho} \frac{\partial \rho}{\partial y} \right)^{1/2} \tag{1.65}$$

The reason why internal waves are seldom of great importance for the sea bed effects discussed in this book is that the upper "well-mixed" layer in which density variation is negligible is typically about 100 m thick. On the other hand, internal waves may occur in much shallower water and Southard and Cacchione (1972) have shown that, at least in the laboratory, internal waves are capable of producing sediment transport.

1.9. BREAKING WAVES

1.9.1. Maximum Wave Height

Stokes (1880) showed that, at any rate for an ideal fluid, the largest possible wave has a crest with an included angle of 120°. Making use of this work Miche (1944) suggested that for progressive waves and constant depth

$$\left(\frac{H}{\lambda}\right)_{max} = 0.142 \tanh bd \qquad (1.66)$$

This result is only approximate, becoming less accurate as the depth of the water decreases compared with the wavelength.

There have been many attempts to calculate the maximum height of solitary waves. It is now generally accepted that for an ideal fluid

$$\left(\frac{H}{d}\right)_{max} = 0.83 \qquad (1.67)$$

These results are for water of constant depth. Ippen and Kulin (1954) found experimentally that on sloping beaches the limiting value of H/d could be much larger. For example, for a slope of 1:50, H/d at breaking was 1.2.

Equations (1.66) and (1.67) also neglect the effects of viscosity. For real fluids, the critical value of H/d appears to be somewhat less than the theoretical value. For solitary waves in water of constant depth, it is found experimentally that

$$\left(\frac{H}{d}\right) \simeq 0.78 \qquad (1.68)$$

However, in deep water the limiting value of H/λ is usually observed to be 0.14 which is very close to the value given by (1.66).

1.9.2.   Types of Breaker

Breaking waves may be classified as follows:

1.   Spilling breakers. Low steepness waves which break by continuous spilling of foam down the front face (Fig. 1.6a).
2.   Plunging breakers. Medium steepness waves on medium steepness beaches curl over as shown in Fig. 1.6b.
3.   Surging breakers. These occur with the steepest waves on the steepest beaches. The base of the wave surges up the beach generating considerable foam (Fig. 1.6c).

Galvin (1972) suggested that breaker type depends on the parameter $H_0/(\lambda_0 \tan^2\theta)$ where θ is the beach slope and H_0/λ_0 is the deep water wave steepness. In laboratory tests with plane concrete beaches he obtained

$$5 < \frac{H_0}{\lambda_0 \tan^2\theta}$$

for Spilling Breakers;

$$0.1 < \frac{H_0}{\lambda_0 \tan^2\theta} < 5$$

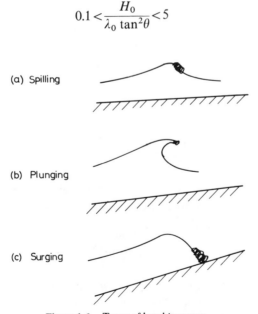

(a) Spilling

(b) Plunging

(c) Surging

Figure 1.6.   Types of breaking wave.

for Plunging Breakers; and

$$\frac{H_0}{\lambda_0 \tan^2\theta} < 0.1$$

for Surging breakers. These limits are only approximate. They were obtained for slopes of 0.05, 0.10 and 0.20 and may not apply outside that range. More fundamentally, the transition from one type of breaker to another is very gradual and estimation of the limit is highly subjective.

Galvin (1972) also describes a fourth category of breaking waves called "collapsing" breakers which foam lower down the forward face than spilling breakers but not right at the base like surging breakers. They may be thought of as a transition stage between plunging and surging breakers.

1.10.   THE MASS TRANSPORT VELOCITY

All of the above theories neglect viscosity. As already mentioned, viscous effects are mainly confined to the thin boundary layers at the bed and at the free surface and consequently do not significantly influence most wave properties. However, viscosity does have a very significant effect on the steady component of velocity induced by the waves. The quantity of greatest interest is the time-mean Lagrangian velocity, that is, the mean velocity of the fluid particles. This is usually referred to as the mass transport velocity.

The mass transport velocity $\bar{u}_{mt}$ may be expressed in terms of the Eulerian velocity u, at a fixed point, by means of Taylor's theorem

$$\bar{u}_{mt} = \overline{u + X\frac{\partial u}{\partial x} + Y\frac{\partial u}{\partial y} + \cdots} \qquad (1.69)$$

where (X, Y) are the coordinates of a fluid particle relative to the point (x, y) at which the Eulerian velocity is being measured and the overbar indicates the time mean.

In the absence of viscous effects, the small-amplitude wave theory gives a first approximation to the mass transport velocity due to progressive waves as

$$\bar{u}_{mt} = \frac{H^2 \omega b}{8 \sinh^2 bd} \cosh 2by \qquad (1.70)$$

For progressive waves the vertical component of the mass transport velocity, $\bar{v}_{mt}$, is zero. For standing waves both components of the mass transport velocity are zero if viscous effects are neglected.

At this level of approximation, the effect of viscosity is to impose additional boundary conditions at the bed and at the free surface. Longuet-Higgins (1953) obtained the following solution for the mass transport velocity in the body of the fluid when viscosity is taken into account:

1. For progressive waves:

$$\bar{u}_{mt} = \frac{H^2\omega b}{16 \sinh^2 bd}\left[2\cosh 2by + 3 + by\left(\frac{3y}{d} - 2\right)\sinh 2bd\right.$$

$$\left. + \frac{3}{d^2}\left(\frac{\sinh 2bd}{2bd} + \frac{3}{2}\right)y(y-2d)\right] \tag{1.71}$$

$$\bar{v}_{mt} = 0 \tag{1.72}$$

2. For standing waves:

$$\bar{u}_{mt} = \frac{3H^2\omega b \sin 2bx}{2\sinh^2 bd(\sinh 4bd - 4bd)}\left[bd\cosh 2bd\cosh 2b(d-y)\right.$$

$$\left. - \tfrac{1}{2}\cosh 2b(d-y)\sinh 2bd - b(d-y)\sinh 2b(d-y)\sinh 2bd\right] \tag{1.73}$$

$$\bar{v}_{mt} = \frac{3H^2\omega b \cos 2bx}{2\sinh^2 bd(\sinh 4bd - 4bd)}$$

$$\times \left[bd\cosh 2bd\sinh 2b(d-y) - b(d-y)\cosh 2b(d-y)\sinh 2bd\right] \tag{1.74}$$

Equations (1.71), (1.72), (1.73), and (1.74) represent what Longuet-Higgins called his "conduction" solution. Since this solution required the nonlinear terms in the equations of motion to be small, the solution was only strictly valid for very small wave heights.

Figure 1.7 shows the mass transport velocity distributions given by (1.70) and (1.71) for one particular value of bd. Equation (1.70) shows a drift of fluid in the direction of wave propagation over the entire depth. In a laboratory channel with closed ends this would be impossible since the net time-mean flow across any section must be zero. Since the equations on which this solution are based are inviscid, an arbitrary constant velocity may be subtracted from the value of $\bar{u}_{mt}$ given by (1.70). If the condition of zero net flow in the direction of wave propagation is to be satisfied, (1.70) should be replaced by

$$\bar{u}_{mt} = \frac{H^2\omega b}{8\sinh^2 bd}\left(\cosh 2by - \frac{\sinh 2bd}{2bd}\right) \tag{1.75}$$

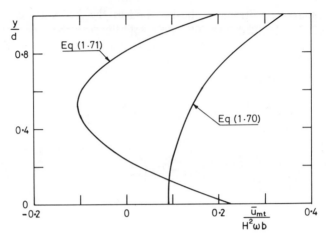

Figure 1.7.   Mass transport velocity profiles for progressive waves ($bd = 1.0$).

There have been numerous measurements of mass transport velocities in wave channels. Those of Russell and Osorio (1957), Mei et al. (1972), and Dyke and Barstow (1981) are fairly typical. Most investigators have found good agreement with Longuet-Higgins' solution in the vicinity of the bed but progressively less good agreement higher up, except for values of bd near unity. The measurements in the vicinity of the bed will be discussed in Chapter 2. Figure 1.8 shows how measurements of the surface velocity compare with theory. Somewhat surprisingly, although all of the measurements were carried out in wave channels with zero net flow in the direction of wave propagation, the best agreement appears to be with (1.70).

For standing waves, (1.73) and (1.74) show that the steady drift takes the form of closed recirculating cells. The velocity is vertically up at the antinodes of the surface profile ($bx = 0$, π, etc.) and vertically down at the nodes ($bx = \pi/2$, $3\pi/2$, etc.). In between, the horizontal flow is toward the nodes near the free surface but away from the nodes near the bed as shown in Fig. 1.9. In the boundary layer at the bed there are further recirculating cells, which will be discussed in Chapter 2.

The experimental support for (1.73) and (1.74) is inconclusive. For example, Mei et al. (1972) observed that on the center line of their wave channel the steady drifts were generally similar to those described above except for a small additional recirculating cell in the vicinity of the water surface at the antinode of the surface profile. This additional recirculating cell became progressively more important as distance from the sidewall of the channel decreased. It seems probable that the extra cell is caused by the boundary layers on the sidewalls. A relatively recent theoretical study of this problem

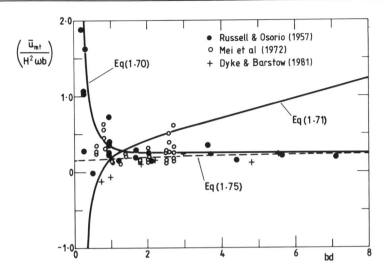

Figure 1.8. The variation with bd of the mass transport velocity at the water surface.

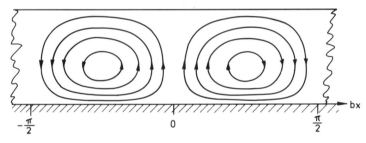

Figure 1.9. Streamlines of the mean flow set up by standing waves when $bd = 1.0$ according to Longuet-Higgins (1953).

by Liu and Davis (1977), assuming two-dimensional flow but allowing for wave attenuation in the direction of propagation, does not show this additional cell.

1.11. LONGSHORE CURRENT

The waves approaching the shore carry momentum with them. The component of momentum parallel to the coast causes a longshore current. This current is of great importance in the transport of sediment along the coast.

Measurements of the longshore current show it is largely confined to the surf zone and that a substantial variation in velocity can exist across that

Table 1.1. SOME PRE-1969 FORMULAS FOR MEAN LONGSHORE CURRENT

Author	Formula for mean longshore current	Principle	Beach profile	Remarks
Putnam, Munk, and Traylor (1949)	$\bar{V} = 1.91 A^{1/3} \left(\dfrac{g H_b^2 \tan\theta \sin 2\alpha_b}{fT} \right)^{1/3}$	Energy approach	Straight slope	A = proportion of wave energy used to produce current
Putnam, Munk, and Traylor (1949)	$\bar{V} = V_0 \left[\left(1 + \dfrac{3.02}{V_0} (g H_b)^{1/2} \sin\alpha_b \right)^{1/2} - 1 \right]$	Momentum conservation	Straight slope	$V_0 = \dfrac{10.44 H_b}{fT} \tan\theta \cos\alpha_b$
Inman, Quinn (1951)	$\bar{V} = \dfrac{1}{V_1} [(1 + V_1^2 (2.28 g H_b)^{1/2} \sin\alpha_b)^{1/2} - 1]^2$	Empirical based on momentum conservation	Straight slope	S.I. units $V_1 = 216.6 \dfrac{H_b}{T} \tan\theta \cos\alpha_b$
Shadrin (1961)	$\bar{V} = \left[1.11 \dfrac{H_b}{T} (g H_b)^{1/2} \left(1 - \dfrac{l_1}{l_2}\right) \right]^{1/2}$	Momentum conservation	Coast with lunate bar	l_1, l_2 are minimum and maximum distances between bar and shoreline
Inman, Bagnold (1963)	$\bar{V} = 1.16 \dfrac{H_b l}{d_b T} \tan\theta \sin 2\alpha_b$	Mass conservation	Coast with bar	l = distance between rip currents
Bruun (1963)	$\bar{V} = \dfrac{Q_{b.v} \cos\alpha_b}{AT}$	Mass conservation	Coast with bar	A = cross section of fluid between bar and shoreline Q_b = volume inflow across bar
Bruun (1963)	$\bar{V} = \left(\dfrac{2g Q_b \tan\theta}{L_b f} \sin 2\alpha_b \right)^{1/2}$	Mass conservation	Coast with bar	L_b = wavelength at breaking Q_b = volume inflow across bar

Author	Equation	Basis	Conditions	Notes
Brebner, Kamphuis (1963)	$\bar{V} = 8.0 \left(\dfrac{H_0^2 \tan\theta}{T}\right)^{1/3} \left[\sin(1.65\alpha_0) + 0.1\sin(3.3\alpha_0)\right]$	Empirical based on momentum conservation	Various	S.I. units
Brebner, Kamphuis (1963)	$\bar{V} = 14.0 \left(\dfrac{H_0^3 \tan^2\theta}{T^2}\right)^{1/4} \left[\sin(1.65\alpha_0) + 0.1\sin(3.3\alpha_0)\right]$	Empirical based on energy analysis	Various	S.I. units
Galvin, Eagleson (1965)	$\bar{V} = gT \tan\theta \sin 2\alpha_b$	Empirical based on mass conservation	Various	
Eagleson (1965)	$\bar{V} = \left(\dfrac{3gn_bH_b^2 \sin\theta}{4fd_b}\right)^{1/2} \sin\alpha_b$	Momentum conservation	Straight slope	Only the final steady state velocity is quoted here, n_b = value of c_g/c at breaking
Sato, Tanaka (1966)	$\bar{V} = 1.6 \left(\dfrac{H_0^{5/3}}{T^{1/3}} \tan\theta \sin 2\alpha_0\right)^{1/3}$	Momentum conservation	Straight slope	
Harrison (1968)	$\bar{V} = 0.241H_b + 0.0318T + 0.0374\alpha_b + 0.0309\tan\theta - 0.17$	Empirical	Various	S.I. units

zone. There is general agreement that the current depends, among other things, on the angle at which the waves approach the shore, the wave height at breaking, and the beach slope. A considerable number of formulas have been proposed. Both Galvin (1967) and Thornton (1969) have written excellent reviews of longshore current formulas. Table 1.1 shows some of the earlier formulas (pre-1969). Galvin (1967) concluded that "a proven prediction of longshore current velocity is not available, and reliable data on longshore currents are lacking over a significant range of possible flows." One reason for this somewhat depressing conclusion is that all formulas, whatever their basis, involve a certain number of empirical coefficients. Formulas generally give good agreement with measurements carried out under conditions similar to those used to determine the empirical coefficients but are not reliable for very different conditions.

The subject received a considerable impetus, at least theoretically, with the publication of papers by Bowen (1969a) and by Thornton (1969), making use of the concept of radiation stress. Longuet-Higgins (1970a, b) published papers along similar lines. Although these papers greatly clarify the mechanisms of longshore drift, they still rely on empirical relations for the bottom friction and the lateral mixing. The main difference between these papers is in the assumptions made about the friction and mixing. In practice they appear to give similar results. All three formulas determine the variation of longshore current with distance from the shore.

Bowen (1969a)

For $x_b < x$,

$$\bar{v} = A\lambda_1 x^{1/2} K_1[\lambda_1 x^{1/2}]$$ (1.76)

For $0 < x < x_b$,

$$\bar{v} = B\lambda_1(1 - K)^{1/2}x^{1/2}I_1[\lambda_1(1 - K)^{1/2}x^{1/2}] + \frac{(1 - K)^2 \tan^2\theta}{8Cd^2} H^2 x \sin 2\alpha_b$$ (1.77)

where K_1 and I_1 are modified first order Bessel functions, A and B are constants to be determined from the condition that $\bar{v}$ and $d\bar{v}/dx$ are continuous at the breaker line, K is the wave set down, λ_1 is a coefficient which expresses the relative importance of bed friction and lateral mixing, C is Bowen's friction factor and x is measured horizontally at right angles to the shore line. In order to use these formulas, it is necessary to be able to estimate both λ_1 and C.

Longuet-Higgins (1970a, b)

If $p \neq 0.4$

For $x_b < x$,

$$\bar{v} = B_2 \bar{v}_0 \left(\frac{x}{x_b}\right)^{p_2} \tag{1.78}$$

For $0 < x < x_b$,

$$\bar{v} = B_1 \bar{v}_0 \left(\frac{x}{x_b}\right)^{p_1} + A\bar{v}_0 \left(\frac{x}{x_b}\right) \tag{1.79}$$

where

$$p_1 = -\frac{3}{4} + \left(\frac{9}{16} + \frac{1}{p}\right)^{1/2}$$

$$p_2 = -\frac{3}{4} - \left(\frac{9}{16} + \frac{1}{p}\right)^{1/2}$$

$$A = (1 - 2.5p)^{-1}$$

$$B = [p(1 - p_1)(p_1 - p_2)]^{-1}$$

$$\bar{v}_0 = \frac{5\pi}{f} \left(\frac{gH_b^3}{d_b^2}\right)^{1/2} \tan \theta \sin \alpha_b$$

If $p = 0.4$

For $x_b < x$,

$$\bar{v} = \frac{10}{49} \bar{v}_0 \left(\frac{x_b}{x}\right)^{5/2} \tag{1.80}$$

For $0 < x < x_b$,

$$\bar{v} = \frac{10\bar{v}_0 x}{49 x_b} - \frac{5\bar{v}_0}{7} \frac{x}{x_b} \ln\left(\frac{x}{x_b}\right) \tag{1.81}$$

The coefficients which have to be estimated in order to be able to use these formulas are the parameter p, which represents the relative importance of horizontal mixing and bed friction, and the friction coefficient f. Longuet-Higgins (1970b) suggested, on the basis of Galvin and Eagleson's (1965) data, that p would usually lie between about 0.1 and 0.4. As shown in Fig.

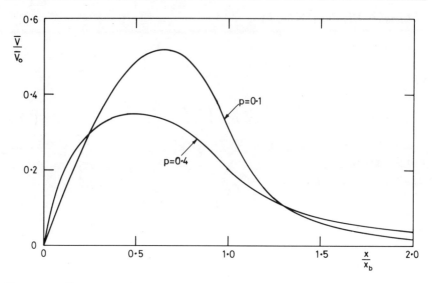

Figure 1.10. Variation of the longshore current with distance from the beach according to Longuet-Higgins (1970b).

1.10 for this range of values of p, the variation in the curve of $\bar{v}/\bar{v}_0$ versus x is remarkably small.

As mentioned previously Thornton's approach is very similar to that of Bowen and Longuet-Higgins. The curves obtained are also similar. However, his equations require numerical solution and therefore will not be further discussed.

For engineering purposes it is useful to have a simple formula for the maximum longshore drift current without having to estimate friction and mixing coefficients. The Coastal Engineering Research Center Shore Protection Manual (1977) recommends (in addition to Galvin and Eagleson's, 1965, formula and a modified version of Bruun's, 1963, formulas) the following formula based on Longuet-Higgins' theoretical expression and the experimental data of Galvin and Eagleson (1965) and Putnam et al. (1949)

$$\bar{V} = 20.7(gH_b)^{1/2} \tan \theta \sin 2\alpha_b \tag{1.82}$$

1.12. RIP CURRENTS

Rip currents are strong narrow currents that flow seaward from the surf zone. They are important both because they are a danger to swimmers, who may be swept out into deep water, and because they can carry significant quantities of sediment in the offshore direction.

According to Bowen (1969b) rip currents are caused by variations in wave set-up from one point on the beach to another point. The wave set-up, or change in mean water level caused by the waves piling up on the beach, varies according to the height of the incoming waves. If the incoming waves are larger at one point on the beach than at another, there will be a longshore pressure gradient. This gradient will produce a current from regions of high waves to adjacent regions of low waves. This flow along the beach causes an outward flowing rip current in regions of low wave height and a more diffuse return current where the waves are large.

There are several reasons for variation in the wave height from one point on the beach to another. The most obvious is wave refraction produced by changes in bottom topography. However, rip currents have also been observed on straight beaches with regular bottom topography. Bowen and Inman (1969) have suggested that in these cases standing edge waves may produce the necessary regular variation in wave height from one point on the beach to another.

Finally, Sonu (1972) has shown that, even when the breaking waves are uniform in height, variations in wave set-up at the beach can be produced by differences in the breaker type caused by changes in the offshore bar pattern from one point to another.

Steady Currents

1.13. GROWING BOUNDARY LAYER OR FULLY DEVELOPED FLOW?

Consider a uniform flow approaching a flat plate with velocity $\bar{U}_1$ as shown in Fig. 1.11. The plate itself is stationary and consequently the fluid in immediate contact with it is also stationary. Away from the plate, the velocity gradually increases until it reaches the value $\bar{U}_1$ of the free stream. The region in which the velocity differs from $\bar{U}_1$ is called the boundary layer. The fluid velocity approaches the free stream value very gradually, therefore the edge of the boundary layer is indeterminate. For convenience, the edge is usually taken as the point at which the fluid velocity reaches 99% of $\bar{U}_1$.

Boundary layers do not grow only from the start of flat plates. Any change in bed roughness or flow conditions can provoke a new boundary layer.

As shown in Fig. 1.11, the thickness of the boundary layer increases with

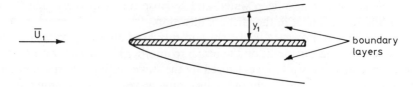

Figure 1.11.   Boundary layer growth along a flat plate.

distance downstream. This means that the velocity distribution within the boundary layer also changes with distance. If the depth of flow is not infinite there may come a point at which the boundary layer fills the whole flow. When this happens there will, after some initial adjustment, be no further change with downstream distance, provided conditions remain unchanged: the flow is "fully developed." For free surface flows it is usually accepted that if x is the distance downstream of the point at which the boundary layer was initiated, the flow is fully developed if $x > 100d$.

1.14.   TRANSITION TO TURBULENCE

It is usual to distinguish a Reynolds number R_a above which small disturbances of the laminar flow are amplified and another R_b below which turbulence is damped out.

For fully developed two-dimensional free surface flow:

$$R_a = 5000$$
$$R_b = 890$$

(1.83)

where the Reynolds number is defined as $\bar{U}d/v$.

For a growing boundary layer at constant pressure:

$$R_a = 420$$

R_b is unknown

(1.84)

where the Reynolds number is $\int_0^d (\bar{U}_1 - u)/v \, dy$.

For a growing boundary layer at constant pressure the Reynolds number $\bar{U}_1 x/v$ is also frequently quoted. The transition condition is

$$\frac{\bar{U}_1 x}{v} = 5 \times 10^5 \text{ to } 3 \times 10^6$$

(1.85)

(the numerical value is strongly influenced by the intensity of turbulence in the free stream and by surface roughness). The distance from the point at which the boundary layer was initiated is x. In many practical applications it is difficult to identify the point at which the boundary layer starts, so (1.84) is more useful.

1.15.   FREE SURFACE LAMINAR FLOW

It is clear from (1.83) that laminar flows will only occur in the sea for extremely weak currents.

For fully developed two-dimensional free surface flow with constant depth the velocity at any height y above the bed is

$$u = u_{max}\left(2 - \frac{y}{d}\right)\frac{y}{d}$$ (1.86)

The mean velocity integrated over a vertical plane is

$$\bar{U} = \tfrac{2}{3}u_{max}$$ (1.87)

For the depth to be constant the bed must slope down at an angle θ to the horizontal. Under these conditions the maximum velocity and the bed slope are related as follows

$$u_{max} = \frac{gd^2}{2\nu}\sin\theta$$ (1.88)

1.16.   TURBULENT FLOW

1.16.1.   Velocity Distribution

It is convenient to split the flow in a boundary layer into the following three regions:

Inner layer
Overlap layer
Outer layer

Since a fully developed flow is merely a boundary layer which fills the whole flow, the same categories apply.

Inner Layer

For smooth beds the inner layer is also referred to as the viscous sublayer or, sometimes, the laminar sublayer. In the immediate vicinity of the bed turbulent eddies are inhibited by the presence of the solid boundary and viscous stresses dominate the motion. The flow in this layer is, however, far from steady since the fluid is constantly being buffeted by turbulent eddies from the flow above. The mean velocity distribution in this layer is

$$\bar{u} = \frac{y\bar{u}_*^2}{\nu} \tag{1.89}$$

Since $\bar{u}_* = (\bar{\tau}_0/\rho)^{1/2}$, (1.89) follows immediately from the relation

$$\bar{\tau} = \mu \frac{\partial \bar{u}}{\partial y} \tag{1.90}$$

and the assumption that the shear stress in this very thin layer is virtually constant.

The thickness of the viscous sublayer is usually taken to be

$$\delta = 11.6 \frac{\nu}{\bar{u}_*} \tag{1.91}$$

When the bed is rough, there is no simple relation for the velocity distribution. There is still a region in which viscous stress dominates but this is lost in the troughs between the bed roughness elements. The local velocity will clearly depend on the shape and arrangement of the roughness elements on the bed.

Overlap Layer

This layer derives its name from the fact that it is the region of overlap between a wall layer and a "defect" layer.

In the wall layer the flow is determined mainly by the shear stress at the bed and hence, by dimensional analysis,

$$\frac{\bar{u}}{\bar{u}_*} = f\left(\frac{\bar{u}_* y}{\nu}\right) \tag{1.92}$$

Equation (1.89) satisfies this relation.

In the defect layer the difference between the local time-mean velocity $\bar{u}$ and the velocity $\bar{U}_1$ in the free stream, that is, the velocity defect, is unaffected by viscosity. Consequently dimensional analysis shows that

$$\frac{\bar{U}_1 - \bar{u}}{\bar{u}_*} = f\left(\frac{y}{y_1}\right) \tag{1.93}$$

where y_1 is the thickness of the boundary layer or the depth of fluid for a fully developed free surface flow.

If the wall layer and the defect layer overlap, (1.92) and (1.93) must be satisfied. This can be done only by an expression of the form

$$\frac{\bar{u}}{\bar{u}_*} = \frac{1}{K} \ln\left(\frac{y}{y_0}\right) \tag{1.94}$$

where y_0 and K are constants. This is the well-known Prandtl–Von Karman formula. The Karman constant K is usually taken to be 0.4. It has been suggested that values as low as 0.2 may be appropriate when the flow is carrying a heavy load of sediment in suspension but Coleman (1981) has reanalyzed the data and shown that a suspended load does not alter the value of K. Coleman's finding that the Karman constant is not affected by the concentration of sediment in suspension is not universally accepted. Many authors have argued (e.g., Wang, 1981) that K is reduced by sediment suspension. The weight of evidence does seem to support Coleman's view.

The constant y_0 must be determined by experiment. Its magnitude depends on the size k_s of the bed roughness compared with the thickness δ of the viscous sublayer. Making use of (1.91) we see that the controlling parameter is the Reynolds number $\bar{u}_* k_s / \nu$.

$\bar{u}_* k_s / \nu < 5$ (hydraulically smooth beds)

Under these circumstances the height k_s, of the bed roughness is small compared with the thickness of the viscous sublayer. It is found that

$$y_0 = \frac{\nu}{9\bar{u}_*} \tag{1.95}$$

and (1.94) thus becomes

$$\bar{u} = 2.5\bar{u}_* \ln\left(\frac{9\bar{u}_* y}{\nu}\right) \tag{1.96}$$

If the velocity distribution is given by (1.96) over the whole depth, then integration gives the mean velocity

$$\bar{U}=2.5\bar{u}_* \ln\left(3.31\frac{\bar{u}_*d}{\nu}\right) \qquad (1.97)$$

$\bar{u}_*k_s/\nu<70$ (hydraulically rough beds)

The roughness height k_s is now much larger than the thickness of the viscous sublayer. Consequently, y_0 should be proportional to k_s. It is found from experiment that

$$y_0=\frac{k_s}{30} \qquad (1.98)$$

Hence

$$\bar{u}=2.5\bar{u}_* \ln\left(\frac{30y}{k_s}\right) \qquad (1.99)$$

In this formula the origin of y for plane beds of sand is usually taken $0.3D_{90}$ below the mean level of the grain crests. On the basis of Jackson's (1981) results, the origin for rippled or duned beds should probably be taken midway between crests and troughs.

Once again, if it were assumed that the velocity was logarithmic over the whole depth the mean velocity would be

$$\bar{U}=2.5\bar{u}_* \ln\left(\frac{11.0d}{k_s}\right) \qquad (1.100)$$

$5<\bar{u}_*k_s/\nu<70$

In this transition region y_0 is a function of both the viscous sublayer thickness and the bed roughness size. Figure 1.12 shows how y_0/k_s varies with $\bar{u}_*k_s/\nu$.

Assuming a logarithmic profile over the whole depth gives the mean velocity as

$$\bar{U}=2.5\bar{u}_* \ln\left(\frac{d}{2.72y_0}\right) \qquad (1.101)$$

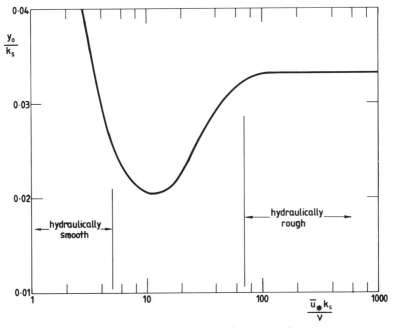

Figure 1.12.   Variation of y_0/k_s with $\bar{u}_* k_s/v$.

Outer Layer

This is the part of the defect layer which does not overlap the wall layer. It is also sometimes called the "wake region." On the basis of a large amount of data for free surface flows in laboratory channels Coleman (1981) suggests the following expression for the velocity distribution:

$$\frac{\bar{U}_1 - \bar{u}}{\bar{u}_*} = -\frac{1}{K}\ln\left(\frac{y}{y_1}\right) + \frac{2P}{K}\left(1 - \sin^2\frac{\pi y}{2y_1}\right) \qquad (1.102)$$

For fully developed flows the thickness y_1 of the boundary layer should be replaced by the depth d and the velocity $\bar{U}_1$ taken as the maximum value of $\bar{u}$. The parameter P varies according to the concentration of sediment in suspension. For clear water Coleman (1981) found P equal to 0.19. For very heavy concentrations of sediment P approaches 1.0. The data for the Karman constant K scatters fairly uniformly around the value 0.4. A similar result was obtained by Itakura and Kishi (1980), who suggested

$$\frac{\bar{U}_1 - \bar{u}}{\bar{u}_*} = -\frac{1}{K}\ln\left(\frac{y}{y_1}\right) + \frac{7g(\rho_s - \rho)W\bar{C}}{\rho \bar{u}_*^3}\, y_1\left(1 - \frac{y}{y_1}\right) \qquad (1.103)$$

where $\bar{C}$ is the mean volumetric concentration of the suspended sediment, averaged over the whole section. In contrast with Coleman's expression, this equation suggests that for clear water the velocity profile remains logarithmic right up to the free surface. On the whole, the experimental results show slightly better agreement with Coleman's formula. Like Coleman, Itakura and Kishi recommend that the value of the Karman constant be taken as 0.4 regardless of the concentration of sediment in suspension.

1.16.2.   Power Law or Log Law?

Some researchers prefer to use a simple power law relationship for turbulent boundary layer and free surface flows. The most frequently quoted is

$$\frac{\bar{u}}{\bar{U}_1} = \left(\frac{y}{y_1} \right)^{1/7} \tag{1.104}$$

where $\bar{U}_1$ is the velocity at the outer edge of the boundary layer and y_1 is the thickness of the layer. For a fully developed free surface flow $\bar{U}_1$ should be replaced by the maximum value of $\bar{u}$ and y_1 by the depth d. This formula must only be regarded as an approximation. As pointed out by Clauser (1956), the exponent in (1.104) may vary between one third and one tenth, depending on the experimental conditions.

Figure 1.13 shows how (1.102) compares with (1.104) and some open-channel measurements made by Coleman (1981). The value of $\bar{U}_1/\bar{u}_*$ for these experiments was 25.6. The power law gives reasonable agreement with experiment over most of the flow but is clearly less satisfactory than (1.102) for this particular application. It is interesting that the experimental results only follow a logarithmic curve, such as the straight line in Fig. 1.13, over a rather restricted range of values of y/d.

It should be emphasized that the situation is complicated in most channels by the existence of secondary flows. Even when the channel is straight the variation in turbulent intensity between the center of the channel and the corners can set up secondary flows capable of producing significant changes in the mean velocity profile.

1.16.3.   Nikuradse Roughness Length

The Nikuradse roughness length k_s is an important parameter because it appears in several widely used formulas. For flat beds of sand or gravel, it is expected that the roughness length would be related to the diameter of the

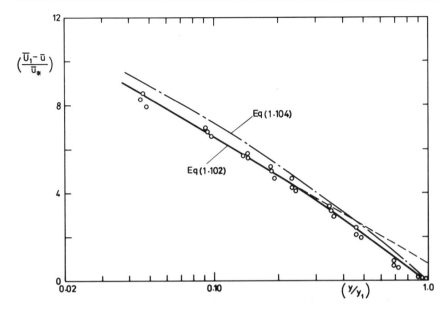

Figure 1.13. Comparison of log and power law velocity profiles with open channel measurements made by Coleman (1981).

largest grains on the surface of the bed. The following values have been suggested:

Ackers-White (1973)	$k_s = 1.25 D_{35}$
Einstein (1950)	$k_s = D_{65}$
Engelund-Hansen (1967)	$k_s = 2D_{65}$
Hey (1979)	$k_s = 3.5 D_{84}$
Kamphuis (1975)	$k_s = 2D_{90}$
Mahmood (1971)	$k_s = 5.1 D_{84}$

It is possible that k_s may vary according to the flow rate since mobile grains might shift to offer minimum resistance to the flow. Van Rijn (1982) reviewed the available data and found no evidence of variation of k_s with flow conditions. He also showed that the scatter of the data was too great to be clear which one, if any, of the suggested expressions is correct. It is possible that some of the data with very large values of k_s/D were for beds which were not completely flat. The Engelund-Hansen expression is probably adequate for most purposes.

For rippled and duned beds the following expressions have been put forward:

Shinohara and Tsubaki (1959):

$$\frac{k_s}{h}=7.5\left(\frac{h}{L}\right)^{0.57}$$

(1.105)

Swart (1976):

$$\frac{k_s}{h}=25\left(\frac{h}{L}\right)$$

(1.106)

Van Rijn (1982)

$$\frac{k_s}{h}=1.1(1-e^{-25h/L})$$

(1.107)

Since Van Rijn's formula is based on the widest range of data it is recommended that it be used in steady flow. Swart included some oscillatory flow data, not considered by Van Rijn, and consequently Swart's expression may be more reliable for flows involving waves.

1.16.4.   Eddy Viscosity And Mixing Length

There have been many attempts to obtain analytical expressions for the velocity distribution in turbulent flows. Some of these theoretical models will be discussed in subsequent chapters. One of the principal difficulties is to obtain a satisfactory relationship between the shear stress and the time-mean velocity. One approach is to assume that the mean flow is the same as laminar flow except that the kinematic viscosity v is replaced by an eddy viscosity ε. For mean flows parallel to the bed

$$\frac{\bar{\tau}}{\rho}=\varepsilon\frac{\partial\bar{u}}{\partial y}$$

(1.108)

Clauser (1956) suggests that for a smooth bed ε varies as follows:

Inner layer $(0<y<11.6v/\bar{u}_*)$:

$$\varepsilon=v$$

(1.109)

Overlap layer $(11.6v/\bar{u}_*<y<0.044\bar{U}_1\overset{*}{\delta}/\bar{u}_*)$:

$$\varepsilon=K\bar{u}_*y$$

(1.110)

Outer layer ($0.044\,\bar{U}_1\dot{\delta}/\bar{u}_* < y$):

$$\varepsilon = 0.018\,\bar{U}_1\dot{\delta} \tag{1.111}$$

Here $\bar{U}_1$ is the velocity at the outer edge of the boundary layer, K is the Karman constant, which Clauser takes equal to 0.41, and $\dot{\delta}$ is the displacement thickness defined as

$$\dot{\delta} = \int_0^\infty \left(1 - \frac{\bar{u}}{\bar{U}_1}\right) dy \tag{1.112}$$

Notice that there is a discontinuity in the eddy viscosity between the inner and overlap layers. This may be avoided by specifying the eddy viscosity in the overlap layer as

$$\varepsilon = K\bar{u}_* \left(y - \frac{11.6v}{\bar{u}_*}\right) + v \tag{1.113}$$

and taking the boundary between the overlap and outer layers as

$$y = 0.044\,\frac{\bar{U}_1\dot{\delta}}{\bar{u}_*} + 9.16\,\frac{v}{\bar{u}_*} \tag{1.114}$$

An alternative approach is to use the mixing length theory of Prandtl and Von Karman. If the velocity is split into time-mean and fluctuating components and then a time mean is taken of the equations of motion, the resulting equations are the same as for a steady flow except for an additional stress

$$\tau_1 = -\overline{\rho u'v'} \tag{1.115}$$

where the overbar indicates the time-mean and u' and v' are the fluctuating components of velocity in the x and y directions. This is called the Reynolds stress. Prandtl suggested that turbulent eddies travel a distance l before giving up their momentum to the surrounding fluid. In that case the fluctuation u' should be equal to the difference between the horizontal component of velocity at the level from which the eddy originated and that at a distance l above at which it ended. Using Taylor's theorem, we obtain

$$u' \simeq -l\frac{\partial \bar{u}}{\partial y} \tag{1.116}$$

It may also be argued that

$$v' \propto -u' \tag{1.117}$$

Absorbing the constant of proportionality into l we obtain

$$\tau_1 = \rho l^2 \left| \frac{\partial \bar{u}}{\partial y} \right| \frac{\partial \bar{u}}{\partial y} \tag{1.118}$$

Von Karman derived the same relation on the basis of dimensional analysis.

To make use of this equation it is necessary to adopt some expression for the mixing length, l. The scale of the turbulent eddies increases with the distance from the wall. The most obvious assumption is

$$l = Ky \tag{1.119}$$

The constant K is the Karman constant.

Outside the viscous sublayer, the Reynolds stress τ_1 due to the turbulence is much larger than the viscous stress. Also, in the wall layer the shear stress is virtually constant at any given value of x. Thus, within the overlap layer,

$$\bar{u}_* = \left(\frac{\tau_1}{\rho} \right)^{1/2} \tag{1.120}$$

Substitution of (1.120) and (1.119) into (1.118) leads to

$$\frac{\bar{u}}{\bar{u}_*} = \frac{1}{K} \ln \left(\frac{y}{y_0} \right) \tag{1.121}$$

This is the same as the expression derived for the overlap layer on dimensional grounds in Section 1.16.1.

1.17. STEADY CURRENTS IN THE MARINE ENVIRONMENT

In the sea there is no such thing as an entirely steady current. Wind and wave conditions and the currents they induce are constantly changing. The outflows from rivers show strong seasonal variations. Even the large-scale ocean currents such as the Gulf Stream and the Pacific Equatorial Countercurrent show significant variations in velocity and direction at any given point. However, the time-scale of the fluctuations is usually large enough

TABLE 1.2.   TYPICAL CURRENT VELOCITIES

Type of current	Typical velocities (m/s)
Tidal current	0–2.0
Large-scale ocean current	0–2.0
Longshore current	0–1.0
Currents caused by wind stress	0–0.1
Mass transport velocity	0–0.05

for most of the different currents to be treated as steady in many situations of practical importance. Table 1.2 indicates the relative magnitude of the fluid velocities associated with different currents.

1.17.1.   Tides And Tidal Currents

Tides

Tides are caused primarily by both the gravitational attraction of the sun and the moon and the opposing centrifugal forces. Because of its proximity to the earth the effect of the moon is usually predominant even though the sun has a far greater mass.

Let us suppose, for the moment, that only the moon is important. The earth and the moon swing around a common axis about 2900 miles from the center of the earth. For this rotation to be stable the gravitational pull of the moon and the centrifugal force opposing it must exactly balance at the center of gravity of the earth. On the side of the earth nearer the moon the gravitational pull of the moon will be greater than the centrifugal force and so the water in the sea will bulge toward the moon. On the other side of the earth the water will bulge away from the moon because the gravitational pull is weaker there than the centrifugal force. For an observer positioned near the equator this process would result in two high tides and two low tides per day. Nearer the poles there would be only one tide per day. The period of tides produced in this way is not exactly 12 hours or 24 hours because as the earth rotates so does the moon. The lunar period is 29.5 days so the period of the so-called semidiurnal tide is $12(1 + 1/29.5) = 12.42$ hours. The period of the "diurnal" tide is 24.83 hours.

In reality the situation is much more complicated. The effect of the sun is not negligible. During part of the lunar month the effects of the sun and moon are in phase. This produces the large spring tides. When the effects of sun and moon are opposed the tides are smaller and are called neap tides. The interval between spring tides is 14.8 days.

The tides are also affected by the tilt of the axis of the earth relative to the sun and moon and also by the changing distances between these bodies during the course of time. Analysis of tidal records reveals over 390 separate components.

In addition, the tides are affected by the land masses surrounding and underlying the seas. In an infinite sea of constant depth the tides would behave like progressive waves. Because their wavelength is so long they are, effectively, shallow water waves. Like all long waves they are relatively easily reflected at the boundaries and consequently resonance or partial resonance is frequently observed. Bed friction reduces tidal amplitude, whereas changing bed and shore topography may increase or decrease it.

Because of these various complications the phase angle and amplitude of the tidal components are usually determined empirically while the period is obtained from astronomical observations.

The tidal range varies enormously from one part of the world to another. In the open ocean it is typically between 0.5 and 1.0 m, but in narrow estuaries and bays may exceed 15 m.

Tidal Currents

Because the tides behave in some places like progressive waves and in others like standing or partially standing waves it might be expected that the currents produced would be similar to those discussed at the beginning of this chapter. However, in addition to all the other complications, the currents are affected by the Coriolis force due to the rotation of the earth. In the Northern Hemisphere the Coriolis force tends to deflect currents to the right, whereas in the Southern Hemisphere the deflection is to the left. Thus a particle of fluid moving with the tide will describe an approximate ellipse during the course of the tidal cycle. In practice this tidal ellipse is usually not closed because of the existence of steady drifts superimposed on the oscillation. These steady drifts may be caused by nontidal currents. In addition, the tide itself generates steady currents both because of the tendency of ebb and flood tides to follow different channels and because of a steady streaming similar to the mass transport current discussed in Section 1.10 (see, e.g., Huthnance, 1981).

Proudman and Doodson (1924) suggested that the velocity components of a tidal current at a given point in the North Sea could be represented by

$$u = u_{max} \cos \omega t \tag{1.122}$$

$$w = w_{max} \sin \omega t \tag{1.123}$$

where u is taken in the direction of the flood tide and w is the horizontal velocity at right-angles to this direction. In view of what has just been said about the existence of steady drifts superimposed on the oscillatory motion, (1.122) and (1.123) should be regarded only as a first approximation.

Tidal currents usually are much stronger near the coast than further out. In the deep sea, tidal velocities are generally not much more than 0.01–0.1 m/s.

Velocity Distribution along a Vertical

Although the tidal current at any given point varies with time, it is frequently possible to approximate the velocity distribution over much of the depth by the steady flow relationships discussed in Section 1.16. On the basis of measurements made over a period of several years Hamilton et al. (1980) concluded that the velocity distribution in tidal currents is adequately represented by (1.94) over at least 85% of the tidal cycle.

On the other hand, several researchers have observed differences between the acceleration and deceleration phases of the tidal cycle. For example, Gordon (1975) observed that the turbulent kinetic energy was greater during the decelerating phase, and Soulsby and Dyer (1981) found that (1.94) somewhat underestimated the values of $\bar{u}_*$ and y_0 in the acceleration phase and overestimated them when the flow was decelerating. Anwar and Atkins (1980) made measurements in a reversing water channel. Although the maximum period was only 550 s, the results are probably qualitatively valid for real tidal flows. They found variations in turbulent kinetic energy similar to those found on site but observed that the velocity profile remained close to that given by (1.94) except in the vicinity of flow reversal. Thus (1.94) is probably adequate for most practical purposes outside the viscous sublayer at the bed and the wake region at the free surface.

1.17.2.   Large-Scale Ocean Currents

The major causes of large-scale ocean currents are uneven heating of the sea and winds (produced by uneven heating of the atmosphere) acting on the water surface. The currents are, of course, also affected by the land masses bounding the oceans and by the Coriolis force due to the rotation of the earth.

The uneven heating of the sea causes the warmer water at low latitudes to rise and spread out over the surface toward the poles. At the same time the denser cold water from the polar regions flows along the bottom toward the equator.

Superimposed on this is the much larger effect of the winds on the water surface. The prevailing winds in the Northern Hemisphere are from the northeast between latitudes 0 and 30°, southwest from 30 to 60°, and northeast again in the region between latitude 60° and the pole. The winds in the Southern Hemisphere are the mirror image of this system.

Figure 1.14 is an idealized sketch of the currents that might be expected from this wind system in an ocean with land masses to east and west. On the whole, the currents tend to follow the wind direction but form recirculating cells because of the land masses on either side of the ocean. It might have been expected that because of the Coriolis force, the currents in the Northern Hemisphere would be deflected to the right of the wind direction. This is not apparent because the deflection of the northeasterly current is opposed by the opposite deflection of the southwesterly current making up the other half of the cell.

Figure 1.15 shows some of the main currents actually observed at the sea surface. As might be expected, the real situation is more complicated than that suggested by Fig. 1.14 but the main features are similar. However, it should be emphasized that the currents are far from steady. Not only are there significant seasonal variations but the path of the current may vary significantly from week to week. For example, the Gulf Stream is observed to form loops which break off into separate eddies. In such an eddy the current may be in the direction opposite to that of the Gulf Stream.

To obtain some idea of the scale of these currents, it is of interest to note

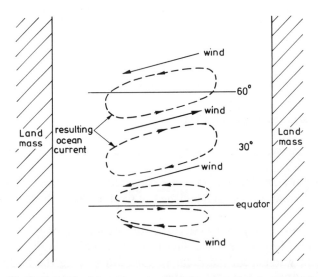

Figure 1.14. Idealized sketch of the currents produced in an enclosed ocean by a given wind system.

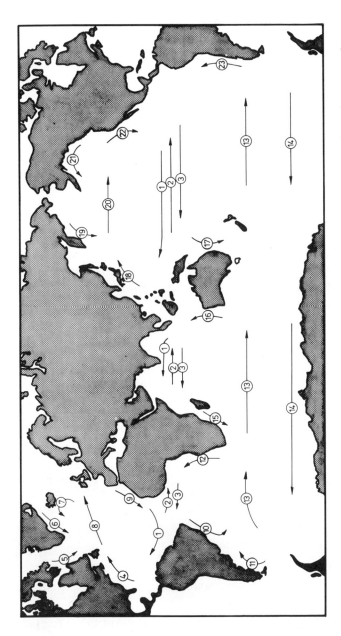

Figure 1.15. Major ocean currents observed at the surface during the northern hemisphere winter: (1) north equatorial current; (2) equatorial countercurrent; (3) south equatorial current; (4) Gulf Stream; (5) Labrador current; (6) East Greenland current; (7) Irminger current; (8) North Atlantic current; (9) Canary current; (10) Brazil current; (11) Falkland current; (12) Benguela current; (13) Antarctic circumpolar current; (14) Antarctic subpolar current; (15) Agulhas current; (16) West Australia current; (17) East Australia current; (18) Kuri Shio current; (19) Oya Shio current; (20) North Pacific current; (21) Alaska current; (22) California current; (23) Peru current.

47

that the Gulf Stream transports around 110 million cubic meters of water per second, which is more than 60 times the amount of water moved by all of the rivers of the world combined. Surface speeds in the Gulf Stream vary from about 0.2 up to almost 2.0 m/s.

Although these large-scale ocean currents are most apparent in deep water their effect is not insignificant in coastal waters.

Waves and Currents

1.18. PREDICTION OF THE CHANGE IN WAVE CHARACTERISTICS PRODUCED BY A KNOWN STEADY CURRENT

The simplest case we can take is that of irrotational flow and a mean current that does not vary with depth. In addition we assume that the variation of the current in the horizontal direction is "slow." In other words,

$$\frac{1}{\omega}\frac{d\bar{U}}{dx}\ll 1 \tag{1.124}$$

The solution for this simple case was given in the classical papers of Longuet-Higgins and Stewart (1961, 1964). The basic equation determining the wave height is

$$\frac{d}{dx}\left[E(\bar{U}+c_g)\right]+S_{xx}\frac{d\bar{U}}{dx}=0 \tag{1.125}$$

where E, c_g, and S_{xx} are given by (1.22), (1.23), and (1.26). After some algebra we obtain

$$\frac{H}{H_0}=\left[\frac{\left(1+\dfrac{2b_0 d_0}{\sinh 2b_0 d_0}\right)\left(1-\dfrac{b\bar{U}}{b_0 c_0}\right)}{\left(\dfrac{b_0}{b}-\dfrac{\bar{U}}{c_0}\right)\left(1+\dfrac{2bd}{\sinh 2bd}\right)+\dfrac{2\bar{U}}{c_0}}\right]^{1/2} \tag{1.126}$$

Here the subscript 0 refers to quantities in the absence of the current but not necessarily in deep water. Physically we imagine the situation to be one in which a steady train of waves propagates over a horizontal bed from a region with no mean current into one in which there is a current. Despite the fact that the bed is horizontal, the depth d is not quite the same as d_0 because of the change in water level produced by the current. The relation between the two depths is

$$d=d_0-\frac{\bar{U}^2}{2g} \tag{1.127}$$

The speed of the waves relative to axes moving with the mean current is the same as that given by (1.16) for stationary axes and zero current. Thus

$$\frac{\omega}{b}=\left(\frac{g}{b}\tanh bd\right)^{1/2}+\bar{U} \tag{1.128}$$

Since we are considering a steady train of waves the frequency ω must be the same as ω_0. Making use of (1.16) and (1.128) we obtain

$$(gb_0\tanh b_0d_0)^{1/2}=(gb\tanh bd)^{1/2}+b\bar{U} \tag{1.129}$$

These formulas are for irrotational flow and a uniform current. Real currents do not satisfy these conditions. Solutions have been obtained for more realistic current profiles (see, e.g., Dalrymple, 1973; Jonsson et al., 1978; Thomas, 1981). These solutions suggest that, for most practical purposes, the assumption of irrotational flow and uniform current is a reasonable first approximation. Figures 1.16 and 1.17 show measurements of the change in

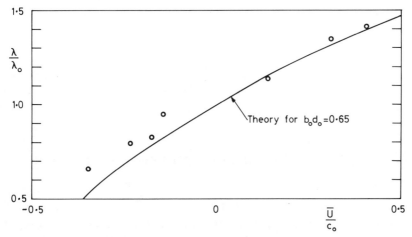

Figure 1.16. The change in wave length produced by a steady current; ∘-measurements of Brevik (1980).

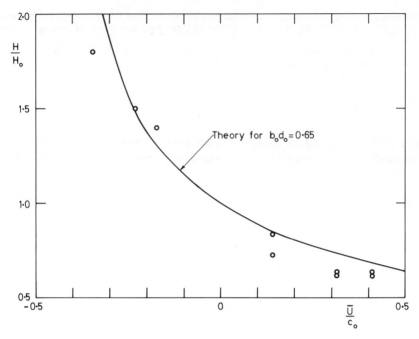

Figure 1.17. The change in wave height produced by a steady current; ∘-measurements of Brevik (1980).

wave height and length produced by currents in a laboratory wave channel. The theoretical curves, obtained from (1.126) and (1.129), are in remarkably good agreement with the measurements.

Figures 1.16 and 1.17 show that when the current is in the same direction as the waves the height is decreased and the wavelength becomes longer. For an opposing current the height is increased and the wavelength decreased. Curves are shown only for one value of *bd*, but those for different values of *bd* are similar.

1.19. PREDICTION OF THE CURRENT PROFILE WHEN THE WAVES ARE KNOWN

This question has been investigated theoretically by Lundgren (1972), Smith (1977), Bakker and Van Doorn (1978), Grant and Madsen (1979), and Fredsoe (1981). There appears to be general agreement on the following three points which are also consistent with available experimental evidence:

1. The mean velocity profile may be split into two sections: an inner region close to the bed which is affected by turbulence produced in the wave-induced boundary layer and an outer region above it. (The flow in the inner region will be discussed in more detail in Chapter 2.)

2. The turbulence in the outer region is unaffected by the waves. Consequently, the mean velocity profile is given by

$$\frac{\bar{u}}{\bar{u}_*} = \frac{1}{K} \ln\left(\frac{y}{y_0}\right) \tag{1.94}$$

However, the values of $\bar{u}_*$ and y_0 in this formula are not the same as those for a current alone. Although the wave-induced turbulence does not extend up into this outer layer, it does affect the boundary conditions for the velocity distribution. In view of the findings for steady currents discussed in Section 1.16, it is not to be expected that (1.94) would hold right up to the free surface.

3. For rough beds the waves reduce the mean current in the outer layer. Figure 1.18 shows a typical example. (As anticipated, these measure-

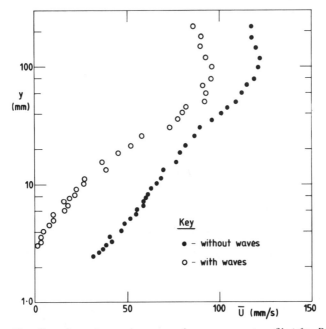

Figure 1.18.   The effect of superimposed waves on the mean current profile (after Bakker and Van Doorn, 1978).

ments show that the velocity profile is not logarithmic right up to the free surface). A similar reduction in mean velocity was also observed by Brevik (1980) for smooth beds. On the other hand, Kemp and Simons (1982) did not observe any clear trend in their smooth bed measurements of the mean velocity profile. This may be because their mean currents were smaller than those of Brevik.

All of the theoretical models mentioned above provide methods for calculating the new values of $\bar{u}_*$ and y_0 to be used in (1.94). Some further discussion of these theoretical models is contained in Section 2.10.

At present there are not enough experimental measurements to show which, if any, of the available formulas is reliable. Brevik and Aas (1980) found poor agreement between their measurements and the formulas of Lundgren and of Grant and Madsen. This disagreement may have been because the currents used in their experiments were relatively strong. (Measurements by Kemp and Simons, 1982, show support for Grant and Madsen's assumption of linear variation in eddy viscosity in the outer region.) Bakker and Van Doorn obtained good agreement between their method and their own experiments. Fredsoe also found good agreement between his method and Bakker and Van Doorn's measurements.

Alternatively, y_0 may be estimated directly from experimental results such as those shown in Fig. 1.19. Knowledge of y_0 and the velocity at some height is sufficient to determine the velocity profile with the aid of (1.94). In

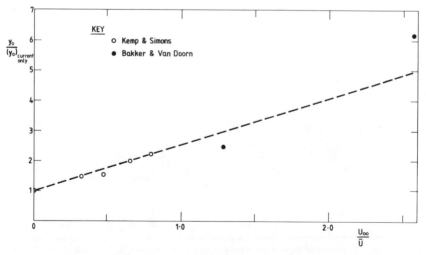

Figure 1.19.   The variation of y_0 with $U_\infty/\bar{U}$.

addition to the measurements of Bakker and Van Doorn, Brevik and Aas, Brevik, and Kemp and Simons mentioned above, experiments have also been carried out by Van Hoften and Karaki (1976) and Thomas (1981).

REFERENCES

Ackers, P. and White, W. (1973). Sediment transport: new approach and analysis. *Proc. A.S.C.E. J. Hydraul. Div.* **99** (HY11): 2041–2060.

Anwar, H. O. and Atkins, R. (1980). Turbulence measurements in simulated tidal flow. *Proc. A.S.C.E. J. Hydraul. Div.* **106** (HY8): 1273–1289.

Bakker, W. T. and Van Doorn, T. (1978). Near bottom velocities in waves with a current. *Proc. 16th Conf. Coastal Eng. Hamburg*, pp. 1394–1413.

Bowen, A. J. (1969a). The generation of longshore currents on a plane beach. *J. Mar. Res.* **37**: 206–215.

Bowen, A. J. (1969b). Rip currents, 1: Theoretical investigations. *J. Geophys. Res.* **74**: 5467–5478.

Bowen, A. J. and Inman, D. L. (1969). Rip currents, 2: Laboratory and field observations. *J. Geophys. Res.* **74**: 5479–5490.

Boussinesq, J. (1872). Théorie des ondes et des remous qui se propagent le long d'un canal réctangulaire horizontal, en communiquant au liquide contenu dans ce canal des vitesses sensiblement parallèles de la surface au fond. *J. Math. Pures Appliques.* Ser. 2. **17**: 55–108.

Brebner, A. and Kamphuis, J. W. (1963). Model tests on the relationship between deep-water wave characteristics and longshore currents. Queens University. Canada. Dept of Civil Eng. Rep. 13.

Brevik, I. (1980). Flume experiment on waves and currents. 2. Smooth bed. *Coastal Eng.* **4**: 89–110.

Brevik, I. and Aas, B. (1980). Flume experiment on waves and currents. 1. Rippled bed. *Coastal Eng.* **3**: 149–177.

Bruun, P. (1963). Longshore currents and longshore troughs. *J. Geophys. Res.* **68**: 1065–1078.

Chaplin, J. R. (1980). Developments of stream-function theory. *Coastal Eng.* 3: 179–205.

Chappelear, J. E. (1961). Direct numerical calculation of wave properties. *J. Geophys. Res.* **66**: 501–508.

Clauser, F. H. (1956). The turbulent boundary layer. In *Advances in Applied Mechanics*, Vol. 4. Academic Press, New York, pp. 1–51.

Coastal Engineering Research Center. (1977). *Shore Protection Manual*, 3rd ed. U.S. Army Corps of Engineers.

Cokelet, E. D. (1977). Steep gravity waves in water of arbitrary uniform depth. *Philos. Trans. Roy. Soc. Ser. A.* **286**: 183–230.

Coleman, N. L. (1981). Velocity profiles with suspended sediment. *J. Hydraul. Res.* **19** (3): 211–229.

Dalrymple, R. A. (1973). Water wave models and wave forces with shear currents. Coastal Oceanog. Eng. Lab. Univ. Florida. Tech. Rep. 20.

Dean, R. G. (1965). Stream function representation of non-linear ocean waves. *J. Geophys. Res.* **70** (18): 4561–4572.

Dean, R. G. (1970). Relative validities of water wave theories. *Proc. A.S.C.E. J. Waterw. Harbors Coastal Eng. Div.* **96** (WW1): 105–119.

Dean, R. G. (1974). Evaluation and development of water wave theories for engineering application. C.E.R.C. Spec. Rep. 1.

Dyke, P. P. and Barstow, S. F. (1981). Wave induced mass transport: theory and experiment. *J. Hydraul. Res.* **19** (2): 89–106.

Eagleson, P. S. (1965). Theoretical study of longshore currents on a plane beach. M.I.T. Hydrodynam. Lab. Tech. Rep. 82.

Einstein, H. A. (1950). The bed-load function for sediment transport in open channel flows. U.S. Dept. Agric. Soil Conserv. Serv. Tech. Bull. 1026.

Engelund, F. A. and Hansen, E. (1967). A monograph on sediment transport in alluvial streams. *Tek. Forlag.* Copenhagen.

Fredsoe, J. (1981). Mean current velocity distribution in combined waves and current. Inst. Hydrodyn. Hydraul. Eng. Tech. Univ. Denmark. Prog. Rep. **53**.

Gaillard, D. D. (1904). Wave action in relation to engineering structures. U.S. Army. Prof. Paper 31. Washington.

Galvin, C. J. (1967). Longshore current velocity: a review of theory and data. *Rev. Geophys.* **5** (3): 287–304.

Galvin, C. J. (1972). Wave breaking in shallow water. In *Waves on Beaches*, R. E. Meyer, Ed. Academic Press, New York, pp. 413–456.

Galvin, C. J. and Eagleson, P. S. (1965). Experimental study of longshore currents on a plane beach. C.E.R.C. Tech. Memo **10**.

Gerstner, F. (1802). *Theorie der Wellen*. Abhandlungen der königlichen bömischen Gesellschaft der Wissenschaften, Prague.

Goda, Y. (1970). A synthesis of breaker indices. *Trans. Jpn. Soc. Civil Eng.* **2**: 227–230.

Gordon, C. M. (1975). Sediment entrainment and suspension in a turbulent tidal flow. *Mar. Geol.* **18**: 57–64.

Grant, W. D. and Madsen, O. S. (1979). Combined wave and current interaction with a rough bottom. *J. Geophys. Res.* **84** (C4): 1797–1808.

Hamilton, D., Sommerville, J. H., and Stanford, P. N. (1980). Bottom currents and shelf sediments, southwest of Britain. *Sed. Geol.* **26**: 115–138.

Harrison, W. (1968). Empirical equation for longshore current velocity. *J. Geophys. Res.* **73** (22): 6929–6936.

Hey, R. D. (1979). Flow resistance in gravel-bed rivers. *Proc. A.S.C.E. J. Hydraul. Div.* **105** (HY4): 365–379.

Housley, J. G. and Taylor, D. C. (1957). Application of solitary wave theory to shoaling oscillatory waves. *Trans. A.G.U.* **38** (1): 56.

Huthnance, J. M. (1981). On mass transports generated by tides and long waves. *J. Fluid Mech.* **102**: 367–387.

Inman, D. L. and Bagnold, R. A. (1963). Littoral processes. In *The Sea*, Vol. 3. M. N. Hill, Ed. Wiley, New York, pp. 529–533.

Inman, D. L. and Quinn, W. H. (1952). Currents in the surf zone. *Proc. 2nd Conf. Coastal Eng.*, pp. 24–36.

Ippen, A. T. and Kulin, G. (1954). The shoaling and breaking of the solitary wave. *Proc. 5th Conf. Coastal Eng. Grenoble.*

Isaacson, M. (1978). Mass transport in shallow water waves. *Proc. A.S.C.E. J. Waterw. Port Coastal Ocean Div.* **104** (WW2): 215–225.

Itakura, T. and Kishi, T. (1980). Open channel flow with suspended sediments. *Proc. A.S.C.E. J. Hydraul. Div.* **106** (HY8): 1325–1343.

Jackson, P. S. (1981). On the displacement height in the logarithmic velocity profile. *J. Fluid Mech.* **111**: 15–25.

Jonsson, I. G., Brink-Kjaer, O. and Thomas, G. P. (1978). Wave action and set-down for waves on a shear current. *J. Fluid Mech.* **87**: 401–416.

Kamphuis, J. W. (1975). Friction factors under oscillatory waves. *Proc. A.S.C.E. J. Waterw. Harbors Coastal Eng. Div.* **101** (WW2): 135–144.

Kemp, P. H. and Simons, R. R. (1982). The interaction between waves and a turbulent current. Waves propagating with the current. *J. Fluid Mech.* **116**: 227–250.

Le Mehaute, B. (1976). *An Introduction to Hydrodynamics and Water Waves.* Springer Verlag, Dusseldorf.

Liu, A. K. and Davis, S. H. (1977). Viscous attenuation of the mean drift in water waves. *J. Fluid Mech.* **81**: 63–84.

Longuet-Higgins, M. S. (1953). Mass transport in water waves. *Philos. Trans. Roy. Soc.* Ser. A. **245**: 535–581.

Longuet-Higgins, M. S. (1970a). Longshore currents generated by obliquely incident sea waves. I. *J. Geophys. Res.* **75** (33): 6778–6789.

Longuet-Higgins, M. S. (1970b). Longshore currents generated by obliquely incident sea waves. II. *J. Geophys. Res.* **75** (33): 6790–6801.

Longuet-Higgins, M. S. and Stewart, R. W. (1961). The changes in amplitude of short gravity waves on steady non-uniform currents. *J. Fluid Mech.* **10**: 529–549.

Longuet-Higgins, M. S. and Stewart, R. W. (1964). Radiation stress in water waves: a physical discussion with applications. *Deep-Sea Res.* **11**: 529–562.

Lundgren, H. (1972). Turbulent currents in the presence of waves. *Proc. 13th Conf. Coastal Eng. Vancouver*, pp. 623–634.

Mahmood, K. (1971). Water Manage. Tech. Rep. 11. Colorado State Univ. Fort Collins.

Mei, C. C., Liu, P. L-F., and Carter, T. G. (1972). Mass transport in water waves. M.I.T. Dept. Civil Eng. Ralph M. Parsons Lab. Rep. 45.

Miche, R. (1944). Mouvements ondulatoires des mers en profondeur constante ou décroissante. *Annales Ponts Chaussées* **114**: 25–78, 131–164, 270–292, 369–406.

Naheer, E. (1977). Stability of bottom armoring under the attack of solitary waves. Cal. Inst. Tech. W.M. Keck Lab. Rep. KH-R-34.

Proudman, J. and Doodson, A. T. (1924). The principal constituent of the tides of the north sea. *Philos. Trans. Roy. Soc.* Ser. A. **224**: 185–219.

Putnam, J. A., Munk, W. A., and Traylor, M. A. (1949). The prediction of longshore currents. *Trans. A.G.U.* **30**: 337–345.

Rienecker, M. M. and Fenton, J. D. (1981). A Fourier approximation method for steady water waves. *J. Fluid Mech.* **104**: 119–137.

Russell, R. C. H. and Osorio, J. D. C. (1957). An experimental investigation of drift profiles in a closed channel. *Proc. 6th Conf. Coastal Eng. Miami*, pp. 171–193.

Sato, S. and Tanaka, N. (1966). Field investigations on sand drifts at Kashima Harbour facing the pacific Ocean. *Proc. 10th Conf. Coastal Eng. Tokyo*, pp. 595–614.

Shadrin, I. F. (1961). The possibility of predicting longshore currents in tideless seas. Dynamics and morphology of sea coasts. *Trans. Inst. Oceanol. Acad. Sci., USSR*, pp. 350–364.

Shinohara, K. and Tsubaki, T. (1959). On the characteristics of sand waves formed upon the beds of the open channels and rivers. Rep. Res. Inst. Appl. Mech. Kyushu Univ. Vol 7 (25).

Smith, J. D. (1977). Modeling of sediment transport on continental shelves. In *The Sea*, Vol 6. E. D. Goldberg, I. N. McCave, J. J. O'Brien, and J. H. Steele, Eds. Wiley, New York, pp. 538–578.

Sonu, C. J. (1972). Field observation of nearshore circulation and meandering currents. *J. Geophys. Res.* **77** (18): 3232–3247.

Soulsby, R. L. and Dyer, K. R. (1981). The form of the near-bed velocity profile in a tidally accelerating flow. *J. Geophys. Res.* **8** (C9): 8067–8074.

Southard, J. B. and Cacchione, D. A. (1972). Experiments on bottom sediment movement by breaking internal waves. In *Shelf Sediment Transport*. D. J. P. Swift, D. B. Duane, and O. H. Pilkey, Eds. Dowden, Hutchinson & Ross, Stroudsburg, Pennsylvania, pp. 83–97.

Stokes, G. G. (1880). On the theory of oscillatory waves. *Math. Phys. Papers. I.* Cambridge University Press, Cambridge, p. 227.

Swart, D. H. (1976). Coastal sediment transport. Computation of longshore transport. Delft Hydraul. Lab. Rep. r968. Part 1.

Swart, D. H. and Loubser, C. C. (1978). Vocoidal theory for all non-breaking waves. *Proc. 16th Conf. Coastal Eng. Hamburg*, pp. 467–486.

Thornton, E. B. (1969). Longshore current and sediment transport. Univ. Florida. Dept. Coastal Oceanogr. Eng. Tech. Rep. 5.

Thomas, G. P. (1981). Wave-current interactions: an experimental and numerical study. Part 1. Linear waves. *J. Fluid Mech.* **110**: 457–474.

Van Hoften, J. D. A. and Karaki, S. (1976). Interaction of waves and a turbulent current. *Proc. 15th Conf. Coastal Eng. Hawaii*, pp. 404–422.

Van Rijn, L. C. (1982). Equivalent roughness of alluvial bed. *Proc. A.S.C.E. J. Hydraul. Div.* **108** (HY10): 1215–1218.

Wang, S.-Y. (1981). Variation of Karman constant in sediment-laden flow. *Proc. A.S.C.E. J. Hydraul. Div.* **107** (HY4): 407–417.

Wiegel, R. L. (1964). *Oceanographical Engineering*. Prentice-Hall, Englewood Cliffs, New Jersey.

Two

FLUID VELOCITIES
AND PRESSURES
NEAR AND IN THE SEA BED

Waves Alone

Most of the theoretical results outlined in this chapter were obtained using small-amplitude wave theory. This means that, to a first approximation, the velocity just outside the boundary layer is assumed to vary sinusoidally with time. In many situations this is not correct, either because higher harmonics are relatively important (e.g., in shallow water or near wave breaking) or because the real situation involves several different wave components. However, once the solution for the simple case is known the extension to more complicated situations is often relatively straightforward.

In addition to the assumption that small-amplitude wave theory is valid, it will generally be assumed that the waves are progressing in water of constant depth without change of form.

Where appropriate, the corresponding results obtained on the basis of different assumptions are quoted.

2.1. TRANSITION

One of the most important factors determining the velocity distribution is whether the flow is laminar or turbulent. Not surprisingly, there have been many investigations of the conditions under which transition takes place.

2.1.1. Smooth Beds

Table 2.1 summarizes the experimental results for the critical value of R at which transition from laminar to turbulent oscillatory flow occurs. This table includes both the results for flat beds and those for circular pipes for which the Stokes parameter βd_2 is large. If $1/\beta$, which is a measure of the thickness of the viscous boundary layer, is small compared with the pipe diameter d_2 the velocity distribution within the viscous layer in a pipe is almost identical with that for a flat plate.

Collins' (1963) critical value is based on observations of the mass transport velocity in the boundary layer at the bed of a wave flume. He observed that when a certain limit is passed the mass transport velocity begins to deviate from the theoretical expression calculated by Longuet-Higgins (1953) (Section 2.2.1). Collins suggested that this deviation was an indication of the

TABLE 2.1. EXPERIMENTAL RESULTS FOR THE CRITICAL VALUE OF R FOR TRANSITION IN OSCILLATORY FLOW

Author	Apparatus	Critical value of R	$(\beta d_2)_{max}$	Method
Li (1954)	Oscillating plate	1.6×10^5	—	Dye dispersion
Vincent (1957)	Wave flume	$\geqslant 1.6 \times 10^5$	—	Dye dispersion
Collins (1963)	Wave flume	1.3×10^4	—	Mass transport velocity
Sergeev (1966)	Circular pipe	1.2×10^5	56	Flow visualization, power measurement
Riedel et al. (1972)	Water tunnel	10^4–6×10^5	—	Measurement of bed friction
Merkli and Thomann (1975)	Resonant tube	4×10^4	100	Hot wire, flow visualization
Hino et al. (1976)	Circular pipe	1.5×10^5	12.4	Hot wire
Tromans (1978)	Circular pipe	1.4×10^5	26.6	Hot wire

onset of turbulence. However, Sleath (1972), Isaacson (1976b), and Dore (1982) showed that this deviation is a purely laminar effect and is not caused by turbulence. The low value of R obtained by Collins should consequently be disregarded.

A much lower value for transition than that shown in Table 2.1 is often attributed to Vincent (1957). The lower value was, in fact, obtained by Vincent for rough beds. Vincent did not obtain turbulent flow in any of his tests with smooth beds and concluded that for a hydraulically smooth bed the critical value of R would be at least 1.6×10^5.

The value of R quoted by Merkli and Thomann (1975) is also open to some doubt. The tube they used for their experiments was slightly wavy. They also experienced difficulties with compressibility effects and disturbance of the flow by their probe.

The results of Hino et al. (1976) are particularly interesting. They observed that even at values of R significantly higher than those shown in Table 2.1 the flow is not turbulent during the whole cycle. Turbulence sets in soon after the velocity passes its maximum and disappears when the flow reverses. Hino et al. also found that at values of R lower than those given in Table 2.1, the flow showed signs of unsteadiness. However, this unsteadiness was of very small amplitude and did not significantly perturb the flow. In these respects it was different from the turbulence found at Reynolds numbers above the critical value. Similar results were obtained by Merkli and Thomann (1975) and Tromans (1978). Whether this preliminary unsteadiness is inherent in the nature of the flow or whether it is caused by some imperfection in the experimental apparatus is not clear at the present time.

It should be mentioned that the velocity used to define R in the pipe flow experiments of Sergeev and of Hino et al. was the cross-sectional average velocity rather than the free-stream velocity. However, for large βd_2 the difference is not significant.

There have also been a number of attempts to calculate the critical value of R analytically. Collins (1963) carried out a stability analysis using a quasi-steady approximation, that is, the time-varying velocity at any given instant is assumed to be steady. However, Von Kerczek and Davis (1972) found that there is a numerical error in this calculation. When this is corrected the critical value of R is found to be 1.58×10^5.

Von Kerczek and Davis (1972, 1974) and Davis and Von Kerczek (1973) have also attempted to calculate the critical condition by use of energy stability theory and by numerical integration of the full time-dependent equations of motion. This work shows that the boundary layer will be unconditionally stable for $R < 293$ but does not provide a definite value for the actual value of R at which the transition takes place.

We conclude that there is at the present time no reason to doubt the value for transition to turbulence originally proposed by Li (1954):

$$R = 1.6 \times 10^5 \qquad (2.1)$$

This is in reasonable agreement with the value of $R = 1 \times 10^5$ recommended by Jonsson (1980) for design purposes.

2.1.2.   Flat Beds of Sand or Gravel

If the intensity of flow is gradually increased, the usual sequence of events is as follows. At very low Reynolds numbers the flow follows the contours of the bed roughness and there is no sign of turbulence. However, when the Reynolds number exceeds a certain limit jets of fluid start to be thrown up from the bed when the flow reverses at the end of each half-cycle. These jets of fluid have been observed by many investigators (e.g., Vincent, 1957, Lhermitte, 1958, George and Sleath, 1978) and are caused by the ejection as the flow reverses of the vortices which form around the bed roughness elements. Strictly speaking, this formation and ejection of vortices is not turbulence. However, it produces mixing of the fluid near the bed and modification of the velocity profile in the same way as turbulence. Also, actual turbulence probably sets in soon after. Consequently, for most practical purposes, the appearance of these jets of fluid may be taken as the start of transition.

Figure 2.1 shows the experimental results obtained for transition over flat beds of sand or gravel together with the curves proposed by various investigators.

The measurements of Li (1954) and Manohar (1955) were made with trays of sediment oscillated in still water, whereas those of Vincent (1957) and Lhermitte (1958) were carried out in wave flumes. Lhermitte suggested that the much earlier transition that he and Vincent observed was caused by a fundamental difference between the two experimental arrangements. It may be readily shown (see Section 2.2.1) that, relative to axes fixed in the bed, the velocity distribution close to a bed oscillating in its own plane in still water is identical, for a given value of x, to the first-order solution for waves over a stationary bed. This result holds true for both smooth and rough beds provided the roughness length is small compared with the length of the waves. However, second-order effects, such as the mass transport velocity in the boundary layer over a flat bed, are not reproduced in an oscillating tray rig. Nevertheless, in most natural situations these effects are small and consequently it seems unlikely that they would have much influence on the transition from laminar to turbulent flow.

The most likely explanations for the discrepancy between the various

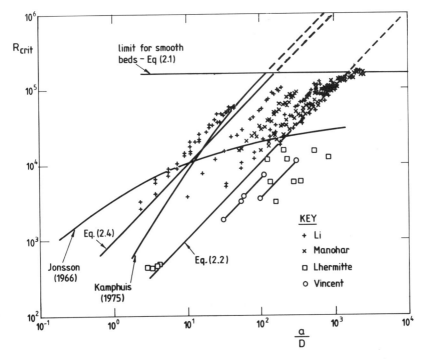

Figure 2.1. Critical value of R for transition for flat beds of sand or gravel.

results seen in Fig. 2.1 are the absence of a single objective criterion for transition and the variability of the experimental conditions. Vincent took transition to be when the jets of fluid first began to appear and consequently his results probably indicate the start of the transition process. Other investigators observed the dispersion of the traces left by crystals of dye falling through the fluid. Results obtained in this way would depend on the height above the bed at which the trace was being observed. Also, the nature of the bed itself could introduce considerable variation: a few particularly large grains of sediment near the measuring point might produce a significant difference in the observation. The difficulty of achieving consistent results was pointed out by Kalkanis (1964). Using the same oscillating tray rig as Li and Manohar he found transition at a value of U_∞/v about five times smaller than would have been expected from their observations.

The formula originally put forward by Manohar for relatively fine sediments is

$$R = 104(a/D) \tag{2.2}$$

For coarse sediments he proposed

$$R = 17,800(a/D^{0.2})$$ (2.3)

where a and D are measured in feet.

In the light of his own experiments, Kalkanis (1964) suggested that Li's results for relatively coarse sediments should be disregarded and that (2.2) might hold for all flat beds of sand or gravel.

Kajiura (1968) derived a relationship very similar to (2.2) for the start of the transition process but suggested that fully developed turbulence was not obtained until

$$R = 1000(a/D)$$ (2.4)

Also shown in Fig. 2.1 are the curve of Kamphuis (1975) and the RL curve of Jonsson (1966). These curves were originally expressed in terms of the roughness length k_s rather than the median grain size D. Since all authors give details of grain size but few have measured k_s, D is probably a more reliable basis for comparison at the present time. Kamphuis' curve has been converted with the aid of his published grain size distributions and in Jonsson's formula it has been assumed that $k_s = 2D$. Jonsson (1980) suggested that for two-dimensional bed roughness k_s should be taken equal to half the wavelength of the bed roughness. Both Li and Manohar used well-sorted sediments. Consequently, as far as their experiments are concerned, the assumed value of k_s is not significantly different from the $2D_{90}$ value suggested by Kamphuis. Jonsson's RS curve is not shown since, in his 1980 paper, he states that this curve is speculative and recommends the formulas of Kajiura or Kamphuis instead. Kamphuis' curve represents the limit beyond which his friction coefficient curves ceased, for given a/D, to depend on R. It will be seen in Chapter 5 that this limit is not necessarily connected with transition to turbulence.

There have been no flat bed experiments at very small values of a/D but the rippled bed results discussed later suggest that none of these formulas are likely to hold for a/D less than unity. In addition, since transition for a rough bed can hardly occur at a higher value of R than for a smooth bed, they should not be extended beyond $R = 1.6 \times 10^5$.

Although the experimental results shown in Fig. 2.1 are far from conclusive, it seems likely that, as suggested by Kalkanis, (2.2) gives a reasonable estimate for the start of the transition process. This equation is also consistent with the results of velocity measurements for this sort of bed (Sleath, 1982). Just how high the Reynolds number has to be for the turbulence to be fully developed is not clear at the present time. In the absence of further information it is suggested that (2.4) be used as a rough estimate.

2.1.3. Rippled Beds

Measurements have been made with a hot-wire anemometer over rippled beds in an oscillating tray apparatus by Sleath (1975). The velocity close to the bed was conditionally sampled at the same instant during each cycle and the mean and root mean square velocity were determined. Figure 2.2 shows the results obtained for a root mean square fluctuation in velocity equal to 5% of U_∞. The solid line in Fig. 2.2 was drawn to give the best fit to the measurements. Its equation is

$$\left(\frac{U_\infty L}{v}\left(\frac{h}{L}\right)^{1.16}-108.2\right)\left(\frac{a}{L}\left(\frac{h}{L}\right)^{1.16}-0.042\right)=0.58 \qquad (2.5)$$

One interesting feature of these results is that there appears to be a limiting value of a/L below which turbulence does not occur. For example, for $h/L=0.15$, (2.5) shows that the root mean square fluctuation in velocity is always less than $0.05\,U_\infty$ if a/L is less than 0.38. Of course, this limit applies only to turbulence generated by the ripple profile. Turbulence would still be generated by the individual grains of sand on the bed if the limits discussed in Section 2.1.2 were exceeded.

When a/L is large, (2.5) reduces to

$$R=108.2\,\frac{(a/L)}{(h/L)^{1.16}} \qquad (2.6)$$

This equation is similar in form to (2.2) and (2.4).

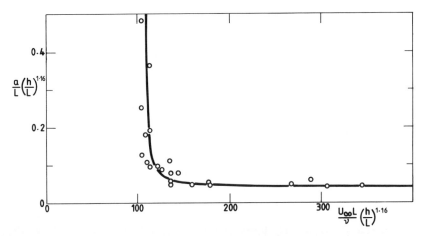

Figure 2.2. Limiting condition for which the r.m.s. fluctuation in velocity is equal to $0.05U_\infty$.

Measurements of transition to turbulence have also been made with beds covered with round, or half-round rods by Li (1954), Manohar (1955), and Kalkanis (1964). As for the beds of sand or gravel, the experimental results are not conclusive. The best estimate for transition appears to be

$$R = 640(a/D) \tag{2.7}$$

2.2. THE VELOCITY DISTRIBUTION IN LAMINAR FLOW

2.2.1. Flat Beds

Small-Amplitude Wave Theory

If the flow is assumed to be two dimensional, the Navier–Stokes equation for the horizontal component of velocity is

$$\frac{\partial u}{\partial t} + u\frac{\partial u}{\partial x} + v\frac{\partial u}{\partial y} = -\frac{1}{\rho}\frac{\partial p}{\partial x} + v\left(\frac{\partial^2 u}{\partial x^2} + \frac{\partial^2 u}{\partial y^2}\right) \tag{2.8}$$

We are interested in the flow very close to the bed. Because the boundary layer is so thin it is reasonable, as a first approximation, to assume that the flow is parallel to the bed. This means that the vertical velocity v and derivatives in the x direction may be neglected. Thus

$$\frac{\partial u}{\partial t} = -\frac{1}{\rho}\frac{\partial p}{\partial x} + v\frac{\partial^2 u}{\partial y^2} \tag{2.9}$$

The other consequence of a very thin boundary layer is that the pressure may be assumed to be constant across it. From (2.9) the pressure gradient just outside the boundary layer is given by

$$-\frac{1}{\rho}\frac{\partial p}{\partial x} = \frac{\partial u_0}{\partial t} \tag{2.10}$$

Thus, assuming that the pressure is the same in the boundary layer, (2.9) becomes

$$\frac{\partial}{\partial t}(u - u_0) = v\frac{\partial^2 u}{\partial y^2} \tag{2.11}$$

Just outside the boundary layer the velocity u_0 must be the same as that given in Chapter 1 for irrotational flow. The first-order solution for this velocity is given by (1.18). At the bed the velocity is zero. Since the flow is periodic in time and space it is logical to look for a solution to (2.11) of the form

$$u = \text{real part } [f(y)e^{i(\omega t - bx)}] \tag{2.12}$$

Substituting into (2.11) and making use of (1.18) for u_0, we obtain

$$\frac{\partial^2 f}{\partial y^2} - \frac{i\omega}{v} f = -\frac{i\omega}{v} U_\infty \tag{2.13}$$

Integrating and applying the boundary conditions gives

$$u = U_\infty [\cos(\omega t - bx) - e^{-\beta y} \cos(\omega t - bx - \beta y)] \tag{2.14}$$

where $\beta = (\omega/2v)^{1/2}$. Figure 2.3 shows the velocity profile at various phases during the cycle. The phase at which the velocity is maximum varies with height above the bed. This is illustrated more clearly by Fig. 2.4, which shows how the amplitude and phase of the maximum velocity vary with βy. We see that the phase of the maximum velocity at the bed is 45° ahead of that in the free stream. Also shown in this figure are experimental measurements of the velocities in the boundary layer above a smooth bed in a wave flume. The agreement between theory and experiment is good.

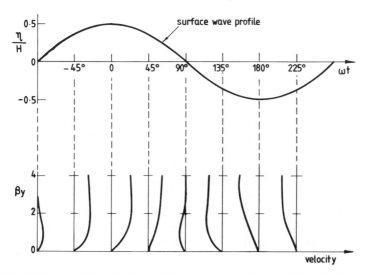

Figure 2.3.   Velocity profiles in the boundary layer at various phases in the cycle of oscillation.

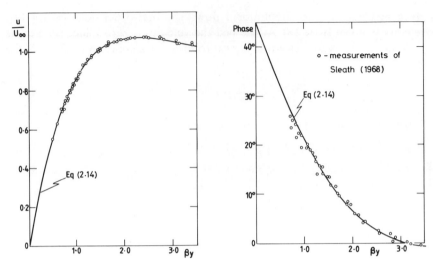

Figure 2.4. Amplitude and phase of the maximum velocity in the boundary layer.

The thickness of the oscillatory boundary layer is proportional to $1/\beta$. The constant of proportionality depends on the definition adopted for the edge of the boundary layer. Jonsson (1980) suggests that the constant should be $\pi/2$, which corresponds to the smallest value of βy at which $u/U_\infty = 1$ in Fig. 2.4, but other values have been proposed (e.g., Manohar 1955).

As stated in Section 2.1.2, there are strong similarities between the velocity distribution obtained in the boundary layer above a flat bed under wave action and that above a plate oscillating in still fluid. The solution for the horizontal component of velocity above a flat plate oscillating in its own plane in a tank of still fluid was given by Stokes (1851) as

$$u = U_\infty e^{-\beta y} \cos(\omega t - \beta y) \tag{2.15}$$

where the motion of the plate is simple harmonic.

This expression is for axes fixed in space. If the axes are fixed in the bed, (2.15) becomes

$$u = U_\infty [\cos \omega t - e^{-\beta y} \cos(\omega t - \beta y)] \tag{2.16}$$

In other words, the velocity distribution at any fixed value of x is the same as the first approximation for waves over a stationary bed given by (2.14). However, as mentioned, this agreement does not extend to the second approximation.

The first approximation for waves over a stationary bed (2.14) was obtained on the assumption that the nonlinear terms in the equations of motion are negligible. A second approximation is obtained by assuming that the nonlinear terms are small but not negligible. The solution contains terms involving $\cos 2(\omega t - bx)$ and also terms which are independent of time. These time-independent terms are of particular interest because the steady flow which they represent, although weak, transports sediment and pollutants from one place to another.

The solution for the component of the Eulerian velocity (i.e., the velocity measured by a stationary probe) which is independent of time is

$$\bar{u} = \frac{U_\infty^2 b}{4\omega} \left[3 + 2e^{-\beta y}(1 - \beta y) \sin \beta y - 2e^{-\beta y}(2 + \beta y) \cos \beta y + e^{-2\beta y} \right] \quad (2.17)$$

More often, particularly if we are concerned with the transport of sediment or pollutants, we are interested in the time-independent Lagrangian velocity. This is the velocity of the fluid particles themselves and usually is called the mass transport velocity. With the aid of Taylor's theorem and (2.14) and (2.17) the solution for the mass transport velocity is found to be

$$\bar{u}_{mt} = \frac{U_\infty^2 b}{4\omega} (5 - 8e^{-\beta y} \cos \beta y + 3e^{-2\beta y}) \quad (2.18)$$

This solution was first obtained by Longuet-Higgins (1953).

Figure 2.5 shows how the time-mean Eulerian velocity and the mass transport velocity vary within the boundary layer. The maximum value of $\bar{u}_{mt}$ is $1.391\, U_\infty^2 b/\omega$.

Experimental measurements of the mass transport velocity near the bed have been made in wave flumes by Caligny (1878), Bagnold (1947), Allen and Gibson (1959), Collins (1963), Mei et al. (1972), and others. All of these studies show general agreement with (2.18), although discrepancies are apparent when the waves are no longer well approximated by small-amplitude theory. For example, Fig. 2.6 shows the results obtained by Collins for the maximum mass transport velocity in the boundary layer at the bed. At small values of U_∞^2/ω there is close agreement between the measured value of $\bar{u}_{mt}$ and that given by (2.18). However, at higher values of U_∞^2/ω the measured values fall consistently below the theoretical curve. This discrepancy between theory and experiment is due to the neglect of higher order terms; (2.18) is only a first approximation.

A second approximation to (2.18) has been obtained by Dore (1982). However, one problem with higher order solutions is that real waves on site usually consist of a number of different components. Provided each component has a different wavelength and period, the first approximation

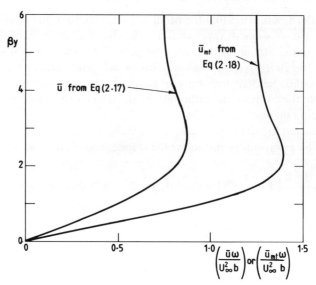

Figure 2.5. Variation of the time-mean Eulerian and mass transport velocities with height.

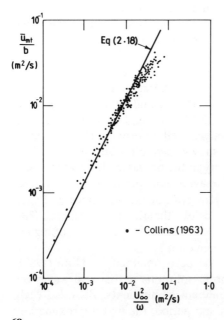

Figure 2.6. Measurements of the maximum mass transport velocity near the bed.

to the combined mass transport velocity may be obtained by summation of the contributions from each individual component separately. This does not hold for higher order approximations. Nor does it hold when two of the components have the same wavelength or period as, for example, with standing waves.

The solution given for the mass transport velocity by Longuet-Higgins (1953) for the case of standing waves is

$$\bar{u}_{mt} = \frac{U_\infty^2 b}{8\omega} \sin 2bx(-3 + 8e^{-\beta y} \sin \beta y + 3e^{-2\beta y}) \qquad (2.19)$$

In this case the wave height to be used in the expression for U_∞ is that of the standing wave, that is, twice that of the incident waves. We see that very close to the bed the fluid particles drift toward the nodes of the water surface profile and away from the antinodes (which occur at $bx = 0, \pi, 2\pi,$ etc.). However, further out, the flow is in the opposite direction. The mean flow in the boundary layer thus forms a series of closed cells.

Measurements of the mass transport velocity in the boundary layer at the bed have been carried out for standing waves by Noda (1968). These show general agreement with (2.19), although there are discrepancies for very small waves and also for very large ones. The discrepancy between theory and experiment for the very small waves is probably less significant than that with the large waves because experimental problems, such as the elimination of wave reflection and parasitic drifts, become relatively more important as wave height decreases. For the large waves, the discrepancies are probably due to the effect of higher order terms which were neglected in the derivation of this first approximation. Measurements have also been made by Mei et al. (1972) and Dore (1976), who showed that there are recirculating cells of fluid above those in the boundary layer.

The more general case of the short-crested waves which are formed from oblique reflections has been studied by Hunt and Johns (1963), Mei et al. (1972), Dore (1974), and Hsu et al. (1979, 1980).

Shallow-Water Waves

If the flow is assumed to be two-dimensional, the basic equation which governs the motion is still (2.8). Following Keulegan (1948) we assume, once again, that since the boundary layer is so thin it is reasonable to neglect v and derivatives in the x direction as a first approximation. Thus (2.11) applies to this case also. The velocity is zero at the bed and tends to the value given by irrotational theory outside the boundary layer. For solitary waves this irrotational velocity, which we will denote by u_0, is given to a first approximation by (1.44). Equation (2.11) may be solved with the aid of a Fourier integral. The solution given by Keulegan is

$$u = u_0 - \frac{2}{\pi^{1/2}} \int_0^\infty u_1 e^{-\xi^2} d\xi \qquad (2.20)$$

where u is the horizontal velocity at any point x and u_1 is the corresponding velocity at $x + cy^2/4v\xi^2$. The parameter ξ is a variable of integration.

Solitary waves produce only a single finite displacement of the fluid particles so there is no direct equivalent of the mass transport velocity observed with periodic waves. However, cnoidal waves, which are the periodic waves obtained from shallow-water theory, do induce a mass transport velocity. Isaacson (1976a, 1976b) has calculated first- and second-order solutions for this velocity. As might be expected, as the parameter bd decreases toward zero the solution given by small-amplitude wave theory becomes progressively less accurate.

2.2.2.   Rippled Beds

Explicit analytical solutions for oscillatory flow over rippled beds are only available for ripples of small height to length ratio. It is convenient to work in terms of the curvilinear coordinates (ξ, η), which are defined in terms of Cartesian coordinates (x, y) as

$$\xi = x + \frac{h}{2} e^{-k\eta} \sin k\xi$$

$$(2.21)$$

$$\eta = y - \frac{h}{2} e^{-k\eta} \cos k\xi$$

where y is measured from the mean bed level as shown by Fig. 2.7. If we take

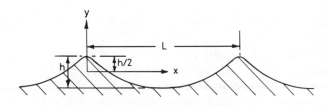

Figure 2.7.   Definition sketch for ripple profile.

the bed to be $\eta = 0$ we see that its profile is

$$y = \frac{h}{2}\cos k\xi \qquad (2.22)$$

When the height to length ratio h/L is very small the bed profile is sinusoidal, but as h/L gets larger the crests become more pointed and the troughs flatter. This is very similar to what is observed with real ripples in oscillatory flow.

For this bed profile, a first approximation for the oscillatory component of velocity when the orbital amplitude of the fluid outside the boundary layer a is small compared with L is

$$u = U_\infty[\cos(\omega t - bx) - e^{-\beta\eta}\cos(\omega t - bx - \beta\eta)] \qquad (2.23)$$

This is the same as the expression for a flat bed (2.14), except that y is replaced by η.

When the solution is carried to a higher order in a/L, we obtain terms independent of time. If the surface waves are very long, so that the steady drift found with progressive waves over a flat bed is negligible, the mass transport velocity in the vicinity of the ripple is

$$\bar{u}_{mt} = \text{real part} \left\{ U_\infty \frac{h}{L}\frac{a}{L} 2\pi^2 i[Ae^{-(c+\mathring{\alpha})\eta} + Be^{-(k+\mathring{\alpha})\eta} + (A+B)e^{-k\eta} \right.$$

$$\left. + Ck\eta e^{-k\eta}]\frac{\sin k\xi}{(c-k)} \right\} \qquad (2.24)$$

where
$$c^2 = \alpha^2 + k^2$$
$$A = (\alpha c + 2\beta^2)(3\beta^2 - k^2)/ic^2 k$$
$$B = 2(\alpha k + 2\beta^2)(\alpha - ik)/(\beta^2 + 2\alpha k + 2ik^2)$$
$$C = A(c + \mathring{\alpha} - k)/(c + \mathring{\alpha}) + B\mathring{\alpha}/(\mathring{\alpha} + k)$$

where $\mathring{\alpha}$ is the complex conjugate of α. Figure 2.8 shows that this steady current produces recirculating cells of fluid. For small values of βL there are only two recirculating cells for each ripple but when βL is large, which is almost always the case for real ripples on the sea bed, there are four. In all cases, the flow in the immediate vicinity of the bed is directed from the ripple trough towards the adjacent crest. The existence of these recirculating cells has been experimentally verified by Kaneko and Honji (1979).

The solution represented by (2.23) and (2.24) was first obtained by Lyne (1971). Sleath (1974a) considered the case where the waves are finite in

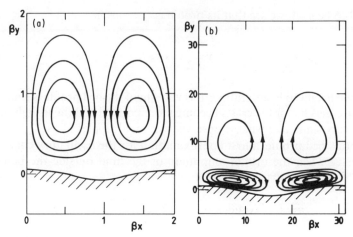

Figure 2.8.   Streamlines of the mean drift close to a rippled bed. (a) $\beta L = 1.9$; (b) $\beta L = 31.4$.

length and consequently the net drift in the direction of wave propagation is not negligible. Matsunaga et al. (1981) extended Lyne's solution to a higher order in ripple steepness h/L. These solutions are probably not of great practical importance since most naturally occurring ripples do not satisfy the condition $a/L \ll 1$ for which these solutions were obtained. Lyne (1971) also obtained a solution for $a/L \gg 1$ but, once again, it is limited to ripples of very small height.

It seems likely that only a numerical method will provide a solution over the whole range for which ripples occur. Two methods are currently available. One is put forward by Sleath (1973), which consists of a finite-difference solution of the full equations of motion. Du Toit and Sleath (1981) showed that, at least in laminar flow, this method gives good agreement with experiment. Longuet-Higgins (1981) used the discrete vortex method but, at present, details of the agreement with measured velocities are not available. Since the method is essentially inviscid, it is unlikely to give good agreement in the viscous boundary layer at the bed.

2.3.   OSCILLATORY VELOCITIES IN TURBULENT FLOW

2.3.1.   Flat Beds

The term "flat" is used here to include both completely smooth beds and plane beds of sand or gravel. The results for rippled beds are considered in the next section.

There are, of course, no analytical solutions for turbulent flow but several different models have been put forward. Agnew (1965), Jonsson (1966, 1980), Kajiura (1968), Bakker (1974), Johns (1975, 1977), and Brevik (1981) have all proposed theoretical models based on assumptions which have been found to give good results in unidirectional flows.

Kajiura's Model

Probably the most consistent and detailed oscillatory boundary layer theory available is by Kajiura (1968). If the mean flow is parallel to the bed, (2.8) may be reduced to

$$\frac{\partial u}{\partial t} = -\frac{1}{\rho}\frac{\partial p}{\partial x} + \frac{\partial \tau}{\partial y} \tag{2.25}$$

The shear stress τ is expressed in terms of an eddy viscosity ε:

$$\tau = \rho\varepsilon\frac{\partial u}{\partial y} \tag{2.26}$$

Following Clauser (Section 1.16.4), Kajiura splits the flow into inner, overlap, and outer layers in which ε varies as follows:

1. Smooth beds:

$$\left.\begin{array}{ll} \text{for } 0<y<12v/\hat{u}_*, & \varepsilon=v \\ \text{for } 12v/\hat{u}_*<y<\Delta, & \varepsilon=K\hat{u}_*y \\ \text{for } \Delta<y, & \varepsilon=K\hat{u}_*\Delta \end{array}\right\} \tag{2.27}$$

2. Rough beds:

$$\left.\begin{array}{ll} \text{for } 0<y<k_s/2, & \varepsilon=0.185K\hat{u}_*k_s \\ \text{for } k_s/2<y<\Delta, & \varepsilon=K\hat{u}_*y \\ \text{for } \Delta<y, & \varepsilon=K\hat{u}_*\Delta \end{array}\right\} \tag{2.28}$$

Here $\hat{u}_*$ is the maximum value of the shear velocity $(\tau_0/\rho)^{1/2}$ at the bed and Δ is the thickness of the wall layer. Kajiura takes

$$\Delta=0.05\frac{\hat{u}_*}{\omega} \tag{2.29}$$

The values chosen for the various coefficients are not quite the same as those suggested by Clauser for steady flows. For example, the thickness of the inner layer is taken by Kajiura as $12v/\hat{u}_*$ instead of $11.6v/\bar{u}_*$. In view of the lack of data about oscillatory boundary layers these differences are probably not significant.

The velocity outside the boundary layer is

$$u_0 = U_\infty \cos \omega t \tag{2.30}$$

Thus, using (2.10), (2.25) becomes

$$\frac{\partial u}{\partial t} = - U_\infty \omega \sin \omega t + \frac{\partial \tau}{\partial y} \tag{2.31}$$

Substitution of (2.26) gives

$$\frac{\partial u}{\partial t} = - U_\infty \omega \sin \omega t + \rho \varepsilon \frac{\partial^2 u}{\partial y^2} + \rho \frac{\partial u}{\partial y} \frac{\partial \varepsilon}{\partial y} \tag{2.32}$$

Making use of the expressions for the eddy viscosity, (2.32) may be solved for each of the three layers. The constants of integration are evaluated by making the velocity and the velocity gradient continuous at the boundaries between the layers. The solution is straightforward but algebraically very laborious.

It will be seen from (2.27) and (2.28) that if $12v/\hat{u}_* \geqslant 0.05\hat{u}_*/\omega$ for a smooth bed, or if $k_s/2 \geqslant 0.05\hat{u}_*/\omega$ for a rough bed, the overlap layer disappears. Making use of Kajiura's solution these limits may be written as follows:

1. Overlap layer disappears for smooth beds if

$$R < 4.7 \times 10^4 \tag{2.33}$$

2. Overlap layer disappears for rough beds if

$$\frac{a}{k_s} < 115 \tag{2.34}$$

Kajiura suggested a limiting value "somewhere around" 33 instead of 115 in (2.34). However, the value of 115, which was calculated by Horikawa and Watanabe (1968), is in better agreement with Kajiura's results.

For the case in which the overlap layer disappears Kajiura assumes that ε is given by the inner layer expression up to $y = 12v/\hat{u}_*$ for smooth beds, or

$y=k_s/2$ for rough beds, and by the outer layer expression beyond that point. Following the method outlined in Section 2.2.1 we find the solution to (2.32):

For $0<y<\delta$:

$$u=\text{real part}\left[U_\infty(1-e^{\alpha_1 y}+A_1 \sinh \alpha_1 y)e^{i\omega t}\right] \qquad (2.35)$$

For $y>\delta$:

$$u=\text{real part}\left[U_\infty(1-A_2 e^{-\alpha_2 y})e^{i\omega t}\right] \qquad (2.36)$$

where

$$A_1=\frac{(\alpha_1+\alpha_2)e^{\alpha_1\delta}}{(\alpha_1 \cosh \alpha_1\delta+\alpha_2 \sinh \alpha_1\delta)} \qquad (2.37)$$

and

$$A_2=\frac{\alpha_1 A e^{(\alpha_2-\alpha_1)\delta}}{(\alpha_1+\alpha_2)} \qquad (2.38)$$

For a smooth bed

$$\delta=12v/\hat{u}_*$$
$$\alpha_1=(i\omega/v)^{1/2} \qquad (2.39)$$
$$\alpha_2=(i\omega^2/0.05K\hat{u}^2_*)^{1/2}$$

For a rough bed

$$\delta=k_s/2$$
$$\alpha_1=(i\omega/0.185K\hat{u}_*k_s)^{1/2} \qquad (2.40)$$
$$\alpha_2=(i\omega^2/0.05K\hat{u}^2_*)^{1/2}$$

When the overlap layer does not disappear the solution is much more complicated. Kajiura (1968) provides a number of useful graphs which facilitate calculation of the velocity profile but care is required when using them since some are not entirely correct. In many situations what is required from a solution for the velocity distribution is an estimate of the bed shear stress. We discuss Kajiura's results in this respect in Chapter 5.

One of the main uncertainties about Kajiura's model is the assumption that the eddy viscosity does not vary with time. Horikawa and Watanabe (1968) found that the eddy viscosity does vary significantly during the course of the wave cycle. Despite this, Kajiura's method shows quite good agreement with experiment, particularly at high Reynolds numbers.

Other Eddy Viscosity Models

Some simplification of Kajiura's three-layer model may be possible at very high values of R or a/k_s. Under these circumstances the inner layer may be relatively unimportant. This is the idea behind Brevik's (1981) model. Like Kajiura, Brevik makes use of a time-independent eddy viscosity but, unlike Kajiura, he considers only the overlap layer and the outer layer. The eddy viscosities assumed by Brevik in these two layers are the same as those chosen by Kajiura except that different values of Δ are considered. The one which gives the best agreement with experimental data is

$$\Delta = \delta_1/2 \tag{2.41}$$

where δ_1 is the boundary layer thickness defined by Jonsson (1980).

Although this approach produces some simplification, the solution still involves Kelvin functions and is consequently far from straightforward. In addition, the results are only compared with the two experiments carried out by Jonsson (1963) and Jonsson and Carlsen (1976) so it is not clear what effect the approximations have at lower Reynolds number.

Agnew (1965) also proposed a two-layer model. The inner layer was assumed to be laminar so that ε was equal to the kinematic viscosity v (as assumed for the inner layer over a smooth bed by Kajiura). In the outer layer the eddy viscosity was taken to be constant. However, no guidance was given as to how the value of the eddy viscosity in the outer layer should be determined for given flow conditions. Knight (1975) has developed Agnew's model for the case where the depth of flow is not necessarily large compared with the thickness of the boundary layer.

Mixing Length Models

Bakker (1974) also starts from (2.25) but instead of making use of eddy viscosity he takes

$$\tau = \rho l^2 \frac{\partial u}{\partial y}\left|\frac{\partial u}{\partial y}\right| \tag{2.42}$$

where the mixing length l is given by

$$l = Ky \tag{2.43}$$

As pointed out in Chapter 1, these expressions give good results in steady flows for the overlap layer. They are not applicable to the viscous sublayer and, from steady flow results, it seems unlikely that they would hold in the wake region above the overlap layer. On the other hand, they do have the advantage that the eddy viscosity, or its equivalent, is not now assumed constant during the course of the wave cycle.

An inconvenience of this approach is that, because of the nonlinearity of the equations when (2.42) is substituted into (2.25), a solution must be obtained numerically. There has consequently been little enthusiasm by other workers to compare their experimental results with the predictions of this model and it is still unclear whether it provides any significant advantages over Kajiura's model.

Johns (1975, 1977) also makes use of mixing length theory, but in a more sophisticated form due to Launder and Spalding (1972). This involves solution of the energy equation as well as the momentum equation. Once again, the solution is numerical and, once again, only a single layer is considered. It is not clear whether the results give any better agreement with experiment than Bakker's or Kajiura's methods.

If the solution is to be numerical in any case, there is no real difficulty in extending this sort of model to cover the viscous sublayer and outer layer as well as the overlap layer. This has been done, for example, by Cebeci (1977). Since this model was proposed for combined steady and oscillatory flow, discussion of it will be deferred to Section 2.10.

Jonsson's Model

Jonsson starts from the idea that for fully developed turbulent oscillatory flow there is, as in steady flow, a wall region in which the velocity distribution is determined by local conditions and a defect layer in which the velocities are independent of viscosity. Thus, by dimensional analysis, for the wall layer (assuming the bed to be rough)

$$\frac{u}{\hat{u}_*} = f\left(\frac{y}{k_s}\right) \tag{2.44}$$

For the defect layer

$$\frac{u - u_0}{\hat{u}_*} = f\left(\frac{y}{\delta}\right) \tag{2.45}$$

where δ is the thickness of the boundary layer and u_0 is the velocity in the free stream outside it.

If there is an overlap between the wall layer and the defect layer it follows, in the same way as for steady flow, that provided the variation in phase within the boundary layer is not great (2.44) and (2.45) can only be satisfied simultaneously by a relation of the form

$$\frac{u}{\hat{u}_*}=\frac{1}{K}\ln\left(\frac{y}{y_0}\right)\cos(\omega t+\phi_0) \tag{2.46}$$

where ϕ_0 is independent of height but varies with a/k_s. From comparison with experiment Jonsson (1980) suggests $\phi_0=25°$ when $a/k_s=100$ and $\phi_0=11°$ when $a/k_s=1000$. For rough beds the constant y_0 is equal to $k_s/30$, as for steady flow.

It also follows from the compatibility of (2.44) and (2.45) that, provided once again that variation in phase is small,

$$\frac{\hat{u}_*}{U_\infty}=\frac{0.4}{\ln(27\delta/k_s)} \tag{2.47}$$

To obtain the thickness δ of the boundary layer Jonsson assumes that the velocity is logarithmic over the whole boundary layer, not just in the overlap layer. Substituting (2.46) and (2.47) into (2.31) and integrating gives an expression for δ which depends on the phase ωt. Taking δ_1 to be the value of δ when $\omega t=0$ leads to

$$\frac{30\delta_1}{k_s}\log\left(\frac{30\delta_1}{k_s}\right)=1.2\frac{a}{k_s} \tag{2.48}$$

The constant 1.2 on the right-hand side of (2.48) was obtained from experiment. (The calculated value was 1.64.)

Jonsson's analysis of available experimental results provided good support for the existence of wall and defect regions in oscillatory flows. However, the usefulness or otherwise of the explicit relationships quoted above depends on how large a portion of the boundary layer is occupied by the overlap region for which the velocity distribution may be expected to be logarithmic. Jonsson found that for his own test at $a/k_s=124$ the overlap layer was extremely small. This is not, perhaps, surprising in view of (2.34), which gives the limit for which the overlap layer disappears entirely. The smallness of the overlap at $a/k_s=124$ tends to confirm (2.34) as opposed to Kajiura's original estimate for the limit.

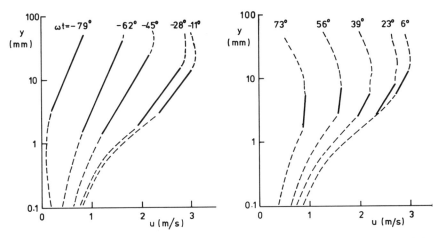

Figure 2.9.   Velocity profiles in a turbulent oscillatory boundary layer (after Hino et al., 1983).

Figure 2.9 shows some measurements made for smooth beds in oscillatory flow by Hino et al. (1983). The broken curves represent the measured velocity profiles and the heavy lines indicate the segments to which it was possible to fit a logarithmic distribution. The value of R for this test was 3.8×10^5, which is well above the limit given by (2.33). Even so, it is clear that the logarithmic profile extends over only a limited part of the velocity profile. Hino et al. also found that the value of K obtained for the logarithmic segment of the profile differed markedly from 0.4 when the flow was accelerating but this may be only because the logarithmic profile was not well defined during that part of the cycle.

Jonsson's model has been further developed by Fredsoe (1981b), but still with the assumption that the velocity distribution outside the viscous sublayer is logarithmic.

Empirical Relationships

The theoretical models discussed above are probably most nearly correct at very high Reynolds numbers. It was observed by Hino et al. (1976) that at moderate Reynolds numbers the flow might be turbulent during part of the cycle and laminar during another part. It is not clear how high the Reynolds number has to be for the flow to be turbulent throughout the cycle but this condition was not reached in any of Hino et al.'s measurements with smooth beds, which extended up to $R = 1.2 \times 10^6$. In Section 2.1.2 it was suggested that (2.4) might be taken as a rough estimate for fully developed turbulence over flat beds of sand or gravel but the real limit could be much higher.

For rough beds there is another reason why the models based on steady flow assumptions are probably not very satisfactory at moderate values of the Reynolds number: the vortices which form around the grains of sediment on the bed and are then ejected when the flow reverses cause considerable mixing from one fluid layer to another. This effect may be expected to produce significant modification of the velocity profile in the early stages of turbulence. Even at very high Reynolds numbers the various assumptions carried over from steady flow are probably unrealistic in the vicinity of flow reversal: in oscillatory flow turbulent eddies and hence turbulent stresses may be present even when the velocity gradient is passing through zero.

For these reasons it may sometimes be preferable to use an empirical relationship if this can be done without extrapolation. Kalkanis (1957, 1964) carried out tests with an oscillating tray rig and proposed a set of empirical equations for the velocity distribution. More recently Sleath (1982) carried out more experiments with flat beds of sand and gravel in a similar apparatus. The revised relationship proposed by Sleath is

$$u = U_\infty \left[\cos \omega t - \hat{u} e^{-\beta y / X_1} \cos \left(\omega t - \frac{\beta y}{X_2} - \phi \right) \right] \qquad (2.49)$$

where X_1, X_2, $\hat{u}$, ϕ are constants for given test conditions. For $U_\infty D/v > 700$ and $a/D > 70$ the experiments give

$$X_1 = 0.2(U_\infty D/v)^{1/2}$$
$$X_2 = 5.0$$
$$\hat{u} = 0.48 U_\infty \qquad (2.50)$$
$$\phi = 22.5°$$

Equation (2.49) is the velocity distribution in an "outer" layer which corresponds approximately with the overlap and outer layers identified by other investigators. Very close to the bed (i.e., within a grain diameter or so of the bed) the velocities follow a different distribution. As yet, there is no satisfactory empirical relationship for this inner layer, although Sleath (1982) suggested that the laminar relationship (2.14) might be used as a rough approximation. The range covered by the experiments on which (2.49) is based is $184 < U_\infty D/v < 3240$ and $4.5 < a/D < 241$.

It is of interest to note that the way in which the amplitude of the velocity falls off with height in (2.49) is consistent with Kajiura's result for his outer layer. In this region he assumed the eddy viscosity to be constant and consequently the defect velocity must decay exponentially with height.

2.3.2. Rippled Beds

The models of Jonsson, Kajiura, Bakker, and Johns are concerned only with
the mean velocity averaged in the horizontal direction. The effective bed
profile in these models is a horizontal plane fixed at some given level below
the crests of the bed roughness. Consequently these models cannot be
expected to predict the detailed variation of velocity in the immediate
vicinity of a rippled bed. On the other hand, since some of the data on which
they are based was for two-dimensional bed roughness, they might be expected to predict the mean velocities averaged in the horizontal direction
for this sort of bed.

The particularly poor agreement between the experimental results and
Velocities have been measured in oscillatory flow over fixed ripples by
Jonsson (1963), Horikawa and Watanabe (1968), and Sawamoto et al. (1980)
and for both fixed and active ripples by Nakato et al. (1977) and Du Toit and
Sleath (1981). Figure 2.10 shows an example of the results obtained for active
ripples by Du Toit and Sleath. The flow in this case was turbulent and the
measured velocities which are shown here are the mean of 30 recorded
cycles which were superimposed with the aid of a phase marker. Two curves
are given for the measured velocities. The full curve is the velocity which
was actually measured whereas the broken curve in one half-cycle is the
mirror image of the full curve in the other half-cycle. It might be thought
that if the flow outside the boundary layer is simple harmonic (which it was)
and if the mean ripple profile is symmetrical, the horizontal velocity directly
above a crest or a trough should be equal in magnitude but opposite in sign
during one half-cycle to that in the other half-cycle. Under these circumstances the difference between the full and broken curves would provide an
indication of the experimental error. However, it is possible that the vortices
formed during one half-cycle might affect those formed during the next,
resulting in a situation in which the two half-cycles were not identical even
when averaged over many cycles. The fact that the full and broken curves are
nearly the same shows that this effect, if it exists at all, is small.

Also shown in Fig. 2.10 are the predictions of various models. The curves
attributed to Kalkanis were obtained from his empirical formula for two-
dimensional roughness, with the roughness length taken equal to the ripple
wavelength. This assumption gave the best agreement with experiment.

The particularly poor agreement between the experimental results and
Kajiura's method is surprising in view of the reasonable agreement which
this method shows with the results of Kalkanis (1964) and Jonsson (1963).
In parallel experiments in oscillating trays Du Toit and Sleath (1981) found
that Kajiura's method gave good agreement with the measured velocity
amplitude but very poor agreement with the phase. It is this error in phase
which produces the very large discrepancy with experiment when the bed is

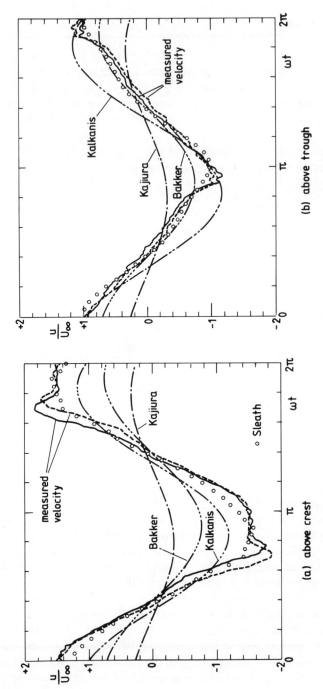

Figure 2.10. Comparison of measured and predicted velocities close to an active bed of ripples.

stationary, as for Fig. 2.10. It should also be pointed out that although the flow was turbulent in these tests, it was probably less turbulent than in Jonsson's and Kalkanis' experiments with rigid beds.

Also surprising is the good agreement with the results obtained using Sleath's numerical model. This model is essentially the same as that put forward by Sleath in 1973, except that the computations have been carried out for a more realistic bed profile [(2.21) with $\eta=0$]. The method consists of a time-marching finite-difference solution of the full Navier–Stokes equations for two-dimensional flow. Since the model assumes laminar flow the agreement with the measurements in Fig. 2.10 is unexpected. It may be that, as suggested above, the flow is not strongly turbulent under these conditions: the agreement was found to be less good under more severe conditions obtained with fixed beds. It may also be that the mixing of the fluid produced by the vortex in the lee of the ripple is large compared with that produced by the turbulent eddies and that, consequently, turbulence is of less importance for rippled beds than for plane ones.

A numerical model has also been proposed by Longuet-Higgins (1981) based on the discrete-vortex method. As mentioned in Section 2.2.2, no velocity records are available for comparison with experiment at the present time. Although Longuet-Higgins suggests that this model should be more suitable at high Reynolds numbers, it should be noted that since the vortices are shed at finite intervals turbulence cannot be adequately reproduced.

There is no comparison with Jonsson's model in Fig. 2.10 because there is no overlap layer under these conditions. Consequently, the assumptions in Jonsson's formulas for bed shear velocity and boundary layer thickness are not realistic.

2.4. MASS TRANSPORT VELOCITIES IN TURBULENT FLOW

2.4.1. Smooth Beds

In an appendix to a paper by Russell and Osorio (1957), Longuet-Higgins showed that if the eddy viscosity is independent of time the mass transport velocity just outside the boundary layer will be the same as that for laminar flow given by (2.18). Johns (1970) confirmed this result and obtained the actual distribution of the mass transport velocity within the boundary layer if the eddy viscosity is assumed to have a given variation with height. He also obtained a solution for standing waves. A similar solution, also making use of eddy viscosity varying with height, was obtained by Noda (1971). More recently Johns (1977) put forward another model which makes use of an extension of mixing length theory due to Launder and Spalding (1972).

This predicts the mass transport velocity outside the boundary layer to be only $U_\infty^2 b/2\omega$ instead of $5 U_\infty^2 b/4\omega$ given by the laminar solution (2.18). The maximum mass transport velocity within the boundary layer is also significantly less than the laminar value. Finally, Wang and Liang (1974) made use of Kalkanis' (1964) empirical formula for turbulent flow over smooth beds to calculate the mass transport velocity for random waves. Apart from the use of Kalkanis' formula, no allowance is made for the effect of the turbulence on the flow so the final result is somewhat doubtful. However, the calculation is of considerable interest in that it shows how mass transport velocity may be determined for something other than the sinusoidal waves usually considered. It is clear from these investigations that the solution obtained for the mass transport velocity depends critically on the assumption made about the structure of the turbulence. As yet, there are not enough experimental results to provide adequate guidance on this question, although those measurements that are available (Horikawa and Watanabe, 1968; Hino et al., 1976) indicate that it is not correct to assume eddy viscosity to be independent of time.

To some extent this is an academic question since smooth beds are rarely found on site and very few laboratory flumes are large enough to produce turbulent boundary layers when the bed is smooth. At the present time there appear to be no measurements of the effect of turbulence on the mass transport velocities with smooth beds. As pointed out in Section 2.1.1, the reduction in the mass transport velocity observed by Collins (1963) is due to the effect of higher order terms and not turbulence.

2.4.2. Rough Beds

The theoretical calculations of Longuet-Higgins, Johns, and others, for smooth beds presumably apply also to turbulent flow over rough beds. For this case there are considerably more experimental results available.

Brebner et al. (1966) found that bed roughness appeared to increase the mass transport velocity for small waves but decrease it for large waves. This agrees with the observation of Bijker et al. (1974) that waves of small steepness show increased mass transport velocities over rippled beds and waves of large steepness show a decrease. It is possible that part of the decrease observed for large waves is caused by the effect of higher order terms, as for the measurements of Collins (1963), rather than to the roughness of the bed. However, Lhermitte (1958) has observed mass transport velocities near a rough bed which were totally reversed in direction and this cannot be attributed solely to higher order terms in the smooth bed solution. In addition, a laminar calculation by Sleath (1973) shows a decrease in the mass transport velocity near a rough bed when the second harmonic increases in importance, as is the case for steeper waves. The fact that this effect is found in a laminar calculation suggests that it may be associated with vortex formation by the bed roughness rather than turbulence.

All of the foregoing measurements were made with dye or neutrally buoyant beads. Dispersion of the dye and vertical drift of the beads make such measurements very difficult to carry out accurately. These problems can be overcome by the use of some form of anemometer. Measurements have been made with a laser Doppler anemometer by Beech (1978). Beech's results show considerable scatter and do not cover a very wide range of flow conditions but are not inconsistent with those of Brebner et al. (1966) and Bijker et al. (1974).

These results are all for the unidirectional drift near the bed. However, in addition to the unidirectional drift there is also a recirculating flow in the immediate vicinity of the roughness element. Du Toit and Sleath (1981) made measurements with a laser Doppler anemometer close to rippled beds. They found that the recirculating drifts were similar, in turbulent flow, to those predicted by laminar theory, that is, toward the adjacent ripple crest in the immediate vicinity of the bed and away from the crest further out. However, the drifts were stronger than those calculated using Sleath's numerical model for laminar flow.

2.5. PERMEABLE BEDS

The flow produced by waves in permeable beds has been studied by Putnam (1949), Reid and Kajiura (1957), Hunt (1959), Murray (1965), Sleath (1970), Liu (1973, 1977), Moshagen and Torum (1975), Prevost et al. (1975), Massel (1976), Yamamoto (1977), Yamamoto et al. (1978), Madsen (1978), Puri (1980), and others. Most investigators assumed that the flow obeys Darcy's law:

$$u = -\frac{K}{\mu}\frac{\partial p}{\partial x}$$

$$v = -\frac{K}{\mu}\frac{\partial p}{\partial y}$$

(2.51)

The coefficient K in this equation is usually referred to as the specific permeability. To avoid confusion it should be noted that some authors make use of the coefficient of permeability k where

$$k = \frac{Kg}{\nu}$$

(2.52)

In S.I. units K is in square meters and k is in meters per second.

If the fluid, grains, and grain skeleton are incompressible,

$$\frac{\partial u}{\partial x} + \frac{\partial v}{\partial y} = 0 \tag{2.53}$$

Thus the pressure obeys Laplace's equation

$$\nabla^2 p = 0 \tag{2.54}$$

Percolation into and out of the bed will cause the waves to lose energy and consequently to attenuate as they propagate in toward the shore. However, this attenuation is usually slow enough for the pressure fluctuation at the bed surface to be assumed periodic, at least as a first approximation. Periodic solutions of Laplace's equation are well known. For the case of progressive waves over a uniform horizontal bed of constant depth d_1 we find the fluctuating component of pressure in the bed to be

$$p = \frac{H\rho g \cosh b(y + d_1)}{2 \cosh bd \cosh bd_1} \cos(\omega t - bx) \tag{2.55}$$

In some situations, particularly when the bed is laid in successive layers, the permeability in the horizontal direction may be different from that in the vertical direction. When (2.55) is modified to take account of this effect the results of tests carried out in wave flumes (Sleath, 1970) show good agreement with the theory.

It has been suggested (e.g., Nakamura et al., 1973; Moshagen and Torum, 1975; Prevost et al., 1975) that the much larger waves which are found on site could produce deformation of the grain skeleton or even of the fluid. As yet, there has been no experimental confirmation of this effect for beds of silt, sand, or gravel because the very large waves which would be necessary are not obtainable in the laboratory. However, Yamamoto et al. (1978) have pointed out that when air is trapped in the bed significant modifications to (2.55) may be observed with small waves.

Yamamoto et al. assume that both the water and air in the pores and the grains and grain skeleton deform elastically. The general solution allowing for these effects is complex. There are two special cases of particular interest.

No Air Is Trapped in the Pores

Under these circumstances the compressibility of the water in the pores is very much less than the compressibility of the grain skeleton. The solution for the fluctuating component of the pressure in the bed in this case is

$$p = p_0 e^{by} \cos(\omega t - bx) \tag{2.56}$$

where

$$p_0 = \frac{H\rho g}{2 \cosh bd} \tag{2.57}$$

Equation (2.56) is for an infinitely deep bed of sediment. The corresponding expression for a bed of depth d_1 is obtained by replacing e^{by} by $\cosh b(y + d_1)/ \cosh bd_1$.

We see that the pressure distribution is the same as that obtained on the assumption that the grain skeleton is completely rigid. The solution is also the same as that obtained by Prevost et al. (1975) on the assumption that the soil is an elastic continuum and no fluid flow takes place in the soil.

Although the pressure distribution is the same as for a rigid bed, the fact that the grain skeleton is not rigid means that there must be movement of the bed in response to the fluctuation in pressure. The displacements (X, Y) of any point in the bed from its mean position (x, y) is given by

$$X = \frac{p_0}{2bG} by \, e^{by} \sin(\omega t - bx)$$

$$Y = - \frac{p_0}{2bG} (1 - by) e^{by} \cos(\omega t - bx) \tag{2.58}$$

where G is the shear modulus of the sediment.

The motion of a particle in the bed is thus an ellipse. At the surface of the bed ($y = 0$) the ellipse degenerates into a pure up and down motion.

The effective stresses in the bed are related to the strains by Hooke's law:

$$\sigma_x = 2G \left[\frac{\partial X}{\partial x} + \left(\frac{v_2}{1 - 2v_2} \right) \left(\frac{\partial X}{\partial x} + \frac{\partial Y}{\partial y} \right) \right]$$

$$\sigma_y = 2G \left[\frac{\partial Y}{\partial y} + \left(\frac{v_2}{1 - 2v_2} \right) \left(\frac{\partial X}{\partial x} + \frac{\partial Y}{\partial y} \right) \right] \tag{2.59}$$

$$\tau_{xy} = G \left(\frac{\partial X}{\partial y} + \frac{\partial Y}{\partial x} \right)$$

where σ_x and σ_y are the effective normal stresses in the x and y directions, τ_{xy} is the shear stress in the y direction on the plane perpendicular to the

x axis, and v_2 is Poisson's ratio for the sediment. Substitution from (2.58) into (2.59) gives

$$\sigma_x = -\sigma_y = -p_0 by\, e^{by} \cos(\omega t - bx)$$

$$\tau_{xy} = p_0 by\, e^{by} \sin(\omega t - bx) \qquad (2.60)$$

Significant Amounts of Air Trapped in the Pores

When air is trapped in the pores the compressibility of the air/water mixture may be much greater than that of the grain skeleton. For example, if sand is 90% saturated with water at atmospheric pressure the modulus of elasticity K' of the air/water mixture is 10^6 N/m^2. The shear modulus G for very dense sand might be 5×10^8 N/m^2, which is 500 times greater than K'.

In the limit as $G/K' \to \infty$ the fluctuating component of the pressure in the bed is

$$p = \text{real part} \left[p_0\, e^{b'y}\, e^{i(\omega t - bx)} \right] \qquad (2.61)$$

where

$$b'^2 = b^2 + \frac{i\omega\mu}{K} \frac{n}{K'} \qquad (2.62)$$

and n is the porosity. Once again the solution for a finite bed is obtained by replacing $e^{b'y}$ by $\cosh b'(y+d_1)/\cosh b'd_1$. This solution is essentially the same as that obtained by Nakamura et al. (1973) and Moshagen and Torum (1975) assuming rigid sediment but compressible fluid.

For situations in which K' is small compared with G, b' will often be significantly larger than b. Consequently, the pressure will fall off much faster than predicted by (2.55) or (2.56). This could have significant implications for the stability of the sediment or any structure resting on the bed. Equation (2.61) also shows that when air is trapped in the pores there is a phase shift of the pressure fluctuation with distance below the surface, whereas (2.55) and (2.56) predict no change in phase.

Although the pressure falls off much faster when air is trapped in the pores, the bed displacements and effective stresses do not. This is because they contain terms varying like e^{by} as well as terms involving $e^{b'y}$.

Yamamoto et al. also carried out experiments in a laboratory wave channel. With relatively coarse sand they obtained good agreement with (2.55). However, for a sand of median diameter 0.2 mm the pressure fell off significantly faster than predicted by (2.55), as shown in Fig. 2.11. Also

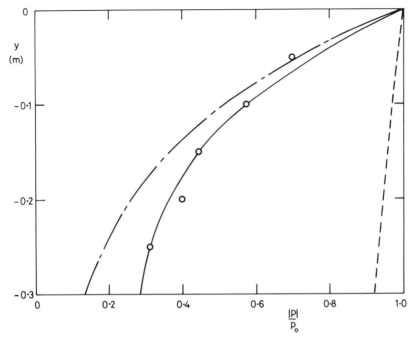

Figure 2.11. Variation of the amplitude of the fluctuating pressure with distance below the surface of the bed. —— Yamamoto et al. (1978) complete solution; ——— (2.61); --- (2.55); ∘-measured pressures.

shown are the curve corresponding to (2.61) and the curve obtained from Yamamoto et al.'s complete solution. In fact, no direct measurements of bed porosity, permeability, and so on, were made, so these two curves are based on parameters obtained by comparison between theory and experiment. Consequently, the good agreement with Yamamoto et al.'s complete solution should be treated with caution. Nevertheless, it is clear that the significant departures from the distribution predicted by (2.55) can be explained by small amounts of air trapped in the pores. It was estimated that in this test the amount of air trapped in the pores was 2% by volume. This would be insufficient to ensure $G \gg K'$, which is why agreement with (2.61) is not good. The depth of the bed for the experiment shown in Fig. 2.11 was 0.5 m. The difference between the curve obtained from (2.61) for an infinite bed and that allowing for the actual depth of the bed is negligible.

The flow into and out of the bed has little effect on the oscillatory velocities in the boundary layer above the bed provided the parameter $V_0/(4\omega v)^{1/2}$ is small (Sleath, 1968). Since percolation velocities are generally very small this condition is usually satisfied in situations of practical importance. On the other hand, the effect of bed permeability on the mass transport velocity is much more significant. This problem has been investigated by Liu (1977) and Sleath (1978). It is found that just outside the boundary layer at the bed the mass transport velocity is

$$\bar{u}_{mt} = \frac{U_\infty^2 b}{4\omega}\left(5 + \frac{4\beta^3 K}{b}\tanh bd_1\right) \qquad (2.63)$$

The first term inside the parentheses is the same as that obtained from Longuet-Higgins' solution (2.18) and the second represents the effect of bed permeability. Since v is approximately 10^{-6} m^2/s for sea water and a typical value of K for a coarse sand might be 10^{-9} m^2, we see that the effect of bed permeability may be extremely significant.

At the interface between the fluid and the porous bed the mass transport velocity falls to

$$\bar{u}_{mt} = \frac{U_\infty^2 b}{4\omega}\left(\frac{2\beta^3 K}{b}\tanh bd_1\right) \qquad (2.64)$$

Within the bed there is another boundary layer in which the mass transport velocity falls from the value given by (2.64) to zero (to a first approximation).

2.6. SLOPING BEDS

Russell and Osorio (1957) made measurements of the mass transport velocity with a bed of slope 1/20 in a wave flume. They found no significant difference between the maximum measured velocity near the bed and that given by Longuet-Higgins' theory (2.18). These results are in reasonable agreement with the theory developed by Bijker et al. (1974) and by Lau and Travis (1973) for mass transport over sloping beds. This theory predicts that the change in the mass transport velocity produced by bed slope will generally be very small (less than 20% in most situations). However, Bijker et al.'s experiments showed much lower mass transport velocities over sloping beds. It is possible that, as with Collins' experiments for flat beds, this discrepancy is caused by the neglect of higher order terms in the solution. A correction was made for higher harmonics but some of their waves would have been more adequately described by cnoidal theory. In addition, their measurements were carried out with neutrally buoyant beads. This method does not give very reliable results in the vicinity of the bed.

Near the breaking point both Russell and Osorio and Bijker et al. found the mass transport velocity at the bed to be in the opposite direction to that predicted by (2.18), that is, offshore rather than onshore.

Since the theory predicts little change in the mass transport velocity close to sloping beds it is not surprising that the predicted change in the oscillatory component of velocity near the bed is also very small.

Steady Currents Alone

2.7. THE VELOCITY DISTRIBUTION

2.7.1. Smooth Beds

The velocity distribution near the bed may be obtained from the equations in Chapter 1. In laminar free surface flow (1.86), (1.87), and (1.88) apply. If the flow is turbulent, (1.89) applies within the viscous sublayer and (1.94) further out.

2.7.2. Rough Beds

When $\bar{u}_*k_s/v > 5$ the bed is too rough for (1.89) to remain valid. It is usually assumed that for flat beds of sand or gravel (1.94) applies down to the level of the grain crests but little is known about the velocity distribution below that level.

For rippled beds the flow is qualitatively similar to that over a series of backward-facing steps. Figure 2.12 shows some measurements made by Raudkivi (1963) and Sheen (1964) over natural and artificial rippled beds. Figure 2.12a gives the horizontal component of the time-mean velocity. In the lee of the crest there is a vortex which causes reverse flow in the immediate vicinity of the bed. The vortex is very unsteady and this is one reason why the value of u'^2 shown by Fig. 2.12b rises so sharply just downstream of the crest. In addition, the shear layer coming off the crest is highly unstable. Visual observations suggested that the mean flow reattached at about six ripple heights downstream of the crest. Since the ripple height was 22.4 mm this gives reattachment 0.13 m from the crest. The fact that the mean shear stress as shown by Fig. 2.12c is not quite zero at this point is probably due to the difficulty of measuring fluctuating shear stresses: because of the unsteadiness of the lee vortex the point of reattachment fluctuates and consequently the shear stress constantly changes direction.

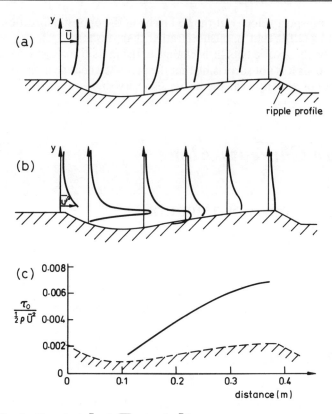

Figure 2.12. Profiles of (a) $\bar{U}$; (b) $\overline{u'^2}$; (c) $\tau_0/\frac{1}{2}\rho\bar{U}^2$ for a rippled bed in steady flow (after Raudkivi, 1963, and Sheen, 1964).

Waves and Currents

2.8. TRANSITION

The question of transition from laminar to turbulent flow in combined steady and oscillatory flows is of interest in many fields in addition to coastal engineering. Much of the attention, so far, has concentrated on the situation where the steady current is stronger than the oscillatory flow.

Figure 2.13 shows the results obtained by Sarpkaya (1966) for combined steady and oscillatory flow in a straight pipe. When the oscillatory velocity U_∞ is very small compared with the steady current $\bar{U}$ the critical Reynolds number is 2200. This is the usual value obtained in steady pipe flow where no particular care has been taken to remove disturbances at the inlet. As U_∞ is increased the critical Reynolds number initially rises and then, for any given value of the parameter βd_2, falls steadily. Generally similar results have been obtained by Gilbrech and Combs (1963) and Tromans (1978) for pipes and by Obremski and Fejer (1967) for boundary layers growing along a flat plate. These results are also in qualitative agreement with the findings of linear stability analyses for combined steady and oscillatory flow in parallel-sided channels. (See Davis, 1976, for a review of work carried out before 1975 and Von Kerczek, 1982, for more recent work.)

The parameter βd_2 is the ratio of the pipe diameter to a measure of the oscillatory boundary layer thickness. If pipe diameter is replaced by water depth this parameter would be far larger than the values shown in Fig. 2.13 for most combined wave plus current situations of engineering importance. Figure 2.13 suggests that, for any given value of $U_\infty/\bar{U}$, the critical Reynolds number decreases with increasing βd_2. However, Ramaprian and Tu (1980) showed that this is true only for values of βd_2 less than about 16. Beyond this value the critical Reynolds number increases steadily, with increasing βd_2, toward the steady-flow value.

We saw in Section 1.14 that the lower critical value of $\bar{U}d/\nu$ for a steady flow in a wide open channel is 890. If the foregoing results for pulsating flow

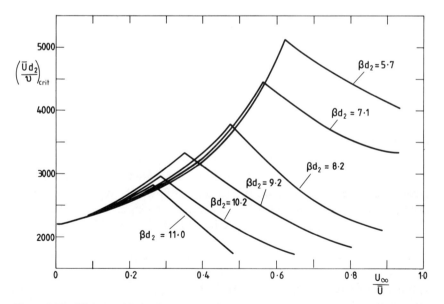

Figure 2.13. The critical Reynolds number for transition to turbulence in combined steady and oscillatory flow (after Sarpkaya, 1966).

in pipes apply to the case of waves plus currents, this would be the appropriate value of the Reynolds number for transition in the body of the fluid. Unfortunately there is a shortage of firm data for the case of waves plus currents. It is possible that waves have a stabilizing effect on the flow so that the critical value of $\bar{U}d/\nu$ may be higher than 890. However, unless it is very significantly higher, it is clear that in most situations of practical importance the steady current would have to be extremely weak for the flow to remain laminar in the body of the fluid.

Although it would seem that even rather weak steady currents will provoke transition, the actual intensity of the turbulence may be low. Under these circumstances the flow in the oscillatory boundary layer at the bed might remain laminar even though the flow in the fluid above was turbulent. Collins (1964) carried out experiments on combined steady plus oscillatory flows in a laboratory wave channel. In some of his tests the flow in the boundary layer at the bed apparently remained laminar even though the value of $\bar{U}d/\nu$ exceeded 14,000.

Ramaprian and Tu's measurements show that in the initial stages of transition the turbulence varies during the course of a cycle of oscillation in a manner similar to that found by Hino et al. (1976) for pure oscillatory flow: turbulence is observed during part of the cycle followed by laminar flow during another part.

2.9.   THE VELOCITY DISTRIBUTION IN LAMINAR FLOW

2.9.1.   Flat Beds

Combined steady and oscillatory flow over a flat bed has been studied by Lighthill (1954). He concludes that if the frequency of oscillation is high enough, a reasonable first approximation to the velocity distribution is provided by the assumption that the oscillatory and steady currents are unaffected by each other. In this context a high frequency is one that produces an oscillatory boundary layer which is thin compared with the steady flow length scale. For combined wave plus current flows, the oscillatory boundary layer is only a few millimeters thick while the length scale of the steady flow is the depth of water. Consequently, Lighthill's condition is very well satisfied.

This conclusion is confirmed by the work of Cebeci (1977), who obtained a numerical solution for the problem of combined steady and oscillatory laminar flow over a flat bed. Figure 2.14 shows how the phase lead of the bed shear stress with respect to the free stream velocity varies with $\omega x/\bar{U}_1$. This calculation is for a boundary layer at constant pressure, so that $\bar{U}_1$

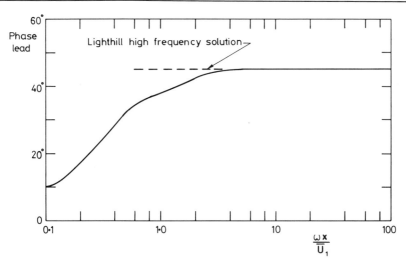

Figure 2.14.   Phase lead of the wall shear stress over the oscillating velocity outside the boundary layer (after Cebeci, 1977).

is the steady velocity just outside the boundary layer and x is the horizontal distance from the point at which the boundary layer was initiated. For values of $\omega x/\bar{U}_1 > 3.0$ the difference between Lighthill's high-frequency approximation and the exact solution is negligible. For combined waves and currents the effective value of $\omega x/\bar{U}_1$ would almost always be very much greater than 3.0.

Numerical solutions are inconvenient and, it would appear, unnecessary for the case of waves plus currents. Assuming, as a first approximation, that the oscillatory and steady currents are unaffected by each other, Collins (1964) gives the velocity distribution in the immediate vicinity of the bed as

$$u = U_\infty[\cos(\omega t - bx) - e^{-\beta y}\cos(\omega t - bx - \beta y)] \pm \bar{U}_0[0.4\beta y - 0.04(\beta y)^2] \quad (2.65)$$

In this expression $\bar{U}_0$ is the steady current at a height $5/\beta$ above the bed. The current is assumed to be collinear with the direction of wave propagation. If the current is at an angle to the direction of wave propagation, it is necessary to take the vector sum of the contributions due to the waves and the current separately.

Equation (2.65) is only a first approximation. If we move on to a second approximation we find that the assumption that there is no interaction between the contributions from the waves and the current is no longer correct. Collins (1964) obtained the following expression for the mass transport velocity:

$$\bar{u}_{mt} = \frac{U_\infty^2 b}{4\omega} (5 - 8 e^{-\beta y} \cos \beta y + 3 e^{-2\beta y})$$

$$\pm \bar{U}_0 [0.4\beta y - 0.04(\beta y)^2] \left\{ 1 + \frac{b}{\omega} [\bar{U}_0 + 0.6\beta y - 0.06(\beta y)^2] \right\} \qquad (2.66)$$

Once again, this expression is obtained for currents which are collinear with the direction of wave propagation.

Collins also measured the drift velocities due to combined waves and currents in a wave flume. The results follow a trend similar to those shown for waves alone in Fig. 2.6. At low wave heights there is good agreement between theory and experiment. For larger wave heights the measured velocities are lower than those given by (2.66). Collins suggests that the discrepancy for larger wave heights may be caused by turbulence but it seems more likely that, as was the case for waves alone, it is attributable to the neglect of higher order terms in the solution.

2.9.2. Rough Beds

The measurements of George and Sleath (1979) show that once vortex or jet formation takes place around the bed roughness elements there is significant nonlinear interaction between the oscillatory and steady currents. Up to this point it is probably reasonable to treat the oscillatory and steady flows as independent, or at any rate as a first approximation.

2.10. THE VELOCITY DISTRIBUTION IN TURBULENT FLOW

When the flow is turbulent there must be interaction between the steady and oscillatory components: the turbulence generated by one component will affect the velocity distribution of the other and vice versa. Under these circumstances it is no longer reasonable to assume that the combined flow is the sum of the two components separately.

Theoretical solutions for combined wave plus current flows have been put forward by Lundgren (1972), Smith (1977), Bakker and Van Doorn (1978), Grant and Madsen (1979), Tanaka and Shuto (1981), Fredsoe (1981a, 1982) and Christoffersen (1982). The main problem in obtaining a solution is to define the relation to assume between shear stress and fluid velocity. There is very little experimental information in this field, so any assumption is bound to be somewhat arbitrary. As an example, we will consider the approach adopted by Smith for currents collinear with the direction of wave propagation. This approach is very similar to that of Grant and Madsen and Tanaka and Shuto, who also consider the case of currents at an arbitrary angle to the waves.

Like Kajiura (1968), Smith makes use of an eddy viscosity which does not vary with time. For the bed layer, in which both wave- and current-generated turbulence are important, he assumes

$$\varepsilon = K(\bar{u}_{*s} + \hat{u}_{*w})y \tag{2.67}$$

where $\bar{u}_{*s}$ is the shear velocity for the steady current and $\hat{u}_{*w}$ is the amplitude of the oscillatory component of the shear velocity. Substitution of this expression into (2.25) and integration gives

$$u = \frac{\bar{u}_{*s}^2}{K(\bar{u}_{*s} + \hat{u}_{*w})} \ln\left(\frac{y}{y_0}\right) + U_\infty \left[\cos \omega t - \left(\frac{\ker \xi \ker \xi_0 + \kei \xi \kei \xi_0}{\ker^2 \xi_0 + \kei^2 \xi_0}\right) \cos \omega t - \left(\frac{\ker \xi \kei \xi_0 - \kei \xi \ker \xi_0}{\ker^2 \xi_0 + \kei^2 \xi_0}\right) \sin \omega t \right] \tag{2.68}$$

where ker and kei are zero-order Kelvin functions, $\xi = 2[\omega y/K(\bar{u}_{*s} + \hat{u}_{*w})]^{1/2}$, $\xi_0 = 2[\omega y_0/K(\bar{u}_{*s} + \hat{u}_{*w})]^{1/2}$ and y_0 is given by (1.95) and those that follow in Chapter 1. Smith (1977) presents a number of graphs which make the use of (2.68) less laborious and also indicate methods for evaluation of the various coefficients.

An interesting feature of (2.68) is that the time-mean velocity distribution is logarithmic in this bed layer. This is also the conclusion reached by Bakker and Van Doorn, Grant and Madsen, and Fredsoe, although each proposes a somewhat different equation. There is good experimental support for a logarithmic profile in the outer layer away from the bed (as discussed in Chapter 1), but most measurements do not extend close enough to the bed to show a clear logarithmic profile in the inner layer as well. Kemp and Simons (1982) found that for smooth beds there is also a viscous sublayer in which the time-mean velocity varies linearly with height. Although Kemp and Simons' measurements show good support for a variation in eddy viscosity similar to that given by (2.67) in the outer layer, they suggested that a constant eddy viscosity might be more appropriate in the bed layer.

Apart from Kemp and Simons, measurements of this sort of flow have been made by Van Hoften and Karaki (1976), Bakker and Van Doorn (1978), Brevik and Aas (1980), Brevik (1980), Iwagaki and Asano (1980), Thomas (1981), and Van Doorn (1981). These measurements do not provide a clear indication as to which of the available formulas for the bed layer is the most reliable.

There have also been many studies of the related problem of combined steady and oscillatory boundary layer flows over flat plates and airfoils. In this situation the oscillatory velocity is usually considered to be small compared with the steady flow. By way of example, we will consider the two-layer model of Cebeci (1977). In the inner layer Cebeci takes

$$\tau = \rho l^2 \frac{\partial u}{\partial y} \left| \frac{\partial u}{\partial y} \right| \tag{2.69}$$

and

$$l = Ky(1 - e^{-y/A}) \tag{2.70}$$

where

$$A = \frac{26v}{u_*} \left(1 + \frac{11.8v}{\rho u_*^3} \frac{\partial p}{\partial x}\right)^{-1/2} \tag{2.71}$$

In the outer layer

$$\tau = \rho \varepsilon \frac{\partial u}{\partial y} \tag{2.72}$$

where

$$\varepsilon = \frac{0.0168}{1 + 0.55B} \int_0^\infty (\bar{U}_1 - u)dy \tag{2.73}$$

and

$$B = 1 - \exp[-0.0118(R_\theta - 425)^{1/2} - 0.000689(R_\theta - 425)] \tag{2.74}$$

In the inner layer Cebeci's model is thus similar to that of Bakker (1974) discussed in Section 2.3.1. However, the modified expression for the mixing length means that this model also accounts for the viscous sublayer. At the same time, the expressions for the outer layer extend the solution over the outer wake region also. The model is thus, at least in theory, a significant advance on that of Bakker. Whether it would actually give better results in practice is not clear since computations have not been made for comparable situations.

The success of a model such as this clearly depends to a large extent on the detailed assumptions made for the eddy viscosities and mixing lengths. For example, (2.73) is different from the eddy viscosity used by Kajiura (1968) in the outer layer but the justification for using one expression rather than another is not clear. Numerical models making different assumptions for the eddy viscosity or mixing length distribution have been put forward by Ackerberg and Phillips (1972), Kuhn and Nielsen (1973), Nash and Patel (1975), McCroskey and Philippe (1975), and Telionis and Tsahalis (1976). An excellent review of their work and related work is given by Telionis (1981). Several of the numerical models, including that of Cebeci outlined above, predict the experimental results reasonably well. However, the experimental scatter is too great to allow a clear decision as to which of the available numerical models is the most satisfactory.

2.11. EXAMPLES

1.   Progressive waves of height 3 m and period 15 s are propagating in water of depth 20 m over a horizontal bed. The bed consists of a layer of 0.8 mm sand of uniform thickness 10 m and specific permeability $K = 3 \times 10^{-10}$ m^2 overlying solid rock. Assuming small-amplitude wave theory to apply and taking kinematic viscosity $v = 10^{-6}$ m^2/s:

(a)   What is the amplitude of the horizontal component of velocity just outside the boundary layer at the bed? By iteration from (1.16),

$$b = 0.0318 \text{ m}^{-1}$$

Thus from (1.19) the amplitude of the horizontal component of velocity just outside the boundary layer is

$$U_\infty = 0.924 \text{ m/s}$$

(b)   Is the boundary layer laminar or turbulent? The parameters governing transition to turbulence for flat beds of sand or gravel are

$$R = \frac{U_\infty^2}{\omega v} = 2.04 \times 10^6$$

$$\frac{a}{D} = \frac{U_\infty}{\omega D} = 2.76 \times 10^3$$

From Fig. 2.1 the flow in the boundary layer at the bed is clearly turbulent. Of course, the bed might be rippled rather than flat. Since this would increase the bed roughness, it does not alter the conclusion that the flow is turbulent.

(c)   What would have been the maximum mass transport velocity in the boundary layer at the bed if the bed had been smooth and impermeable and the flow laminar? From (2.18) the maximum mass transport velocity in a laminar boundary layer over a smooth impermeable bed is

$$(\bar{u}_{mt})_{max} = 1.391 \frac{U_\infty^2 b}{\omega}$$

$$= 0.090 \text{ m/s}$$

(d)   What is the additional mass transport velocity at the outer edge of the boundary layer due to bed permeability? At the outer edge of the boundary layer the increase in mass transport velocity due to bed permeability is given by (2.63) as

$$\bar{u}_{mt} = \frac{U_\infty^2 b}{\omega} \frac{\beta^3 K}{b} \tanh bd_1$$

$$= 0.018 \text{ m/s}$$

(e)   What is the amplitude of the fluctuating component of pressure 5 m below the surface of the bed? From (2.55) the amplitude of the fluctuating pressure 5 m below the bed surface is

$$p = \frac{H\rho g \cosh b(y + d_1)}{2 \cosh bd \cosh bd_1}$$

$$= 11.7 \text{ KN/m}^2$$

This answer, and also that to (d), assumes that fluid, grains, and grain skeleton are all rigid. From (2.58) we see that the grain skeleton may be assumed rigid if

$$\frac{p_0}{G} \ll 1$$

The shear modulus G might be about 10^8 N/m^2, whereas from (2.57) p_0 is equal to 12.2×10^3 N/m^2. Thus

$$\frac{p_0}{G} = 1.2 \times 10^{-4}$$

which is, indeed, very small.

The modulus of elasticity of sea water is approximately 2.3×10^9 N/m^2. The ratio of p_0 to this modulus is extremely small and consequently compressibility of the fluid may be neglected. This assumes that there is no gas trapped in the pores.

Finally, the grains of sediment are much less easily compressed than the grain skeleton. Thus if the skeleton is effectively rigid, the grains themselves are even more so.

2.   In water of depth 30 m the steady current is observed to have a surface velocity of 1 m/s. If the bed is flat and horizontal and consists of 0.4 mm of sand, what is the fluid velocity 0.5 m above the bed? What is the mean velocity? Take the kinematic viscosity to be $\nu = 10^{-6}$ m^2/s.

Let us assume that the velocity profile is logarithmic over the whole depth of flow. Although, as pointed out in Section 1.16, this will not be entirely correct even if the flow is fully developed, the error in the near bed and mean velocities is unlikely to be large. Corrections may subsequently be calculated by iteration if necessary.

It is also necessary to make some initial assumption about the nature of the bed. In the present case the sand is relatively fine and consequently it is reasonable to start with the assumption that the bed is hydraulically smooth. Thus, from (1.96), at the free surface

$$1 = 2.5\bar{u}_* \ln \left(\frac{9\bar{u}_* \times 30}{10^{-6}} \right)$$

thus

$$\bar{u}_* = 0.0254 \text{ m/s}$$

Bearing in mind the results quoted in Section 1.16.3, we take k_s equal to twice the grain size. Thus

$$\frac{\bar{u}_* k_s}{\nu} = 20.3$$

This is outside the range for hydraulically smooth beds. Had it been well above the hydraulically smooth limit of $\bar{u}_* k_s / \nu < 5$, the next step would have been to assume that the bed was hydraulically rough and see what that gave. In the present case there is little hope that the hydraulically rough equations would apply and consequently we turn directly to Fig. 1.12. As a first step we assume

$$\frac{\bar{u}_* k_s}{\nu} = 20.3$$

Hence, from Fig. 1.12,

$$\frac{y_0}{k_s} = 0.0227$$

At the free surface (1.94) gives

$$1 = 2.5\bar{u}_* \ln\left(\frac{30}{0.0227 \times 0.8 \times 10^{-3}}\right)$$

Hence

$$\bar{u}_* = 0.0279 \text{ m/s}$$

$$\frac{\bar{u}_* k_s}{v} = 22.3$$

A second approximation could now be obtained by using this value of $\bar{u}_* k_s/v$ in Fig. 1.12 and repeating the calculation. However, since the change in the value of y_0/k_s is small the present approximation is probably adequate. Thus, from (1.94), the velocity at $y = 0.5$ m is

$$\bar{u} = 2.5 \times 0.0279 \times \ln\left(\frac{0.5}{0.0227 \times 0.8 \times 10^{-3}}\right) = 0.71 \text{ m/s}$$

and the mean velocity, from (1.101), is

$$\bar{U} = 2.5 \times 0.0279 \times \ln\left(\frac{30}{2.72 \times 0.0227 \times 0.8 \times 10^{-3}}\right) = 0.93 \text{ m/s}$$

REFERENCES

Ackerberg, R. C. and Phillips, J. H. (1972). The unsteady boundary layer on a semi-infinite flat plate due to small fluctuations in the magnitude of the free-stream velocity. *J. Fluid Mech.* **51**: 137–157.

Agnew, R. (1965). A two layer theory for unsteady flow. *Proc. 2nd Australas. Conf. Hydraul. Fluid Mech.*, pp. A97–A115.

Allen, J. and Gibson, D. H. (1959). Experiments on the displacement of water by waves of various heights and frequencies. *Proc. Inst. Civ. Eng.* **13**: 363–386.

Bagnold, R. A. (1947). Sand movement by waves: some small scale experiments with sand of very low density. *J. Inst. Civ. Eng.*: 447–469.

Bakker, W. T. (1974). Sand concentration in oscillatory flow. *Proc. 14th Conf. Coastal Eng. Copenhagen*, pp. 1129–1148.

Bakker, W. T. and Van Doorn, T. (1978). Near bottom velocities in waves with a current. *Proc. 16th Conf. Coastal Eng. Hamburg*, pp. 1394–1413.

Beech, N. W. (1978). Boundary layers due to gravity waves. Ph.D. Thesis. Univ. Nottingham.

Bijker, E. W., Kalkwijk, J. P. T., and Pieters, T. (1974). Mass transport in gravity waves on a sloping bottom. *Proc. 14th Conf. Coastal Eng. Copenhagen*, pp. 447–465.

Brebner, A., Askew, J. A., and Law, S. W. (1966). Effect of roughness on mass-transport of progressive gravity wave. *Proc. 10th Conf. Coastal Eng. Tokyo*, pp. 175–184.

Brebner, A. and Collins, J. I. (1961). The effect on mass transport of the onset of turbulence at the bed under periodic gravity waves. *ASME-EIC Hydraul. Conf. Montreal*, Pap. 61-EIC-8.

Brevik, I. (1980). Flume experiment on waves and currents. 2. Smooth bed. *Coastal Eng.* **4**: 89–110.

Brevik, I. (1981). Oscillatory rough turbulent boundary layers. *Proc. A.S.C.E. J. Waterway Port Coastal Ocean Div.* **107** (WW3): 175–188.

Brevik, I. and Aas, B. (1980). Flume experiment on waves and currents. 1: Rippled bed. *Coastal Eng.* **3**: 149–177.

Caligny, A. (1878). Expériences sur les mouvements des molécules liquides des ondes courantes, considérées dans leur mode d'action sur la marche des navires. *Compt. Rendu Acad. Sci. Paris.* **87**: 1019–1023.

Cebeci, T. (1977). Calculation of unsteady two-dimensional laminar and turbulent boundary layers with fluctuations in external velocity. *Proc. Roy. Soc.* Ser. A. **355**: 225–238.

Christoffersen, J. B. (1982). Current depth refraction of dissipative water waves. Inst. Hydrodyn. Hydraul. Eng. Tech. Univ. Denmark. Series paper 30.

Collins, J. I. (1963). Inception of turbulence at the bed under periodic gravity waves. *J. Geophys. Res.* **68** (21): 6007–6014.

Collins, J. I. (1964). Effect of currents on mass transport of progressive water waves. *J. Geophys. Res.* **69** (6): 1051–1056.

Davis, S. H. (1976). The stability of time-periodic flows. *Ann. Rev. Fluid Mech.* **8**: 57–74.

Davis, S. H. and Von Kerczek, C. (1973). Reformulation of energy stability theory. *Arch. Ration. Mech. Anal.* **52**: 112.

Dore, B. D. (1974). The mass transport velocity due to interacting wave trains. *Meccanica* **9**: 172–178.

Dore, B. D. (1976). Double boundary layers in standing surface waves. *Pure Appl. Geophys.* **114**: 629–637.

Dore, B. D. (1982). On the second approximation to mass transport in the bottom boundary layer. *Coastal Eng.* **6**: 93–120.

Du Toit, C. G. and Sleath, J. F. A. (1981). Velocity measurements close to rippled beds in oscillatory flow. *J. Fluid Mech.* **112**: 71–96.

Fredsoe, J. (1981a). Mean current velocity distribution in combined waves and current. Inst. Hydrodyn. Hydraul. Eng. Tech. Univ. Denmark, Prog. Rep. **53**.

Fredsoe, J. (1981b). A simple model for the wave boundary layer. Inst. Hydrodyn. Hydraul. Eng. Tech. Univ. Denmark, Prog. Rep. 54.

Fredsoe, J. (1982). Calculation of mean current profile in combined wave-current motion by application of the momentum equation. Inst. Hydrodyn. Hydraul. Eng. Tech. Univ. Denmark, Prog. Rep. 55, 56.

George, C. B. and Sleath, J. F. A. (1978). Oscillatory laminar flow above a rough bed. *Proc. 16th Conf. Coastal Eng. Hamburg*, pp. 898–910.

George, C. B. and Sleath, J. F. A. (1979). Measurements of combined oscillatory and steady flow over a rough bed. *J. Hydraul. Res.* **17** (4): 303–313.

Gilbrech, D. A. and Combs, G. D. (1963). Critical Reynolds numbers for incompressible pulsating flows in tubes. In *Developments in Theoretical and Applied Mechanics*, Vol. 1. Plenum Press, New York, pp. 292.

Grant, W. D. and Madsen, O. S. (1979). Combined wave and current interaction with a rough bottom. *J. Geophys. Res.* **84** (c4): 1797–1808.

Hino, M., Sawamoto, M., & Takasu, S. (1976). Experiments on transition to turbulence in an oscillatory pipe flow. *J. Fluid Mech.* **75**: 193–207.

Hino, M., Kashiwayanagi, M., Nakayama, A., and Hara, T. (1983). Experiments on the turbulent statistics and the structure of a reciprocating oscillatory flow. *J. Fluid Mech.* (in press).

Horikawa, K. and Watanabe, A. (1968). Laboratory study on oscillatory boundary layer flow. *Coastal Eng. Jpn.* **11**: 13–28.

Hsu, J. R. C., Tsuchiya, Y., and Silvester, R. (1979). Third-order approximation to short crested waves. *J. Fluid Mech.* **90**: 179–196.

Hsu, J. R. C., Silvester, R., and Tsuchiya, Y. (1980). Boundary-layer velocities and mass transport in short-crested waves. *J. Fluid Mech.* **99**: 321–342.

Hunt, J. N. (1959). On the damping of gravity waves propagated over a permeable surface. *J. Geophys. Res.* **64**: 437–442.

Hunt, J. N. and Johns, B. (1963). Currents induced by tides and gravity waves. *Tellus.* **15**: 343–351.

Isaacson, M. de St. Q. (1976a). Mass transport in the bottom boundary layer of cnoidal waves. *J. Fluid Mech.* **74**: 401–413.

Isaacson, M. de St. Q. (1976b). The second approximation to mass transport in cnoidal waves. *J. Fluid Mech.* **78**: 445–457.

Iwagaki, Y. and Asano, T. (1980). Water particle velocity in wave-current system. *Coastal Eng. Japan.* **23**: 1–14.

Johns, B. (1970). On the mass transport induced by oscillatory flow in a turbulent boundary layer. *J. Fluid Mech.* **43**: 177–185.

Johns, B. (1975). The form of the velocity profile in a turbulent shear wave boundary layer. *J. Geophys. Res.* **80** (36): 5109–5012.

Johns, B. (1977). Residual flow and boundary shear stress in the turbulent bottom layer beneath waves. *J. Phys. Oceanogr.* **7**: 733–738.

Jonsson, I. G. (1963). Measurements in the turbulent wave boundary layer. *Proc. 10th Congr. IAHR. London*, pp. 85–92.

Jonsson, I. G. (1966). Wave boundary layers and friction factors. *Proc. 10th Conf. Coastal Eng. Tokyo*, pp. 127–148.

Jonsson, I. G. (1980). A new approach to oscillatory rough turbulent boundary layers. *Ocean Eng.* **7**: 109–152.

Jonsson, I. G. and Carlsen, N. A. (1976). Experimental and theoretical investigations in an oscillatory turbulent boundary layer. *J. Hydraul. Res.* **14** (1): 45–60.

Kajiura, K. (1968). A model of the bottom boundary layer in water waves. *Bull. Earthquake Res. Inst.* **46**: 75–123.

Kalkanis, G. (1957). Turbulent flow near an oscillating wall. Beach Erosion Board. Tech. Memo. 97.

Kalkanis, G. (1964). Transportation of bed material due to wave action. U.S. Army C.E.R.C. Tech. Memo. 2.

Kamphuis, J. W. (1975). Friction factors under oscillatory waves. *Proc. A.S.C.E. J. Waterw., Harbors Coastal Eng. Div.* **101** (WW2): 135–144.

Kaneko, A. and Honji, H. (1979). Double structures of steady streaming in the oscillatory viscous flow over a wavy wall. *J. Fluid Mech.* **93**: 727–736.

Kemp, P. H. and Simons, R. R. (1982). The interaction between waves and a turbulent current. Waves propagating with the current. *J. Fluid Mech.* **116**: 227–250.

Keulegan, G. H. (1948). Gradual damping of solitary waves. *J. Res. Nat. Bur. Standards.* **40**: 487–498.

Knight, D. W. (1975). Velocity and shear stress distributions in oscillatory flow. *Proc. 16th Congr. I.A.H.R. Sao Paulo. Brazil*, pp. 66–72.

Kuhn, G. D. and Nielsen, J. N. (1973). Studies of an integral method for calculating time-dependent turbulent boundary layers. Nielsen Eng. Res. Inc. Rep. NEAR TR 57.

Lamb, H. (1932). *Hydrodynamics.* 6th ed. Cambridge University Press, Cambridge.

Lau, J. and Travis, B. (1973). Slowly varying Stokes waves and submarine longshore bars. *J. Geophys. Res.* **78** (21): 4489–4497.

Launder, B. E. and Spalding, D. B. (1972). *Mathematical Models Of Turbulence.* Academic Press, New York.

Lhermitte, P. (1958). Contribution à l'étude de la couche limite des houles progressives. C.O.E.C. Imprimerie Nationale. Paris. No. 136.

Li, H. (1954). Stability of oscillatory laminar flow along a wall. Beach Erosion Board. Tech. Memo 47.

Lighthill, M. J. (1954). The response of laminar skin friction and heat transfer to fluctuations in stream velocity. *Proc. Roy. Soc. Ser. A.* **224**: 1–23.

Liu, P. L-F. (1973). Damping of water waves over porous bed. *Proc. A.S.C.E. J. Hydraul. Div.* **99** (HY12): 2263–2271.

Liu, P. L-F. (1977). Mass transport in water waves propagated over a permeable bed. *Coastal Eng.* **1**: 79–96.

Longuet-Higgins, M. S. (1953). Mass transport in water waves. *Philos. Trans. Roy. Soc. Ser. A* **245** (903): 535–581.

Longuet-Higgins, M. S. (1981). Oscillating flow over steep sand ripples. *J. Fluid Mech.* **107**: 1–35.

Lundgren, H. (1972). Turbulent currents in the presence of waves. *Proc. 13th Conf. Coastal Eng. Vancouver*, pp. 623–634.

Lyne, W. H. (1971). Unsteady viscous flow over a wavy wall. *J. Fluid Mech.* **50**: 33–48.

Madsen, O. S. (1978). Wave-induced pore pressures and effective stresses in a porous bed. *Geotechnique*, **28** (4): 377–393.

Manohar, M. (1955). Mechanics of bottom sediment movement due to wave action. Beach Erosion Board. Tech. Memo. 75.

Massel, S. R. (1976). Gravity waves propagated over permeable bottom. *Proc. A.S.C.E. J. Waterw. Harbors Coastal Eng. Div.* **102** (WW2): 111–121.

Matsunaga, N. Kaneko, A. and Honji, H. (1981). A numerical study of steady streamings in oscillatory flow over a wavy wall. *J. Hydraul. Res.* **19** (1): 29–42.

McCroskey, W. J. and Philippe, J. J. (1975). Unsteady viscous flow on oscillating airfoils. *A.I.A.A. J.* **13**: 71–79.

Mei, C. C., Liu, P. L-F. and Carter, T. G. (1972). Mass transport in water waves. M.I.T. Dept Civil Eng. Ralph M. Parsons Lab. Rep. 146.

Merkli, P. and Thomann, H. (1975). Transition to turbulence in oscillating pipe flow. *J. Fluid Mech.* **68**: 567–575.

Moshagen, H. and Torum, A. (1975). Wave-induced pressures in permeable seabeds. *Proc. A.S.C.E. J. Waterw. Harbors Coastal Eng. Div.* **101** (WW1): 49–58.

Murray, J. D. (1965). Viscous damping of gravity waves over a permeable bed. *J. Geophys. Res.* **70** (10): 2325–2331.

Nakamura, H., Onishi, R., and Minamide, H. (1973). On the seepage in the seabed due to waves. *Proc. 20th Japan Soc. Civil Eng. Coastal Eng. Conf.*, pp. 421–428. (in Japanese)

Nakato, T., Locher, F. A., Glover, J. R. and Kennedy, J. F. (1977). Wave entrainment of sediment from rippled beds. *Proc. A.S.C.E. J. Waterw. Port Coastal Ocean Div.* **103** (WW1): 83–99.

Nash, J. F. and Patel, V. C. (1975). Calculations of unsteady turbulent boundary layers with flow reversal. NASA. CR-2546.

Noda, H. (1968). A study on mass transport in boundary layers in standing waves. *Proc. 11th Conf. Coastal Eng. London*, pp. 227–247.

Noda, H. (1971). On the oscillatory flow in turbulent boundary layers. *Bull. Disaster Prev. Res. Inst.* Kyoto Univ. **20**, Pt. 3 (176): 127–144.

Obremski, H. J. and Fejer, A. A. (1967). Transition in oscillating boundary layer flows. *J. Fluid Mech.* **29**: 93–111.

Prevost, J. H., Eide, O., and Anderson, K. H. (1975). Discussion of "Wave induced pressures in permeable seabeds" (by H. Moshagen and A. Torum). *Proc. A.S.C.E. J. Waterw. Harbors Coastal Eng. Div.* **101** (WW4): 464–465.

Puri, K. K. (1980). Damping of gravity waves over porous bed. *Proc. A.S.C.E. J. Hydraul. Div.* **106** (HY2): 303–312.

Putnam, J. A. (1949). Loss of wave energy due to percolation in a permeable sea bottom. *Trans. A.G.U.* **30** (3): 349–356.

Ramaprian, B. R. and Tu, S-W. (1980). An experimental study of oscillatory pipe flow at transitional Reynolds numbers. *J. Fluid Mech.* **100**: 513–544.

Raudkivi, A. J. (1963). Study of sediment ripple formation. *Proc. A.S.C.E. J. Hydraul. Div.* **89** (HY6): 15–33.

Reid, R. O. and Kajiura, K. (1957). On the damping of gravity waves over a permeable sea bed. *Trans. A.G.U.* **38** (5): 662–666.

Riedel, H. P., Kamphuis, J. W. and Brebner, A. (1972). Measurement of bed shear stress under waves. *Proc. 13th Conf. Coastal Eng. Vancouver*, pp. 587–603.

Russell, R. C. H. and Osorio, J.D.C. (1957). An experimental investigation of drift profiles in a closed channel. *Proc. 6th Conf. Coastal Eng. Miami*, pp. 171–193.

Sarpkaya, T. (1966). Experimental determination of the critical Reynolds number for pulsating Poiseuille flow. *Trans. A.S.M.E. D. J. Basic Eng.* **88**: 589–598.

Sawamoto, M., Yamashita, T., and Kurita, T. (1980). Vortex Formation over rippled bed under oscillatory flow. Tokyo Inst. of Technology. Dept Civil Eng. Rep. 27.

Sergeev, S. I. (1966). Fluid oscillations in pipes at moderate Reynolds numbers. *Fluid Dyn.* **1** (1): 121–122.

Sheen, S. J. (1964). Turbulence over a sand ripple. M. Eng. Thesis. Univ. Auckland. New Zealand.

Sleath, J. F. A. (1968). The effect of waves on the pressure in a bed of sand in a water channel and on the velocity distribution above it. Ph.D. Thesis. Univ. Cambridge.

Sleath, J. F. A. (1970). Wave-induced pressures in beds of sand. *Proc. A.S.C.E. J. Hydraul. Div.* **96** (HY2): 367–378.

Sleath, J. F. A. (1972). A second approximation to mass transport by water waves. *J. Mar. Res.* **30** (3): 295–304.

Sleath, J. F. A. (1973). A numerical study of the influence of bottom roughness on mass transport by water waves. *Proc. Int. Conf. Numer. Methods Fluid Dyn. Southampton.*

Sleath, J. F. A. (1974a). Mass transport over a rough bed. *J. Mar. Res.* **32** (1): pp. 13–24.

Sleath, J. F. A. (1974b). Stability of laminar flow at sea bed. *Proc. A.S.C.E. J. Waterw. Harbors Coastal Eng. Div.* **100** (WW2): 105–122.

Sleath, J. F. A. (1975). Transition in oscillatory flow over rippled beds. *Proc. I.C.E. Pt. 2.* **59**: 309–322.

Sleath, J. F. A. (1978). Discussion of "Mass transport in water waves propagated over a permeable bed" (by P.L-F. Liu 1977). *Coastal Eng.* **2**: 169–171.

Sleath, J. F. A. (1982). The effect of jet formation on the velocity distribution in oscillatory flow over flat beds of sand or gravel. *Coastal Eng.* **6**: 151–177.

Smith, J. D. (1977). Modeling of sediment transport on continental shelves. In *The Sea*, Vol. 6. E. D. Goldberg, I. N. McCave, J. J. O'Brien, and J. H. Steele, Eds. Wiley-Interscience, New York, pp. 539–578.

Stokes, G. G. (1851). On the effect of the internal friction of fluids on the motion of pendulums. *Trans. Camb. Philos. Soc.* **9**: 20–21.

Tanaka, H. and Shuto, N. (1981). Friction coefficient for a wave-current coexistent system. *Coastal Eng. Japan.* **24**: 105–128.

Telionis, D. P. (1981). *Unsteady Viscous Flows.* Springer-Verlag, New York.

Telionis, D. P. and Tsahalis, D. Th. (1976). Unsteady turbulent boundary layers and separation. *A.I.A.A. J.* **14**: 468–474.

Thomas, G. P. (1981). Wave-current interactions: an experimental and numerical study. Part 1. Linear waves. *J. Fluid Mech.* **110**: 457–474.

Tromans, P. S. (1978). Stability and transition of periodic pipe flows. Ph.D. Thesis. Univ. Cambridge.

Van Doorn, T. (1981). Experimental investigation of near-bottom velocities in water waves without and with a current. Delft Hydraul. Lab. Rep. M1423. Part 1.

Van Hoften, J. D. A. and Karaki, S. (1976). Interaction of waves and a turbulent current. *Proc. 15th Conf. Coastal Eng. Hawaii*, pp. 404–422.

Vincent, G. E. (1957). Contribution to the study of sediment transport on a horizontal bed due to wave action. *Proc. 6th Conf. Coastal Eng. Miami*, pp. 326–355.

Von Kerczek, C. H. (1982). The instability of plane Poiseuille flow. *J. Fluid Mech.* **116**: 91–114.

Von Kerczek, C. and Davis, S. H. (1972). The stability of oscillatory Stokes layers. *Stud. Appl. Math.* **51.3**: 239–252.

Von Kerczek, C. and Davis, S. H. (1974). Linear stability analysis of oscillatory Stokes layers. *J. Fluid Mech.* **62**: 753–773.

Wang, H. and Liang, S. S. (1974). Sediment transport in random waves at constant depth. *Proc. 14th Conf. Coastal Eng. Copenhagen*, pp. 795–811.

Yamamoto, T. (1977). Wave induced instability in seabeds. *Proc. A.S.C.E. spec. conf: Coastal Sediments '77. Charleston*, pp. 898–913.

Yamamoto, T. H., Koning, L., Sellmeijer, H., and Van Hijum, E. (1978). On the response of a poro-elastic bed to water waves. *J. Fluid Mech.* **87**: 193–206.

Three

SEDIMENT PROPERTIES

It is helpful to have some idea of the properties of sediment before discussing how the sediment is moved around on the sea bed.

3.1. SIZE

Sediment grain sizes vary widely. For purposes of discussion and comparison it is convenient to classify sediments into size ranges. Various classifications have been proposed. Table 3.1 is the classification suggested by the sub-committee on Sediment Terminology of the American Geophysical Union as reported by Lane (1947). This classification is an extension of the well-known Wentworth scale.

Particles of sediment have a wide range of shapes so the use of the term "particle diameter" in Table 3.1 is not unambiguous. Possible definitions of diameter are:

1. Sieve diameter.
2. The diameter of the sphere having the same volume.
3. The length of either the short, intermediate, or long grain axes or some combination of these lengths.
4. The diameter of the smooth sphere of the same density and with the same fall velocity.

TABLE 3.1. SIZE CLASSIFICATION OF SEDIMENT PARTICLES (AMERICAN GEOPHYSICAL UNION)

Class Name	Particle Diameter	
	Millimeters	Microns
Boulders		
Very large	4096–2048	
Large	2048–1024	
Medium	1024–512	
Small	512–256	
Cobbles		
Large	256–128	
Small	128–64	
Gravel		
Very coarse	64–32	
Coarse	32–16	
Medium	16–8	
Fine	8–4	
Very fine	4–2	
Sand		
Very coarse	2–1	2000–1000
Coarse	1–0.5	1000–500
Medium	0.5–0.25	500–250
Fine	0.25–0.125	250–125
Very fine	0.125–0.062	125–62
Silt		
Coarse	0.062–0.031	62–31
Medium	0.031–0.016	31–16
Fine	0.016–0.008	16–8
Very fine	0.008–0.004	8–4
Clay		
Coarse	0.004–0.002	4–2
Medium	0.0020–0.0010	2–1
Fine	0.0010–0.0005	1–0.5
Very fine	0.0005–0.00024	0.5–0.24

Sand and gravel are most commonly classified according to their sieve diameters, that is, the mesh size of the sieve through which the grains just pass. The fourth classification, usually referred to as the equivalent fall diameter or sedimentation diameter, is more commonly used for silt and clay.

A natural sample of sediment contains grains of a range of sizes. Because of the need to compare measurements with different samples of sediment, there have been many attempts to identify one particular size as characteristic of the whole sample. Frequently used are:

1. The median grain size, D.
2. The geometric mean, D_g.
3. The grain size corresponding to some fraction such as D_{90}, D_{65}.

The median grain size is the size for which 50% by weight of the sample is finer, or coarser. The diameters D_{90} and D_{65} are the sizes for which 90% and 65%, respectively, by weight of the sample is finer. The geometric mean is usually taken to be

$$D_g = (D_{84.1} D_{15.9})^{1/2} \tag{3.1}$$

in which $D_{84.1}$ and $D_{15.9}$ are the grain sizes for which 84.1% and 15.9% by weight of the sediment is finer.

Another classification commonly used by earth scientists is the phi scale:

$$\phi = -\log_2 D_m \tag{3.2}$$

where D_m is the grain diameter in millimeters. The mean value of ϕ for any given sample is usually denoted by M_ϕ.

In addition to the characteristic diameter it is common to specify the nature or spread of the size distribution as follows:

$$\text{skewness} = \frac{\log(D_g/D)}{\sigma_g} \tag{3.3}$$

$$\text{2nd skewness} = \frac{\log(D_{95}D_5/D^2)^{1/2}}{\sigma_g} \tag{3.4}$$

$$\text{kurtosis} = \frac{\log(D_{16}D_{95}/D_5 D_{84})^{1/2}}{\sigma_g} \tag{3.5}$$

where σ_g is the standard deviation of the log (grain size) distribution of the sample. It is often found that the distribution of grain sizes is approximately log-normally distributed. If this is the case, the standard deviation of the log (grain size) distribution is given by

$$\sigma_g = \log \left(\frac{D_{84.1}}{D_{15.9}} \right)^{1/2} \tag{3.6}$$

3.2. SHAPE

There have been many attempts to characterize the shape of sediment particles by one or more parameters but none is wholly satisfactory. One of the more widely used is the shape factor:

$$S.F. = \frac{D_1}{(D_2 D_3)^{1/2}} \tag{3.7}$$

where D_1, D_2, D_3 are respectively the lengths of the shortest, intermediate, and longest mutually perpendicular axes.

3.3. DENSITY, SPECIFIC GRAVITY, AND SPECIFIC WEIGHT

The specific weight γ is the weight per unit volume. It is related to density ρ by

$$\gamma = \rho g \tag{3.8}$$

In S.I. units if γ is expressed in kg/m^3, ρ is in $kg \cdot sec^2/m^4$.

The specific gravity is the ratio of the specific weight to that of water at $4°C$. The specific gravity of a sediment is a function of its mineral composition. Quartz is the mineral most commonly found in sediments and consequently the specific gravity of sands is usually very close to 2.65. However, other minerals may be present in significant quantities so caution is required when using this value unless the specific gravity has been measured for the sediment in question.

It is often important to know the weight of a given volume of deposited sediment. This depends on the porosity n of the sample and whether the pores are full of water or air. If ρ_1 is the density of the bed, ρ_s that of the dry sediment, and ρ that of the fluid occupying the pores, then

$$\rho_1 = (1-n)\rho_s + n\rho \tag{3.9}$$

This formula implies that all of the pores are filled with the same fluid, whether it be air or water. If the pores were only partially filled with water, ρ would have to be taken as the mean density of the water and air mixture occupying the pore spaces.

There are several empirical formulas for the specific weight of sediment deposits. In S.I. units, the formula suggested by Lane and Koelzer (1953) is

$$\gamma = 818(P+2)^{0.13} \tag{3.10}$$

TABLE 3.2.   VALUES OF CONSTANTS IN (3.12)

Condition	Sand γ_0	B	Silt γ_0	B	Clay γ_0	B
Sediment always submerged	1500	0	1040	91.4	480	260
Moderate reservoir drawdown	1500	0	1190	43.3	740	170
Considerable reservoir drawdown	1500	0	1270	16.0	960	96
Reservoir normally empty	1500	0	1310	0	1250	0

where γ is the specific weight in kg/m^3 and P is the percentage by weight of the sediment which is coarser than 0.05 mm.

Komura's (1963) formula may be written

$$\gamma = 2004 - 144D^{0.21} \tag{3.11}$$

where γ is in kg/m^3 and the median diameter D is in meters.

Both (3.10) and (3.11) are for recently deposited sediments. For silt and clay the specific weight increases with time. Lane and Koelzer suggested the following empirical relation on the basis of measurements on sediments deposited in reservoirs:

$$\gamma = \gamma_0 + B \log T \tag{3.12}$$

where γ is the specific weight after T years and γ_0 and B are given by Table 3.2 in kg/m^3.

Lane and Koelzer suggested that where the sediment consisted of more than one of the classes shown in Table 3.2 the specific weights obtained for each class from (3.12) should be combined in proportion to their relative weights in the sample. The alternative of combining the results by volume rather than by weight does not produce significantly different answers when allowance is made for the uncertainty inherent in an empirical formula of this sort.

3.4.   FALL VELOCITY

3.4.1.   Fall Velocity of a Sphere in an Infinite Still Fluid

The fall velocity W is the final equilibrium velocity reached by the falling sphere. Under these circumstances the drag of the fluid must exactly balance the force due to gravity tending to pull the sphere down:

$$\frac{\pi D^3}{6}(\rho_s - \rho)g = C_D \frac{\pi D^2}{4}\rho\frac{W^2}{2} \tag{3.13}$$

Figure 3.1 shows how the drag coefficient C_D varies with Reynolds number WD/ν for a sphere in an infinite fluid. In the Stokes region, that is, for $WD/\nu < 0.1$,

$$C_D = \frac{24}{(WD/\nu)} \tag{3.14}$$

Consequently, substituting in (3.13),

$$W = \frac{gD^2}{18\nu}\left(\frac{\rho_s - \rho}{\rho}\right) \tag{3.15}$$

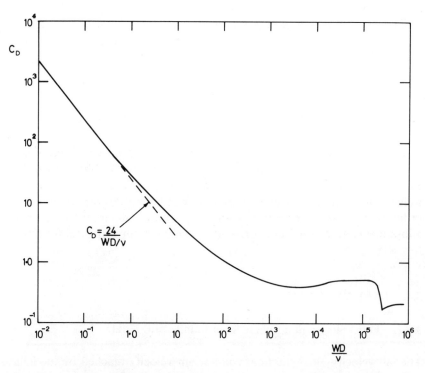

Figure 3.1. Variation of C_D with Reynolds number for a sphere falling in an infinite fluid.

Figure 3.1 also shows that, for $400 < WD/v < 200,000$, C_D is almost constant. From (3.13) this would give

$$W = \text{const} \times \left(\frac{\rho_s - \rho}{\rho} gD \right)^{1/2} \tag{3.16}$$

3.4.2. Influence of Shape

The expressions obtained for a sphere are not directly applicable to grains of sediment because of the difference in shape.

Figure 3.2 shows how the shape factor (S.F.) affects the fall velocity. These curves were calculated for water at 20°C from the curves suggested by the U.S. Inter-Agency Committee on Water Resources (1957) on the basis of a large number of experiments with natural sediments. Note that the effect of variations in shape on the fall velocity is much less significant for small grain sizes than for large. Moreover, the curve for a shape factor equal to unity is not identical with that for a sphere. The reason for this is that a single shape factor cannot completely define the particle shape: both a cube and a sphere have a shape factor of unity even though their shapes are very different. Thus the natural sediments for which the curves shown in Fig. 3.2 were obtained could have shape factors equal to unity without being spherical.

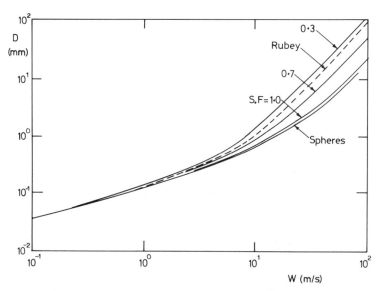

Figure 3.2. Variation of fall velocity with grain size and shape factor for isolated particles of sediment.

Approximate formulas may be obtained for relatively coarse and relatively fine sediments. For quartz sand in water at 20°C we have, for $90 > D > 3$ mm,

$$\text{S.F.} = 1.0 \qquad W = 6.5D^{1/2}$$
$$\text{S.F.} = 0.7 \qquad W = 4.2D^{1/2} \tag{3.17}$$
$$\text{S.F.} = 0.3 \qquad W = 2.8D^{1/2}$$

And for $D < 0.1$ mm,

$$W = 92 \times 10^4 D^2 \tag{3.18}$$

In these formulas W is in m/s and D in meters. The upper limit on D for (3.17) corresponds to a value of $WD/v = 200,000$. It is seen from Fig. 3.1 that at higher values of the Reynolds number the drag coefficient for a sphere is no longer approximately constant. This is because of transition to turbulence in the boundary layer which significantly alters the pattern of flow and hence the fluid drag.

Also shown in Fig. 3.2 is the well-known curve proposed by Rubey (1933) for particles of sand. It would seem that his measurements were made with relatively flat sediments.

3.4.3. Effect of Temperature

A change in temperature modifies the coefficient of viscosity of the fluid and hence the Reynolds number WD/v. It is clear from Fig. 3.1 that a change in Reynolds number will have a significant effect on the drag coefficient and hence the fall velocity at small values of WD/v but a relatively small effect in the range $400 < WD/v < 200,000$.

Figure 3.3 shows how the fall velocity W_θ for quartz spheres in fluid of temperature $\theta°$C compares with the value W_{20} for fluid at 20°C. As anticipated, the smallest diameters, corresponding to the lowest Reynolds numbers, show the largest effect of temperature.

Temperature also has an effect on the density of the water. However, the change in density is so small compared with the change in kinematic viscosity that density variation may be neglected for all practical purposes.

3.4.4. Effect of Sediment Concentration

The curves discussed thus far have been for an isolated grain in an infinite fluid. In practice, the presence of other grains will modify the fall velocity. A small cloud of grains in an otherwise clear fluid will fall faster than a single

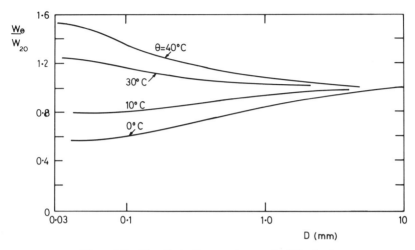

Figure 3.3. The effect of temperature on the fall velocity.

grain. On the other hand, in a uniform suspension the fall velocity of any given grain will be less than that of an isolated grain in a clear fluid. This is because the fall of one grain causes a compensating upflow of fluid elsewhere, which impedes the fall of other grains.

The case of particles dispersed throughout the fluid is the situation most commonly encountered in practice. Figure 3.4 shows the results obtained by McNown and Lin (1952) for this case. These curves are based on a theoretical analysis but showed good agreement with experiment for concentrations

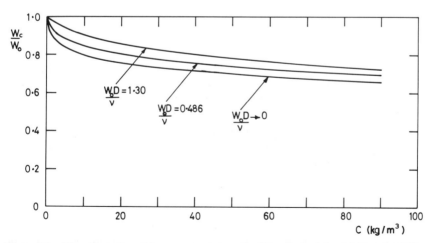

Figure 3.4. The effect of particle concentration on the fall velocity (after McNown and Lin, 1952).

ranging from 1.0 up to 60 kg/m^3. In Fig. 3.4 W_C is the fall velocity at concentration C and W_0 is that in clear fluid. It would seem that quite small concentrations of sediment may significantly reduce the fall velocity.

More recently Richardson and Jeronimo (1979) suggested

$$\frac{W_C}{W_0} = (1 - C)^n \qquad (3.19)$$

where C is the volumetric concentration and the exponent n varies from 4.6 at low Reynolds numbers to 2.3 at high Reynolds numbers. This formula does not give good agreement with the curves in Fig. 3.4, possibly because (3.19) is based on data for fluidized beds and is consequently intended for larger values of C than those shown in Fig. 3.4.

The curves of McNown and Lin and the formula of Richardson and Jeronimo are for a uniform dispersion of noncohesive particles. In some fluids, particles of silt and clay tend to collect together in flocs. The fall velocity of the flocs is many times greater than that of the individual particles so that, under these circumstances, an initially uniform suspension of particles may produce accelerated settling.

3.4.5. Effect of Turbulence

At very small Reynolds numbers the drag exerted by the fluid on a body in a stream is directly proportional to the relative velocity. Thus random fluctuations in velocity will have no effect on the mean drag, which will remain proportional to the mean velocity. On the other hand, in the region where C_D is approximately constant, drag is proportional to the square of the velocity. Under these circumstances the mean drag will no longer be proportional to the mean velocity if random fluctuations are present.

Thus the effect of turbulence on the fall velocity should be negligible at very small Reynolds numbers. However, at values of WD/ν greater than about 10 the turbulence would be expected to reduce the fall velocity.

Unfortunately, because of the difficulty of predicting turbulence intensities and length scales in any given situation it is not yet possible to determine the reduction in fall velocity due to turbulence in advance in situations of practical importance.

3.5. ANGLE OF REPOSE

If sediment is placed in an open box and carefully leveled and the box is then gradually tilted, there is observed to be a certain angle of tilt beyond which the sediment becomes unstable. This angle is what most engineers call the angle of repose ϕ. On the other hand, several authors have pointed out that there are really two characteristic angles of rest. For example, Allen (1970) distinguishes between the "angle of initial yield" and the "residual angle of shearing" ϕ_r. The angle of initial yield is the same as the angle of repose ϕ defined above, whereas ϕ_r is the angle of the final slope after avalanching has ceased.

Allen (1970) carried out experiments with uniform spheres ranging in diameter from 0.08 up to 3 mm and obtained

$$\phi \backsimeq 33°$$
$$\phi_r \backsimeq 23°$$

(3.20)

These results were confirmed by Statham (1974) except for two tests with spheres of diameter 11 and 17 mm which show somewhat larger values of ϕ and ϕ_r. Since the critical angle ought not to vary with diameter for uniform spheres it is possible that the limited size of Statham's apparatus or the non-sphericity of the ballotini used may have affected the results for the two largest spheres.

The angle of repose ϕ is usually identified with the friction angle used in soil mechanics. For any natural sediment its value is strongly dependent on how closely packed the sample is. Cornforth (1973) suggests values of ϕ for natural sediments ranging from about 28 up to 36° when porosity is maximum and from about 45 up to 53° at minimum porosity. These results are consistent with Allen's and Statham's measurements with uniform spheres: the porosity of avalanching spheres is greater than that of a stationary bed and consequently ϕ_r is less than ϕ.

Curves have also been presented "until more exact relationships can be determined" by Lane (1955). He specifies ϕ in terms of sediment diameter and shape. For sediment of diameter 8 mm he shows ϕ ranging from 22° for very round grains up to 34° for very angular particles, whereas for a diameter of 25 mm the range is from 32° up to about 39°. Lane's curves were subsequently revised by Simons and Albertson (1960) as seen in Fig. 3.5. However, since there is no allowance for the porosity of the sediment they should probably still be treated with caution.

Another set of curves is proposed by Simons and Senturk (1977). These show ϕ as a function of grain size and sediment composition. For example, the experimental results for sand range from 31 up to 42° with changing diameter while the results for lignite lie between 50 and 60°. There is no allowance for the porosity of the sample or for the shape of the grains.

In view of these conflicting results it is clearly desirable to measure ϕ directly.

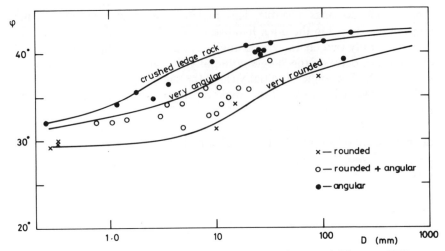

Figure 3.5.   Angle of repose of sand and gravel (after Simons and Albertson, 1960).

3.6.   PERMEABILITY AND POROSITY

The permeability of a bed of sediment is usually defined in terms of the flow produced by a given pressure gradient [see (2.51)]. For laboratory tests the U.S. Geological Survey defines the coefficient of permeability k as equal to the flow of water at 60°F in gal/day through a cross-sectional area of 1 ft² under a hydraulic gradient of 1 ft/ft. The definition for use in the field is the flow of water in gal/day through a cross section of aquifer 1 ft thick and 1 mile wide under a hydraulic gradient of 1 ft/mile at field temperature.

No formula for permeability in terms of the properties of the sediment is universally accepted but one of the most widely used is that of Fair and Hatch (1933):

$$K = \frac{1}{A \left[\dfrac{(1-n)^2}{n^3} \left(B \sum \dfrac{P}{100 D_{gm}} \right)^2 \right]} \tag{3.21}$$

where K is the specific permeability, n is porosity, A is a packing factor equal to about 5, B is a sand shape factor varying from 6.0 for spherical grains to 7.7 for angular grains, P is the percentage of sand held between two adjacent sieves, and D_{gm} is the geometric mean of the mesh sizes of the two sieves.

The relationship between the coefficient of permeability k and the specific permeability K is given by (2.52).

The porosity is defined as

$$n = \frac{\text{volume of voids in a sample of sediment}}{\text{total volume of the sample}} \qquad (3.22)$$

Todd (1959) suggests the following typical values of porosity:

Material	Porosity
Soils	0.5–0.6
Clay	0.45–0.55
Silt	0.40–0.50
Medium to coarse mixed sand	0.35–0.40
Uniform sand	0.30–0.40
Fine to medium mixed sand	0.30–0.35
Gravel	0.30–0.40
Gravel and sand	0.20–0.35
Sandstone	0.10–0.20
Shale	0.01–0.10
Limestone	0.01–0.10

REFERENCES

Allen, J. R. L. (1970). The avalanching of granular solids on dunes and similar slopes. *J. Geo.* **78**: 326–351.

Cornforth, D. H. (1973). Prediction of drained strength of sands from relative density measurements. Am. Soc. Test. Mat. Spec. Tech. Pub. 523; pp. 281–303.

Fair, G. M. and Hatch, L. P. (1933). Fundamental factors governing the streamline flow of water through sand. *J. Am. Water Works Assoc.* **25**: 1551–1565.

Komura, S. (1963). Discussion of "Sediment transportation mechanics: Introduction and Properties of Sediment," Prog. rep. Task Comm. Prep. Sediment. Man. *Proc. A.S.C.E. J. Hydraul. Div.* **89** (HY1): 263–266.

Lane, E. W. (1947). Report of subcommittee on sediment terminology. *Trans. A.G.U. Washington D.C.* **28**(6): 936–938.

Lane, E. W. (1955). Design of stable channels. *Trans A.S.C.E.* **120**: 1234–1279.

Lane, E. W. and Koelzer, V. A. (1953). Density of sediments deposited in reservoirs. In "A study of methods used in measurement and analysis of sediment loads in streams." St Paul. U.S. Eng. Dist.St. Paul, Minnesota. Rep. 9.

McNown, J. S. and Lin, P. N. (1952). Sediment concentration and fall velocity. *Proc. 2nd Midwest. Conf. Fluid Mech. Ohio State Univ.*, pp. 401–411.

Richardson, J. F. and Jeronimo, M.A. daS. (1979). Velocity-voidage relations for sedimentation and fluidization. *Chem. Eng. Sci.* **34**: 1419–1422.

Rubey, W. W. (1933). Settling velocities of gravel sand and silt particles. *Am. J. Sci.* **25** (148): 325–338.

Simons, D. B. and Albertson, M. L. (1960). Uniform water conveyance channels in alluvial material. *Proc. A.S.C.E. J. Hydraul. Div.* **86** (HY5): 33–99.

Simons, D. B. and Senturk, F. (1977). Sediment transport technology. Water Res. Pub. Fort Collins, Colorado.

Statham, I. (1974). The relationship of porosity and angle of repose to mixture proportions in assemblages of different sized materials. *Sedimentology* **21**: 149–162.

Todd, D. K. (1959). *Ground Water Hydrology.* John Wiley & Sons, New York.

U.S. Interagency Committee On Water Resources. (1957). Some fundamentals of particle size analysis, a study of methods used in measurement and analysis of sediment loads in streams. St. Anthony Falls Hydraul. Lab. Minneapolis, Minnesota.

Four

BED FORMS

The flow of water over a bed of sand often distorts the bed into a pattern of regular or irregular waves. This is observed both in steady and oscillatory flows. The bed forms which are produced by the interaction of the flow and the sediment are of considerable practical importance since near-bed currents, sediment transport, and wave height attenuation are all significantly affected by the bed profile.

Waves Alone

4.1. SUMMARY OF BED FORM TYPES

Different observers have given different names to what are, essentially, the same bed forms. In order to avoid confusion Fig. 4.1 shows the classification adopted in this book together with some of the other names found in the literature.

In addition to the bed forms shown in Fig. 4.1, the bed may also be flat. In oscillatory flow, plane beds are found at very high sediment transport rates ("sheet flow"). The bed may also be plane when there is no movement of the sediment but this is not always the case: if the bed was rippled just before the fluid velocity fell below the limit for sediment movement "fossil" or "relic" ripples may remain on the bed.

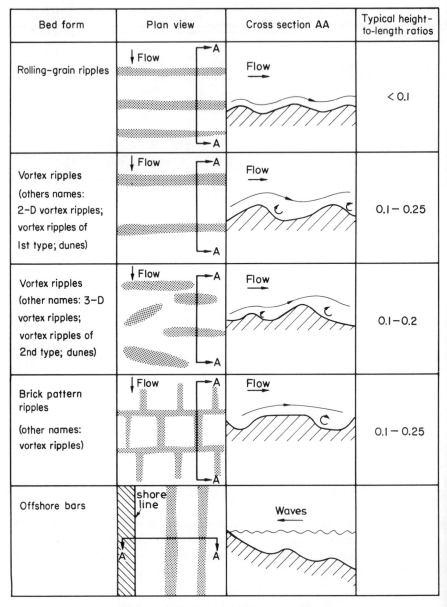

Bed form	Plan view	Cross section AA	Typical height-to-length ratios
Rolling-grain ripples	Flow	Flow	< 0.1
Vortex ripples (others names: 2-D vortex ripples; vortex ripples of 1st type; dunes)	Flow	Flow	0.1 − 0.25
Vortex ripples (other names: 3-D vortex ripples; vortex ripples of 2nd type; dunes)	Flow	Flow	0.1−0.2
Brick pattern ripples (other names: vortex ripples)	Flow	Flow	0.1 − 0.25
Offshore bars	shore line	Waves	

Figure 4.1. Bed forms produced by oscillatory flows.

4.2. ROLLING-GRAIN RIPPLES

Bagnold (1946) classified the bed forms produced by the action of progressive waves on horizontal beds into two main groups: those which have a large enough height to length ratio to form vortices in the lee of the crest he called "vortex ripples," and those which are too small for vortex formation he described as "rolling-grain" ripples. We adopt the same terminology here.

Rolling-grain ripples are the first to appear on an initially plane bed subjected to wave action (provided there are no obstructions on or near the bed capable of producing vortex formation). The distinguishing feature of these ripples is their low height to length ratio. One reason why rolling-grain ripples are not found with large height to length ratios is that when this ratio exceeds about 0.1 the boundary layer separates behind the crests and vortex formation takes place. When this occurs vortex ripples will gradually spread over the bed surface, destroying the rolling-grain ripples. This situation is illustrated in Fig. 4.2. Rolling-grain ripples are the small-amplitude bed forms on the right but vortex ripples are just starting to spread in from the left.

Because vortex ripples are much more vigorous than rolling-grain ripples, the latter are only stable where vortex ripples will not form. This means that

Figure 4.2.   A bed of rolling-grain ripples being invaded by vortex ripples.

rolling-grain ripples are rarely stable at low to moderate sediment transport rates. At very high sediment transport rates vortex formation is inhibited and only rolling-grain ripples are found.

4.2.1. Ripple Profile

When fully developed, rolling-grain ripples are usually two dimensional and regular. The ripple profile is approximately sinusoidal, although there is considerable variation during the course of the wave cycle.

4.2.2. Mechanism of Formation

Let us suppose that the bed is initially slightly wavy. Then a steady drift of fluid is set up in addition to the oscillatory motion as discussed in Section 2.2.2. Figure 2.8 shows the streamlines of this steady drift for the situation when the wavelength L of the ripples is much larger than the orbital amplitude a of the fluid outside the bed boundary layer. In reality ripples are not observed with very small values of a/L but the steady drifts set up at higher values of a/L are similar.

The important feature of these steady drifts is that in the vicinity of the bed they are directed from the ripple trough toward the ripple crest. Consequently, any sediment in motion at the bed will tend to be carried toward the ripple crests and away from the troughs provided the particles of sediment are not too large. Under these circumstances the ripples will tend to grow.

The reason why the particles of sediment must not be too large is that, as shown by Fig. 2.8, the steady drift further away from the bed is away from the crest and toward the trough. Thus if the particle projects too far into this outer region, it will tend to drift toward the trough rather than the crest. In other words, there is a limiting value of βD beyond which rolling-grain ripples will not form.

The ripples will not, of course, continue to grow indefinitely. The tendency of the steady drift to carry particles of sediment toward the crest is opposed by the component of the gravity force acting down the slope. As the ripples get steeper the gravity force becomes relatively stronger and consequently there is a limiting height beyond which the ripples will not grow for given wave conditions.

So far we have assumed that the bed is initially slightly wavy. In fact, any initial disturbance is sufficient to start the process. Even a single grain of sediment projecting from the bed will do. For example, suppose the bed is entirely flat apart from a triangular ridge at right angles to the flow so that the bed profile is for $\beta|x| < 1,$ $y = h(1 - \beta|x|)$

for $\beta|x| > 1,$ $y = 0$ (4.1)

We have taken the ridge to be of height h (assumed small) and to extend a distance $1/\beta$ on either side of the crest. Since $1/\beta$ is typically of the order of a millimeter in most natural situations this disturbance is comparable to that produced by a few grains of sand piled together. The profile of the ridge may be expressed as a Fourier integral

$$y = \frac{h}{\pi} \int_0^\infty \frac{2\beta}{k^2} \left(1 - \cos\frac{k}{\beta}\right) \cos kx \, dk$$ (4.2)

Each element of this Fourier integral is a sinusoidal disturbance of the bed, which will set up a mean drift as seen in Fig. 2.8. The drift produced by our isolated ridge will be the combined drift due to the sum of all of these sinusoidal disturbances. With the aid of (2.24) we obtain the streamlines shown in Fig. 4.3.

We see that in the vicinity of the ridge the time-mean flow near the bed tends to carry sediment toward the ridge, thus the ridge would tend to grow. Further away, the flow near the bed is in the opposite direction. This outer

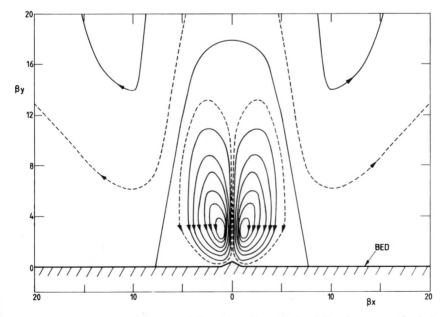

Figure 4.3. Streamlines of the mean drift produced by an isolated disturbance on a flat bed.

flow would consequently tend to pile sand up into a new ridge on either side of the initial ridge. Once these new ridges start to form they generate drifts similar to those seen in Fig. 4.3; consequently, the ripple pattern will gradually spread over the whole bed.

4.2.3. Theoretical Work

Attempts to predict the wavelength of rolling-grain ripples analytically have been made by Uda and Hino (1975), Sleath (1976), and Kaneko (1981).

Sleath considered only the case of very mobile sediments, that is, those which are sufficiently light when set in motion to move at the same velocity as the surrounding fluid. For the case $a/L \ll 1$ he took the fluid velocity to be given by (2.23) and (2.24). He further assumed the ripples that form are those for which the drift of fluid (and hence of sediment) toward the crest is maximum. He concluded that, for any given sediment (i.e., constant ρ_s and D),

$$\beta L = \text{const} \tag{4.3}$$

This equation can also be written

$$\frac{a}{L} = \text{const} \times R^{1/2} \tag{4.4}$$

According to Kaneko (1981) a similar conclusion was reached by Uda and Hino (1975).

For the case $a/L \gg 1$ Sleath made use of the solution for the velocity distribution given by Lyne (1971). He also assumed a simple power law relationship between sediment transport rate and fluid velocity in order to allow for the differing quantities of sediment in motion at any instant. Assuming, once again, the ripples that form are those for which the drift of sediment toward the crest is maximum he found

$$\frac{a}{L} = 0.93(\beta D)^{-0.658} \tag{4.5}$$

Kaneko (1981) considered only the case of a/L small compared with unity. He obtained a higher order (in a/L) solution for the velocity numerically and assumed that the ripples which formed would be those for which the bed shear stress at the crest was maximum. The relationship he obtained may be written

$$\frac{a}{L} = \frac{R^{0.74}}{60.6} \tag{4.6}$$

The difficulty with the two solutions for a/L small compared with unity [(4.4) and 4.6)] is that rolling-grain ripples usually form at much larger values of a/L. Ripples with values of a/L significantly less than unity, to which these solutions are restricted, are rare. Consequently, whatever their other merits, these equations are not of great practical importance.

On the other hand, (4.5), for $a/L \gg 1$, is at least in a more relevant range. However, the assumption that the grains of sediment are either at rest or move at the same velocity as that which the fluid would have had in the absence of any sediment transport is unrealistic, particularly for relatively heavy or large grains.

Consequently, it would seem that the various theoretical models do not at the present time allow rolling-grain ripple geometries to be predicted with confidence.

4.2.4.   Experimental Results for Ripple Geometry

Most investigators have been principally concerned with vortex ripples. However, if we define rolling-grain ripples as those with height to length ratios less than 0.1, measurements of this sort of ripple have been made by Manohar (1955), Inman (1957), Yalin and Russell (1962), Kennedy and Falcon (1965), Horikawa and Watanabe (1967), Carstens et al. (1969), Mogridge and Kamphuis (1972), Dingler (1975), Sleath and Ellis (1978), Nielsen (1979), and others. In fact, all of Manohar's results fall in this regime, which may be one reason why other investigators, more concerned with vortex ripples, have found it difficult to reconcile his measurements with theirs.

Mogridge and Kamphuis (1972) suggested that ripple geometry was determined by four dimensionless groups:

$$\frac{(\rho_s - \rho)gD^3}{\rho v^2}, \quad \frac{\rho D}{(\rho_s - \rho)gT^2}, \quad \frac{a}{D}, \quad \frac{\rho_s}{\rho}$$

If the mass-transport velocity is negligible, these are the same as the dimensionless groups suggested by Yalin and Russell (1962), with the addition of ρ_s/ρ.

Figure 4.4 shows how a/L varies with $\rho D/(\rho_s - \rho)gT^2$. At low values of $\rho D/(\rho_s - \rho)gT^2$ the experimental points follow a single curve with relatively little scatter. A regression analysis for the four dimensionless groups (Sleath, 1976) shows that in this region the other three groups are unimportant. However, for values of $\rho D/(\rho_s - \rho)gT^2$ greater than about 5×10^{-5} the experimental scatter is more significant. This region corresponds to the very mobile sediments to which the theory leading up to (4.5) is supposed to apply. It seems likely that in this region $\rho D/(\rho_s - \rho)gT^2$ is not the only

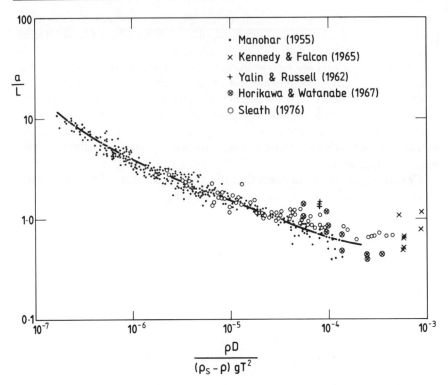

Figure 4.4. Variation of a/L with $\rho D/(\rho_s - \rho)gT^2$.

important dimensionless group. At the present time, however, the single curve shown in Fig. 4.4 is probably sufficient for design purposes.

Although it is not difficult to measure the wavelength of rolling-grain ripples, measurements of their height are much more of a problem because of the smallness of the height and because of the movement of the crest during the course of the cycle. Consequently, empirical formulas for ripple hieght show much greater scatter. Most investigators agree that the height is determined by some measure of the sediment transport rate. Nielsen (1979) found that the parameter

$$\psi = \frac{\hat{\tau}_0}{(\rho_s - \rho)gD} \tag{4.7}$$

gave the best correlation. The formulas he obtained (for both rolling-grain and vortex ripples) were

$$\frac{h}{L}=0.182-0.24\psi^{3/2} \tag{4.8}$$

for laboratory tests and

$$\frac{h}{L}=0.342-0.34\psi^{1/4} \tag{4.9}$$

for actual site conditions. He suggested that different formulas are required for the two cases because natural waves are much less regular than those used in the laboratory.

4.3. VORTEX RIPPLES

The essential feature of vortex ripples is the vortex which forms in the lee of each crest. These are the ripples most commonly found at low to moderate sediment transport rates.

4.3.1. Ripple Profile

At low sediment transport rates, vortex ripples are usually two dimensional. An exception to this rule is provided by the so-called brick-pattern ripples discussed in Section 4.3.5. Figure 4.5 is a photograph of two-dimensional vortex ripples. This bed was obtained for the same test conditions as those for Fig. 4.2, but for Fig. 4.5 the test was continued for an extra half hour. This was long enough for the vortex ripples, which are just starting to appear in Fig. 4.2, to take over the entire bed. Figure 4.6 shows two measured ripple profiles. We see that the profile of the 0.2-mm sand is very well approximated by the relation

$$y=\frac{h}{2}\cos k\xi \tag{2.22}$$

where ξ is given by (2.21) with $\eta=0$. The ripple profile in the coarser sand is more nearly sinusoidal. In general, the coarser the sand the more rounded the crests. In addition, the profile becomes more nearly sinusoidal as the height to length ratio of the ripple decreases.

The measurements shown in Fig. 4.6 were made when the flow had come to rest. That is why the profiles are symmetrical about the crest. During the course of an actual cycle the crest tends to move first to one side and then, as the flow reverses, to the other. This makes the upstream face of the ripple

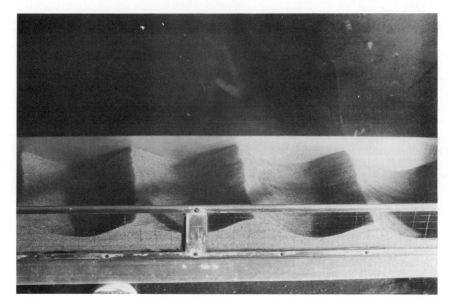

Figure 4.5. Two-dimensional vortex ripples.

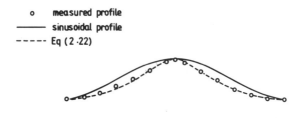

o   measured profile
——— sinusoidal profile
– – – – Eq (2·22)

(a) $D = 0.2$ mm, $h/L = 0.17$, $L = 0.14$ m

(b) $D = 1.14$ mm, $h/L = 0.18$, $L = 0.21$ m

Figure 4.6. Mean profiles of vortex ripples.

slightly flatter than that shown in Fig. 4.6 and, in addition, a cliff of sediment tends to form just downstream of the crest as indicated by the dashed line in Fig. 4.7.

The two-dimensional vortex ripple profile is usually associated with relatively steep ripples (typically $0.15 < h/L < 0.25$). As the sediment transport rate increases, these ripples become progressively more three dimensional and the steepness decreases. Figure 4.8 is an example of the sort of bed obtained at relatively high sediment transport rates (but not high enough to produce rolling-grain ripples). It should be emphasized that this bed was obtained after a prolonged period of oscillatory flow. Even at these relatively high sediment transport rates, a two-dimensional bed will usually form at the start of a test. However, after two or three hours, three-dimensional effects become progressively more pronounced and the two-dimensional profile is lost. This may explain why some investigators (e.g., Bagnold, 1946)

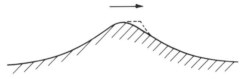

Figure 4.7.   The difference between mean and instantaneous ripple profiles.

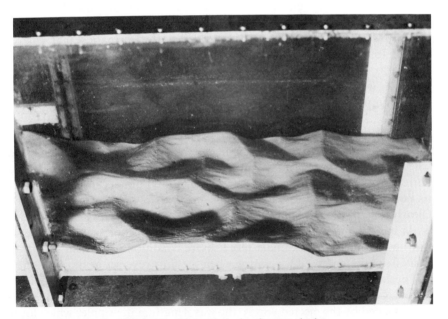

Figure 4.8.   Three-dimensional vortex ripples.

appear not to have observed three-dimensional effects even at relatively high sediment transport rates. When measurements are made in oscillating trays it is not possible to continue the test very long at high sediment transport rates without significant loss of sediment. Under these circumstances the three-dimensional bed would not have time to establish itself. There is also some evidence to suggest that relatively narrow flumes or oscillating trays may inhibit the formation of three-dimensional effects. In addition, particularly with very light sediment, the interval between two-dimensional vortex ripples and the reappearance of rolling-grain ripples at very high sediment transport rates is sometimes so restricted that three-dimensional ripples might not be detected.

4.3.2. Mechanism of Formation

It is not difficult to see why vortex ripples form. Both the primary flow on the upstream face of the crest and the reverse flow in its lee tend to carry sediment up toward the top of the crest. This process is opposed by gravity forces which tend to carry the grains back down the slope and by the erosion of sediment by the flow over the crest. Both of these opposing effects become progressively more important as ripple height increases and this explains why there is a limiting steepness for any given set of conditions.

However, it is less clear why ripples form at only one wavelength, for given experimental conditions, since the foregoing argument implies that the bed is unstable to all wavelengths provided vortex formation takes place. Presumably, the wavelength which actually forms is the one that gives the greatest transport of sediment toward the crest. At low sediment transport rates the wavelength of the ripples is usually directly proportional to the orbital amplitude of the fluid outside the boundary layer. The constant of proportionality varies hardly at all with grain size or density and only very slowly with the Reynolds number R of the flow. This suggests that the wavelength is controlled by the vortex which is shed at the end of each half-cycle when the flow reverses. At the end of the half-cycle in which it is ejected this vortex is in the vicinity of an adjacent ripple. At this point it can, depending on its position, either help or impede the transport of sediment up the crest. Clearly, one particular value of a/L will give maximum growth.

At low sediment transport rates there is no significant exchange of sediment between crests but, under more severe conditions, sediment is carried away from the bed with the vortex when the flow reverses at the end of the half cycle. Where this sediment falls clearly influences the growth rate of the ripples. Consequently, when a significant amount of sediment is carried up from the bed by the ejected vortex, the wavelength of the ripples which form will no longer be a function only of the orbital amplitude of the fluid.

This explains why vortex ripples can maintain themselves on a bed of sediment. However, for such a ripple to establish itself in the first place there must be some obstruction on or near the bed which is capable of forming vortices. This existing obstruction may be rolling-grain ripples which have grown so steep that vortices begin to form in their lee or it may be some other surface feature such as a pebble lying on the bed. However, in the latter case vortex ripples will spread over the bed only if rolling-grain ripples are also possible. The spread of vortex ripples over the bed appears to require the assistance of the rolling-grain mechanism to pile the sediment into ridges on either side of the initial disturbance from which the new vortex ripples will grow. This is illustrated by Fig. 4.9. In this case the isolated disturbance consisted of a thin vertical wall of height 0.02 m running across the bed. The fluid velocity was sufficient to cause general movement of the sediment but the grain size was too large for rolling-grain ripples to form. The isolated obstruction caused vigorous vortex formation. The bed was initially flat but after a few minutes sand had been scooped in against the wall by these vortices as shown in Fig. 4.9. However, vortex ripples did not spread across the bed. The photograph, which was taken after prolonged oscillation, shows that the vortices from the initial disturbance did produce a slight ridge of sand on either side. But without the assistance of the rolling-grain mechanism these ridges did not grow large enough to generate vortices.

Figure 4.9. The bed profile on either side of a vertical barrier placed normal to the flow.

4.3.3. Theoretical Models

There has been very little theoretical work on vortex ripple formation, probably because the nonlinearity of the flow mechanisms makes solution of the equations of motion much more difficult than for rolling-grain ripples.

However, Sleath (1975) presented some calculations based on his numerical solution for flow over rippled beds (see Section 2.2.2). He considered only the case of rather low sediment transport rates for which there is negligible exchange of sediment from one ripple to the next. He assumed that under these circumstances the ripples which formed would be those with the maximum rate of migration toward the crest of the fluid particles in the immediate vicinity of the bed. The equation obtained was

$$\frac{a}{L} = 0.49 R^{0.032} \tag{4.10}$$

The most doubtful part of the derivation of this equation is probably the assumption that the fluid velocities are given by Sleath's numerical solution since this assumes laminar flow, whereas the flow over active ripples is almost always turbulent. (However, it was pointed out in Section 2.3.2 that the solution agreed well with experiment even when the flow was turbulent.) The assumption that the sediment moves in the same way as the fluid particles is also questionable.

Figure 4.10 shows a comparison between (4.10) and the measurements of

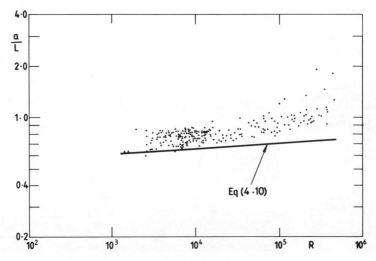

Figure 4.10. Comparison of (4.10) with the measurements of Mogridge and Kamphuis (1972).

Mogridge and Kamphuis (1972). Most of these measurements are for the relatively low sediment transport rates assumed in the derivation of (4.10). In view of the dubious assumptions, the agreement between theory and experiment could have been worse. There is clearly considerable room for further work in this field.

4.3.4. Experimental Results for Ripple Geometry

In contrast with the lack of theoretical work there have been numerous experimental studies of vortex ripples. Measurements have been made by Hunt (1882), Forel (1883), Darwin (1883), Bagnold (1946), Scott (1954), Inman (1957), Yalin and Russell (1962), Homma et al. (1965), Kennedy and Falcon (1965), Horikawa and Watanabe (1967), Carstens et al. (1969), Mogridge and Kamphus (1972), Chan et al. (1972), Dingler (1975), Lofquist (1978), Sleath and Ellis (1978), Nielsen (1979), Kaneko (1981), and many others.

Once again, it may be assumed that ripple geometry is determined by the four dimensionless groups:

$$\frac{(\rho_s - \rho)gD^3}{\rho v^2}, \quad \frac{\rho D}{(\rho_s - \rho)gT^2}, \quad \frac{a}{D}, \quad \frac{\rho_s}{\rho}$$

Mogridge and Kamphuis' experiments showed that, at any rate at relatively low sediment transport rates, $(\rho_s - \rho)gD^3/\rho v^2$ and ρ_s/ρ were unimportant. We saw in Section 4.2.4 that the same was also true at very high sediment transport rates for rolling-grain ripples. This suggests that a single curve of L/D versus a/D for constant $\rho D/(\rho_s - \rho)gT^2$ may be plotted covering both vortex and rolling-grain ripples. Figure 4.11 shows the result.

Each curve in Fig. 4.11 may be split into three separate sections. This is most clearly seen for relatively small values of $\rho D/(\rho_s - \rho)gT^2$. At small values of a/D the value of L/D increases steadily with a/D and the ratio a/L is nearly constant. This section of the curve corresponds to two-dimensional or brick-pattern ripples and relatively low sediment transport rates. This is followed by a region in which L/D ceases to rise rapidly, and at small values of $\rho D/(\rho_s - \rho)gT^2$ even falls, as a/D increases. In this region the ripples become progressively more irregular, the value of a/L increases, and the ripple steepness h/L decreases. Finally, at still higher values of a/D, the value of L/D starts to rise steadily again and a/L is again nearly constant for any given value of $\rho D/(\rho_s - \rho)gT^2$. This third region corresponds to rolling-grain ripples. The sediment transport rate is high. As a/D increases the ripple steepness falls steadily toward zero.

As the value of $\rho D/(\rho_s - \rho)gT^2$ in Fig. 4.11 gets larger, the intermediate region between the two rising sections of the curve becomes steadily more restricted. In the curve for $\rho D/(\rho_s-\rho)gT^2 = 200 \times 10^{-6}$ the intermediate section has completely disappeared. This suggests that for this value of $\rho D/(\rho_s-\rho)gT^2$ only rolling-grain ripples will form. One of Mogridge and Kamphuis' series of tests was made at a value of $\rho D/(\rho_s-\rho)gT^2 = 196 \times 10^{-6}$. In none of these tests did the height to length ratio of the ripples exceed 0.12 and in most it was significantly less than the value of 0.1 which we have taken as the limit for rolling-grain ripples.

The curves in Fig. 4.11 are based on the design curves of Mogridge and Kamphuis, the correlation between a/L and $\rho D/(\rho_s-\rho)gT^2$ shown for rolling-grain ripples in Fig. 4.4, and the experimental results of Inman (1957) and others. Lofquist (1978) showed that there is good agreement between the various investigators about the curves in the region corresponding to two-dimensional or brick-pattern ripples (i.e., the initial rising part of the curves). There may be, as shown by Fig. 4.10, some variation in a/L with R. Also both Bagnold (1946) and Lofquist (1978) drew attention to the fact that the measured wavelength may be affected to some extent by overcrowding or "overextension" of the ripples, but, on the whole, the deviation from the curve in Fig. 4.11 is small. Similarly, the experimental evidence for the shape of the curves in the third region, corresponding to rolling-grain ripples, appears from Fig. 4.4 to be strong although it is possible that other dimension-

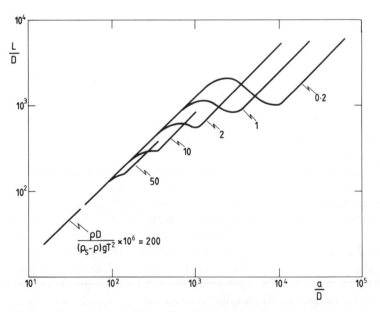

Figure 4.11. Variation of L/D with a/D for vortex and rolling-grain ripples.

less groups may not be negligible at relatively large values of $\rho D/(\rho_s - \rho)g T^2$. However, there is still disagreement about the shape of the curves in the intermediate region where L/D ceases to rise or even falls with increasing a/D.

Yalin and Karahan (1978) pointed out that Mogridge and Kamphuis' results show little influence of either ρ_s/ρ or $(\rho_s - \rho)/\rho$. If these parameters are unimportant, we may eliminate two of the four dimensionless groups and write

$$\frac{L}{D} = f\left(\beta D, \frac{a}{D}\right) \qquad (4.11)$$

It might seem from this that βD would be a more appropriate independent variable than $\rho D/(\rho_s - \rho)g T^2$ in Fig. 4.11. However, Mogridge and Kamphuis' tests were almost entirely confined to the low-sediment transport region, corresponding to the initial rising section of the curves. Consequently, their results do not justify the neglect of ρ_s/ρ and $(\rho_s - \rho)/\rho$ outside this region. In this low-sediment transport region either dimensionless group is equally good because the experimental results collapse onto a single curve in any case.

It could also be argued that U_∞/W might be an important parameter in the intermediate region since sediment is lifted clear of the bed under these conditions. Nielsen (1979) obtained the following empirical formula:

$$\frac{a}{L} = 0.5 + 0.004\left(\frac{U_\infty}{W}\right)^2 \qquad (4.12)$$

However, some of the laboratory data for very fine sediment did not follow this curve well and so he recommended that for regular waves (such as those found in the laboratory)

$$\frac{a}{L} = \left[2.2 - 0.345\left(\frac{\rho U_\infty^2}{(\rho_s - \rho)g D}\right)^{0.34}\right]^{-1} \qquad (4.13)$$

Although this formula gives good agreement with laboratory data, it is not satisfactory for site data. Nielsen suggested that this was because waves are much more irregular on site. Since both U_∞/W and $\rho U_\infty^2/(\rho_s - \rho)g D$ may be expressed as functions of a/D and $\rho D/(\rho_s - \rho)g T^2$, (4.12) and (4.13) are not inconsistent with Fig. 4.11.

Empirical formulas have also been put forward by Homma et al. (1965) and Horikawa and Watanabe (1967). The more recent formula is

$$\frac{a}{L} = 0.05 R^{0.332} \qquad (4.14)$$

This formula was based on limited data, some of which were for vortex ripples and some for rolling-grain ripples. It should consequently be treated with caution.

The argument over the form of the curves in the intermediate region is further complicated by the fact that this is the regime where the ripples tend to become three-dimensional. Carstens et al. (1969) found that ripples become three-dimensional when

$$\frac{a}{D} > 775 \tag{4.15}$$

This limit is based on tests with sand at a period $T = 3.56$ sec. On the basis of further tests with sand of diameter 0.18 mm, but with widely varying period, Lofquist (1978) suggested that this limit should be modified to

$$\frac{a}{DT} = 222 \ \mathrm{sec}^{-1} \tag{4.16}$$

Bearing in mind the values of D and ρ_s for which this relation was obtained we conclude that the ripples become three dimensional as soon as they start to leave the rising part of the curve in Fig. 4.11. However, Lofquist

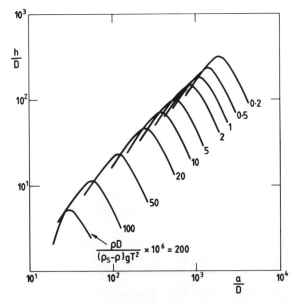

Figure 4.12.   Variation of h/D with a/D (after Mogridge and Kamphuis, 1972).

found that (4.16) did not hold for his tests with 0.21-mm sand. These tests suggested that at smaller values of T [larger values of $\rho D/(\rho_s - \rho)gT^2$] the limiting value of a/D was larger than that given by (4.16).

Hino (1968) showed that at high wavenumbers the spatial spectra of steady-flow ripples decay like the reciprocal of the cube of the wavenumber. Bliven et al. (1977) found that a similar relationship applied to three-dimensional ripples produced by waves alone provided the parameter $\omega W/g$ exceeded approximately 100. For smaller values of this parameter the decay rate was somewhat faster.

Figure 4.12 shows Mogridge and Kamphuis' design curves for ripple height. One problem with these curves is that they do not extend to very large values of a/D. At values of a/D larger than those shown in Fig. 4.12, (4.8) and (4.9) should be used.

4.3.5. Brick-Pattern Ripples

As mentioned in Section 4.3.1, vortex ripples at relatively low sediment transport rates are either regular two dimensional or form what Bagnold (1946) described as a brick pattern. The brick pattern is usually found when the orbital amplitude of the fluid outside the boundary layer is small. Figure 4.13 is a typical example.

The mechanism of brick-pattern ripple formation appears to be basically

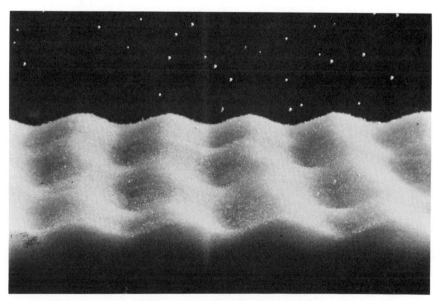

Figure 4.13. Brick-pattern ripples.

the same as that of two-dimensional vortex ripples. The only difference is that, in the case of brick-pattern ripples, the lee vortex breaks up into a series of horseshoe vortices, as in Fig. 4.14, rather than one continuous transverse vortex. This figure shows the vortex pattern at one particular instant in the flow cycle. When the flow reverses this pattern is destroyed and a similar pattern establishes itself on the other side of the transverse crests. The transverse crest is formed by the combined action of the primary flow and the lee vortex, both of which tend to carry sediment toward the crest. However, the trailing arms of the horseshoe vortex tend to push sediment sideways. This forms the "bridges" between the transverse crests.

Two factors limit the formation of the brick pattern. First of all the spacing between the "bridges" is observed to be not less than the spacing between the transverse ripples. (Bagnold suggested that the spacing between bridges was an integral multiple of the wavelength in the direction of oscillation but the measurements of Sleath and Ellis, 1978, do not confirm this result.) Thus a first condition for the appearance of the brick pattern is that the width of the flume, for the case of laboratory measurements, is no less than twice the ripple wavelength in the direction of oscillation. The limiting condition is

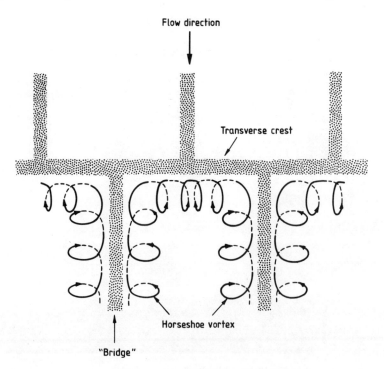

Figure 4.14. Sketch showing the pattern of vortices formed by brick-pattern ripples.

twice the ripple wavelength rather than just equal to it because, as seen in Fig. 4.14, the bridges are offset. Thus, in one of the flow directions there must be at least two complete horseshoe vortices. In fact the flume width must be somewhat greater than this minimum since, otherwise, the sidewalls would still inhibit the rotation in the trailing arms of the horseshoe vortex.

A second limitation on the formation of the brick pattern is the sediment transport rate. The brick pattern disappears when a significant amount of sediment is swept from the crest over the lee vortex rather than remaining in close contact with the bed. It is clear from Fig. 4.14 that the trailing arms of the horseshoe vortex only push sediment out toward the bridges when the sediment is not too far from the bed. Further from the bed, the flow in the vortex is in the opposite direction. Consequently, the sediment swept from the transverse crest over the lee vortex will tend to be carried by the trailing arms of the horseshoe vortex away from the bridges.

Under conditions when the brick pattern is not inhibited by either of the two factors mentioned both two-dimensional and brick-pattern ripples can form. However, it would seem that the brick pattern is the more stable state since, even when the bed forms two-dimensional ripples initially it will always change to brick pattern in due course if the conditions are appropriate. Transition from brick-pattern to two-dimensional ripples is not observed.

Bagnold (1946) suggested that brick-pattern ripples occur when the orbital amplitude a is less than about $L_0/6$. Here L_0 is the maximum wavelength a given sediment can form. Bagnold did not observe any influence of frequency of oscillation on wavelength. It is clear from Fig. 4.11 that although the effect of frequency is negligible on the rising part of the curve it is far from negligible for the maximum wavelength. Perhaps L_0 should be interpreted as the maximum wavelength of vortex ripples for a given value of $\rho D/(\rho_s-\rho)gT^2$. In that case the measurements of Sleath and Ellis (1978) suggest that $L_0/2$ would be a more appropriate limit. However, it should be remembered that the brick pattern does not suddenly disappear when a exceeds a given limit. In fact, some trace of the brick pattern may still be found at much higher orbital amplitudes than those at which bridges first show signs of weakening. Despite these reservations a limiting value of a equal to some fraction of L_0 does seem reasonable since, as a approaches L_0, significant quantities of sediment start to be swept over the lee vortex rather than remaining close to the bed.

4.4. DUNES AND ANTIDUNES

In steady flow both ripples and dunes are observed. Both are steep enough for vortex formation to occur in their lee and both may be two dimensional.

However, in pure oscillatory flow at constant depth only one two-dimensional vortex-forming bed form is observed. This bed form has been described as ripples in the preceding sections because this is the name most frequently used in the literature. However, some investigators (e.g., Carstens et al., 1969) have used the name dunes. It should be emphasized that as far as wave action is concerned both ripples and dunes are the same bed form. Of course, in the sea it is possible to observe small wavelength ripples superimposed on large wavelength dunes, but in that case the dunes are formed by tides or other quasi-steady currents.

Another bed form which is commonly observed in steady flow is antidunes. Antidunes formed by wave action are chiefly observed on beaches where extensive trains are created by backwash on seaward-facing slopes and by overwash beyond bar crests. Allen (1982) describes them under these circumstances as having wavelengths between 0.3 and 1.2 m and heights ranging from a few millimeters up to about a centimeter. Apart from this, antidunes are rarely observed in purely oscillatory flow and consequently further discussion is deferred to Sections 4.12 and 4.13.

4.5. LIMITS ON RIPPLE FORMATION

Initial Motion Condition

The most obvious condition for ripple formation is that the sediment must be in movement. This means that ripples will form only on an initially plane bed if the velocity exceeds the critical value for initial motion (see Chapter 6). Manohar (1955) found that, on average, the velocity at which ripples first form on a plane bed was about. $1.24 U_c$ where U_c is the critical velocity for initial motion of the sediment. Carstens et al. (1969) suggested that ripples first formed at $1.16 U_c$. In most situations it is probably sufficient to assume that ripples may form on a plane bed if the velocity exceeds U_c.

However, if the bed is initially rippled, changes in profile in response to changed wave conditions may take place at much lower fluid velocities because the velocity over the crest of a ripple is significantly greater than the mean velocity at that level. Lofquist (1978) suggests that the ripples will still be active down to velocities as small as $0.2 U_c$.

Sheet Flow

There is a limit on the maximum velocity since ripples disappear at very high sediment transport rates. Carstens et al. (1969) found that ripples disappeared when

$$\frac{a}{D} = 1700 \qquad (4.17)$$

On the other hand, Kennedy and Falcon (1965), using Inman's (1957) site data, found the limit to be

$$\frac{a}{D} = 8000 \qquad (4.18)$$

The disagreement between these two values suggests that a/D is not, by itself, a sufficient criterion.

More recently, Dingler and Inman (1976) suggested

$$\frac{\rho U_\infty^2}{(\rho_s - \rho)gD} = 240 \qquad (4.19)$$

This may be compared with the limit proposed in an earlier paper by Carstens (1966):

$$\frac{\rho U_\infty^2}{(\rho_s - \rho)gD} = 169 \qquad (4.20)$$

Nielsen (1979) found better agreement with the experimental results when the zero height condition was defined in terms of the Shields parameter ψ. For laboratory measurements he suggested that ripples disappear when

$$\psi = 0.83 \qquad (4.21)$$

Bearing in mind that

$$\psi = \frac{\hat{\tau}_0}{(\rho_s - \rho)gD} = f_w \frac{\rho U_\infty^2}{(\rho_s - \rho)gD} \qquad (4.22)$$

we see that Nielsen's zero height condition is not very different from that of Dingler and Inman.

None of the foregoing formulas show any explicit effect of viscosity. However, viscosity does appear in the formula put forward by Manohar (1955), which may be written

$$\frac{\rho U_\infty^2}{(\rho_s - \rho)gD} \times \left(\frac{U_\infty D}{\nu} \right)^{1/2} = 2000 \qquad (4.23)$$

Viscosity also comes into the formula suggested by Chan et al. (1972), which may be expressed as

$$\frac{\rho U_\infty^2}{(\rho_s-\rho)gD} \times (\beta D)^{0.8} = 43.6 \tag{4.24}$$

Insufficient data make a definite choice between these various expressions impossible. However, it should be borne in mind that in deriving his formula, Manohar made extensive use of averaging and this may have obscured possible dependence on a/D. Also, the experiments of Chan et al. were carried out in a pipe that was only 5.1 cm in diameter, which could have influenced the results. On the other hand, Lofquist (1978) showed that the various formulas give surprisingly similar results for the conditions of Dingler's (1975) observations of sheet flow.

βD Limit

It was suggested in Section 4.2.2 that there should be a maximum value of βD beyond which rolling-grain ripples would not form. The experimental results suggest that the limit is

$$\beta D \simeq 3.5 \tag{4.25}$$

There also appears to be a similar limit for vortex ripples. Mogridge and Kamphuis did not obtain ripples at values of βD greater than

$$\beta D \simeq 1.5 \tag{4.26}$$

These limits on βD explain why it is sometimes found that coarse sediments will not form ripples.

a/L Limit

The minimum value of a/L for vortex ripple formation appears to be

$$\frac{a}{L} \simeq 0.4 \tag{4.27}$$

The reason for this limit is that in an oscillatory flow separation of the boundary layer, and hence formation of a vortex, cannot take place if the orbital motion of the fluid is too small compared with the length scale of the roughness. There is no theoretical limit on the value of a/L at which rolling-grain ripples will form. Sleath and Ellis observed values of a/L down to 0.3 and Kaneko (1981) obtained rolling-grain ripples at $a/L=0.25$.

4.6.   RIPPLE GROWTH TIME

So far, only equilibrium ripples have been considered. But wave conditions on site can change rapidly. How long must conditions remain stable for ripples to reach an equilibrium state? The answer depends on the intensity of sediment motion. Lofquist (1978) found that when the velocity was just above the initial motion value the number of wave cycles n required for equilibrium ripples to form was given by

$$n=\frac{a}{D}\qquad(4.28)$$

On the other hand, Dingler and Inman (1976) observed that for intense sediment motion only a few waves were necessary to change the bed profile.

4.7.   OFFSHORE BARS

4.7.1.   Experimental Results

The preceding results have been for horizontal beds of sediment in water of constant depth. However, for waves approaching a coast there is another bed form of great engineering importance. This is the offshore bar. These bars run parallel to the coast and are usually found close to the plunge point of the breakers. In tidal seas it is the plunge line associated with low water that is the most important.

Some beaches show several bars (Bascom, 1951, records a maximum of three on the Pacific coast of the United States) and some do not have bars at all. Those which do are sometimes called winter or storm profiles because they tend to form during bad weather. This sort of profile is associated with beach erosion. Beach profiles without well-defined bars are sometimes referred to as normal, step, or summer profiles and are associated with onshore deposition. In addition to wave steepness, bar formation is also affected by the grain size of the sediment: the finer the sediment the more likely bars are to form. Figure 4.15 shows the limiting conditions for bar formation proposed by various investigators. Nayak (1970) found that bar formation was also affected by the specific gravity of the sediment. The curve attributed to him in Fig. 4.15 is that for sand of specific gravity 2.65.

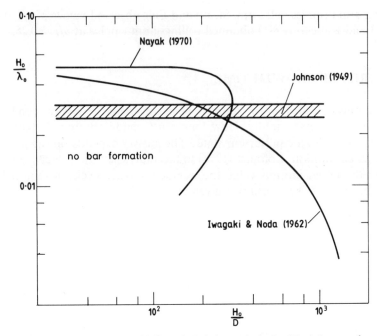

Figure 4.15.   Limiting value of H_0/λ_0 and H_0/D beyond which offshore bars are formed.

The disagreement between Johnson's (1949) recommendations and those of Iwagaki and Noda (1962) is probably just a question of available data: the latter investigators had much more data to work with. (In addition to their own tests, Iwagaki and Noda made use of the results of Rector, 1954, Watts, 1954, and Saville, 1957.) The significantly different trend of Nayak's curve at low values of H_0/λ_0 is more troublesome. However, Nayak used only his own test results so it is possible that there was some peculiarity in his experimental arrangement which produced this discrepancy. Nayak's curve has not been confirmed by other investigators.

Sunamura and Horikawa (1974) carried out further tests. The limit between their Type II and Type III profiles, which is approximately equivalent to the limit between bar and normal profiles, is

$$\frac{H_0}{\lambda_0} = 2.3(\tan \theta)^{-0.162}\left(\frac{H_0}{D}\right)^{-0.4} \tag{4.29}$$

At first sight this would appear to confirm the general trend of Iwagaki and Noda's curve, but it should be remembered that the beach slope θ may also be influenced by H_0/λ_0 and H_0/D.

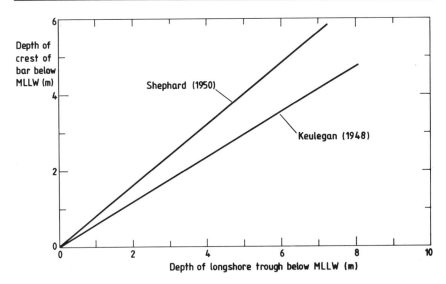

Figure 4.16. The way in which the depth of water above the crest of a bar varies with depth above the trough.

In all problems involving sediment transport there is the question of whether it is better to use grain size D or fall velocity W as a measure of sediment properties. Dean (1973) suggested that the limit between bar and normal profiles was determined by H_0/λ_0 and WT/λ_0. The limiting condition for bar formation which he proposed reduces to

$$\frac{H_0}{WT} = 0.85 \tag{4.30}$$

This is in reasonable agreement with the limiting values of H_0/WT between 0.7 and 1.5, depending on wave steepness, recommended by the CERC Shore Protection Manual (1977).

Figure 4.16 shows how the depth of water above the crest of the bar varies with depth above the trough according to Keulegan (1948) and Shephard (1950). Shephard's curve is based on several thousand data points from various coasts in California and Keulegan's is based on laboratory data. Measurements for the Tokai and Niigata coasts in Japan reported by Homma et al. (1959) scatter fairly evenly between these two curves.

4.7.2. Mechanism of Bar Formation

Carter et al. (1973) suggest that offshore bars are caused by the mass transport current associated with partial reflection of the waves by the beach.

For standing waves the mass transport current in the immediate vicinity of the bed is directed away from the antinodes and toward the nodes of the water surface profile. On the other hand, the mass transport velocity close to the bed is in the direction of the beach for progressive waves (in the absence of breaking and provided the bed roughness is not too great). Even when beach reflectivity is low the combination of the standing and progressive wave drifts should produce buildup of sediment at the nodes and erosion at the antinodes. However, Carter et al. found that it was only when the reflection coefficient of the beach was high enough for the reverse drift in the standing wave to exceed the forward drift in the progressive wave at certain points that recognizable bars were formed.

Carter et al.'s theory was developed only for horizontal beds. Lau and Travis (1973) showed that the conclusions apply equally well to sloping beds. However, there is another factor which should be borne in mind. This is that the theory does not apply to breaking waves. Russell and Osorio (1957) and Bijker et al. (1974) found that on a sloping beach the mass transport velocity near the bed was onshore before breaking but offshore after. This effect, which is independent of wave reflection from the beach, would explain why bars are usually found close to the plunge line of breakers.

Offshore bars frequently fluctuate in height in the longshore direction. Bowen and Inman (1971) suggested that the interaction between the incoming waves and standing edge waves would produce lunate or crescentic bars. They also suggested that edge waves are responsible for beach cusps. These ideas have been taken up in several further papers. Huntley and Bowen (1978) give a good review of this work.

4.7.3. Beach Profile

There is a link between bar formation and beach profile. Profiles with longshore bars tend to have a milder foreshore slope than those without. Figure 4.17 shows a curve due to Dalrymple and Thompson (1976) for foreshore slope θ in terms of the parameter H_0/WT used by many investigators to characterize bar formation. This curve is based on the experimental results of Rector (1954), Eagleson et al. (1963), Nayak (1970), Raman and Earattupuzha (1972), Van Hijum (1974), and Thompson (1976).

As in the case of bar formation, there is disagreement as to whether grain size D or fall velocity W is the more relevant parameter. Kemp and Plinston (1968) produced a curve similar to that of Dalrymple and Thompson but using $H_b/TD^{1/2}$ instead of H_0/WT. (H_b is the breaking wave height.) Work has also been carried out on beach profiles by Waters (1939), Bagnold (1940), Bascom (1951), Larras (1959), Eagleson et al. (1961), Sitarz (1963), Motta (1963), Carter et al. (1973), and many others. Wiegel (1964) summarizes

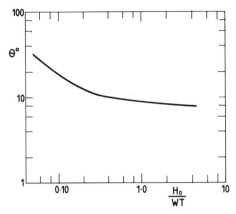

Figure 4.17.   The variation of beach slope with H_0/WT (after Dalrymple and Thompson, 1976).

much of the earlier work. In view of the scatter of available measurements it is difficult to reach any firm conclusion about the relative merits of different methods. Figure 4.17 is probably adequate for design purposes for the time being.

Since fall velocity increases with grain size we see from Fig. 4.17 that, other things being equal, steeper foreshores are associated with coarser sediment, smaller deep-water wave heights, and longer wave periods, and vice versa.

Steady Currents Alone

4.8.   SUMMARY OF BED FORM TYPES

Figure 4.18 shows schematically the principal bed forms produced by steady currents in the sea. In addition, the following bed forms are observed in rivers and channels but are of limited relevance to the sea bed effects with which we are concerned here: braid bars, transverse bars, scroll, side, and point bars; and chutes and pools.

As in oscillatory flow, the bed may also be plane. At high sediment transport rates, plane beds occur as an intermediate regime between dunes and antidunes. In this regime the bed is frequently unstable with sand waves and washed-out dunes covering part of the bed and a flat bed over the remainder. The bed may also be plane when the fluid velocities are too low to produce any sediment movement at all. However, in this case the state of the bed

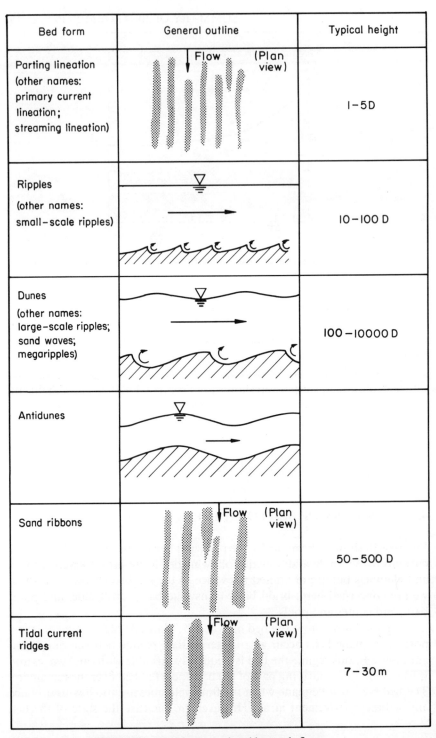

Bed form	General outline	Typical height
Parting lineation (other names: primary current lineation; streaming lineation)	Flow (Plan view)	1–5D
Ripples (other names: small-scale ripples)		10–100 D
Dunes (other names: large-scale ripples; sand waves; megaripples)		100–10000 D
Antidunes		
Sand ribbons	Flow (Plan view)	50–500 D
Tidal current ridges	Flow (Plan view)	7–30 m

Figure 4.18. Bed forms produced by steady flows.

depends, as for oscillatory flow, on the bed regime just before the velocity dropped below the limit for sediment motion.

For a complete treatment of the bed forms found in steady flow the reader is referred to the excellent books by Allen (1968, 1982), Simons and Senturk (1977), and Yalin (1977).

4.9. BED REGIME BOUNDARIES

There have been many attempts to determine the boundaries between the different bed regimes. Table 4.1 lists some of the variables that have been used as a basis for comparison.

None of the charts produced so far has proved entirely successful. It is probably overoptimistic to expect a single pair of variables or group of variables to determine the transition from one bed form to another over the entire range of possible flow conditions.

It is generally accepted that the initial motion of sediment is determined by the parameters $\tau_0/(\rho_s-\rho)gD$ and $\bar{u}_*D/\nu$. Thus at very low sediment transport rates these two parameters are likely to be important for bed form geometry. This is the basis of Chabert and Chauvin's plot seen in Fig. 4.19.

Although $\tau_0/(\rho_s-\rho)gD$ and $\bar{u}_*D/\nu$ are important at low sediment transport rates they are certainly not sufficient under more severe flow conditions. Figure 4.20 shows the plot suggested by Simons and Richardson. These

TABLE 4.1.   VARIABLES USED TO CATEGORIZE THE DIFFERENT BED REGIMES

Investigator	Variables
Shields (1936)	$\tau_0/(\rho_s-\rho)gD$; $\bar{u}_*D/\nu$
Liu (1957)	$\bar{u}_*/W$; $\bar{u}_*D/\nu$
Albertson et al. (1958)	$\bar{u}_*/W$; $\bar{u}_*D/\nu$
Bogardi (1958)	$gD/\bar{u}_*^2$; D
Garde and Albertson (1959)	$\tau_0/(\rho_s-\rho)gD$; $\bar{U}/(gd)^{1/2}$
Chabert and Chauvin (1963)	$\tau_0/(\rho_s-\rho)gD$; $\bar{u}_*D/\nu$
Garde and Raju (1963)	$\rho S/(\rho_s-\rho)$; R/D
Reynolds (1965)	d/L; $\bar{U}/(gd)^{1/2}$
Simons and Richardson (1966)	$\tau_0\bar{U}$; D
Athaullah (1968)	$\bar{u}_*/W$; S
Senturk (1973)	$\tau_0/(\rho_s-\rho)gD$; WD/ν
Holtorff (1982)	d/L; $\bar{U}/(gd)^{1/2}$

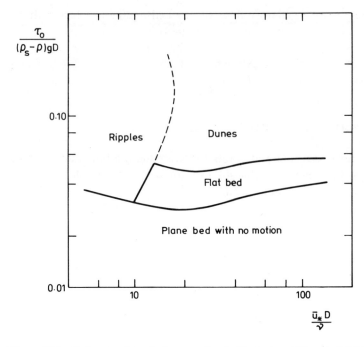

Figure 4.19.   Bed regime boundaries according to Chabert and Chauvin (1963).

limits are based on extensive laboratory and site data. Agreement with available data is good except near the flat bed–dune boundary where some measurements for the Mississippi river are incorrectly predicted. Clearly $\tau_0 \bar{U}$ and D are not sufficient at very low sediment transport rates. Also, since Fig. 4.20 does not make use of dimensionless variables it should be employed only for beds of sand.

Neither Fig. 4.19 nor Fig. 4.20 makes any reference to parting lineation. The small scale of this bed form and its orientation parallel to the flow makes it of little importance in calculations of bed roughness or sediment transport and consequently most engineers prefer to ignore it. Parting lineation is chiefly observed on plane beds at relatively high sediment transport rates. However, Allen (1968) also observed parting lineation on the backs of ripples and dunes, indicating that it may occur over a very wide range of conditions.

Sand ribbons and tidal ridges are also omitted from Figs. 4.19 and 4.20. Relatively little is known about the conditions necessary for their formation but they are normally found to coexist with dunes.

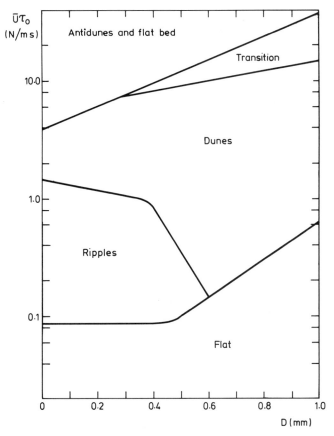

Figure 4.20.   Bed regime boundaries according to Simons ad Richardson (1966).

4.10.   PARTING LINEATION

A steady current transporting sediment across a plane bed of the same sediment will frequently produce streamwise streaks on the surface. These streaks consist of low parallel ridges rarely exceeding a few grain diameters in height. Allen (1964) observed ridges with transverse spacing between about 5 and 13 mm and up to 300 mm long. This bed form is usually referred to as parting lineation, although the terms primary current lineation and streaming lineation have also been used. It has been described by Sorby (1859) and many others.

Allen (1982) suggests that parting lineation is associated with the bursting streaks observed in turbulent boundary layers. It would seem that these boundary layer streaks have approximately the correct transverse spacing and, as shown by Grass (1971), are capable of collecting sand into similar patterns. If this explanation for their formation is correct, it would seem that parting lineation may form in any turbulent flow over a mobile bed.

In the marine environment parting lineations are most frequently observed in the swash zone on the beach.

4.11. RIPPLES

As seen in Fig. 4.18, the ripple profile is asymmetrical in the flow direction. A relatively gentle upstream slope is followed by a steep lee slope. While the bed is active, the downstream slope is usually at an angle of between 40 and 52° to the horizontal. This is, of course, greater than the angle of repose of sand in still water, which is typically of the order of about 33° to the horizontal. The reason why the downstream slope is so steep is that a vortex in the lee of the ripple tends to push the sediment back up toward the crest.

The geometry of ripples viewed from above is very variable. Figure 4.21 provides some examples. It should be emphasized that Fig. 4.21 is highly idealized—in real life ripples are rarely regular. The type of ripple formed

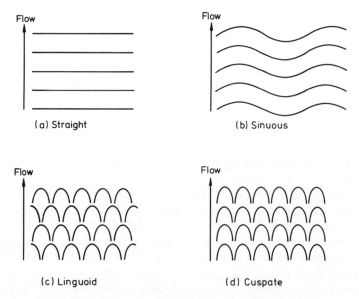

(a) Straight

(b) Sinuous

(c) Linguoid

(d) Cuspate

Figure 4.21.   Examples of ripple geometry (viewed from above).

appears to be determined mainly by the flow velocity and relative roughness. Allen (1977) proposed the following empirical relationship between the ripple wavelength L in the direction of the mean flow and the transverse distance L_z between streamwise features:

$$\frac{L}{L_z} = 5.85 \left[\frac{\bar{U}}{(gd)^{1/2}} \frac{h}{d} \right]^{0.412} \left(1 + \frac{d}{w} \right)^{1.71} \tag{4.31}$$

Very small values of L/L_z correspond to straight-crested ripples. As L/L_z increases the three dimensionality of the ripple geometry also increases. Thus it would appear that straight-crested ripples are more likely to occur at low values of the Froude number $\bar{U}/(gd)^{1/2}$ and in relatively wide channels (small d/w). Equation (4.31) also suggests that straight-crested ripples are associated with relatively smaller values of the ripple height h.

4.11.1.   Theoretical Models

In comparison with dunes, there has been relatively little theoretical work on ripples. One of the earliest attempts to model the deformation of a bed of sediment by a steady flow was that of Exner (1925). Since this model may also be applied to the formation of dunes discussion is postponed to Section 4.12. More recently, Richards (1980) extended the models of Engelund (1970) and Fredsoe (1974), which are also discussed in Section 4.12. The use of an eddy viscosity increasing with height, rather than constant as assumed by Engelund and Fredsoe, results in two unstable bed forms. Richards attributes one of these to dunes and the other to ripples.

According to Richards, ripples form because a flat bed is unstable. On the other hand, Raudkivi (1963) has attributed ripple formation to a chance piling up of sediment, which then propagates downstream. Williams and Kemp (1971) suggest that ripple formation is associated with the action on the bed of turbulent bursts in the boundary layer.

In view of this disagreement over the basic mechanism it is perhaps not surprising that no model has yet achieved anything other than qualitative agreement with experiment.

4.11.2.   Empirical Results

Several authors have suggested empirical formulas for the ripple geometry. According to Yalin (1964):

$$L = 1000D \tag{4.32}$$

and

$$\frac{h}{d} = \left(\frac{\tau_0 - \tau_c}{6\tau_0} \right) \tag{4.33}$$

Equation (4.33) suggests that h/d cannot exceed 1/6. However, Simons and Richardson (1960) report values of this parameter as high as 1/2 and the ratio 1/3 is not uncommon.

Allen (1963) found (S.I. units):

$$\log d = 0.8271 \log h + 0.8901 \tag{4.34}$$

and

$$\log h = 0.9508 \log L - 1.0867 \tag{4.35}$$

These equations may also be written as

$$h = 0.08 d^{1.2} \tag{4.36}$$

$$h = 0.08 L^{0.95} \tag{4.37}$$

Goswami (1967) suggests (S.I. units)

$$h = 0.047 L^{0.87} \tag{4.38}$$

Of the formulae presented by Allen and Goswami, only (4.35) and hence (4.37) are specifically for ripples. The other equations are based on data for dunes as well as ripples.

4.12. DUNES

Dunes, like ripples, have a relatively gentle upstream slope and a steep downstream slope (see Fig. 4.18). Here again, there is a vortex in the lee of the crest and this counterflow maintains the downstream slope at, or a little above, the angle of equilibrium of the sediment while the flow remains the same as that for which the dune was formed. However, whereas ripples do not show any noticeable effect on the free surface, dunes usually produce a slight dip in the water surface above the crest and a slight rise in water level above the trough. For a rigid isolated bump in the bed this type of water surface profile is only found for Froude numbers less than unity. Because dunes are not rigid and not isolated they are sometimes found at Froude numbers greater than unity but are most commonly observed in subcritical flows.

There is some disagreement about whether ripples and dunes really are fundamentally different. Dunes certainly are very much bigger than ripples. Also, in some flows ripples are found superimposed on the backs of dunes, which suggests that different mechanisms are responsible for their formation. Finally, a change in the depth of flow has different effects on the wavelength of ripples and dunes and also, at least when the grain size is less than 0.3 mm, on the resistance to flow. Against this there is the fact that their profiles are very similar and that each is characterized by a vortex in the lee of the crest. Most engineers and geologists would probably accept that they are fundamentally different but, for example, Vanoni et al. (1961) saw little reason for distinguishing between them.

Dunes also show considerable variation in plan view as indicated in Fig. 4.22. At low velocities of flow straight-crested forms are more common but under more severe conditions the bed becomes increasingly three dimensional. It should be emphasized that Fig. 4.22 is only an indication of possible dune configurations: in real life dunes are rarely regular, there is a continuous progression between different types, and the line of dunes is not necessarily normal to the mean flow direction.

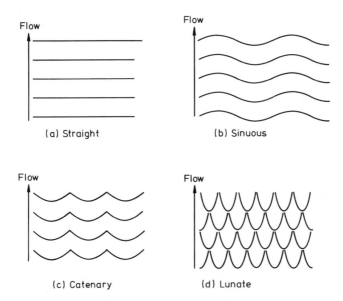

Figure 4.22.   Examples of dune geometry (viewed from above).

4.12.1. Theoretical Models

There have been numerous attempts to study theoretically the formation of dunes and antidunes on erodible beds. The first serious attempt was that of Exner (1925). Exner's model is based on three equations:

1. A continuity equation for sediment transport

$$(1-n)\frac{\partial \eta}{\partial t}+\frac{\partial q_s}{\partial x}=0 \tag{4.39}$$

where η is here the height of the bed profile above some reference level and n is the porosity of the bed.

2. An equation for the fluid velocity

$$\bar{U}=\frac{Q}{d} \tag{4.40}$$

where Q is the flow rate per unit width and d is the water depth at any given value of x.

3. An equation relating sediment transport rate to fluid velocity:

$$q_s=\text{const} \times \bar{U} \tag{4.41}$$

Eliminating q_s and $\bar{U}$ between (4.39), (4.40), and (4.41) gives an equation for the bed profile η as a function of time. The assumptions represented by (4.40) and (4.41) are extremely crude and consequently Exner's model is not likely to give realistic results. However, it does predict some observed features of bed profiles such as the progressive steepening of the lee face of an initially sinusoidal perturbation to the bed.

There have been many attempts to improve this model. These have concentrated on more realistic descriptions of the velocity distribution to replace (4.40) and of the sediment transport relation to replace (4.41).

Anderson (1953), Kennedy (1963), Reynolds (1965), Falcon (1969), Hayashi (1970), Gradowczyk (1968), and Parker (1975) made use of the potential flow solution for an ideal inviscid fluid over a wavy bed. Engelund (1970), Fredsoe (1974b) and Richards (1980) used approximations to the logarithmic velocity distribution, observed in real flows, with an inviscid perturbation for the waviness of the bed.

There has also been considerable improvement in the description of the sediment transport. Kennedy (1963) introduced a power law relationship between sediment transport rate and local velocity. Engelund (1970) made use of the Meyer-Peter and Muller (1948) formula for bed load transport and an approximation to Rouse's solution for suspended load. Fredsoe (1974b) introduced a correction for bed load transport to allow for the effect of bed slope.

Two other modifications have been made to Exner's original model. The first was the introduction of a lag between a change in fluid velocity and the corresponding change in sediment transport rate. This idea was suggested by Kennedy (1963). The second, also initiated by Kennedy (1963), was the use of linear stability analysis. For given flow conditions, the small perturbation to the bed profile assumed in all of the above models may be unstable for a range of wavelengths. Kennedy suggested that the wavelength which actually formed was that with the maximum growth rate. Engelund and his colleagues have calculated neutral stability curves.

Explicit expressions for the wavelength of the dunes or antidunes have been obtained as follows:

Anderson (1953):

$$\frac{gd}{\bar{U}^2} = kd\left(\tanh kd - \frac{2}{\sinh 2kd}\right) \qquad (4.42)$$

Kennedy (1963) for zero delay distance:

$$\frac{\bar{U}^2}{gd} = \frac{2 + kd \tanh kd}{(kd)^2 + 3kd \tanh kd} \qquad (4.43)$$

Tsuchiya and Ishizaki (1967):

$$\frac{\bar{U}}{(gd)^{1/2}} = \left(\frac{2 \tanh 2kd}{kd}\right)^{1/2} - \left(\frac{\tanh kd}{kd}\right)^{1/2} \qquad (4.44)$$

Holtorff (1982)—antidunes only:

$$\frac{\bar{U}^2}{gd} = \frac{1}{kd \tanh kd} \qquad (4.45)$$

Mercer (1971) pointed out that Anderson assumed bed profile and water surface to be in phase. Thus (4.42) only applies to antidunes. For dunes the corresponding expression would be

$$\frac{gd}{\bar{U}^2} = kd\left(\tanh kd + \frac{6}{\sinh 2kd}\right) \qquad (4.46)$$

Expressions have also been obtained for the upper limit for the formation of two-dimensional bed forms:

Kennedy (1963):

$$\frac{\bar{U}^2}{gd} = \frac{1}{kd} \tag{4.47}$$

Reynolds (1965)

$$\frac{\bar{U}^2}{gd} = \frac{\coth kd}{kd} \tag{4.48}$$

Gradowczyk (1968):

$$\frac{\bar{U}^2}{gd} \simeq 1.77 \tag{4.49}$$

Kennedy (1963), Reynolds (1965), and Tsuchiya and Ishizaki (1967) all found the limit between dunes and antidunes to be

$$\frac{\bar{U}^2}{gd} = \frac{\tanh kd}{kd} \tag{4.50}$$

Figure 4.23 shows a comparison between some of the theoretical curves and experimental measurements. Kennedy's equation (4.43) agrees well with the data for antidunes but less well for dunes. Except for values of kd less than unity, Mercer's curve for dunes is very close to that of Kennedy. This is not altogether surprising since most of the assumptions made by Mercer were very similar to those of Kennedy. Neither of the other curves gives good agreement with the experimental data. Kennedy suggested that the very considerable scatter of the data for dunes was attributable to the fact that some of the measurements were for three-dimensional bed forms. It is also possible that Froude number is not the only parameter determining the wavelength of the dunes. This is in agreement with the theoretical results of Engelund (1970) and his colleagues who showed that both dunes and anti-dunes could form over a range of Froude numbers for any given value of kd. For dunes, the maximum-growth curve was found to be particularly sensitive to the value of $\bar{U}/\bar{u}_*$ (see Fredsoe, 1974b). At the present time, it would seem that although there is good agreement between theory and experiment for antidunes, the various available theories are still not capable of accurate prediction of the wavelengths of dunes.

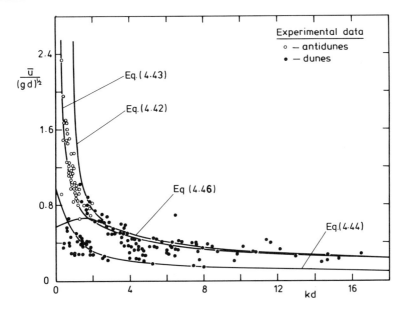

Figure 4.23. Comparison of formulas for dune/antidune wavelength with the measurements from various sources collected by Kennedy (1963).

All of the theoretical results discussed thus far have been for two-dimensional bed forms. Reynolds (1965) studied three-dimensional bed forms assuming potential flow for the velocity distribution. Figure 4.24 shows the regime boundaries he obtained for one particular class of three-dimensional profiles. Reynolds' results support Kennedy's suggestion that the wavelength might be significantly different if the bed form were three-dimensional rather than two-dimensional. Engelund and Fredsoe studied oblique dunes (see, e.g., Fredsoe, 1974a) and Callander (1969) found alluvial beds to be unstable to all three-dimensional disturbances when kd is very small. Although available theoretical models are capable of predicting many observed features, agreement between theory and experiment for three-dimensional bed forms is still far from perfect.

A number of researchers have also obtained expressions for the height h of the bed form. For example, Raichlen and Kennedy (1965) suggest

$$h = \frac{2}{nk}\left(\frac{\bar{U}-\bar{U}_c}{\bar{U}}\right)\left(\frac{\tanh kd - \bar{U}^2 k/g}{1-(\bar{U}^2 k/g)\tanh kd}\right) \tag{4.51}$$

where n is the exponent of the relation between velocity and sediment transport rate and $\bar{U}_c$ is the critical value of $\bar{U}$ for initial motion of the sediment.

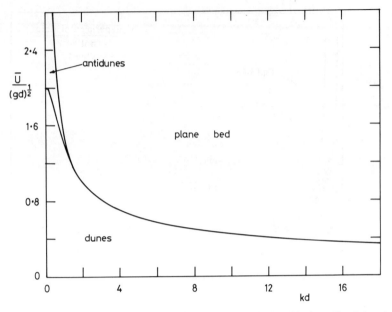

Figure 4.24. Regime boundaries for one class of three-dimensional bed profiles [after A. J. Reynolds, Waves on the erodible bed of an open channel. *J. Fluid Mech.* (1965), **22**, pt. 1, Fig. 8].

More recently Fredsoe (1982), using a small-perturbation technique, obtained

$$\frac{h}{(2d - h - 2\bar{U}^2/g)} = \frac{Q_{sb}}{4\tau_0(dQ_s/d\tau_0)} \tag{4.52}$$

where Q_{sb} and Q_s are, respectively, the bed load and total load sediment transport rates.

4.12.2. Empirical Results

Yalin (1964) suggested the following empirical formula:

$$L = 5d \tag{4.53}$$

This is in reasonable agreement with the expression given by Hino (1968) for the "prevailing dune length":

$$L = 7d \tag{4.54}$$

Neither (4.53) nor (4.54) gives good agreement with the experimental results seen in Fig. 4.23. It would seem from the theoretical work of Kennedy, Engelund, and others, that L/d ought to vary with Froude number. An empirical formula that does take account of variation in Froude number has been suggested by Swart (1976):

$$L = d \exp\left(\frac{3.12\bar{U}}{(gd)^{1/2}} - 1.28\right) \qquad (4.55)$$

As far as the dune height is concerned, it will be remembered that the formulas of Allen, (4.36), and of Goswami, (4.38), apply to dunes as well as to ripples. Allen (1963) also suggested the following expression (S.I. units):

$$h = 0.08 L^{0.74} \qquad (4.56)$$

Yalin's formula (4.33) for the height of ripples may also apply to dunes. A revised version of that formula was suggested by Gill (1971):

$$\frac{h}{d} = \left(\frac{1 - \bar{U}^2/gd}{2nb}\right)\left(\frac{\tau_0 - \tau_c}{\tau_0}\right) \qquad (4.57)$$

in which n is the exponent in a bed load equation of the Meyer-Peter and Muller type and b is a numerical coefficient related to the cross-sectional shape of the bed form. A further revision of Yalin's formula, this time in essentially graphical form, is given by Yalin and Karahan (1979).

Finally, Fredsoe (1975) suggested

$$\frac{h}{L} = \frac{1}{8.4}\left(1 - \frac{0.06}{\psi} - 0.4\psi\right)^2 \qquad (4.58)$$

where ψ is the Shields parameter $\tau_0/(\rho_s - \rho)gD$.

4.12.3.   Spectral Analysis

Rippled and duned beds on site are frequently irregular. Although three-dimensionality is less marked in laboratory channels, particularly in narrow ones because of the restraining effect of the sidewalls, it may still be significant. An attempt to study this effect has been made by various authors.

On the basis of dimensional analysis Hino (1968) suggested that the spectral density of the wavenumber k should fall off like k^{-3}. This result has been confirmed experimentally for high wavenumbers by Nordin (1971).

However, at low wavenumbers Nordin found that each set of data followed a separate curve without any consistent pattern.

As pointed out by Engelund and Fredsoe (1982) it is the low wavenumbers, that is, the longer wavelengths, which are particularly important in calculations of the bed friction and energy loss. Engelund (1969) has examined this low wavenumber region. Currently available data are insufficient to determine the range over which Engelund's curve is applicable.

A problem with spectral analysis methods is that the significance of the high-wavenumber components is not always obvious. A bed profile which was entirely regular apart from a single discontinuity would have a spectral density decaying like k^{-3} (Engelund and Fredsoe, 1982). Likewise, a second peak in the power spectrum such as that observed experimentally by Jain and Kennedy (1974) might be due to a second distinct bed form or might, as pointed out by Plate (1971), only represent a harmonic due to the non-sinusoidal shape of the basic sand wave.

4.13.   ANTIDUNES

Figure 4.18 is an idealized sketch of an antidune profile. One of the main differences between this sketch and one for dunes is that the water surface is in phase with that of the bed. For rigid beds a water surface profile in phase with an isolated bump on the bed is found when the Froude number $\bar{U}/(gd)^{1/2} > 1$. It is thus to be expected that antidunes would mainly occur at Froude numbers greater than unity although, because the bed is not rigid and the bump not isolated, this will not be exactly true. In fact, potential flow theory shows that for a sinusoidal bed the boundary between surface profiles in phase and surface profiles out of phase is

$$\frac{\bar{U}^2}{gd} = \frac{\tanh kd}{kd} \qquad (4.50)$$

This is the same as the equation suggested by Kennedy (1963) and others as the boundary between dunes and antidunes. It is in good agreement with the experimental results shown in Fig. 4.23.

Figure 4.23 also shows that Kennedy's theoretical expression for kd in terms of Froude number (4.43) is in close agreement with experimental results for antidunes. The theretical model assumed potential flow and a sinusoidal bed profile. Antidunes are much more nearly sinusoidal than dunes. Also antidunes, unlike dunes, do not have a lee vortex and consequently the streamlines are much closer to those of a potential flow. It is thus hardly surprising that the agreement between theory and experiment should be better than for dunes.

Unlike dunes, which always move downstream, antidunes may move either upstream or downstream. Engelund (1970) suggested that sediment transport was predominantly in suspension for antidunes, whereas bed load was more important for dunes.

4.14. SAND RIBBONS

Sand ribbons are bed waves with ridges parallel to the mean flow direction (see Fig. 4.18). They have been observed in laboratory flumes (e.g., by Guy et al., 1966), in the desert (Bagnold, 1954) and in the sea (Stride, 1963). Bagnold's desert ribbons were 1–3 m wide, spaced 4–60 m apart in the transverse direction, and were less than 2 cm high. Those observed in the sea by Stride were similar but somewhat larger. Their width ranged from 30 to 300 m and their transverse spacing was about 150–350 m.

The reason for the formation of sand ribbons is not entirely clear. Bagnold (1954) suggested that they originated in a chance piling up of sand. This mound of sediment generated helical vortices with axes in the mean flow direction which then piled up sediment downstream. Allen (1968) refers to the possibility that secondary flows similar to those observed in laboratory channels are responsible for sand ribbon formation. The variation in bed shear stress between the center of the channel and the corners causes a variation in turbulence intensity which in turn produces a secondary flow at right angles to the main stream. He suggests that the absence of wall-like boundaries in the desert and in the sea makes this theory unattractive. On the other hand, it is possible that the variation in bed level might by itself produce a similar effect.

4.15. TIDAL CURRENT RIDGES

Tidal current ridges, like parting lineation and sand ribbons, are aligned parallel to the mean flow direction. According to Off (1963), tidal current ridges are 8–65 km long, have heights of 7.5–30 m, and a regular spacing at right angles to the mean flow of 1.6–10 km.

Off suggested that the geometry of tidal current ridges was related to that of freshwater streams. Figure 4.25 shows a comparison of Leopold and Maddock's (1953) data for rivers with Off's data for current ridges. Despite the very great scatter, it does look as if the data from the two sources is more or less continuous. However, it would clearly be dangerous to extrapolate formulas established for rivers to estimate the geometry of tidal current ridges.

Thus far, tidal current ridges have only been observed in broad shallow seas subject to strong (0.5–2 m/s) currents.

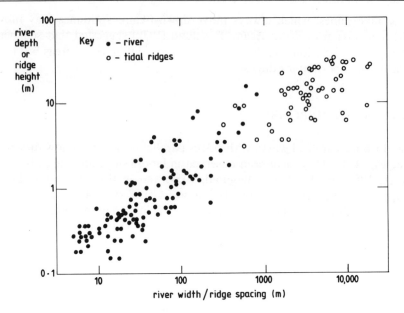

Figure 4.25. Comparison of Leopold and Maddock's (1953) data for rivers with Off's (1963) data for tidal current ridges (after Allen, 1963).

Waves and Currents

4.16.   CURRENT DOMINATION VERSUS WAVE DOMINATION

If the steady current is very weak, the ripple geometry will be given by the various formulas for waves alone. Similarly, for very strong currents wave action will have little effect on the ripple geometry. The limits for the wave-dominated, transition, and current-dominated regimes suggested by various workers are summarized in Table 4.2. The limits attributed to Natarajan and Bliven et al. are intended as a rough indication only. Neither set out to derive a limit and their experiments covered only a restricted range of $\bar{U}/U_\infty$.

Clearly, the decision as to where the boundary between one regime and the other lies is very subjective so the quoted values should be treated with caution. This is illustrated by the different limits proposed by Bijker and by Swart even though they used the same data.

TABLE 4.2. LIMITS FOR RIPPLE GEOMETRY REGIMES

Author	Wave Dominated	Transition	Current Dominated
Bijker (1967)	$U_\infty/\bar{u}_* > 20$	$20 > U_\infty/\bar{u}_* > 6$	$U_\infty/\bar{u}_* < 6$
Natarajan (1969)	$(\bar{U}/U_\infty < 0.27)$		
Swart (1976)	$U_\infty/\bar{u}_* > 10$	$10 > U_\infty/\bar{u}_* > 3$	$U_\infty/\bar{u}_* < 3$
Bliven et al. (1977)	$(\bar{U}/U_\infty < 1.6)$		
Amos and Collins (1978)	$U_\infty/\bar{u}_* > 10$	$10 > U_\infty/\bar{u}_* > 1$	$U_\infty/\bar{u}_* < 1$

4.17. BED GEOMETRY IN COMBINED FLOWS

4.17.1. Ripples

Changes in Bed Geometry Produced by Currents Collinear with the Waves

Natarajan's (1969) experiments did not extend to values of $\bar{U}/U_\infty$ greater than 0.25. In this range the ripple profile tended to become more asymmetrical as the steady current increased: flatter upstream slope and steeper downstream. However, there was little change in ripple height or wavelength.

Similar results were obtained by Bliven et al. (1977). Their experiments were carried out in a wave channel and the ripples were predominantly three-dimensional. They observed little change in the root-mean-square ripple height or in the shape of the spatial spectral density distribution as $\bar{U}/U_\infty$ varied from 0 up to about 1.6. However, there was some slight increase in dominant ripple wavelength L with increasing mean current: the parameter Lg/W^2 rose by about 40% as $\bar{U}/U_\infty$ was increased from 0 to 6.0.

Changes in Bed Geometry Produced by Currents at Right Angles to the Direction of Wave Propagation

When the current is at right angles to the direction of wave propagation the effect on the ripple geometry is more marked. Figure 4.26 is a sketch of the ripple patterns formed under these circumstances.

In the regime where the ripples induced by waves alone are regular and two-dimensional, the amplitude L_1 and the length L_2 of the wavy indentations grow steadily with increasing current. For values of $\bar{U}/U_\infty$ less than about 0.27, it is possible to detect a slight decrease in the wavelength L and a slight increase in the steepness h/L of the ripples as the steady current is

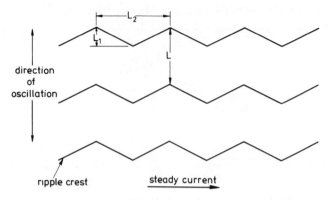

Figure 4.26.   Plan view of ripple crests in combined steady and oscillatory flow.

increased. Under these circumstances the mean profile of the ripples in the direction of oscillation remains more or less symmetrical.

4.17.2.   Dunes

In the sea, the wavelength of the dunes formed by steady flows or tidal currents is usually so much larger than that of the ripples formed by the waves that there is no competition between them: the ripples form readily on top of the dunes. Thus, at first sight, it would seem that the dunes should be unaffected by wave action. However, this is not entirely certain since oscillatory motion does make the sediment more mobile than might otherwise be the case and this may have some effect on dune geometry.

If the dunes formed by steady or tidal currents in the sea were totally unaffected by wave action, the steady flow formulas given in Section 4.12 would imply very large wavelengths and heights. Stride (1963) gives details of measurements around the coasts of Britain which do, indeed, show very large dunes. Dune heights of up to 20 m and wavelengths of up to 1000 m were observed, although not necessarily at the same point.

The steady flow formulas based only on depth do not show very good agreement with the measurements. For example, Stride records wavelengths between 200 and 400 m at depths of 90 and 125 m, whereas (4.53) would predict wavelengths of 450 and 625 m at these two depths. Equation (4.54) predicts even larger wavelengths. Unfortunately data on local currents are not available so it is not possible to say whether the discrepancy is due to the Froude number effects, which are allowed for by other steady flow formulas.

On the other hand, the steady flow formulas linking dune height to length do agree well with measurements in the sea, as shown by Fig. 4.27. This agreement is all the more remarkable when the fact that the currents are much less

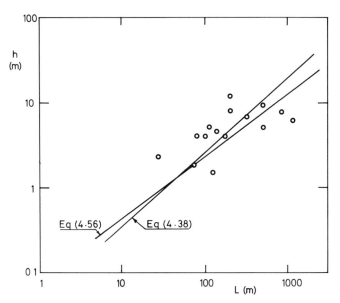

Figure 4.27. Comparison of steady flow formulas with measurements of dune height and length in the sea made by Off (1963).

uniform in time and space in the marine environment is borne in mind. Both (4.38) and (4.56) show the height to length ratio of dunes to decrease with increasing wavelength. Since dunes in the sea are generally larger than those commonly observed in steady flows it is to be expected that their profile would be less steep. In fact, downstream slopes of marine dunes rarely exceed about 12° to the horizontal and upstream slopes are usually about half this value.

4.18. EXAMPLES

1. Progressive waves of height 3 m and period 15 s are propagating in water of depth 20 m. The bed is horizontal and consists of sand of median diameter 0.8 mm. There is no superimposed steady current. What will be the wavelength and height of the ripples formed?

Following the methods outlined in Example 1 of Section 2.11 we obtain

$$b = 0.03181 \text{ m}^{-1}$$
$$U_\infty = 0.924 \text{ m/s}$$
$$a/D = 2.76 \times 10^3$$

also

$$\frac{\rho D}{(\rho_s - \rho)gT^2} = \frac{0.8 \times 10^{-3}}{1.65 \times 9.81 \times (15)^2} = 0.220 \times 10^{-6}$$

Hence, from Figs. 4.11 and 4.12,

$$\frac{L}{D} = 2000$$

$$\frac{h}{D} = 200$$

Thus the bed form is vortex ripples of length 1.6 m and height 0.16 m. For the specified conditions these ripples would probably be three-dimensional.

2.   A steady current in water of depth 20 m over a horizontal bed has a surface velocity of 1 m/s. If wave effects are negligible what bed forms might be expected if the sediment is sand of median diameter 0.8 mm?

The first step would be to check that the bed actually is mobile. The procedure for doing this will be outlined in Chapter 6. Let us assume that the current is strong enough to move the sediment. In that case it cannot be assumed when calculating the velocities and shear stresses that the bed will necessarily be plane. From Fig. 4.20 it would seem that the most likely probability once the bed is in motion is that dunes will form. We will take this as a first approximation.

At this stage we do not know velocities and shear stresses so we can only use formulas that do not make use of these variables. Yalin's (4.53) for dunes gives

$$L = 100 \text{ m}$$

whereas Hino's expression gives

$$L = 140 \text{ m}$$

A combination of Allen's (4.36) and (4.56) gives

$$L = 129 \text{ m}$$

$$h = 2.91 \text{ m}$$

Taking $h=2.9$ m and $L=130$ m, (1.107) gives

$$k_s=1.36 \text{ m}$$

As a first guess we assume that the bed is hydraulically rough. From (1.99) applied to the free surface

$$1=2.5\bar{u}_* \ln\left(\frac{30 \times 20}{1.36}\right)$$

Thus

$$\bar{u}_*=0.0657 \text{ m/s}$$

$$\frac{\bar{u}_* k_s}{\nu}=89 \times 10^3$$

Since $\bar{u}_* k_s/\nu$ is greater than the limit of 70, the assumption that the bed is hydraulically rough is justified. If that had not been the case it would have been necessary to iterate using Fig. 1.12 and (1.94) as in a previous example. From (1.100)

$$\bar{U}=0.84 \text{ m/s}$$

Thus the Froude number is

$$\frac{\bar{U}}{(gd)^{1/2}}=0.060$$

Also, since $\bar{u}_*=(\tau_0/\rho)^{1/2}$ it follows that

$$\bar{U}\tau_0=3.63 \text{ N/m} \cdot \text{s}$$

and

$$\frac{\tau_0}{(\rho_s-\rho)gD}=\frac{(\bar{u}_*)^2}{1.65 \times 9.81 \times 0.8 \times 10^{-3}}=0.33$$

Since

$$\frac{u_* D}{\nu}=52.6$$

both Fig. 4.19 and 4.20 show the bed regime to be dunes as assumed in the first place. Had this not been the case it would have been necessary to repeat the calculation for some other bed form.

We are now in a position to see what wavelengths are predicted by the various formulas that take account of Froude number.

Kennedy's (4.43) predicts

$$L = 0.45 \text{ m}$$

whereas (4.44) of Tsuchiya and Ishizaki gives

$$L = 2.64 \text{ m}$$

These are theoretical expressions. Swart's empirical (4.55) predicts

$$L = 6.7 \text{ m}$$

These values of wavelength are all much lower than those given by the formulas which make no allowance for fluid velocity. One reason is that the Froude number is very low. It is clear from Fig. 4.23 that under these circumstances a very small change in Froude number corresponds to a very large change in the predicted wavelength. Thus equations which are based solely on Froude number are likely to be unreliable. On the other hand it has to be admitted that there is very little experimental evidence in this range so that the empirical formulas are probably unreliable also. Clearly, direct measurements on site would be highly desirable.

3. Waves of height 3 m and period 15 s are propagating in the same direction as a mean current with surface velocity 1 m/s in water of depth 20 m. The bed is horizontal and consists of sand of median diameter 0.8 mm. What bed forms are to be expected?

After checking that the bed is mobile, the next step is to find out whether the ripples which form are current or wave dominated or in the transition regime between. From the results given in the preceding examples we find

$$\frac{U_\infty}{\bar{u}_*} = 14.1$$

Thus, from Table 4.2, it would appear that the ripples would probably be wave dominated. Consequently, from Example 1, three-dimensional vortex ripples are to be expected with average length 1.6 m and height 0.16 m.

In addition to these ripples, the steady current will also form dunes. Example 2 of this section suggested that the wave length of these dunes might be anywhere between 0.4 and 140 m. However, in view of the size of the ripples produced by the waves, it is unlikely that dunes would form in this combined flow with a wavelength of less than about 10 m: smaller dunes would have to compete with the relatively vigorous wave-induced ripples.

REFERENCES

Albertson, M. L., Simons, D. B., and Richardson, E. V. (1958). Discussion of "Mechanics of sediment-ripple formation" by H. K. Liu. *Proc. A.S.C.E. J. Hydraul. Div.* **84** (HY1): 1558.

Allen, J. R. L. (1963). Asymmetrical ripple marks and the origin of water-laid closets of cross-strata. *Liverpool and Manchester Geol. J.* **3**: 187–236.

Allen, J. R. L. (1964). Primary current lineation in the lower old red sandstone (Devonian), Anglo-Welsh basin. *Sedimentology* **3**: 89–108.

Allen, J. R. L. (1968)' *Current Ripples*. North-Holland, Amsterdam.

Allen, J. R. L. (1977). The plan shape of current ripples in relation to flow conditions. *Sedimentology* **24**: 53–62.

Allen, J. R. L. (1982). *Sedimentary Structures. Their Character and Physical Basis*, Vol. 1. Elsevier, Amsterdam.

Amos, C. L. and Collins, M. B. (1978). The combined effects of wave motion and tidal currents on the morphology of intertidal ripple marks: the Wash, *U.K. J. Sediment. Petrol.* **48** (3): 849–856.

Anderson, A. G. (1953). The characteristics of sediment waves formed by flow in open channels. *Proc. 3rd Midwestern Conf. Fluid Mech. Univ. Minn.*

Athaullah, M. (1968). Prediction of bed forms in erodible channels. Ph.D. Thesis. Dept. Civil Eng. Colorado State Univ. Fort Collins, Colorado.

Bagnold, R. A. (1940). Beach formation by waves, some model-experiments in a wave tank. *J. Inst. Civ. Eng.* **15**: 27–52.

Bagnold, R. A. (1946). Motion of waves in shallow water. Interaction of waves and sand bottoms. *Proc. Roy. Soc. Ser. A* **187**: 1–15.

Bagnold, R. A. (1954). *The Physics Of Blown Sand And Desert Dunes*. 2nd ed. Methuen & Co., London.

Bascom, W. J. (1951). The relationship between sand size and beach-face slope. *Trans. A.G.U.* **32** (6): 866–874.

Bijker, E. W. (1967). Some considerations about scales for coastal models with movable bed. Delft Hydraul. Lab. Publ. 50.

Bijker, E. W., Kalkwijk, J. P. T., and Pieters, T. (1974). Mass transport in gravity waves on a sloping bottom. *Proc. 14th Conf. Coastal Eng. Copenhagen*, pp. 447–465.

Bliven, L., Huang, N. E., and Janowitz, G. S. (1977). An experimental investigation of some combined flow sediment transport phenomena. Cent. Mar. Coastal Stud. North Carolina State Univ. Rep. 77-3.

Bogardi, J. L. (1958). Some recent advances in the theory of sediment movement. *Hydrol. J.* **38** (4): 241–252.

Bowen, A. J. and Inman, D. L. (1971). Edge waves and crescentic bars. *J. Geophys. Res.* **76** (36): 8662–8671.

Callander, R. A. (1969). Instability and river channels. *J. Fluid Mech.* **36**: 465–480.

Carstens, M. R. (1966). Similarity laws for localised scour. *Proc. A.S.C.E. J. Hydraul. Div.* **92** (HY3): 13–36.

Carstens, M. R., Neilson, F. M., and Altinbilek, H. D. (1969). Bed forms generated in the laboratory under an oscillatory flow: analytical and experimental study. C.E.R.C. Tech. Memo 28.

Carter, T. G., Liu, P. L-F., and Mei, C. C. (1973). Mass transport by waves and offshore bed forms. *Proc. A.S.C.E. J. Waterw. Harbors Coastal Div.* **99** (WW2): 165–184.

Chabert, J. and Chauvin, J. L. (1963). Formation de dunes et de rides dans les modéles fluviaux. *Bull. CREC.* **4**.

Chan, K. W., Baird, M. H. I., and Round, G. F. (1972). Behaviour of beds of dense particles in a horizontally oscillating liquid. *Proc. Roy. Soc. Ser. A.* **330**: 537–559.

Coastal Engineering Research Center. (1977). Shore protection manual. U.S. Army Corps Eng.

Dalrymple, R. A. and Thompson, W. W. (1976). Study of equilibrium beach profiles. *Proc. 15th Conf. Coastal Eng. Hawaii*, pp. 1277–1296.

Darwin, G. H. (1883). On the formation of ripple marks in sand. *Proc. Roy. Soc. Ser. A.* **36**: 18–43.

Dean, R. G. (1973). Heuristic models of sand transport in the surf zone. *Proc. Conf. Eng. Dynamics in the Surf Zone.* Sydney. 7 pp.

Dingler, J. R. (1975). Wave formed ripples in nearshore sands. Ph.D. Thesis. Dept. Oceanogr. Univ. Cal., San Diego.

Dingler, J. R. and Inman, D. L. (1976). Wave-formed ripples in nearshore sands. *Proc. 15th Conf. Coastal Eng. Hawaii*, pp. 2109–2126.

Eagleson, P. S., Glenne, B. and Dracup, J. A. (1961). Equilibrium characteristics of sand beaches in the offshore zone. Beach Erosion Board. Tech. Memo 126.

Eagleson, P. S., Glenne, B. and Dracup, J. A. (1963). Equilibrium characteristics of sand beaches. *Proc. A.S.C.E. J. Hydraul. Div.* **89** (HY1): 35–57.

Engelund, F. (1969). On the possibility of formulating a universal spectrum for dunes. *Tech. Univ. Denmark. Inst. Hydrodyn. Hydraul. Eng. Prog. Rep.* **18**: 1–4.

Engelund, F. (1970). Instability of erodible beds. *J. Fluid Mech.* **42**: 225–244.

Engelund, F. and Fredsoe, J. (1982). Sediment ripples and dunes. *Annual Review of Fluid Mechanics.* **14**: 13–37.

Exner, F. M. (1925). Uber die wechselwirkung zwischen wasser und geschiebe in flussen. *Sitzenberichte Akad. Wiss. Wien.* **3–4**: 165.

Falcon, M. (1969). Theoretical description of free surface two-phase flow over a wavy bed. Cent. Univ. Venezuela. Caracas. Hydraul. Lab. Bull. 2: 87–102.

Forel, F. A. (1883). Les rides de fond étudiées dans le lac Léman. *Arch. Sci. Phys. Nat. Geneva,* **7**.

Fredsoe, J. (1974a). The development of oblique dunes. Part 4. Tech. Univ. Denmark. Inst. Hydrodyn. Hydraul. Eng. Prog. Rep. 34, pp. 25–29.

Fredsoe, J. (1974b). On the development of dunes in erodible channels. *J. Fluid Mech.* **64**: 1–16.

Fredsoe, J. (1975). The friction factor and height-length relations in flow over a dune-covered bed. Tech. Univ. Denmark. Inst. Hydrodyn. Hydraul. Eng. Prog. Rep. 37, 31–36.

Fredsoe, J. (1982). Shape and dimensions of stationary dunes in rivers. *Proc. A.S.C.E. J. Hydraul. Div.* **108** (HY8): 932–947.

Garde, R. J. and Albertson, M. L. (1959). Sand waves and regimes of flow in alluvial channels. *Proc. 8th Congr. IAHR. Montreal.* **4** (28-S11): 1–7.

Garde, R. J. and Raju, K. G. R. (1963). Regime criteria for alluvial channels. *Proc. A.S.C.E. J. Hydraul. Div.* **89** (HY6): 153–164.

Gill, M. A. (1971). Height of sand dunes in open channel flows. *Proc. A.S.C.E. J. Hydraul. Div.* **89** (HY12): 2067–2074.

Gradowczyk, M. H. (1968). Wave propagation on the erodible bed of an open channel. *J. Fluid Mech.* **33**: 93–112.

Grass, A. J. (1971). Structural features of turbulent flow over smooth and rough boundaries. *J. Fluid Mech.* **50**: 233–255.

Goswami, A. C. (1967). Geometric study of ripples and dunes. M.S. Thesis. Dept. of Civil Eng. Colorado State Univ., Colorado.

Guy, H. P., Simons, D. B., and Richardson, E. V. (1966). Summary of alluvial channel data from flume experiments 1956–1961. U.S. Geol. Surv. Prof. Pap. 462-i.

Hayashi, T. (1970). Formation of dunes and antidunes in open channels. *Proc. A.S.C.E. J. Hydraul. Div.* **96** (HY2): 431–439.

Hino, M. (1968). Equilibrium-range spectra of sand waves formed by flowing water. *J. Fluid Mech.* **34**: 565–573.

Holtorff, G. (1982). Resistance to flow in alluvial channels. *Proc. A.S.C.E. J. Hydraul. Div.* **108** (HY9): 1010–1028.

Homma, M., Horikawa, K., and Kajima, R. (1965). A study on suspended sediment due to wave action. *Coastal Eng. Jpn.* **8**: 85–103.

Homma, M., Horikawa, K., and Sonu, C. (1959). Coastal sediment transport and beach profile change. *Proc. 6th Conf. Coastal Eng. Jpn.* pp. 78–88 (in Japanese).

Horikawa, K. and Watanabe, A. (1967). A study on sand movement due to wave action. *Coastal Eng. Jpn.* **10**: 39–57.

Hunt, A. R. (1882). On the formation of ripplemark. *Proc. Roy. Soc.* **34**: 1–18.

Huntley, D. A. and Bowen, A. J. (1978). Beach cusps and edge waves. *Proc. 16th Conf. Coastal Eng. Hamburg*, pp. 1378–1393.

Inman, D. L. (1957). Wave-generated ripples in nearshore sands. Beach Erosion Board. Tech. Memo 100.

Iwagaki, Y. and Noda, H. (1962). Laboratory study of scale effects in two dimensional beach processes. *Proc. 8th Conf. Coastal Eng. Mexico*, pp. 194–210.

Jain, S. C. and Kennedy, J. F. (1974). The spectral evolution of sedimentary bed forms. *J. Fluid Mech.* **63**: 301–314.

Johnson, J. W. (1949). Scale effects in hydraulic models involving wave motion. *Trans. A.G.U.* **30** (4): 517–525.

Kaneko, A. (1981). Oscillation sand ripples in viscous fluids. *Proc. Jpn. Soc. Civil Eng.* **307**: 113–124.

Kemp, P. H. and Plinston, D. T. (1968). Beaches produced by waves of low phase difference. *Proc. A.S.C.E. J. Hydraul. Div.* **94** (HY5): 1183–1195.

Kennedy, J. F. (1963). The mechanics of dunes and antidunes in erodible-bed channels. *J. Fluid Mech.* **16**: 521–544.

Kennedy, J. F. and Falcon, M. (1965). Wave-generated sediment ripples. M.I.T. Hydrodyn. Lab. Rep. 86.

Keulegan, G. H. (1948). An experimental study of submarine bars. Beach Erosion Board. Tech. Memo 3.

Lamb, H. (1932). *Hydrodynamics*, 6th ed. Cambridge Univ. Press, Cambridge.

Larras, J. (1959). Les profils d'équilibre des fonds de sable sous la mer. *Ann. Ponts Chaussées.* July-Aug.

Lau, J. and Travis, B. (1973). Slowly varying Stokes waves and submarine longshore bars. *J. Geophys. Res.* **78** (21): 4489–4497.

Leopold, L. B. and Maddock, T. (1953). The hydraulic geometry of stream channels and some physiographic implications. U.S. Geol. Surv. Prof. Pap. 252.

Liu, H. K. (1957). Mechanics of sediment-ripple formation. *Proc. A.S.C.E. J. Hydraul. Div.* **183** (HY2): 1–23.

Lofquist, K. E. B. (1978). Sand ripple growth in an oscillatory-flow water tunnel. C.E.R.C. Tech. Pap. 78-5.

Lyne, W. H. (1971). Unsteady viscous flow over a wavy wall. *J. Fluid Mech.* **50**: 33–48.

Manohar, M. (1955). Mechanics of bottom sediment movement due to wave action. Beach Erosion Board. Tech. Memo 75.

Mercer, A. G. (1971). Analysis of alluvial bed forms. In *River Mechanics*, Vol. 1, H. W. Shen, Ed. Colorado State Univ. Fort Collins, Colorado, pp. 10.1–10.26.

Mogridge, G. R. and Kamphuis, J. W. (1972). Experiments on bed form generation by wave action. *Proc. 13th Conf. Coastal Eng. Vancouver*, pp. 1123–1142.

Motta, V. F. (1963). The correlation between wave steepness and the type of equilibrium beach profiles formed by waves with constant period in a tideless sea. *1st Latin American Hydraul. Congr. Brazil.*

Natarajan, P. (1969). Sand movement by combined action of waves and currents. Ph.D. Thesis. Imperial College. London.

Nayak, I. V. (1970). Equilibrium profiles of model beaches. *Proc. 12th Conf. Coastal Eng. Washington*, pp. 1321–1339.

Nielsen, P. (1979). Some basic concepts of wave sediment transport. Inst. of Hydrodyn. Hydraul. Eng. Tech. Univ. of Denmark. Series Pap. 20.

Nordin, C. F. (1971). Statistical properties of dune profiles. U.S. Geol. Surv. Prof. Pap. 562-F.

Off, T. (1963). Rhythmic linear sand bodies caused by tidal currents. *Bull. Amer. Assoc. Petrol. Geol.* **47** (2): 324–341.

Parker, G. (1975). Sediment inertia as cause of river antidunes. *Proc. A.S.C.E. J. Hydraul. Div.* **101** (HY2): 211–221.

Plate, E. (1971). Limitations of spectral analysis in the study of wind-generated surface waves. *Proc. 1st Int. Symp. Stochastic Hydraul. Pittsburgh*, pp. 522–539.

Raichlen, F. and Kennedy, J. F. (1965). The growth of sediment bed forms from an initially flattened bed. *Proc. 11th Congress IAHR Leningrad.* **3**: (3.7).

Raman, H. and Earattupuzha, J. J. (1972). Equilibrium conditions in beach wave interaction. *Proc. 13th Conf. Coastal Eng. Vancouver*, pp. 1237–1256.

Raudkivi, A. J. (1963). Study of sediment ripple formation. *Proc. A.S.C.E. J. Hydraul. Div.* **89** (HY6): 15–36.

Rector, R. L. (1954). Laboratory study of equilibrium profile of beaches. Beach Erosion Board. Tech. Memo 41.

Reynolds, A. J. (1965). Waves on the erodible bed of an open channel. *J. Fluid Mech.* **22**: 113–133.

Richards, K. J. (1980). The formation of ripples and dunes on an erodible bed. *J. Fluid Mech.* **99**: 597–618.

Russell, R. C. H. and Osorio, J. D. C. (1975). An experimental investigation of drift profiles in a closed channel. *Proc. 6th Conf. Coastal Eng. Miami*, pp. 171–193.

Saville, T. (1957). Scale effects in two dimensional beach studies. *Proc. 7th Cong. IAHR. Lisbon.* 10 pp.

Scott, T. (1954). Sand movement by waves. Beach Erosion Board. Tech. Memo 48.

Senturk, F. (1973). A new category of bed configurations: anti-ripples. *Proc. 15th Cong. IAHR Istanbul*, **5**: 95–100.

Shephard, F. P. (1950). Longshore-bars and longshore-troughs. Beach Erosion Board Tech. Memo 15.

Shields, A. (1936). Anwendung der aehnlichkeits mechanik und der turbulenzforschung auf die geschiebebewegung. *Mitt. Preuss. Versuchanst. Wasserbau Schiffbau. Berlin.* **26**: 1–26.

Simons, D. B. and Richardson, E. V. (1960). Resistance to flow in alluvial channels. *Proc. A.S.C.E. J. Hydraul. Div.* **86** (HY5): 73–99.

Simons, D. B. and Richardson, E. V. (1966). Resistance to flow in alluvial channels. U.S. Geol. Surv. Prof. Pap. 422-J.

Simons, D. B. and Senturk, F. (1977). *Sediment Transport Technology.* Water Resources Publications. Fort Collins, Colorado.

Sitarz, J. A. (1963). Contribution à l'étude de l'évolution des plages à partir de la connaissance des profils d'équilibre. *Centre Rech. d'Etud. Océanogr. Paris.* **5**.

Sleath, J. F. A. (1975). A contribution to the study of vortex ripples. *J. Hydraul. Res.* **13** (3): p. 315–328.

Sleath, J. F. A. (1976). On rolling-grain ripples. *J. Hydraul. Res.* **14** (1): 69–81.

Sleath, J. F. A. and Ellis, A. C. (1978). Ripple geometry in oscillatory flow. Univ. Cambridge. Dept of Engineering. Rep. A/Hydraul./TR2.

Sorby, H. C. (1859). On the structures produced by the currents present during the deposition of stratified rocks. *Geologist* **2**: 137–147.

Stride, A. H. (1963). Current-swept sea floors near the southern half of Great Britain. *Q. J. Geol. Soc. London*, **119**: 175–199.

Sunamura, T. and Horikawa, K. (1974). Two dimensional beach transformation due to waves. *Proc. 14th Conf. Coastal Eng. Copenhagen*, pp. 920–938.

Swart, D. H. (1976). Coastal sediment transport. Computation of longshore transport. Delft Hydraul. Lab. Rep. R968. Part 1.

Thompson, W. W. (1976). A study of equilibrium beach profiles. M.C.E. Thesis. Univ. Delaware.

Tsuchiya, A. and Ishizaki, K. (1967). The mechanics of dune formation in erodible-bed channels. *Proc. 12th Congress IAHR Fort Collins.* **1**: 479–486.

Uda, T. and Hino, M. (1975). A solution of oscillatory viscous flow over a wavy wall. *Proc. Jpn Soc. Civil Eng.* **237**: 27–36 (in Japanese).

Van Hijum, E. (1974). Equilibrium profiles of coarse material under wave attack. *Proc. 14th Conf. Coastal Eng. Copenhagen*, pp. 939–957.

Vanoni, V. A., Brooks, N. H., and Kennedy, J. F. (1961). Lecture notes on sediment transportation and channel stability. Report KH-R-1. Cal. Inst. Tech., California.

Waters, C. H. (1939). Equilibrium studies of sea beaches. M.S. Thesis. Univ. of Cal., Berkeley.

Watts, G. M. (1954). Laboratory study of the effect of varying wave periods on beach profiles.

Beach Erosion Board. Tech. Memo 53.

Wiegel, R. L. (1964). *Oceanographical Engineering*. Prentice-Hall, Englewood Cliffs, New Jersey.

Williams, P. B. and Kemp, P. H. (1971). Initiation of ripples on flat sediment beds. *Proc. A.S.C.E. J. Hydraul. Div.* **97** (HY4): 505–522.

Yalin, M. S. (1964). Geometrical properties of sand waves. *Proc. A.S.C.E. J. Hydraul. Div.* **90** (HY5): 105–119.

Yalin, M. S. (1977). *Mechanics of Sediment Transport*, 2nd ed. Pergamon Press, Oxford.

Yalin, M. S. and Karahan, E. (1978). On the geometry of ripples due to waves. *Proc. 16th Conf. Coastal Eng. Hamburg*, pp. 1776–1786.

Yalin, M. S. and Karahan, E. (1979). Steepness of sedimentary dunes. *Proc. A.S.C.E. J. Hydraul. Div.* **105** (HY4): 381–392.

Yalin, M. S. and Russell, R. C. H. (1962). Similarity in sediment transport due to waves. *Proc. 8th Conf. Coastal Eng. Mexico*, pp. 151–167.

Five

BED FRICTION,
ENERGY DISSIPATION,
FORCES ON BODIES
ON OR NEAR THE BED

Waves Alone

It is often important to know how the heights of the waves change as they move toward the coast. Wave height measurements may be available at one point and required at another. One influence on the change in height of the waves is the dissipation of energy which occurs in the boundary layer above the sea bed or in the bed itself.

For rough beds there is a close link between the mean force exerted by the bed on the fluid, which is ultimately responsible for the energy dissipation, and the horizontal forces on the individual particles of sediment. A knowledge of the forces on individual particles on or near the bed is important in a study of sediment transport.

As in other parts of this book most of the available results for oscillatory flow relate, either implicitly or explicitly, to small-amplitude waves. Some work has also been done on solitary waves, which is described in Sections 5.1.5 and 5.4.4.

181

5.1.   BED FRICTION AND ENERGY DISSIPATION FOR SMOOTH BEDS IN LAMINAR FLOW

5.1.1.   Impermeable Beds

Consider a steady train of waves progressing in still water of constant depth over a horizontal bed. The shear stress on the bed ($y=0$) is

$$\tau_0 = \mu \left(\frac{\partial u}{\partial y} \right)_{y=0} \tag{5.1}$$

Thus for small-amplitude waves, (2.14) in Section 2.2.1 gives

$$\tau_0 = \mu U_\infty \beta \sqrt{2} \cos \left(\omega t - bx + \frac{\pi}{4} \right) \tag{5.2}$$

The shear stress on the bed varies sinusoidally with time and its maximum occurs 45° before the maximum of the velocity outside the boundary layer. This might have been anticipated from the fact that the phase of the velocity very close to the bed is 45° ahead of that outside the boundary layer (Fig. 2.4).
    If we define a friction factor f_w as

$$f_w = \frac{\hat{\tau}_0}{\frac{1}{2} \rho U_\infty^2} \tag{5.3}$$

Equation (5.2) gives

$$f_w = \frac{2}{R^{1/2}} \tag{5.4}$$

   Similarly, making use of (5.1) and (2.15), we find that the shear stress on a flat plate oscillating with simple harmonic motion in its own plane is

$$\tau_0 = - \mu U_\infty \beta \sqrt{2} \cos \left(\omega t + \frac{\pi}{4} \right) \tag{5.5}$$

Since this plate is oscillating with a velocity $U_\infty \cos \omega t$, the work done per second and per unit area on the fluid by the plate—the energy dissipation—is

$$P = - \tau_0 U_\infty \cos \omega t \tag{5.6}$$

The mean rate of energy dissipation (averaged over one cycle) is

$$\bar{P} = \frac{1}{T} \int_0^T P \, dt \tag{5.7}$$

From (5.5), (5.6), and (5.7)

$$\bar{P} = \frac{\mu U_\infty^2 \beta}{2} \tag{5.8}$$

It is easy to show that, with a change of sign, (5.6) also gives the energy per unit area of bed dissipated in the boundary layer in the case of small-amplitude waves. This result holds true because the pressure gradient, in the case of the waves, is 90° out of phase with the free-stream velocity and consequently does not contribute to the energy dissipation. Thus the mean rate of energy dissipation in the boundary layer per unit area of bed is given by (5.8) for small-amplitude waves also.

It is convenient to express this energy dissipation in terms of a non-dimensional coefficient. Various definitions have been suggested. We use the "energy dissipation factor," which was defined by Jonsson (1980) as

$$f_e = \frac{3\pi \bar{P}}{2\rho U_\infty^3} \tag{5.9}$$

It will be seen that

$$f_e = 2\bar{C}_D = \frac{\bar{\bar{f}}}{4} = \frac{3\pi}{4} f_1 = 3K = 3C_f = \frac{6}{\pi^2} C_g = \frac{3\pi}{4} \hat{C} \cos \theta_1 \tag{5.10}$$

where $\bar{C}_D$, $\bar{\bar{f}}$, f_1, K, C_f, C_g, $\hat{C} \cos \theta_1$ are the friction coefficients used by Longuet-Higgins (1981), Carstens et al. (1969), Lofquist (1980), Bagnold (1946), Sleath (1976), Zhukovets (1963), and Kajiura (1968), respectively.

From (5.8) and (5.9)

$$f_e = \frac{3\pi}{4(2R)^{1/2}} \tag{5.11}$$

The energy dissipation is equal to the rate of change of the energy flux:

$$\bar{P} = - \frac{d}{dx} (Ec_g) \tag{5.12}$$

where E is mean wave energy per unit surface area and c_g is the group velocity. For small-amplitude waves this gives

$$\bar{P} = \frac{\rho g H}{8} \frac{\omega}{b} \left(1 + \frac{2bd}{\sinh 2bd} \right) \frac{dH}{dx} \tag{5.13}$$

For waves advancing in still water it is usual to assume that the variation in height with distance may be represented, locally, by

$$H = H_i e^{-a_0 x} \tag{5.14}$$

where H_i is the wave height at $x = 0$ and a_0 is a wave attenuation coefficient. Bearing in mind that

$$U_\infty = \frac{\omega H}{2 \sinh bd} \tag{5.15}$$

we obtain from (5.8), (5.14), and (5.13)

$$a_1 = \frac{b^2}{\beta(2bd + \sinh 2bd)} \tag{5.16}$$

where a_1 is the component of a_0 attributable to energy dissipation in the boundary layer at the bed.

The above solutions are only a first approximation, since only the first-order relationships for small-amplitude waves have been used and no allowance was made for the fact that if the wave height is gradually changing as the waves advance toward the coast, the wavelength will change gradually as well. A solution which takes account of this variation in wavelength has been obtained by Carry (1956). This solution also takes account of the energy dissipation in the body of the fluid, above the boundary layer. Neglecting terms involving $(b/\beta)^3$ and above Carry found

$$a_0 = \frac{b^2}{\beta(2bd + \sinh 2bd)} \left\{ 1 + \frac{2b}{\beta} \left[\sinh 2bd + \frac{8bd + 6 \sinh 2bd + \sinh 4bd}{4(2bd + \sinh 2bd)^2} \right] \right\} \tag{5.17}$$

Since b/β is extremely small (much less than 10^{-3} in most situations of practical importance) we see that (5.16) does give a very good first approximation within the limits of small-amplitude theory. The fact that (5.16), which gives the attenuation due to the boundary layer at the bed only, is such a good approximation indicates that the contribution to the attenuation from the rest of the fluid must be very small except when the depth is large. For infinite depth,

$$a_0 = \frac{4b^3 v}{\omega} \tag{5.18}$$

This is the same as the expression obtained by Lamb (1932) when allowance is made for variation in space rather than in time.

Carry's solution is for the case of a steady train of waves whose height varies in space but not, at any given point, in time. A solution was obtained by Biesel (1949) for the case of waves whose height varies in time but not, at any given instant, in space. Biesel's extension of this solution to the more useful case of spatially varying waves is only correct as a first approximation. It was Biesel's doubts about his own solution which led him to encourage Carry to produce a solution specifically for the case of spatially varying waves.

For laboratory measurements it is also necessary to know the effect of the sidewalls on the wave height attenuation. Hunt (1952) has obtained a first approximation for waves in a channel of width w. The attenuation coefficient is found to be

$$a_1 = \frac{b^2}{\beta(2bd + \sinh 2bd)} \left(1 + \frac{\sinh 2bd}{wb}\right) \tag{5.19}$$

The attenuation coefficient for standing waves has been calculated by Keulegan (1959). In this case it is more interesting to consider the variation in wave height with time. Assuming

$$H = H_i e^{-a_* t} \tag{5.20}$$

Keulegan obtained

$$a_* = \frac{\omega b}{\beta} \left[\frac{b}{\beta} + \frac{\pi + wb(1 + \pi - 2bd)}{2\pi wb \sinh 2bd} \right] \tag{5.21}$$

As shown by Fig. 5.1, the agreement between the progressive wave theory and laboratory measurements of the attenuation coefficient is not perfect. To some extent this may be attributable to experimental problems. Direct measurements of the shear stress, such as those of Eagleson (1962) and Iwagaki and Tsuchiya (1966), who used a plate mounted flush with the bed, are notoriously sensitive to unbalanced pressure forces on the edges of the

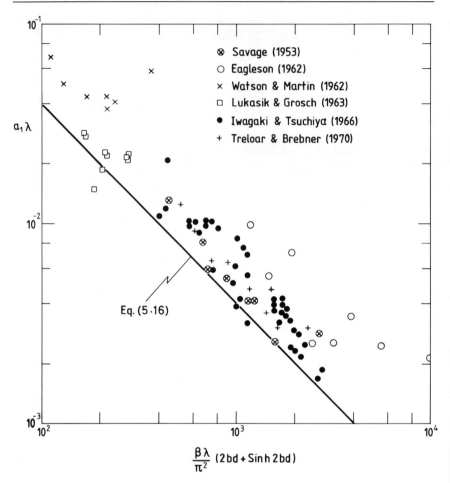

Figure 5.1. Comparison between theory and experiment for wave height attenuation due to bottom friction.

plate. On the other hand, observations of the attenuation of the wave height in laboratory flumes, such as those of Watson and Martin (1962), Lukasik and Grosch (1963), and Treloar and Brebner (1970), require careful correction for sidewall effects. Also, as pointed out by Hunt (1963), in his discussion of the earlier work of Grosch et al. (1960), comparison with the small-amplitude theory must clearly be limited to small-amplitude waves. Grosch (1962) found that higher-order effects were not usually significant if the flow outside the boundary layer remained sinusoidal in time. This conclusion is confirmed by the work of Iwagaki and Tsuchiya (1966) and Teleki (1972). But this would certainly not be true, for example, for cnoidal waves.

However, not all of the observed discrepancy between theory and experiment can be attributed to these experimental difficulties. Van Dorn (1966) suggested that much of the disagreement was caused by contamination of the water surface. Even initially clean water will quickly form a surface film and this can markedly increase the wave height attenuation. It is significant that Keulegan (1959) found reasonably good agreement with his theory for standing waves when the water was kept clean. Unfortunately, there does not seem to be any satisfactory way of estimating the effect of surface contamination in advance.

The foregoing results take no account of wave breaking, which may be a major source of energy dissipation in practice. Also, on site, resonant interactions between different wave components may produce significant changes in the energy of one particular component.

The measurements shown in Fig. 5.1 were all made in laboratory wave tanks. Much closer agreement between smooth bed laminar flow theory and experiment was found by Kamphuis (1975) in an oscillating flow water tunnel. His results are presented in Fig. 5.5.

5.1.2.   Rigid Permeable Beds

The flow into and out of the permeable bed may dissipate considerable energy. The mean rate of energy loss per unit area of bed is given by

$$\bar{P} = \frac{1}{\lambda T} \int_0^T \int_0^\lambda -(vp)_{y=0} \, dx \, dt \tag{5.22}$$

Using (2.51) and (2.55), we find

$$\bar{P} = \frac{K}{v} \frac{\rho g^2 b H^2 \tanh b d_1}{8 \cosh^2 b d} \tag{5.23}$$

If we define a wave attenuation coefficient as in (5.14) we obtain

$$a_2 = \frac{K\omega}{v} \frac{2b}{(2bd + \sinh 2bd)} \tanh b d_1 \tag{5.24}$$

Here a_2 is the component of a_0 attributable to bed permeability and d_1 is the depth of the permeable bed. When d_1 is infinite, (5.24) is the same (provided $K\omega/v$ is small) as the expression obtained by Reid and Kajiura (1957). Very similar expressions using somewhat different approaches have been obtained by Hunt (1959), Murray (1965), and Liu (1973). It should be noted that the expression obtained by Putnam (1949) contains a minor arithmetical error.

It may be shown from (5.24) that for given values of the parameters d, d_1, and K/v there is one particular value of the wave period T for which the attenuation coefficient a_2 is maximum (see Fig. 5.2). For example, for a permeable bed of infinite depth $a_2 v d^{3/2}/K$ is maximum when $T = 7.0(d/g)^{1/2}$. For both smaller and larger values of T the attenuation of the waves is less, because the energy dissipation depends on the product of the pressure $\dot{p}$ on the bed and the velocity v of flow into and out of the bed. As the wave period gets shorter the fluctuation in pressure on the bed becomes progressively less. Consequently the product pv becomes less. On the other hand,

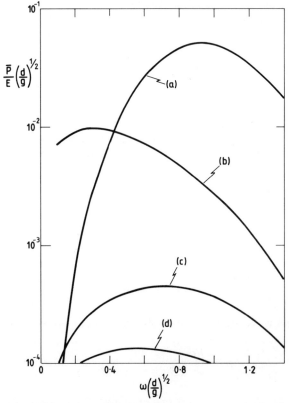

Figure 5.2. Energy dissipation rates for (a) viscous bed [$G=0$, $v_1/(gd^3)^{1/2}=0.1$, $\rho_1/\rho=0.8$, $d_1 = \infty$]; (b) viscoelastic bed [$G/\rho_1\, gd = 10$, $v_1/(gd^3)^{1/2} = 10$, $\rho_1/\rho = 0.5$, $d_1 = \infty$]; (c) permeable rigid bed [$(K/v)(g/d)^{1/2} = 10^{-3}$, $d_1 = \infty$]; (d) laminar boundary layer over rigid impermeable bed [$v/(gd^3)^{1/2} = 10^{-1}$]. [After H. Macpherson. The attenuation of water waves over a nonrigid bed. *J. Fluid Mech.* (1980), **97**, Fig. 7].

as the period becomes larger the pressure fluctuation tends toward a limiting value but the velocity v becomes less because the distance between maximum pressure and minimum pressure (half the wavelength) is increased. Thus for longer waves pv also decreases.

5.1.3. Nonrigid Beds

Thus far it has been assumed that the compressibility of the fluid and of the bed itself may be neglected. This is not always true in practice.

First, the fluid is not entirely incompressible although it would require very large waves (much larger than those obtainable in the laboratory) to produce any significant compression of pure water. However, if air or some other gas is trapped in the porous bed, the effective compressibility of the fluid will be much greater. Under these circumstances, significant modifications of the pressure and velocity distributions in the bed may be found even with waves as small as those used in the laboratory. Although Yamamoto et al. (1978) do not actually calculate the energy dissipation for this case, it is clear from their solution for the velocity and pressure distributions that wave attenuation would be significantly greater than that given by (5.24). The main difficulty is that, in practice, it is not always easy to estimate the amount of gas trapped in the bed.

The assumption that the grain skeleton is rigid may also be incorrect. Even for sand or silt the larger waves found on site could produce some deformation of the skeleton. (For silt the compressibility of the grain skeleton is nearly 1000 times that of pure water.) Under these circumstances the deformation of the bed would be elastic. Prevost et al. (1975), Mallard and Dalrymple (1977), and Yamamoto et al. (1978) showed that, somewhat surprisingly, the pressure within the bed decays with depth in the same way as for a rigid bed (2.55). However, if the bed is elastic, the normal and shear stresses are different and the bed itself has an orbital motion similar to that produced by the waves in the fluid above the bed. If only compressibility of the bed were important, the attenuation coefficient would be zero because a truly elastic bed cannot dissipate energy. In reality, there must still be a flow of water in the bed for the skeleton to deform so that the attenuation coefficient will not be less than that given by (5.24).

For beds of mud the compressibility of the grain skeleton is even greater and marked deformation of the bed may be readily produced in laboratory flumes. However, with this sort of bed the deformation is no longer elastic. Some investigators (e.g., Gade, 1958; Dalrymple and Liu, 1978) assume that the bed behaves like a viscous fluid. More recently, Macpherson (1980) made use of a viscoelastic model. Figure 5.2 shows how the energy dissipation varies with wave frequency, depending on the assumption made. In this figure E is the local wave energy. It should be borne in mind that both viscous and viscoelastic beds are deformed by the surface waves and consequently E is the sum of the wave energy of the bed and of the fluid above. Curves a and b are based on the solution put forward by Macpherson (1980), whereas c and d were calculated from (5.23) and (5.8), respectively.

The most striking feature of Fig. 5.2 is the very large increase in energy dissipation associated with beds of mud, whether they are assumed to be viscoelastic or purely viscous. Observations of rapid wave height attenuation by mud beds have been reported by Gade (1958), Silvester (1974), and Macpherson (1980), who refers to areas off the southwest coast of India where the waves were "almost completely attenuated over a distance of 4 to 8 wavelengths."

The actual dissipation rate depends very much on the values chosen for the viscosity and elasticity of the bed. Unfortunately it is very difficult to determine these quantities in advance for any given bed of mud since much depends on the previous history of the bed. Consequently, the theoretical results provide only an indication of the possible attenuation. Also, at the present time there are very few laboratory results that might provide guidance. Those of Lhermitte (1958) suggest that higher-order effects, particularly a steady drift of the bed in the direction of wave propagation, may be important.

All of the curves in Fig. 5.2 show that the rate of energy dissipation, for given values of d, G, K, v, v_1, etc., rises to a maximum at some intermediate value of the wave frequency. The energy dissipation is less for both very short and very long waves for the same reason as that discussed in connection with (5.24): the effect of very short waves is not felt strongly at the bed but the effect of very long waves is spread over a much larger distance.

5.1.4. Sloping Beds

Teleki and Anderson (1970) made shear stress measurements with Preston tubes on a smooth beach inclined at 1:12.5 in a laboratory channel. Almost all of their measurements were carried out at values of R less than 1.6×10^5 so that the flow was probably laminar. However, the measured values of f_w were approximately twice those given by the theoretical expression for flat beds (5.4) and also approximately twice those given by Kajiura's model for smooth beds. It is not clear whether this apparent increase in shear stress is due to the bed slope or whether it is associated with the very considerable experimental problems of using Preston tubes to measure shear stress under these conditions.

The theoretical solutions of Lau and Travis (1973) and Bijker et al. (1974) for gently sloping beaches suggest that the maximum shear stress will be increased by bed slope but not significantly (except in extreme cases).

5.1.5. Solitary Waves

Following Keulegan (1948) and Ippen and Kulin (1957) we define a friction factor

$$f_{sw} = \frac{\tau_0}{\rho u^2/2} \tag{5.25}$$

For any given value of x, τ_0 is the shear stress on the bed and u is the horizontal component of velocity just outside the boundary layer.

The mean energy dissipation per unit time and per unit width (but not per unit area) is given by

$$\bar{P}_{sw} = \int_{-\infty}^{\infty} \tau_0 u \, dx \tag{5.26}$$

Hence

$$\bar{P}_{sw} = \bar{f}_{sw} \int_{-\infty}^{\infty} \frac{\rho u^3}{2} \, dx \tag{5.27}$$

where $\bar{f}_{sw}$ is the mean value of f_{sw}.

An appropriate Reynolds number is

$$R_{sw} = \int_{0}^{X} \frac{u}{v} \, dx \tag{5.28}$$

where X is the horizontal displacement of a fluid particle:

$$X = \int_{-\infty}^{t} u \, dt \tag{5.29}$$

Substituting in (5.28):

$$R_{sw} = \int_{-\infty}^{t} \frac{u^2}{v} \, dt \tag{5.30}$$

or

$$\bar{R}_{sw} = \int_{-\infty}^{\infty} \frac{u^2}{v} \, dt \tag{5.31}$$

From measurements of wave height attenuation in a laboratory wave channel Ippen and Kulin obtained, for smooth beds,

$$\bar{f}_{sw} = \frac{1.33}{(\bar{R}_{sw})^{1/2}} \qquad (5.32)$$

This is the same as the theoretical expression given by Blasius (1908) for a flat plate in a steady flow with zero pressure gradient if the total horizontal displacement of a fluid particle is taken equal to the distance from the leading edge of the plate.

The integrals in (5.30) and (5.31) are easy to evaluate numerically but for many purposes a more direct method of calculation is desirable. In the derivation of (5.32) Ippen and his colleagues used the following expressions:

$$R_{sw} = \frac{cN^2d}{3vM}\left[1 - \left(1 + 0.5 \operatorname{sech}^2 \frac{Mx}{2d}\right) \tanh \frac{Mx}{2d}\right] \qquad (5.33)$$

and

$$\bar{R}_{sw} = \frac{2cN^2d}{3vM} \qquad (5.34)$$

where the coefficients M and N are given by

$$\frac{H}{d} = \frac{N}{M} \tan \frac{M(d+H)}{2d} \qquad (5.35)$$

$$N = \frac{2}{3} \sin^2 \frac{M(3d+2H)}{3d} \qquad (5.36)$$

Ippen and Mitchell (1957) suggest that for values of H/d between 0 and 0.5, (5.35) and (5.36) are closely approximated by

$$M = \frac{(3Hd)^{1/2}}{(d+0.8H)} \qquad (5.37)$$

$$N = \frac{2H}{(d+1.5H)} \qquad (5.38)$$

Support for (5.32) was provided by measurements with a shear plate carried out by Ippen and Mitchell (1957). However, their measurements showed that although Blasius' solution appeared to hold for the mean friction factor it did not give a good prediction of the variation in friction factor at different positions under the wave.

A theoretical solution for the wave height attenuation was obtained by Keulegan (1948):

$$\frac{dH}{dx} = -0.334 \frac{\nu^{1/2}}{(gd^3)^{1/4}} \left(\frac{H}{d}\right)^{5/4} \qquad (5.39)$$

This expression did not give good agreement with the measurements of Ippen and Kulin. In order to derive this solution Keulegan assumed wave height to be small. Naheer (1977) used an approach similar to that of Keulegan but did not restrict his solution to small wave heights. He obtained

$$\bar{f}_{sw} = \frac{1.52}{(\bar{R}_{sw})^{1/2}} \qquad (5.40)$$

Naheer found good agreement between this expression and smooth bed measurements in a laboratory channel. In view of the difficulties inherent in this sort of experiment the difference between (5.32) and (5.40) is probably not significant.

For solitary waves the celerity c is the same as the group velocity c_g. Thus, from (5.12),

$$\bar{P}_{sw} = -c\frac{dE}{dx} \qquad (5.41)$$

The wave energy E is the sum of the potential and kinetic energies. Making use of (1.48) and (1.49) we find that the relationship between $\bar{f}_{sw}$ and wave height attenuation is

$$\bar{f}_{sw} \int_{-\infty}^{\infty} \frac{u^3}{2}dx = -\frac{(gd)^{3/2}}{(3)^{1/2}} d \left\{ 5\left[\frac{H}{d}\left(1+\frac{H}{d}\right)\right]^{1/2} - \tfrac{1}{2}\ln\left[\frac{1+\left(\dfrac{H}{d+H}\right)^{1/2}}{1-\left(\dfrac{H}{d+H}\right)^{1/2}}\right] \right\} \frac{dH}{dx}$$

$$(5.42)$$

5.2. BED FRICTION AND ENERGY DISSIPATION FOR SMOOTH BEDS IN TURBULENT FLOW

Kajiura (1968) gives the following expression for the friction factor in turbulent flow over a smooth bed at large values of R:

$$\frac{1}{8.1\sqrt{f_w}} + \log\frac{1}{\sqrt{f_w}} = -0.135 + \log\sqrt{R} \qquad (5.43)$$

This expression was obtained from the three-layer model for the velocity distribution discussed in Section 2.3.1. It should only be regarded as an approximation valid in the limit as $R \to \infty$. The "exact" solution is shown in Fig. 5.3. Figure 5.5 shows good agreement between Kajiura's "exact" solution and the measurements of Kamphuis (1975) and also that there is not much difference between that solution and (5.43) for values of R greater than about 10^6.

Kajiura assumed that the bed shear stress varied sinusoidally with time and that the phase difference between it and the fluid velocity outside the

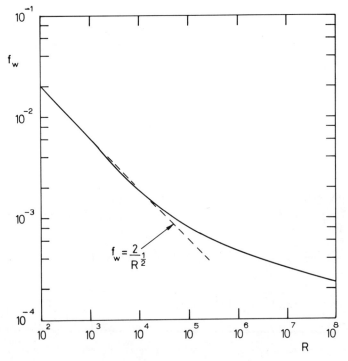

Figure 5.3.   Variation of f_w with R for smooth beds according to Kajiura (1968).

boundary layer was θ_1. Thus, making use of (5.3), (5.6), and (5.7), the mean energy dissipation is given by

$$\bar{P} = f_w \frac{\rho U_\infty^3}{4} \cos \theta_1 \qquad (5.44)$$

The phase angle θ_1 suggested by Kajiura is shown in Fig. 5.4. We see from Fig. 5.3 and 5.4 that Kajiura's expression for energy dissipation is the same at very small values of R as that for laminar flow over a smooth bed.

For small amplitude waves, (5.13) applies whether the flow is laminar or turbulent. Consequently, the wave height attenuation due to bed friction is given by

$$\frac{dH}{dx} = - \frac{4H^2 b^2 f_e}{3\pi \sinh bd(\sinh 2bd + 2bd)} \qquad (5.45)$$

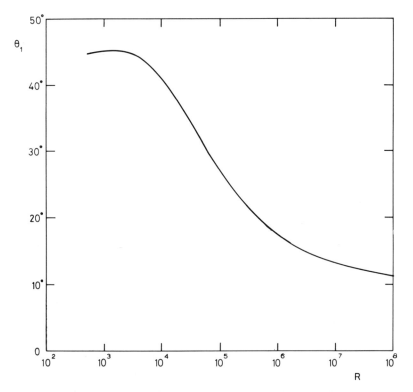

Figure 5.4. Variation of θ_1 with R for smooth beds according to Kajiura (1968).

where f_e is the energy dissipation factor defined by (5.9). From (5.44) Kajiura's expression for smooth beds corresponds to

$$f_e = \frac{3\pi}{8} f_w \cos \theta_1 \qquad (5.46)$$

None of the other models discussed in Section 2.3.1 gives an explicit relation for smooth turbulent flow.

5.3.   ROUGH BEDS—BED FRICTION

5.3.1.   Experimental Results

Probably the most comprehensive series of experimental results are those of Riedel et al. (1972), which have been reanalyzed by Kamphuis (1975). These measurements were made in an oscillating water tunnel with a shear plate mounted flush with the bed. Figure 5.5 shows the design curves suggested by Kamphuis together with the experimental results for smooth beds. These show good agreement with (5.4) for values of R less than about 2×10^5. The friction factor f_w is the same as that defined by (5.3).

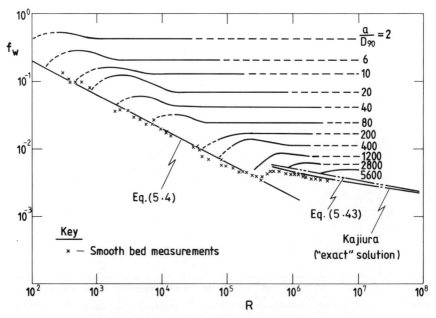

Figure 5.5.   Variation of f_w with R according to Kamphuis (1975).

The rough bed measurements were made with a single layer of sand or gravel glued to the bed. At large values of R, for any given value of a/D_{90}, the value of f_w appears to become more or less constant. If we denote the value of f_w as $R \to \infty$ by f, the expression obtained by Kamphuis for large R may be written

$$\frac{1}{4\sqrt{f}} + \log \frac{1}{4\sqrt{f}} = -0.35 + \frac{4}{3} \log \left(\frac{a}{k_s} \right) \qquad (5.47)$$

Here k_s is the Nikuradse grain roughness, which Kamphuis suggested could be taken equal to $2D_{90}$ for these tests. Appropriate values of k_s for different conditions are discussed in Section 1.16.3.

Measurements have also been made in an oscillating water tunnel by Jonsson (1963) and Jonsson and Carlsen (1976). In this case the bed was roughened with triangular ridges running across the tunnel. Two tests were carried out, each at a sufficiently high value of R for f_w to have reached its asymptotic value. The friction factor was determined from velocity measurements made above a trough between ridges. The semiempirical formula suggested by Jonsson (1963) was

$$\frac{1}{4\sqrt{f}} + \log \frac{1}{4\sqrt{f}} = -0.08 + \log \left(\frac{a}{k_s} \right) \qquad (5.48)$$

This formula was also found to give good agreement with the result of the second test (Jonsson and Carlsen, 1976).

Swart (1976) has suggested the following empirical relationship, which is somewhat easier to use than (5.47) and (5.48):

$$\text{for } \frac{a}{k_s} > 1.57, \qquad f = 0.00251 \exp \left[5.21 \left(\frac{a}{k_s} \right)^{-0.19} \right] \qquad (5.49)$$

$$\text{for } \frac{a}{k_s} \leqslant 1.57, \qquad f = 0.3 \qquad (5.50)$$

5.3.2. Theoretical Work

The theoretical models put forward by Jonsson (1966b, 1980), Kajiura (1968), Bakker (1974), Johns (1975, 1977), and Brevik (1981) for the velocity distribution also allow the shear stress on the bed to be determined. As mentioned in Section 2.3.1, all of these models make use of assumptions about the effect of turbulence which have been found to give good results in steady flows.

Jonsson's equation for the value of f_w as $R \to \infty$ is given above. Of the other models, probably the one that gives the best agreement with available experimental results is that of Kajiura. As in the case of smooth beds the solution obtained by Kajiura for rough beds is presented in graphical form. Figure 5.6 shows Kajiura's solution for the friction factor f_w and Fig. 5.7 the solution for the phase angle θ_1 between bed shear stress and free stream velocity. For very large values of R Kajiura suggested the following approximate expression for f_w:

$$\frac{0.98}{4\sqrt{f_w}} + \log \frac{1}{4\sqrt{f_w}} = -0.25 + \log \left(\frac{a}{k_s} \right) \tag{5.51}$$

It is not necessary to use this approximate formula for values of $a/k_s < 30$ since under these conditions Kajiura's "exact" solution reduces to

$$f_w = 0.35 \left(\frac{a}{k_s} \right)^{-2/3} \tag{5.52}$$

Figure 5.8 shows that (5.47), (5.48), (5.51), and Kajiura's "exact" curve are in surprisingly close agreement over a wide range of values of a/k_s. There is,

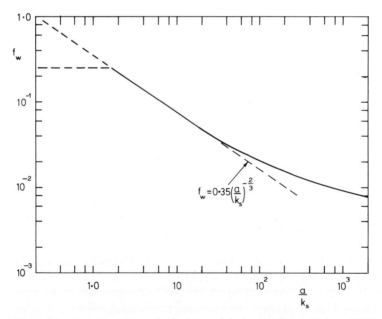

Figure 5.6. Variation of f_w with a/k_s for rough beds according to Kajiura (1968).

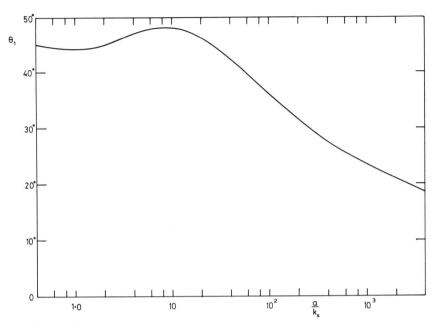

Figure 5.7. Variation of θ_1 with a/k_s for rough beds according to Kajiura (1968).

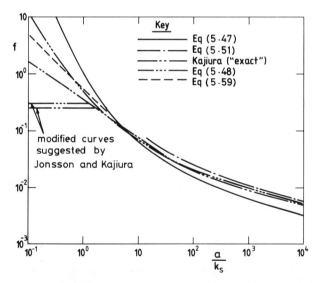

Key
——— Eq (5·47)
—·—·— Eq (5·51)
—··—··— Kajiura ("exact")
—···—···— Eq (5·48)
– – – – Eq (5·59)

modified curves
suggested by
Jonsson and Kajiura

Figure 5.8. Comparison of different formulas for the way in which f (the value of f_w as $R \rightarrow \infty$) varies with a/k_s.

199

however, some uncertainty at very small values of a/k_s. On the basis of Bagnold's test results, Kajiura (1968) and Jonsson (1980) suggested that as $a/k_s \to 0$ the value of f becomes constant rather than continuing to rise. (Jonsson recommends $f = 0.30$ for $a/k_s < 1.57$ and Kajiura gives $f = 0.25$ for $a/k_s < 1.67$.)

To get a clearer idea of the probable behavior of f as $a/k_s \to 0$ let us consider a small segment of bed such as that shown in Fig. 5.9. In this sketch the bed consists of a single layer of sediment glued to a flat plate. This was the experimental situation for Kamphuis' tests. The line BB' is the flat plate, which we will take as $y = -\delta$ and CC' is at $y = \infty$. The control volume $BCC'B'$ is of length l in the direction of the mean flow and unit width perpendicular to it.

The rate of change of the horizontal component of momentum of the fluid within the control volume $BCC'B'$ is equal to the horizontal forces acting on the periphery. Thus the horizontal force on the segment of bed is

$$F = -\rho \frac{\partial}{\partial t} \int_{y=\eta}^{\infty} \int_{x=0}^{l} \int_{z=0}^{1} u \, dz \, dx \, dy - l \int_{y=-\delta}^{\infty} \frac{\partial p}{\partial x} \, dy \qquad (5.53)$$

The first term on the right-hand side of this equation represents the rate of change of the momentum of the fluid. If we make use of a spatial mean velocity $\bar{u}$, averaged in the x and z directions, the lower boundary for the integration in y will have to be replaced by some mean value of η. Let us assume that this mean bed level is AA' and that the distance $AB = \delta$ so that AA' is the line $y = 0$. Then

$$F = -\rho l \frac{\partial}{\partial t} \int_{y=0}^{\infty} \bar{u} \, dy - l \int_{y=-\delta}^{\infty} \frac{\partial p}{\partial x} \, dy \qquad (5.54)$$

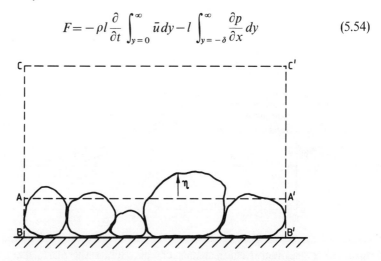

Figure 5.9. Idealized sketch of a layer of sediment glued to a flat plate.

If the bed is stationary and the fluid in the free stream outside the boundary layer has a velocity

$$u_0 = U_\infty \cos \omega t \tag{5.55}$$

then

$$-\frac{1}{\rho}\frac{\partial p}{\partial x} = \frac{\partial u_0}{\partial t} = -U_\infty \omega \sin \omega t \tag{5.56}$$

Substituting back into (5.54) and rearranging, we find

$$F = \rho l \frac{\partial}{\partial t} \int_{y=0}^{\infty} (u_0 - \bar{u})\, dy + l\delta\rho\, U_\infty \omega \sin \omega t \tag{5.57}$$

Let us assume that the mean bed level is 0.3D below the level of the crests so that $\delta = 0.7D$. (For the present argument, the exact value chosen for δ is not particularly important.) Since the horizontal force per unit area on the bed is equal to F/l we have

$$\frac{\tau_0}{\rho U_\infty^2/2} = \frac{2}{U_\infty^2}\frac{\partial}{\partial t} \int_{y=0}^{\infty} (u_0 - \bar{u})\, dy + \frac{0.7D}{a} \sin \omega t \tag{5.58}$$

As $a/k_s \to 0$, $D/a \to \infty$ and consequently the second term on the right-hand side of (5.58) becomes much greater than the first at large values of R. It follows that when $a/k_s \to 0$

$$f \propto \left(\frac{a}{k_s}\right)^{-1} \tag{5.59}$$

Why then do Bagnold's tests apparently show f to be constant at small a/k_s? The answer is that Bagnold measured the energy dissipation, not the friction force. Since the pressure force, which dominates the bed friction at small values of a/k_s, does not contribute to the energy dissipation, it is not surprising that Bagnold's tests should give a different trend from that shown by (5.59).

The fact that at large R the value of f_w is almost totally attributable to the pressure force at small values of a/k_s is of particular relevance to rippled beds. Except when the steepness is very low, natural rippled beds usually form with relatively small values of a/k_s. Thus the force on such beds, measured, say, from trough to trough, should be mainly determined by the pressure gradient in the flow. Bayazit (1969) made measurements of f_w for rippled beds. Unfortunately, insufficient details are given of the ripple geometry for this question to be examined. Sleath (1982b) gives computed curves of f_w for rippled beds.

Both Jonsson (1966b) and Sleath (1982a) proposed curves of f_w versus R for given relative roughness. The only significant difference between these curves and those of Kamphuis shown in Fig. 5.5 is in the vicinity of the smooth bed laminar flow curve. Both Jonsson and Sleath show curves of constant relative roughness which tend to turn up as $R \to 0$. However, since Kamphuis' curves are based on direct measurements it is probably preferable to use them for the time being.

5.4. ROUGH BEDS—ENERGY DISSIPATION

5.4.1. Rippled Beds

Laboratory measurements of the energy dissipation with rippled beds have been made by Bagnold (1946), Inman and Bowen (1962), Zhukovets (1963), Carstens et al. (1969), and Lofquist (1980). Theoretical models (discussed in Sections 2.2.2 and 2.3.2) have been proposed by Sleath (1973) and Longuet-Higgins (1981).

Figure 5.10 shows the values of f_e calculated by Sleath (1982b) for ripples of steepness $h/L = 0.17$. Each curve has a somewhat similar trend. For values of R below that at which (for given βL) vortex formation takes place the value of f_e is not very different from that for a flat bed. However, once vortex formation sets in the value of f_e pulls sharply away from the flat bed curve. Curves for other values of h/L show similar behavior but the actual value of f_e is strongly influenced by ripple steepness, as illustrated in Fig. 5.11. This figure also shows the values of f_e measured by Carstens et al. (1969) and Lofquist (1980) for two-dimensional ripples. Although there is reasonable agreement between theory and experiment there is very considerable scatter. To some extent this scatter may be due to the fact the computed curve is only for $a/L = 0.75$ and $\beta L = 120$, whereas the measurements cover a range of values of a/L and βL. However, it would be wrong to place too much reliance on the computed results which are based on a laminar flow model.

Longuet-Higgins' (1981) model is based on the discrete-vortex method and involves an empirical parameter ε. Provided an appropriate value is chosen for ε, Longuet-Higgins' model gives results similar to those obtained from Sleath's model.

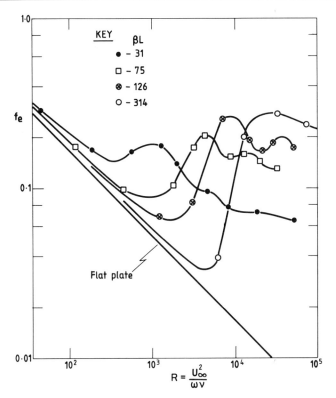

Figure 5.10. Computed curves for the variation in f_e with R for rippled beds (after Sleath, 1982b).

5.4.2. Flat Beds of Sand or Gravel

There is still some controversy about the importance of energy dissipation due to the roughness of the grains of sediment. Vitale (1979) suggests that the grain roughness is a significantly more important source of energy dissipation than the rippling of the bed. This conclusion appears to be supported by Tunstall's (1973) calculations of the proportion of bed energy dissipation attributable to vortex formation. On the other hand, the measurements of Carstens et al. (1969) and the curves calculated by Sleath (1982a) from velocity measurements show values of f_e for flat beds to be less than about 0.1 except at very small values of R (see Fig. 5.12). As shown by Fig. 5.11, the values of f_e measured for two-dimensional rippled beds are usually significantly larger than this. It is probably reasonable to conclude that the roughness of the grains of sediment is not the major contributor to energy

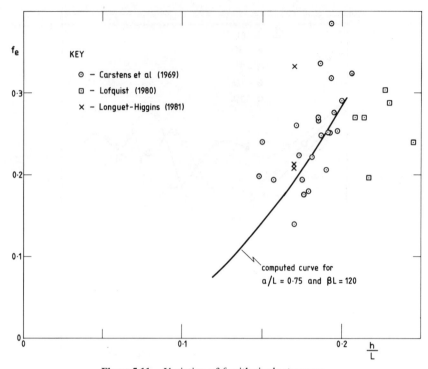

Figure 5.11. Variation of f_e with ripple steepness.

dissipation when the steepness of the ripples is greater than about 0.16 but that it becomes progressively more important as ripple steepness decreases.

The rate of energy dissipation and wave height attenuation due to bed friction may be obtained from (5.44) and (5.45), using the values of f_w and θ_1 suggested by Kajiura, which are seen in Fig. 5.6 and 5.7. Kajiura showed that his model gave reasonable agreement with the experimental results available in 1968. However, since the velocity measurements discussed in Section 2.3.2 suggest that Kajiura's estimate of phase was suspect and since energy dissipation depends on the phase, calculated values should be treated with caution.

5.4.3.   Site Measurements

Table 5.1 lists values of f_e measured on site. These values are for the total wave height attenuation. No allowance has been made for effects such as wave breaking and wind stress. This may be the reason for some of the particularly large values of f_e which were measured. However, most of the

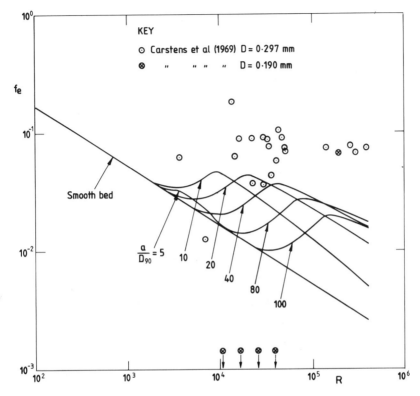

Figure 5.12. Variation of f_e with R for flat beds of sand or gravel (measurements of Carstens et al., 1969; calculated curves of Sleath, 1982a).

TABLE 5.1.   MEASUREMENTS OF WAVE ENERGY DISSIPATION ON SITE

Investigator	Location	Mean f_e	Range of f_e
Bretschneider (1954)	Gulf of Mexico	0.106	0.060–1.934
Iwagaki and	Akita Coast	0.116	0.066–0.190
Kakinuma	Izumisano Coast	0.410	
(1967)	Hiezu Coast (1963)	0.176	0.054–0.380
	Nishikinohama Coast	1.100	0.560–2.460
	Hiezu Coast (1964)	0.094	0.020–0.150
	Takahama Coast	0.100	0.060–0.170

values of f_e are consistent with those obtained for rippled beds in the laboratory as shown in Fig. 5.11.

5.4.4. Solitary Waves

Laboratory measurements of the attenuation of solitary waves over flat beds of gravel have been made by Ippen and Kulin (1957), Ippen and Mitchell (1957), and Naheer (1977). Ippen and Kulin found

$$\bar{f}_{sw} = \frac{1.33}{(\bar{R}_{sw})^{1/2}} \left(1 + 0.0063 \frac{D}{H} \bar{R}_{sw}^{3/4} \right) \tag{5.60}$$

where $\bar{R}_{sw}$ is the Reynolds number defined by (5.31) and $\bar{f}_{sw}$ is the mean value of the friction factor defined by (5.25).

Ippen and Kulin's experiments were carried out with coarse sand and gravel ranging from 1.7 to 6 mm in diameter. The fact that $\bar{f}_{sw}$ was found to depend on Reynolds number suggests that, despite these large grain sizes, the flow near the bed was still not fully developed rough turbulent. Under more severe conditions it might be expected that Reynolds number dependence would disappear. According to Naheer, all of his experiments were in the fully developed rough turbulent regime. He found that Reynolds number dependence, if not totally negligible, was very slight for any given value of D/d. Figure 5.13 shows his results.

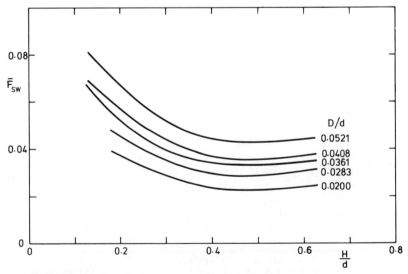

Figure 5.13.   Variation of $\bar{f}_{sw}$ with H/d and D/d according to Naheer (1977).

Ippen and Mitchell's measurements with a shear plate set into the bottom of the wave channel are in general agreement with the above results. For a given bed roughness, they found that $\bar{f}_{sw}$ followed (5.60) at lower Reynolds numbers but that it became constant at higher values of the Reynolds number.

When the value of $\bar{f}_{sw}$ is known, the wave height attenuation may be calculated from (5.42), which applies to rough as well as smooth beds for both laminar and turbulent flow.

5.5. FORCES ON BODIES ON OR NEAR THE BED

Two sorts of body are of particular importance in any study of sea bed effects. First, the widespread use of submarine pipelines has led to an increasing demand for information about the fluid forces exerted on circular cylinders. Second, there is little hope of understanding the way in which the sea moves sediment around without some knowledge of the forces acting on grains of sediment. As yet there have been very few measurements of the forces on individual grains of sediment but a considerable amount may be learned from measurements with spheres.

The forces exerted on a body by the fluid may be split into an in-line force F, parallel to the mean flow direction, a lift L perpendicular to it, and a moment M tending to rotate the body.

5.5.1. The In-Line Force

Bodies Well Away From the Bed

In oscillatory flow it is observed that the in-line force on a stationary body has one component directly in phase with the velocity of the surrounding fluid and another component in phase with the acceleration of the fluid. This may be expressed by the well-known Morison equation (Morison et al., 1950). For spheres

$$F = C_d \tfrac{1}{2}\rho \, \frac{\pi D^2}{4} u_s|u_s| + C_M \rho \, \frac{\pi D^3}{6} \frac{du_s}{dt} \qquad (5.61)$$

and for cylinders

$$F = C_d \tfrac{1}{2}\rho D u_s|u_s| + C_M \rho \, \frac{\pi D^2}{4} \frac{du_s}{dt} \qquad (5.62)$$

It should be noted that in (5.61) F is the total in-line force, whereas in (5.62) it is the force per unit length of the cylinder.

Morison's equation has been frequently attacked. One of the main objections is that if C_d and C_M are assumed to be independent of time, the equation implies that when the fluid velocity varies like $\cos \omega t$ the force F will have only two components: one varying like $\sin \omega t$ and the other like $\cos \omega t |\cos \omega t|$. In reality the measured force is more complicated than this. Sarpkaya (1976a) found that for a pure sinusoidal oscillation the error in the maximum force calculated from Morison's equation did not exceed about 15% if C_d and C_M were correctly chosen. However, details of the force record, such as the relative importance of higher harmonics, are not well predicted by Morison's equation and for more complex fluid motions, such as those found in the sea, the errors could be considerable. Unfortunately, no one has yet produced a better alternative for anything other than very small Reynolds numbers.

Figures 5.14 and 5.15 show how the values of C_d and C_M for spheres vary in oscillatory flow with the Keulegan-Carpenter number $U_0 T/D$ according to Sarpkaya (1975). Here U_0 is the maximum fluid velocity during the course of the cycle. Sarpkaya did not find any consistent variation with Reynolds number. The range of Reynolds numbers in his experiments was $10^3 < U_0 D/\nu < 5.10^4$. In view of the fact that the drag coefficient for a sphere in a steady flow is almost constant in this range, the lack of variation of C_d and C_M with Reynolds number is not surprising. However, it is to be expected that

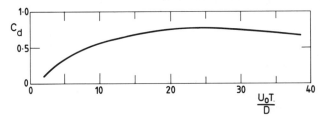

Figure 5.14.   Variation of C_d for a sphere with $U_0 T/D$ (after Sarpkaya, 1975).

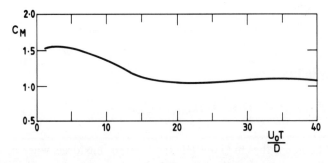

Figure 5.15.   Variation of C_M for a sphere with $U_0 T/D$ (after Sarpkaya, 1975).

Reynolds number dependence would be more important at smaller values of U_0D/v.

Figures 5.16 and 5.17 show the corresponding values of C_d and C_M obtained by Sarpkaya (1976b) for circular cylinders. The fact that different curves are obtained for different values of βD indicates that Reynolds number effects are not negligible. This is more clearly illustrated by Fig. 5.18, which shows increasing Reynolds number dependence as U_0D/v decreases.

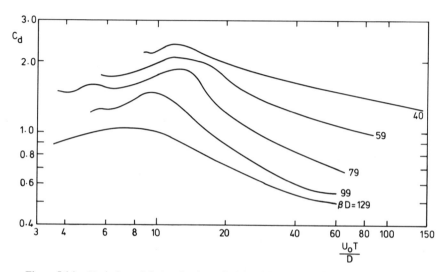

Figure 5.16. Variation of C_d for circular cylinders with U_0T/D (after Sarpkaya, 1976b).

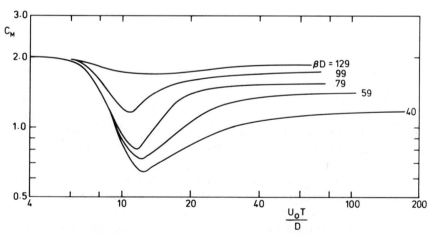

Figure 5.17. Variation of C_M for circular cylinders with U_0T/D (after Sarpkaya, 1976b).

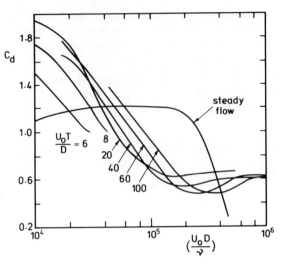

Figure 5.18. The effect of Reynolds number on the value of C_d for circular cylinders (after Sarpkaya, 1976b).

Also shown in Fig. 5.18 is the curve for the drag coefficient of a circular cylinder in steady flow. It is not surprising that this curve is different from those for oscillatory flow since in steady flow shed vorticity is convected quickly downstream whereas in oscillatory flow it is carried backward and forward past the body.

Sarpkaya's curves for C_d and C_M are based on experiments in an oscillatory flow water tunnel. For real waves there is a vertical component of velocity as well as the horizontal component reproduced in the water tunnel. Near the sea bed, however, this vertical component of velocity is sufficiently small to be neglected. In addition, it has to be remembered that real waves are much less regular than the purely sinusoidal motions obtained in a water tunnel. Consequently, the extension of results obtained in the laboratory to situations of practical importance requires caution.

Analytical solutions for the forces on bodies in oscillatory flow fall into two groups. If it is assumed that viscous effects are relatively unimportant, a solution may be obtained by potential flow methods. On the other hand, if viscous effects are assumed to be highly important, it may be reasonable to neglect the nonlinear terms in the equations of motion.

It is found from experiment that the potential flow solution is most nearly correct when the Keulegan-Carpenter number U_0T/D is low. Under these circumstances the flow around the body does not separate. Poisson (1832) found that for potential flow around a stationary sphere in an infinite oscillating fluid

$$C_M = 1.5 \qquad (5.63)$$

For an oscillating sphere in a stationary fluid the equivalent value is

$$C_M = 0.5 \qquad (5.64)$$

The values given by potential flow theory for circular cylinders are

$$C_M = 2.0 \qquad (5.65)$$

for a stationary cylinder and oscillating fluid and

$$C_M = 1.0 \qquad (5.66)$$

when the fluid is stationary and the cylinder oscillating.

The values for stationary and oscillating bodies are different because when the fluid is oscillating there is a mean pressure gradient which drives the flow whereas when the fluid is stationary there is not. It is this mean pressure gradient, acting around the surface of the body, which gives the additional force when the fluid is oscillating and the body stationary.

On the other hand, even when $U_0 T/D$ is small the potential flow solution does not give a realistic value for C_d. The predicted value of C_d is zero. Figure 5.14 appears to suggest that this value would not be too far wrong as $U_0 T/D \to 0$ but, in reality, it is found that as U_0 approaches zero viscous forces become important and C_d rises again.

The other group of solutions, based on the assumption that viscous forces are very important, is most nearly correct at very low Reynolds numbers. The first significant contribution in this group was Stokes' (1851) solution for the in-line force on a sphere oscillating in an infinite fluid. This solution has been obtained in a somewhat different way by Lamb (1932). When the sphere is held stationary and the fluid is oscillating the solution for the in-line force is

$$F = \frac{3\pi D^3 \omega}{4} \left[\frac{1}{\beta D} + \frac{2}{(\beta D)^2} \right] \rho u_s + \left(1.5 + \frac{9}{2\beta D} \right) \frac{\rho \pi D^3}{6} \frac{\partial u_s}{\partial t} \qquad (5.67)$$

Stokes (1851) also obtained the solution for a stationary cylinder in an oscillating fluid:

$$F = \pi D^2 \omega \left[\frac{1}{\beta D} + \frac{1}{(\beta D)^2} \right] \rho u_s + \left(2 + \frac{4}{\beta D} \right) \rho \frac{\pi D^2}{4} \frac{\partial u_s}{\partial t} \qquad (5.68)$$

Comparing (5.61) and (5.62) with (5.67) and (5.68) we see that Morison's equation cannot apply at very low Reynolds numbers if C_d is assumed independent of time.

In addition to the restriction to small Reynolds numbers it is also implicitly assumed in the derivation of (5.67) and (5.68) that the amplitude of the fluid oscillation is small compared with the diameter of the body. In other words the solution holds only for very small values of the Keulegan number $U_0 T/D$. It is of interest that the value of C_M obtained from (5.67) is $(1.5 + 4.5/\beta D)$, which is not too different from the value given by Fig. 5.15 as $U_0 T/D \to 0$, particularly if βD is large. The value of C_M for cylinders given by (5.68) is $(2.0 + 4/\beta D)$. This too agrees well with the experimental results shown in Fig. 5.17 as $U_0 T/D \to 0$.

Equations (5.67) and (5.68) are the solutions for simple harmonic motion of the fluid. More complicated time-varying motions at low Reynolds numbers have been investigated by Boussinesq (1885) and Basset (1888). Basset's solution for the force on a sphere oscillating in still fluid is

$$F = 3\pi\mu D u_s + \frac{\rho\pi D^3}{12}\frac{\partial u_s}{\partial t} + \frac{3\rho(\pi v)^{1/2}}{2}\int_0^t (t-\xi)^{-1/2}\frac{\partial u_s}{\partial \xi}\,d\xi \qquad (5.69)$$

In addition to Sarpkaya (1975), experimental measurements of forces on spheres in unsteady flow have been made by DuBuat (1786), Krishnaiyar (1923), Carstens (1952), Bugliarello (1956), Odar and Hamilton (1964), Hamilton and Lindell (1971), Karanfilian and Kotas (1978), and Grace and Zee (1978). It would seem from these results that (5.61) is adequate for most engineering purposes for values of $U_0 D/v$ between about 100 and 5.10^5 and that (5.67) and (5.69) are valid at very low values of $U_0 D/v$ and $U_0 T/D$. There does not appear to be any general agreement on a formula valid between these two extremes. For example, Odar and Hamilton (1964) proposed an extension of (5.69) for values of $U_0 D/v$ up to about 60, but Schoneborn (1975) showed that this formula underestimates the drag under certain conditions.

There have also been many experimental studies of the forces on cylinders in oscillatory flow. At very low Reynolds numbers the experiments of Martin (1925) and Stuart and Woodgate (1955) showed good agreement with Stokes' theory provided the amplitude of oscillation was less than one tenth of the cylinder diameter.

Comprehensive surveys of the large amount of data for circular cylinders at higher Reynolds numbers have been made by the British Ship Research Association (1976), Hogben et al. (1977), and Sarpkaya and Isaacson (1981).

These suggest that despite its drawbacks (5.62) is probably adequate for most engineering purposes.

It should also be mentioned that several investigators have put forward numerical solutions for flows of this sort. So far, all have involved the so-called discrete vortex method in which point vortices are released in a steady stream into an inviscid flow. However, the solution is sensitive to the point at which vortices are released and the way in which they are assumed to diffuse and coalesce. Consequently, these methods are not yet capable of predicting forces in anything other than very simple situations with any degree of reliability.

All of the preceding results have been for smooth bodies. Figures 5.19 and 5.20 show an example of results obtained by Sarpkaya (1976b) with sand-roughened cylinders in oscillatory flow. At low Reynolds numbers the values of C_d and C_M are not very different from those for smooth cylinders. However, at high Reynolds numbers the effect of surface roughness is marked. The reason for the different curves at higher Reynolds numbers is that surface roughness affects the critical value of U_0D/v at which the flow in the boundary layer becomes turbulent and this in turn affects the pattern of flow around the cylinder and hence C_d and C_M.

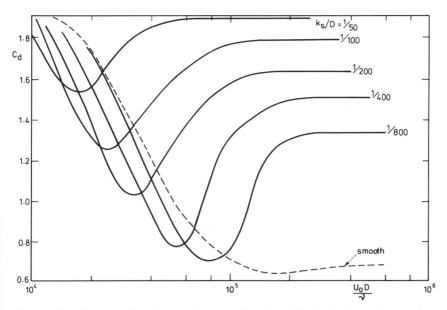

Figure 5.19. The effect of surface roughness on the value of C_d for circular cylinders (after Sarpkaya, 1976b).

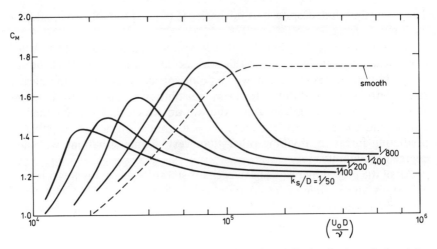

Figure 5.20.   The effect of surface roughness on the value of C_M for circular cylinders (after Sarpkaya, 1976b).

Effect of Boundary Proximity

Figures 5.21 and 5.22 show how C_d and C_M for circular cylinders vary with distance from the bed according to Sarpkaya (1976a). Once again the curves are based on experiments in an oscillatory flow water channel. When the gap ε between the cylinder and the bed is greater than about one cylinder diameter the results are little different from those well away from the bed. However, for smaller gaps the effect of boundary proximity on C_d and C_M is very marked. (In these tests the Reynolds number varied between 4×10^3 and 2.5×10^4 but Reynolds number dependence was not investigated.)

Similar results were obtained by Nath and Yamamoto (1974) in a laboratory wave channel. Nath and Yamamoto also derived the potential flow solution for the inertia coefficient:

$$C_M = 2 + 2 \sum_{j=2}^{\infty} (q_2^2 q_3^2 \ldots q_j^2)^2 \qquad (5.70)$$

where

$$q_1 = 0$$

$$q_n = \left[2\left(1 + \frac{2\varepsilon}{D}\right) - q_{n-1} \right]^{-1} \qquad (5.71)$$

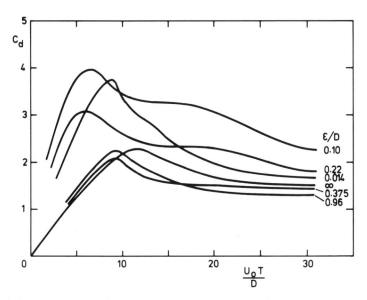

Figure 5.21. The effect of boundary proximity on the value of C_d for circular cylinders (after Sarpkaya, 1976a).

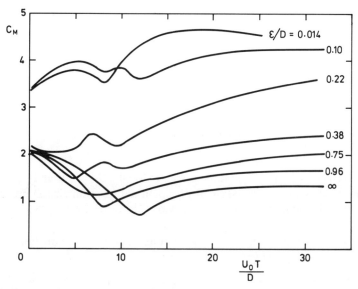

Figure 5.22. The effect of boundary proximity on the value of C_M for circular cylinders (after Sarpkaya, 1976a).

For an oscillating cylinder in a stationary fluid the first term on the right hand side of (5.70) would be 1 rather than 2.

For spheres a first approximation to the potential flow solution for the inertia coefficient is given by Milne Thomson (1968). For a stationary sphere in an oscillating fluid this may be written

$$C_M = 1.5 + \frac{3}{32(1 + 2\varepsilon/D)^3} \tag{5.72}$$

Grains of Sediment on a Flat Bed

The results discussed so far have been for spheres and cylinders. Experiments with regular bodies are obviously much more repeatable, and an analytical solution for such a complicated geometry as a grain of sediment would be difficult to obtain. However, as mentioned at the start of this chapter it is possible to deduce something about the horizontal forces on particles of sediment lying on the bed from measurements of the overall bed friction.

It is usually assumed that the proportion of the total horizontal force on the bed which is borne by an individual particle of sediment is proportional to its cross-sectional area. If the cross-sectional area of an individual grain is $\pi D^2/4$, the horizontal force on the grain is

$$F \propto \tau_0 \times \frac{\pi D^2}{4} \tag{5.73}$$

where τ_0 is the mean horizontal force per unit area acting on the bed.

Figure 5.5 shows that, at sufficiently low values of R, τ_0 is well represented by the laminar solution for a flat bed. Thus from (5.2) and (5.73)

$$F \propto \mu U_\infty \beta D^2 \cos\left(\omega t + \frac{\pi}{4}\right) \tag{5.74}$$

This is basically the result obtained from (5.67) if βD is assumed very small and the local velocity u is assumed proportional to grain size D multiplied by the velocity gradient $\partial u/\partial y$ at the bed. The restriction to "sufficiently" small R implies small βD.

On the other hand, Fig. 5.5 shows that at large R, f_w is constant for any given value of a/k_s. Using (5.73), this means that at large R

$$F \propto \rho U_\infty^2 D^2 f\left(\frac{a}{D}\right) \tag{5.75}$$

This result is consistent with Morison's equation (5.61) with coefficients given by Fig. 5.14 and 5.15.

5.5.2. The Lift

A regular body such as a sphere or circular cylinder will experience lift only if it is near a boundary, or spinning, or in a shear flow, or if the flow is temporarily distorted, for example, by vortex shedding. The thickness of the boundary layer at the bed for wave-induced flows is very thin. Thus for the case of stationary circular cylinders near the sea bed the most important sources of lift are boundary proximity and fluctuations in the flow due to separation first on one side of the cylinder and then on the other.

Lift measurements have been made for circular cylinders by Nath and Yamamoto (1974), Nath et al. (1976), Sarpkaya (1976a), Maull and Milliner (1978), and Maull and Norman (1978). Figures 5.23 and 5.24 show the results obtained by Sarpkaya (1976a) in a water tunnel. The lift coefficient is defined as

$$C_L = \frac{L}{\frac{1}{2}\rho U_0^2 D} \tag{5.76}$$

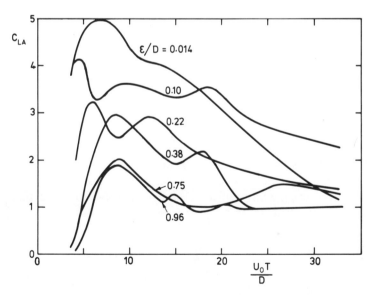

Figure 5.23. Variation of the lift coefficient C_{LA}, for maximum lift away from the bed, with U_0T/D (after Sarpkaya, 1976a).

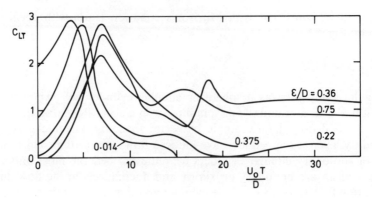

Figure 5.24. Variation of the lift coefficient C_{LT}, for maximum negative lift, with $U_0 T/D$ (after Sarpkaya, 1976a).

where U_0 is the amplitude of the fluid velocity in the tunnel and L is the lift per unit length of cylinder. The coefficient C_{LA} is for the maximum positive lift, that is, away from the bed, while C_{LT} is for the maximum negative lift (toward the bed). For values of $U_0 T/D > 5$ the lift force away from the bed is the most significant but for small values of $U_0 T/D$ lift is predominantly negative. This agrees with the results of other investigators. It also agrees with the predictions of potential flow theory, as might be expected at small values of $U_0 T/D$. Nath and Yamamoto (1974) give the lift coefficient for a cylinder near a plane bed in potential flow as

$$C_L = -4\pi \sum_{j=1}^{\infty} \sum_{k=1}^{\infty} \frac{m_j m_k}{[2(1+2\varepsilon/D) - q_j - q_k]^3} \qquad (5.77)$$

where $m_n = q_2^2 q_3^2 \dots q_r^2$

$m_1 = 1$

and the variables $q_2, q_3, \dots$ are given by (5.71).

The solution holds only when the cylinder does not actually touch the bed. When it does, the lift coefficient suddenly becomes positive, that is, lift is away from the bed. Jeffreys (1929) obtained the potential flow solution for a cylinder in contact with the bed:

$$C_L = \frac{\pi}{3}\left(1 + \frac{\pi^2}{3}\right) \qquad (5.78)$$

In addition to the regular and repeatable variation in lift with velocity characterized by these results, it is also possible to observe an apparently random fluctuation in lift with time. The explanation appears to be that the formation and shedding of one vortex influences the formation of the next, and so on. Thus for a certain time vortices will shed preferentially from one side of the cylinder. Suddenly, perhaps following a slight change in conditions, the vortices start to shed preferentially from the other side. This produces a fluctuation in the lift record.

There is far less information about the lift on spheres in oscillatory flow. There do not appear to be any direct measurements of lift under these conditions at the present time. However, if the results for cylinders are any guide, it is possible that a potential flow solution may also hold for spheres at sufficiently small values of $U_0 T/D$. The solution for the lift on a sphere near a plane bed is the same for oscillatory potential flow as for steady potential flow. The expression suggested by Milne Thomson (1968) is

$$L = -\frac{3}{64}\frac{\rho \pi D^2 u_s^2}{(1+2\varepsilon/D)^4} \tag{5.79}$$

where ε is the gap between the sphere and the wall and u_s is the velocity of the surrounding fluid relative to the sphere at any given instant. This is, in fact, only a first approximation based on the assumption that the distance of the center of the sphere from the wall is large compared with $D/2$. The solution is consequently unreliable as $\varepsilon \to 0$. A second approximation has been obtained by Naheer (1977). Allowing for change in sign, this may be written

$$L = -\frac{3}{64}\frac{\rho \pi D^2 u_s^2}{(1+2\varepsilon/D)^4}\left[1+\frac{1}{8(1+2\varepsilon/D)^2}\right] \tag{5.80}$$

Steady Currents

5.6. BED FRICTION AND FRICTION FACTORS

The bed shear stress is usually expressed nondimensionally with the aid of a friction factor. Many different coefficients are available but one of the most widely used is the Darcy Weisbach friction factor:

$$f = \frac{8\tau_0}{\rho \bar{U}^2} \tag{5.81}$$

In some countries the quantity C_f defined as

$$C_f = \frac{2\tau_0}{\rho \bar{U}^2} \qquad (5.82)$$

is called the Darcy Weisbach friction factor. Also frequently used are the Chezy coefficient

$$C = \left(\frac{2g}{C_f}\right)^{1/2} \qquad (5.83)$$

and the skin friction coefficient, which has the same definition as C_f in (5.82).

For fully developed steady flow the velocity distribution over much of the depth is logarithmic. Using (1.101) and bearing in mind that $\bar{u}_* = (\tau_0/\rho)^{1/2}$, we obtain

$$f = \frac{1.28}{\ln^2(d/2.72 y_0)} \qquad (5.84)$$

In the absence of sediment transport, y_0 is given by Fig. 1.12. Smith (1977) suggests that when sediment transport is significant the value of y_0 should be increased to

$$y_0 = y_{00} + 26.4 \frac{(\tau_0 - \tau_c)}{(\rho_s - \rho)g} \qquad (5.85)$$

where y_{00} is the value of y_0 in the absence of sediment transport.

When the bed is hydraulically rough ($\bar{u}_* k_s / v > 70$) the friction factor depends only on bed roughness. A number of simple power-law relations are available for this situation. One of the more widely used is the Manning-Strickler equation

$$f = 0.122 \left(\frac{k_s}{d}\right)^{1/3} \qquad (5.86)$$

The use of either this expression or (5.84) requires a knowledge of the bed roughness as well as of the mean velocity. On the basis of measurements in tidal channels Sternberg (1972) suggested that bed shear stress could be estimated from the relationship

$$\tau_0 = C_{100} \rho \bar{u}_{100}^2 \qquad (5.87)$$

where $\bar{u}_{100}$ is the value of $\bar{u}$ at a height of 0.1 m above the bed and C_{100} is an empirical coefficient. Sternberg found that for values of $\bar{u}_{100}$ greater than about 0.15 m/s, C_{100} was constant for any given bed. In his measurements the value of C_{100} for the different beds ranged from 2×10^{-3} up to 4×10^{-3} but he suggests that for most purposes a value of C_{100} equal to 3×10^{-3} would give reasonable results when $\bar{u}_{100} > 0.15$ m/s.

5.7. FORCES ON BODIES ON OR NEAR THE BED

It might be expected that in a steady flow the forces on a rigid body would also be steady. In many situations this is not the case because of the effect of vortex shedding. In steady flow past a circular cylinder vortex shedding from the body begins to be apparent at a Reynolds number of about 40. The corresponding Reynolds number for spheres is about 500. When a vortex is shed the flow is disturbed and consequently both the in-line and normal forces on the body also change. For cylinders, vortices tend to shed first on one side and then on the other. This produces a regular fluctuation in the force on the body. For spheres, the dominant mode is often a spiral vortex which induces a sideways force that swings around the body with the vortex. However, small irregularities in the flow or on the sphere can alter this pattern.

The frequency at which vortices are shed from the body is important because it determines the frequency of the fluctuation in the force. The shedding frequency f_0 is usually expressed nondimensionally in terms of the Strouhal number

$$\text{St} = \frac{f_0 D}{\bar{u}_s} \tag{5.88}$$

Figure 5.25 shows how the Strouhal number varies with Reynolds number for circular cylinders. For spheres, vortex shedding is much less regular so no well-defined curve exists. Even for circular cylinders vortex shedding is erratic over much of the range and consequently f_0 has to be taken as the dominant frequency. This is particularly true in the vicinity of $\bar{u}_s D/\nu \approx 4 \times 10^5$ where transition from laminar to turbulent flow takes place in the boundary layer and this is why only broken curves are shown in this region.

Most of the results presented below are for the time-mean force exerted by the steady flow on the body. The fluctuations produced by vortex shedding should also be borne in mind, particularly if the structure of which the body is a part has a resonant frequency.

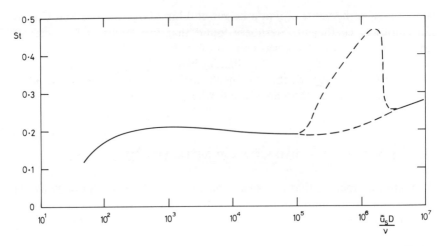

Figure 5.25.   Variation with Reynolds number of the Strouhal number for a circular cylinder.

5.7.1.   The In-Line Force and the Moment

The drag exerted by the steady flow of fluid past an isolated body has been extensively studied. The way in which the drag coefficient for a circular cylinder in an infinite fluid varies with Reynolds number is shown in Fig. 5.26. The corresponding curve for a sphere is shown in Fig. 3.1 and reproduced in Fig. 5.27.

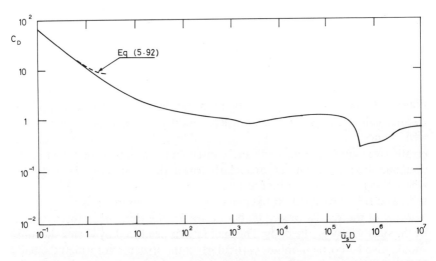

Figure 5.26.   Variation of C_D with Reynolds number for a circular cylinder in an infinite fluid.

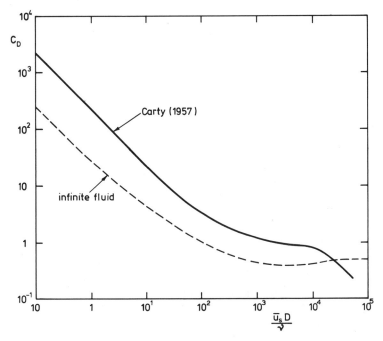

Figure 5.27. Comparison of the curve obtained by Carty (1957) for the variation of C_D with Reynolds number of a sphere rolling down a smooth plane with the curve for a sphere in an infinite fluid.

The drag coefficient is defined for a sphere as

$$C_D = \frac{F}{\frac{1}{2}\rho\bar{u}_s^2(\pi D^2/4)} \qquad (5.89)$$

where $\bar{u}_s$ is the relative velocity of the center of the sphere and the surrounding fluid. For a circular cylinder the drag coefficient is

$$C_D = \frac{F}{\frac{1}{2}\rho\bar{u}_s^2 D} \qquad (5.90)$$

where F is now the force per unit length of the cylinder.

At very low Reynolds numbers ($\bar{u}_s D/\nu < 0.1$) it is found that for a sphere

$$C_D = \frac{24}{(\bar{u}_s D/\nu)} \qquad (5.91)$$

and for a circular cylinder Lamb (1932) gives

$$C_D = \frac{8\pi}{\left(\dfrac{\bar{u}_s D}{v}\right)\left[2.0 - \ln\left(\dfrac{\bar{u}_s D}{v}\right)\right]} \tag{5.92}$$

The curves in Fig. 5.26 and 5.27 are for smooth spheres and cylinders. The principal effect of surface roughness is to alter the point at which the boundary layer on the body becomes turbulent. It is the transition to turbulence which causes the sudden drop in the drag coefficient at a value of $\bar{u}_s D/v$ equal to about 4×10^5. In the vicinity of this transition, surface roughness will clearly be very important but at other Reynolds numbers the change in drag coefficient with surface roughness is slight.

Although the forces on bodies in an infinite fluid are well understood there are two complications in the case in which we are interested here. First, what is the effect of boundary proximity? Second, in the particular case of sediment transport, we need to know how the fact that the grains of sediment are not isolated affects the drag.

Boundary Proximity

Carty (1957) examined the influence of a boundary on the drag on a sphere by rolling a sphere of known size and weight down a smooth plane at a known angle to the horizontal and observing the terminal velocity in various fluids of known properties. Figure 5.27 shows the curve obtained by Carty and also the curve for an isolated sphere in an infinite fluid for purposes of comparison. Carty assumed that the in-line force F exerted by the fluid on the sphere is equal in magnitude to the component of the weight of the sphere resolved parallel to the slope. This assumption, which was also made by Garde and Sethuraman (1969), is discussed further below.

It is seen from Fig. 5.27 that at low values of the Reynolds number the drag coefficient is given by

$$C_D = \frac{215}{(\bar{u}_s D/v)} \tag{5.93}$$

This is significantly different from the result for an isolated sphere at low Reynolds numbers (5.91). Similar experiments were carried out with spheres rolling over rough beds by Garde and Sethuraman (1969). Coleman (1977) suggests that at low Reynolds numbers their results correspond to

$$C_D = \frac{100}{(\bar{u}_s D/v)} \tag{5.94}$$

The case of a sphere rolling down a plane in still fluid is rather different from the case in which we are interested of a stationary body resting on a bed with fluid flowing past it. The case of a stationary sphere on a solid boundary was studied by Young (1960), Coleman (1967, 1972, 1977), and Aksoy (1973). Most of their experiments were carried out for $10^2 < \bar{u}_s D/\nu < 10^4$. Here $\bar{u}_s$ is the velocity of the surrounding fluid at the level of the center of the sphere. In this range of Reynolds numbers there is little difference between Carty's curve for a rolling sphere and that for a sphere in an infinite fluid. The measurements of Young, Coleman, and Aksoy confirm this result. Coleman (1977) did carry out some measurements at smaller values of the Reynolds number. Because of the experimental scatter these measurements are not conclusive but appear to show some increase in C_D caused by boundary proximity. Very tentatively Coleman suggests that at low Reynolds numbers the drag coefficient for a stationary sphere is

$$C_D = \frac{40}{(\bar{u}_s D/\nu)} \tag{5.95}$$

Since the bed in Coleman's experiments was rough this equation for stationary spheres should be compared with (5.94) for rolling spheres.

Values of C_D for spheres resting on both smooth and rough beds were also obtained by Eagleson et al. (1958) from observation of incipient and established motion of sediment in a wave channel. The calculation assumed that the velocity distribution of the fluid was that for a smooth bed in laminar flow and the measurements show considerable scatter. However, they are not inconsistent with the results of other investigators summarized above.

There is, as yet, no analytical solution for large Reynolds numbers but a great number of investigators have studied flows of this sort for very small values of the Reynolds number. Exact solutions, using bipolar spherical coordinates, have been obtained for spheres rotating near, and moving parallel to, a plane wall by Dean and O'Neill (1963) and O'Neill (1964). More recently Lin et al. (1970) gave a general solution for combined translation and rotation of a sphere in a shear flow near a wall. This solution holds both for a sphere actually touching the bed and also for finite separations. For the case of a stationary sphere resting on the bed the drag coefficient is

$$C_D = \frac{40.8}{(\bar{u}_s D/\nu)} \tag{5.96}$$

This solution is very similar to (5.95) but it should be remembered that Coleman's empirical formula is for a sphere on a rough bed.

The analytical solution also allows the moment M to be determined. For a stationary sphere on a smooth bed the moment is

$$M = \pi\mu D^2 \bar{u}_s \qquad (5.97)$$

The solution of Lin et al. may also be applied to the case of a sphere rolling down a smooth plane. In this case some extrapolation of the tabulated coefficients is necessary but the error involved is almost certainly small. The results are

$$C_D = \frac{186}{(\bar{u}_s D/v)} \qquad (5.98)$$

and

$$M = 11\pi\mu D^2 \bar{u}_s \qquad (5.99)$$

At first sight the agreement between (5.93) and (5.98) is highly satisfactory. However, the calculations of Carty (1957) and Garde and Sethuraman (1969) make no allowance for the moment M. In reality the component of the weight of the sphere down the slope is opposed by the combined action of the in-line force F and the moment M. In other words, if the method of Carty and Garde and Sethuraman is used to calculate C_D the theory of Lin et al. would predict a drag coefficient approximately 43% higher than that actually found in the experiments.

The most likely explanation for this discrepancy is that the sphere rolling down the slope is not in close contact with the bed. As the sphere rolls a thin layer of fluid is trapped beneath it. This has two results. First, the theory shows that both the in-line force and the moment exerted by the fluid on the sphere decrease as the separation from the boundary increases. Second, the sphere is more free to slide, rather than roll, down the slope so that the moment is reduced. It is also possible that rolling friction was not entirely negligible in the experiments.

Whatever the reason for the discrepancy between theory and experiment it is clear that boundary proximity can produce significant increase in the drag on a body at low Reynolds numbers but that for $\bar{u}_s D/v > 100$ the increase is small or nonexistent.

For cylinders there is much less information on the effects of boundary proximity. Takaisi (1955) obtained a low Reynolds number solution for the drag on a cylinder moving parallel to a plane wall. When the gap ε is large compared with D this reduces to

$$C_D = \frac{8\pi}{(\bar{u}_s D/v) \ln 2(1 + \varepsilon/D)} \qquad (5.100)$$

More recently, Bagnold (1974) measured the drag on a stationary cylinder at various positions above the bed in a water channel. For $\bar{u}_s D/\nu$ approximately equal to 3×10^3 the value of C_D when the cylinder touched the bed was about 30% greater than that in the free stream. On the other hand, Roshko et al. (1975) at a Reynolds number of 2×10^4 and Gotkun (1975) at Reynolds numbers between 0.9×10^5 and 2.5×10^5 found that C_D when the cylinder actually touched the wall was about 30% less than that in the free stream. They did, however, observe that, for values of the gap ratio ε/D greater than about 0.6, C_D was greater than the free stream value. It was only when ε/D was reduced below this value that C_D decreased.

Nonzero Concentrations of Sediment

The fluid drag on an isolated particle is different from that on a particle in a uniform dispersion of similar particles, as clearly shown by the reduction in fall velocity as concentration increases discussed in Chapter 3. Making use of (3.13) and (3.19), we obtain

$$\frac{(C_D)_W}{(C_D)_0} = \left(\frac{W_0}{W_C}\right)^2 = (1 - C)^{-2n} \tag{5.101}$$

In this equation the drag coefficient $(C_D)_W$ is for a fall velocity W_C in a uniform suspension with volumetric concentration C, whereas the drag coefficient $(C_D)_0$ relates to a fall velocity W_0 in a clear fluid. Richardson and Jeronimo (1979) found n to be equal to 4.6 at low Reynolds numbers and 2.3 at high Reynolds numbers. They also showed that for both low and high Reynolds number flows the drag coefficient $(C_D)_0$ for a clear fluid was related to the drag coefficient $(C_D)_C$ at concentration C with the same relative velocity of fluid and particle as for the clear fluid by

$$\frac{(C_D)_C}{(C_D)_0} = (1 - C)^{-4.6} \tag{5.102}$$

This expression is based on measurements with fluidized beds of spherical particles. As pointed out by Richardson and Jeronimo, the average drag exerted by the fluid on particles which are free to move is less than that obtained for fixed particles. For example, the drag coefficient obtained from (5.102) is almost equal to the low Reynolds number value calculated numerically for a fixed array of spheres by Zick and Homsy (1982) at large values of C but is about 60% below the fixed bed value for $C=0.3$.

When the concentration of sediment is significant the force exerted on an individual grain by its neighbors—for example, by interparticle collisions

—may be much larger than the fluid forces discussed above. This situation was investigated experimentally by Bagnold (1954). He found that the shear stress exerted by one layer of grains on the layer below is given by

Inertial regime ($\rho_s D^2 T/\mu^2 \lambda > 1500$):

$$T = 0.013 \rho_s (\lambda D)^2 \left(\frac{du}{dy}\right)^2 \tag{5.103}$$

Viscous regime ($\rho_s D^2 T/\mu^2 \lambda < 100$):

$$T = 2.2 \lambda^{3/2} \mu \left(\frac{du}{dy}\right) \tag{5.104}$$

with a smooth transition between these two extremes. In these expressions λ is the linear concentration:

$$\lambda = \frac{\text{grain diameter}}{\text{mean distance between grain centers}} \tag{5.105}$$

He also found that

$$T = P \tan \alpha \tag{5.106}$$

where $\tan \alpha$ is equal to 0.32 in the inertial regime and 0.75 in the viscous regime and P is the normal stress, which at any height z above the bed is given by

$$P = \int_z^\infty C \, dy \tag{5.107}$$

Similar experiments have been carried out by Savage and McKeown (1983). Although they confirm the general trend of Bagnold's results they suggest that (5.103) and (5.104) should only be regarded as a first approximation.

5.7.2. The Lift

A first approximation for the lift on a sphere close to a plane boundary in steady flow of an inviscid fluid is given by Milne Thomson (1968) as

$$L = -\frac{3}{64} \frac{\rho \pi D^2 \bar{u}_s}{(1 + 2\varepsilon/D)^4} \tag{5.108}$$

where ε is the gap between the sphere and the wall and $\bar{u}_s$ is the velocity of the surrounding fluid relative to that of the sphere. This is the same as the expression given in Section 5.5.2 for oscillatory flow except that the relative velocity is here assumed to be steady. Naheer's second approximation (see Section 5.5.2) will also apply to steady flow.

Rubinow and Keller (1961) obtained a solution for the force on a sphere spinning with angular velocity Ω and moving with relative velocity $\bar{u}_s$ through an unbounded viscous fluid. The lift is

$$L = \frac{\pi \rho D^3}{8} \Omega \bar{u}_s \tag{5.109}$$

at right angles to the axis of rotation and the direction of propagation.

A low Reynolds number solution has also been obtained by Saffman (1965) for the case of a sphere in a shear flow. The lift is

$$L = 20.3 \rho \bar{u}_s D^2 (\nu K)^{1/2} \tag{5.110}$$

where K is the velocity gradient of the fluid.

Measurements of lift on spheres in steady flows have been described by Young (1960), Swanson (1961), Coleman (1967), Willmarth and Enlow (1969), Thomschke (1971), Chen and Carstens (1973), Aksoy (1973), Bagnold (1974), Davies and Samad (1978), Lee (1979), and Willetts and Murray (1981). Lift measurements for hemispherical bed roughness have been made by Einstein and El Samni (1949) and Chepil (1958). In most cases the Reynolds number was relatively large ($\bar{u}_s D / \nu > 100$).

Most of the experimental results appear to agree that lift is positive (away from the bed) when the sphere is actually touching the bed but that it falls off rapidly the moment the sphere leaves the bed. Figure 5.28 shows that the variation of lift with distance from the bed is extremely complex. Just why the lift should fluctuate with height above the bed is not entirely clear but Willetts and Murray suggest that it is associated with the behavior of the wake, which is in turn influenced by the seepage under the sphere. In Fig. 5.28 C_L is the lift coefficient:

$$C_L = \frac{L}{\frac{1}{2} \rho \bar{u}_s^2 (\pi D^2 / 4)} \tag{5.111}$$

It would seem from the experimental results in Fig. 5.28 that the potential flow solution (5.108) is not applicable to spheres in steady flow even at high Reynolds numbers.

Figure 5.28 suggests that when the sphere is well away from the bed the

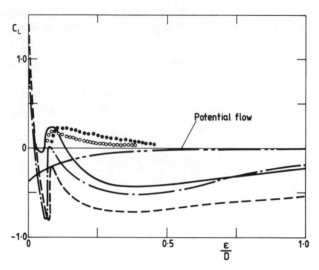

Figure 5.28. Variation of lift coefficient with distance from the bed for a sphere in steady flow. Water tunnel measurements of Willetts and Murray (1981): - - - $\bar{u}_sD/\nu=18,000$; — — — $\bar{u}_sD/\nu=$ 19,000; —— $\bar{u}_sD/\nu=23,000$. Wind tunnel measurements of Thomschke (1971): ● ● ● $\bar{u}_sD/\nu=360,000$; ○ ○ ○ $\bar{u}_sD/\nu=440,000$.

Reynolds number of the flow has a marked effect on the lift coefficient. On the other hand, for spheres actually touching the bed the variation of C_L with Reynolds number appears from Fig. 5.29 to be slight. The experimental scatter is too great for firm conclusions to be drawn but there is no evidence of significant Reynolds number dependence in the range $20 < \bar{u}_sD/\nu < 10^5$. In view of the very sharp variation of C_L with ε/D seen in Fig. 5.28 the scatter in Fig. 5.29 is hardly surprising. Bagnold (1974) showed that even small leakage under the sphere could make a considerable difference to C_L.

Figure 5.29 is for a single sphere resting on a flat bed. Measurements of C_L for a sphere resting on a bed of similar spheres have been made by Coleman (1967) and also by Davies and Samad (1978). The experimental scatter is even greater than that shown in Fig. 5.29 but the values of C_L appear to be generally similar to those for a flat bed when $\bar{u}_sD/\nu$ is greater than about 100. However, both Davies and Samad and Coleman suggest that C_L becomes negative at smaller values of $\bar{u}_sD/\nu$. The scatter is too great for definite conclusions.

The mean value of C_L in Fig. 5.29 appears to be about 0.5, which is considerably greater than the 0.178 obtained by Einstein and El Samni (1949). In fact Chepil (1958) suggested that Einstein and El Samni's value ought really to be 0.0624. The experimental value of C_L obtained by Chepil himself was 0.07. The main reason for these different values is that the experimental

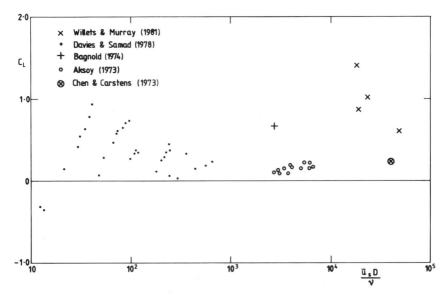

Figure 5.29. Measurements of the lift coefficient for an isolated sphere resting on a plane bed in steady flow.

arrangement is different. The results shown in Fig. 5.29 are for an isolated sphere resting on a plane bed, whereas both Einstein and El Samni's and Chepil's experiments were carried out with hemispheres.

For circular cylinders the potential flow solutions of Nath and Yamamoto (1974) and Jeffreys (1929) [(5.77) and (5.78)] also apply to steady flow. However, in view of the results for spheres seen in Fig. 5.28, it is not to be expected that these solutions would give good agreement with experiment. Measurements of the lift on circular cylinders have been made by Wilson and Caldwell (1970), Bagnold (1974), and Roshko et al. (1975). These studies show that the lift coefficient increases steadily as the distance ε from the wall decreases. This is the opposite of the behavior predicted by Nath and Yamamoto's potential flow solution.

The reason why the potential flow solution gives good agreement with experiment in oscillatory flow for values of $U_0 T/D < 5$ but poor agreement in steady flow is that the theory takes no account of boundary layer separation. At small values of $U_0 T/D$ oscillatory flows do not separate, whereas boundary layer separation occurs in steady flow for all Reynolds numbers greater than about 4.

It is also possible to obtain analytical solutions for the lift on circular cylinders at very low Reynolds numbers. This has been done by Takaisi (1955). When the gap ε between the cylinder and the bed is large compared with D this solution reduces to

$$C_L = \frac{\pi(1 + 2\varepsilon/D)}{[\frac{1}{2} - \ln(2 + 4\varepsilon/D)]^2 - \frac{1}{4}} \tag{5.112}$$

There are no experimental results available at sufficiently low Reynolds numbers to test this expression.

Waves and Currents

5.8. CURRENTS COLLINEAR WITH THE DIRECTION OF WAVE PROPAGATION

5.8.1. The Relationship between Bed Friction and Wave Height Attenuation

This relationship is of interest both because it is often important to know how bed shear will affect the height of the waves approaching a coastal structure and also because one of the main methods of determining bed shear is from measurements of the wave height attenuation.

When there is a superimposed mean current the calculation is considerably more complicated than with waves alone because the change in mean water level with distance cannot be neglected. Even when there is no mean current waves produce a change in mean water level but, at least for small-amplitude waves, this has negligible effect on the attenuation coefficient.

Even more difficult is the question of how to deal with turbulence. It is clear from the discussion in Chapter 2 that unless the steady current is very weak the flow will almost always be turbulent. Very little is known about the interaction between the turbulence and the steady and oscillatory components of velocity. This means that in order to obtain a solution a number of assumptions have to be made which may be unjustified.

This problem has been examined by Jonsson (1966a) and, more recently, by Brevik and Aas (1980). The principal assumptions they make are as follows:

1. The steady current $\bar{U}$ does not vary with height. This assumption is not entirely necessary but simplifies the algebra.

2. The bed shear stress τ_{WC} due to the combined action of waves and currents may be expressed as

$$\tau_{WC} = \rho \frac{f_{WC}}{2} (\bar{U} + U_\infty \cos \omega t) |\bar{U} + U_\infty \cos \omega t| \qquad (5.113)$$

where the friction factor f_{WC} is constant in time and space. This assumption is most open to question.

3. The rate of energy dissipation per unit area is

$$P = \tau_{WC} (\bar{U} + U_\infty \cos \omega t) \qquad (5.114)$$

The energy balance for the mean motion may be written as

$$\frac{d}{dx} \left[\frac{E}{\omega_r} (\bar{U} + c_{gr}) \right] + \left(\frac{\bar{P} - \bar{\tau}_{WC} \bar{U}}{\omega_r} \right) = 0 \qquad (5.115)$$

Here $\bar{P}$ and $\bar{\tau}_{WC}$ are the time-mean values of P and τ_{WC} and ω_r and c_{gr} are the angular frequency and group velocity of the waves in a frame of reference moving with the mean current. Relative to axes moving with the mean flow the waves behave, to the present order of approximation, as if they were in still water. Consequently, ω_r and c_{gr} may be calculated from the expressions for waves in the absence of a mean current given at the beginning of Chapter 1. The value of U_∞ in (5.113) and (5.114) is also given by the expression for waves alone.

Substituting from (5.113) and (5.114) into (5.115) and neglecting the change in depth, which introduces only a second-order correction, we obtain

$$f_{WC} = -\frac{gH}{2\beta_1} (c_{gr} + \bar{U}) \frac{dH}{dx} \qquad (5.116)$$

where

$$\beta_1 = \overline{|\bar{U} + U_\infty \cos \omega t|^3} - \overline{\bar{U}(\bar{U} + U_\infty \cos \omega t)^2} \qquad (5.117)$$

When $\bar{U} \ll U_\infty$, (5.116) becomes

$$f_{WC} = -\frac{3\pi}{8} \frac{gHc_{gr}}{U_\infty^3} \frac{dH}{dx} \qquad (5.118)$$

and when $\bar{U} \gg U_\infty$

$$f_{WC} = -\frac{gH}{2U_\infty^2} \left(1 + \frac{c_{gr}}{\bar{U}} \right) \frac{dH}{dx} \qquad (5.119)$$

5.8.2.   Formulas for Bed Friction

Equation (5.116) allows the attenuation of wave height to be calculated if f_{WC} is known, but how should f_{WC} be determined? If the flow were laminar the bed friction would be equal to the sum of the components due to the steady and oscillatory flows separately. In turbulent flows the situation is much more complex. Jonsson (1966a) suggested that the following expression could be used as a rough approximation:

$$f_{WC} = \frac{U_\infty f_w + \bar{U} C_f}{(U_\infty + \bar{U})} \qquad (5.120)$$

Here f_w is the friction factor for the waves in the absence of any current, discussed in Sections 5.1, 5.2, and 5.3, and C_f is the friction factor for the steady current alone defined by (5.82).

Figure 5.30 shows how the value $(f_{WC})_{\mathrm{calc}}$ of the friction factor obtained from (5.120) compares with the value $(f_{WC})_{\mathrm{meas}}$ obtained, with the aid of (5.116), from measurements of wave height attenuation. All of the measurements were made in laboratory channels. In each case the value of f_w used in (5.120) was that obtained with the same setting of the wave generator in the absence of any current. The overall picture seen in Fig. 5.30 would not be

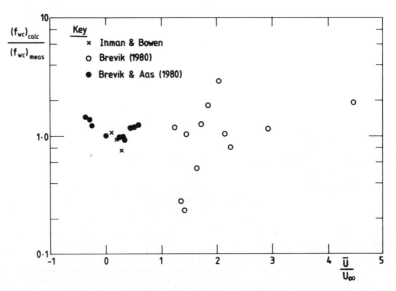

Figure 5.30. Comparison of calculated and measured values of f_{WC}.

significantly different if the actual wave height and period in the combined flow were used to calculate f_w.

Clearly, the value of f_{WC} calculated from (5.120) must equal the measured value when there is no steady current. The close agreement between calculation and measurement shown in Fig. 5.30 in the vicinity of $\bar{U}/U_\infty$ equal to zero is thus only to be expected. At higher values of $\bar{U}/U_\infty$ the calculated value of f_{WC} differs from the measured value by a factor of up to three or four. Whether this is caused by defects in (5.120) or in (5.116) or in the laboratory measurements is not clear. On the other hand, the fact that the points scatter more or less equally on either side of the line of perfect agreement is, perhaps, encouraging. Almost all of the measurements in Fig. 5.30 are for currents in the same direction as that of wave propagation. The three points shown for opposing currents ($\bar{U}/U_\infty$ negative) are not in particularly good agreement with (5.120). For opposing currents it would probably be more logical to use $|\bar{U}|$ in that equation.

The various theoretical models mentioned in Section 2.10 may also be used to predict the value of f_{WC}. This is usually a very laborious process because many of the solutions involve Bessel functions. An example of how this may be done is given by Tanaka and Shuto (1981), who also suggest the following approximate expression, valid for $U_\infty/\omega y_0 > 50$:

$$\left(\frac{f_{WC}}{2}\right)^{1/2} = \frac{0.4}{\left[\ln\left(\dfrac{d}{y_0}\right)-1\right]}\frac{\bar{U}}{U_\infty}$$

$$+\frac{0.4}{\pi\left\{0.25+0.101\left[\ln\left(\dfrac{\omega y_0}{U_\infty}\right)-\frac{1}{2}\ln(f_{WC})+2.42\right]^2\right\}^{1/2}} \tag{5.121}$$

For smooth beds

$$y_0=\frac{0.111\nu}{U_\infty(f_{WC}/2)^{1/2}} \tag{5.122}$$

and for rough beds

$$y_0=\frac{D}{30} \tag{5.123}$$

These expressions appear to give reasonable agreement with available experimental data.

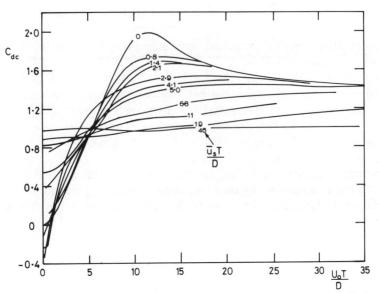

Figure 5.31. Variation of C_{dc} for circular cylinders with $U_0 T/D$ and $\bar{u}_s T/D$ (after Verley and Moe, 1979).

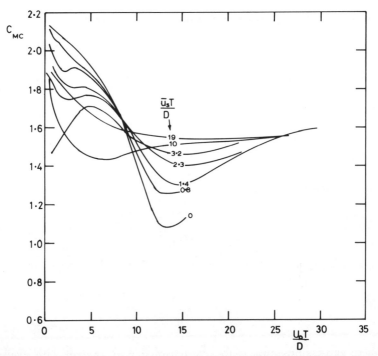

Figure 5.32. Variation of C_{MC} for circular cylinders with $U_0 T/D$ and $\bar{u}_s T/D$ (after Verley and Moe, 1979).

236

5.8.3. Forces on Rigid Bodies

It is customary to determine the force on the body by means of a modified version of Morison's equation. For cylinders

$$F = C_{dc} \tfrac{1}{2} \rho D (\bar{u}_s - U_0 \cos \omega t) |\bar{u}_s - U_0 \cos \omega t| + C_{MC} \rho \frac{\pi D^2}{4} \frac{du_s}{dt} \quad (5.124)$$

Figures 5.31 and 5.32 show how C_{dc} and C_{MC} vary with $U_0 T/D$ and $\bar{u}_s T/D$ according to Verley and Moe (1979). These curves were obtained for values of βD equal to about 30, which is why different curves are not given for different Reynolds numbers. It is clear that a superimposed steady current produces significant variation in C_{dc} and C_{MC} compared with the values obtained for pure oscillatory flow.

Further data are given by Mercier (1973) and Sarpkaya (1977). There is no information yet on the effect of boundary proximity in this sort of flow or on the values of the coefficients to be used for spheres

5.9. CURRENTS AT RIGHT ANGLES TO THE DIRECTION OF WAVE PROPAGATION

5.9.1. Bed Friction

The problem of currents parallel, or at a small angle α, to the line of wave crests has been investigated by Bijker (1966). He assumes that the shear stress on the bed is given by Prandtl's steady flow formula

$$\tau_0 = \rho l^2 \left(\frac{\partial u}{\partial y} \right)^2_{y=0} \quad (5.125)$$

and that the mixing length is

$$l = Ky \quad (5.126)$$

In the viscous sublayer at the bed the velocity distribution will be approximately linear and the shear stress constant. Thus

$$\left(\frac{\partial u}{\partial y} \right)_{y=0} = \frac{u'}{\delta} \quad (5.127)$$

where δ is the thickness of the viscous sublayer and u' is the velocity at height $y = \delta$. Thus, from (5.125), (5.126), and (5.127),

$$\tau_0 = \rho K^2 (u')^2 \tag{5.128}$$

The velocity u' is assumed to be the vector sum of the steady and oscillatory velocity components. The steady current at $y = \delta$ is taken to be $\bar{u}_*/K$ and the oscillatory component to be $p U_\infty \cos \omega t$, where p is a coefficient that has to be determined from experiment. For small values of α the time-mean components of the resultant bed shear stress are found to be closely approximated by

$$\frac{\tau'}{\tau_{0c}} = 1 + (0.046 - 0.018 \cos 2\alpha) \left(\frac{U_\infty}{C_f^{1/2} \bar{U}} \right)^{3/2} \tag{5.129}$$

and

$$\frac{\tau''}{\tau_{0c}} = 0.037 \sin 2\alpha \left(\frac{U_\infty}{C_f^{1/2} \bar{U}} \right)^{5/4} \tag{5.130}$$

where τ' is the component parallel to the mean current, τ'' is that at right angles, and τ_{0c} is here the shear stress due to the current alone. The coefficient p was found from experiment to be 0.45 and the Karman constant K was taken as 0.4.

The experiments used to determine p were carried out in a wave basin and shear stresses were deduced from the slope of the mean water level in the direction of the steady current. This method involves the measurement of very small differences in head and is consequently subject to significant errors. Bijker found that the standard deviation for measurements of the bed roughness was about 50% of the mean value. Even using the experimentally determined value of p, the value of τ' given by (5.129) was observed to differ from the measured value by a factor of up to three or four.

At first sight it may seem slightly surprising that interaction between a steady current and an oscillatory flow produces a shear stress at an angle to the mean current except when the wave and current are directly in line or directly perpendicular. The reason is that the shear stress is proportional to the square of the velocity, as seen in (5.125). During one half-cycle the oscillatory flow has a component in the same direction as the steady current, whereas during the other half-cycle it is in the opposite direction. The fact that the velocity is squared results in a nonzero mean. This resultant shear stress at an angle to the mean current produces refraction of the steady flow.

A somewhat similar formula has been given by Swart (1974) for the case of the longshore drift current:

$$\frac{\tau'}{\tau_{0c}}=1+(1.91-1.32\sin\alpha_b)\left[\frac{\bar{v}}{U_\infty}\left(\frac{C_f}{f_w}\right)^{1/2}\right]^{(1.24-0.08\sin\alpha_b)} \qquad (5.131)$$

5.9.2. Wave Height Attenuation

When the current is at right angles to the direction of wave propagation Bijker's theory gives the time-varying bed shear stress in the direction of wave propagation as

$$\tau_0=0.13C_f^{1/2}\rho\,\bar{U}U_\infty\cos\omega t\left(1+\frac{0.065}{C_f}\frac{U_\infty^2}{\bar{U}^2}\cos^2\omega t\right)^{1/2} \qquad (5.132)$$

Since there is no mean current in the direction of wave propagation the energy dissipation and wave height attenuation may be calculated using (5.132) along with (5.6) and (5.13).

When the current is not quite parallel to the wave crests the refraction of the current makes any calculation of wave height attenuation much more complex. In view of the uncertainties over the nature of the turbulence under these conditions such a calculation is unlikely to be reliable.

5.10. EXAMPLES

1. Progressive waves of height 3 m and period 15 s are propagating in water of depth 20 m over a horizontal bed. The bed consists of sand of median diameter 0.8 mm and there is no superimposed mean current.

(a) What is the amplitude of the bed shear stress? From Example 1 of Section 4.18, the bed is covered with vortex ripples of length 1.6 m and height 0.16 m. The amplitude of the velocity just outside the boundary layer at the bed is

$$U_\infty=0.924 \text{ m/s}$$

Equation (1.106) gives the bed roughness length as

$$k_s=0.4 \text{ m}$$

Thus

$$\frac{U_\infty k_s}{\nu}=370\times10^3$$

It is clear from Fig. 2.1 that the bed is in the fully developed rough turbulent regime. Since

$$\frac{a}{k_s} = \frac{U_\infty}{\omega k_s} = 5.51$$

we see from Fig. 5.8 that there is little difference between the various expressions for the friction factor. A mean value would be

$$f = 0.11$$

Thus the amplitude of the bed shear stress is

$$\hat{\tau}_0 = \tfrac{1}{2}\rho U_\infty^2 f$$
$$= 47.0 \text{ N/m}^2$$

(b)   What is the wave height attenuation due to bed shear? The wave height attenuation due to bed friction may be calculated from (5.45). Making use of Kajiura's model, Fig. 5.7 gives

$$\theta_1 = 47.5°$$

Hence, from (5.46),

$$f_e = \frac{3\pi}{8} \times 0.11 \cos(47.5) = 0.088$$

Thus, from (5.45), the wave height attenuation due to bed shear is

$$\frac{dH}{dx} = -\frac{4 \times 9 \times (0.0318)^2 \times 0.088}{3\pi \sinh(0.636)(1.272 + \sinh 1.272)}$$
$$= -0.17 \times 10^{-3}$$

(c)   What would be the maximum horizontal force on a circular cylinder of diameter 0.25 m mounted with its axis parallel to the wave crests at a height of 1 m above the bed? The horizontal force on the cylinder is given by (5.62). For these waves the amplitude of the fluid velocity at the level of the center of the cylinder is

$$U_0 = \frac{3\pi}{15} \frac{\cosh 0.0318}{\sinh 0.636} = 0.925$$

Thus

$$\frac{U_0 T}{D} = \frac{0.925 \times 15}{0.25} = 55.5$$

$$\beta D = \left(\frac{\pi}{15 \times 10^{-6}}\right)^{1/2} 0.25 = 114$$

$$\frac{\varepsilon}{D} = \frac{0.875}{0.25} = 3.5$$

This value of the gap ratio ε/D is sufficiently large for the effect of boundary proximity to be neglected. Thus from Fig. 5.16 and 5.17

$$C_d = 0.53$$

$$C_M = 1.77$$

From (5.62),

$$F = 0.53 \times 500 \times 0.25 \times (0.925)^2 \cos \omega t |\cos \omega t|$$

$$+ 1.77 \times 1000 \times \pi \times \frac{0.25^2}{4} \times \frac{2\pi}{15} \times 0.925 \sin \omega t$$

$$= 56.7 \cos \omega t |\cos \omega t| + 33.7 \sin \omega t$$

Thus the maximum horizontal force on the cylinder is 61.7 N/m of length.

2. Waves of height 3 m and period 14 s are propagating in the same direction as a steady current with surface velocity 1 m/s. The bed is horizontal and consists of sand of median diameter 0.8 mm. The depth of water is 20 m.

(a) What is the wave height attenuation due to bed shear? From Example 2 of Section 4.18 we have for the current alone

$$\bar{U} = 0.84 \text{ m/s}$$

$$\tau_0 = \rho \bar{u}_*^2 = 4.32 \text{ N/m}^2$$

Consequently, the friction factor for the current alone is

$$C_f = \frac{\tau_0}{\rho \bar{U}^2/2} = 0.0122$$

The wave period of 14 s is for axes fixed in space. For axes moving with the mean current (1.128) gives

$$\frac{2\pi}{14}=(gb \tanh 20b)^{1/2}+0.84b$$

Thus by iteration

$$b=0.0321 \text{ m}^{-1}$$

and

$$\omega_r=0.422 \text{ s}^{-1}$$

where the subscript r indicates that the frequency is relative to axes moving with the current. The group velocity relative to these moving axes is given by (1.23):

$$c_{gr}=\frac{0.422}{2 \times 0.0321}\left(1+\frac{1.284}{\sinh 1.284}\right)=11.64 \text{ m/s}$$

and the velocity just outside the boundary layer by (1.19):

$$U_{\infty}=0.92 \text{ m/s}$$

In this example the wave conditions relative to axes moving with the mean current are almost the same as those in Example 1 of this section. Following the procedure outlined there, we find that the friction factor for waves alone is

$$f_w=0.11$$

Thus Jonsson's (5.120) for the friction factor in the combined flow gives

$$f_{wc}=\frac{0.92 \times 0.11+0.84 \times 0.0122}{(0.92+0.84)}=0.063$$

From (5.117)

$$\beta_1=1.659-0.948=0.711$$

Thus (5.116) gives the wave height attenuation due to bed friction as

$$\frac{dH}{dx} = -\frac{2 \times 0.711 \times 0.063}{9.81 \times 3(11.64 + 0.84)} = -0.24 \times 10^{-3}$$

(b) Estimate the maximum horizontal force on a circular cylinder of diameter 0.25 m mounted with its axis parallel to the wave crests at a height of 1 m above the bed. The amplitude of the oscillatory velocity of the fluid at the level of the center of the cylinder is the same for stationary axes as for axes moving with the mean current:

$$U_0 = \frac{3 \times 0.422 \times \cosh 0.0321}{2 \times \sinh 0.642} = 0.922 \text{ m/s}$$

Thus

$$\frac{U_0 T}{D} = 51.6$$

$$\beta D = \left(\frac{\pi}{14 \times 10^{-6}}\right)^{1/2} 0.25 = 118$$

$$\frac{\varepsilon}{D} = 3.5$$

The gap ratio ε/D is sufficiently large for the effect of boundary proximity to be neglected.

Making use of the values of $\bar{u}_*$ and k_s calculated in Example 2 of Section 4.18, (1.99) gives the mean velocity at the level of the cylinder axis as

$$\bar{u}_s = 2.5 \times 0.0657 \ln\left(\frac{30 \times 1}{1.36}\right) = 0.508 \text{ m/s}$$

Hence

$$\frac{\bar{u}_s T}{D} = 28.4$$

The problem lies in the choice of the values of C_{dc} and C_{MC} to be used in (5.124). If we assume that these coefficients have the same values as for waves alone, Fig. 5.16 and 5.17 give

$$C_{dc} = 0.52$$
$$C_{MC} = 1.77$$

Substituting in (5.124), the maximum horizontal force per meter length of cylinder is

$$F = 137 \text{ N}$$

On the other hand, if we neglect the difference in the value of βD between the present case and that for Fig. 5.31 and 5.32 we obtain (with some extrapolation)

$$C_{dc} = 1.1$$
$$C_{MC} = 1.6$$

Substitution of these values in (5.124) gives the maximum horizontal force per meter length as

$$F = 282 \text{ N}$$

In each case the major contribution to the force comes from the term involving the coefficient C_{dc}. Figure 5.31 shows that for large values of $\bar{u}_s T/D$, as in the present case, the value of C_{dc} is almost independent of Keulegan-Carpenter number $U_0 T/D$. It would seem that under these conditions the drag component of the in-line force is behaving as if the flow were effectively steady. This suggests that C_{dc} may be estimated from the steady flow curve for C_D. The Reynolds number for maximum velocity relative to the cylinder is

$$\frac{u_s D}{\nu} = 3.6 \times 10^5$$

From Fig. 5.26, this is very close to the transition at which the drag coefficient drops suddenly. Thus the value of C_{dc} on this basis would be between 1.0 and about 0.3, which is not too far from the values obtained from Fig. 5.16 and 5.31.

REFERENCES

Aksoy, S. (1973). Fluid force acting on a sphere near a solid boundary. *Proc. 15th Congress IAHR Istanbul*; pp. 217–224.

Bagnold, R. A. (1946). Motion of waves in shallow water. Interaction of waves and sand bottoms. *Proc. Roy. Soc. Ser. A.* **187**: 1–15.

Bagnold, R. A. (1954). Experiments on a gravity-free dispersion of large solid spheres in a newtonian fluid under shear. *Proc. Roy. Soc. Ser. A.* **225**: 49–64.

Bagnold, R. A. (1974). Fluid forces on a body in shear flow; experimental use of stationary flow. *Proc. Roy. Soc. Ser. A.* **340**: 147–171.

Bakker, W. T. (1974). Sand concentration in oscillatory flow. *Proc. 14th Conf. Coastal Eng. Copenhagen*, pp. 1129–1148.

Bassett, A. B. (1888). On the motion of a sphere in a viscous fluid. *Phil. Trans. Roy Soc. Ser. A.* **179**: 43–63.

Bayazit, M. (1969). Resistance to reversing flows over movable beds. *Proc. A.S.C.E. J. Hydraul. Div.* **95** (HY4): 1109–1128.

Biesel, F. (1949). Calcul de l'amortissement d'une houle dans un liquide visqueux de profondeur finie. *La Houille Blanche* **4**: 630–634.

Bijker, E. W. (1966). The increase of bed shear in a current due to wave motion. *Proc. 10th Conf. Coastal Eng. Tokyo*, pp. 746–765.

Bijker, E. W., Kalkwijk, J. P. T., and Pieters, T. (1974). Mass transport in gravity waves on a sloping bottom. *Proc. 14th Conf. Coastal Eng. Copenhagen*, pp. 447–465.

Blasius, H. (1908). Grenzschichten in Flüssigkeiten mit kleiner Reibung. *Z. Math. Phys.* **56**: 1–37.

Boussinesq, J. (1885). Sur la resistance qu'oppose un liquide ... au mouvement varie d'une sphère solide ... *Compt. Rendu Acad. Sci. Paris.* **100**: 935–937.

Bretschneider, C. L. (1954). Field investigation of wave energy loss of shallow water ocean waves. Beach Erosion Board. Tech. Memo 46.

Brevik, I. (1980). Flume experiments on waves and currents. II. Smooth bed. *Coastal Eng.* **4**: 89–110.

Brevik, I. (1981). Oscillatory rough turbulent boundary layers. *Proc. A.S.C.E. J. Waterw. Port Coastal Ocean Div.* **107** (WW3): pp. 175–188.

Brevik, I. and Aas, B. (1980). Flume experiments on waves and currents. I. Rippled bed. *Coastal Eng.* **3**: 149–177.

British Ship Research Association (1976). A critical evaluation of the data on wave force coefficients. Br. Ship Res. Assoc. Wallsend upon Tyne, Contract Rep. W-278.

Bugliarello, G. (1956). La resistenza al moto accelerato di sfere in acqua. *Ric. Sci.* **26**: 437–461.

Carry, C. (1956). Calcul de l'amortissement d'une houle dans un liquide visqueux en profondeur finie. *La Houille Blanche* **11**: 75–79.

Carstens, M. R. (1952). Accelerated motion of spherical particles. *Trans. A.G.U.* **33**: 713–721.

Carstens, M. R., Neilson, F. M. and Altinbilek, H. D. (1969). Bed forms generated in the laboratory under an oscillatory flow: analytical and experimental study. C.E.R.C. Tech. Memo. No. 28.

Carty, J. J. (1957). Resistance coefficients for spheres on a plane boundary. B.Sc. Thesis. Dept. Of Civil Eng. M.I.T.

Chen, C. and Carstens, M. R. (1973). Mechanics of removal of a spherical particle from a flat bed. *Proc. 15th Cong. IAHR Istanbul*, pp. 147–158.

Chepil, W. S. (1958). The use of evenly spaced hemispheres to evaluate aerodynamic forces on a soil surface. *Trans. A.G.U.* **39**: 397–404.

Coleman, N. L. (1967). A theoretical and experimental study of drag and lift forces acting on a sphere resting on a hypothetical streambed. *Proc. 12th Congress IAHR. Fort Collins*, pp. 185–192.

Coleman, N. L. (1972). The drag coefficient of a stationary sphere on a boundary of similar spheres. *La Houille Blanche* **27**: 17–21.

Coleman, N. L. (1977). Extension of the drag coefficient function for a stationary sphere on a boundary of similar spheres. *La Houille Blanche* **32**: 325–328.

Dalrymple, R. A. and Liu, P. L-F. (1978). Waves over soft muds: a two layer model. *J. Phys. Oceanogr.* **8**: 1121–1131.

Davies, T. R. H. and Samad, M. F. A. (1978). Fluid dynamic lift on a bed particle. *Proc. A.S.C.E. J. Hydraul. Div.* **104** (HY8): 1171–1182.

Dean, W. R. and O'Neill, M. E. (1963). A slow motion of viscous liquid caused by the rotation of a solid sphere. *Mathematika* **10**: 13–24.

Du Buat, P. L. G. (1786). *Principes d'Hydraulique*, 2nd ed., Vol. 2. L'Imprimerie de Monsieur, Paris, pp. 226–259.

Eagleson, P. S. (1962). Laminar damping of oscillatory waves. *Proc. A.S.C.E. J. Hydraul. Div.* **88** (HY3): 155–181.

Eagleson, P. S., Dean, R. G. and Peralta, L. A. (1958). The mechanics of the motion of discrete spherical and bottom sediment particles due to shoaling waves. Beach Erosion Board. Tech. Memo. 104.

Einstein, H. A. and El Samni, S. A. (1949). Hydrodynamic forces on a rough wall. *Rev. Mod. Phys.* **21** (3): 520–524.

Engelund, F. A. and Hansen, E. (1972). *A Monograph on Sediment Transport*. Teknisk Forlag, Copenhagen.

Gade, H. G. (1958). Effects of a non-rigid, impermeable bottom on plane surface waves in shallow water. *J. Mar. Res.* **16**: 61–82.

Garde, R. J. and Sethuraman, S. (1969). Variation of the drag coefficient of a sphere rolling along a boundary. *La Houille Blanche* **24**: 727–732.

Gotkun, S. (1975). The drag and lift characteristics of a cylinder placed near a plane surface. M.S. Thesis Naval Postgraduate School. Monterey. California.

Grace, R. A. and Zee, G. T. Y. (1978). Further tests on ocean wave forces on sphere. *Proc. A.S.C.E. J. Waterw. Harbor Coastal Ocean Div.* **104** (WW1): 83–88.

Grosch, C. E. (1962). Laminar boundary layer under a wave. *Phys. Fluids.* **5**: 1163–1167.

Grosch, C. E., Ward, L. W., and Lukasik, S. J. (1960). Viscous dissipation of shallow water waves. *Phys. Fluids.* **3**: 477–479.

Hamilton, W. S. and Lindell, J. E. (1971). Fluid force analysis and accelerating sphere tests. *Proc. A.S.C.E. J. Hydraul. Div.* **97** (HY6): 805–817.

Hogben, N., Miller, B. L., Searle, J. W., and Ward, G. (1977). Estimation of fluid loading on offshore structures. *Proc. Inst. Civil Eng.* **63** (2): 515–562.

Hunt, J. N. (1952). Amortissement par viscosité de la houle sur un fond incliné dans un canal de largeur finie. *La Houille Blanche* **7**: 836–842.

Hunt, J. N. (1959). On the damping of gravity waves propagated over a permeable surface. *J. Geophys. Res.* **64**: 437–442.

Hunt, J. N. (1963). Dissipation in water waves. *Phys. Fluids.* **7**: 156–157.

Inman, D. L. and Bowen, A. J. (1962). Flume experiments on sand transport by waves and currents. *Proc. 8th Conf. Coastal Eng. Mexico,* pp. 137–150.

Ippen, A. T. and Kulin, G. (1957). The effect of boundary resistance on solitary waves. *La Houille Blanche* **12**: 390–407.

Ippen, A. T. and Mitchell, M. M. (1957). The damping of the solitary wave from boundary shear measurements. M.I.T. Hydrodyn. Lab. Tech. Rep. 23.

Iwagaki, Y. and Kakinuma, T. (1967). On the bottom friction factors off five Japanese coasts. *Coastal Eng. Jpn.* **10**: 13–22.

Iwagaki, Y. and Tsuchiya, Y. (1966). Laminar damping of oscillatory waves due to bottom friction. *Proc. 10th Conf. Coastal Eng. Tokyo,* pp. 149–174.

Jeffreys, H. (1929). On the transport of sediment by streams. *Proc. Camb. Philos. Soc.* **25**: 272–276.

Johns, B. (1975). The form of the velocity profile in a turbulent shear wave boundary layer. *J. Geophys. Res.* **80** (36): 5109–5012.

Johns, B. (1977). Residual flow and boundary shear stress in the turbulent bottom layer beneath waves. *J. Phys. Oceanogr.* **7**: 733–738.

Jonsson, I. G. (1963). Measurements in the turbulent wave boundary layer. *Proc. 10th Congress IAHR. London,* pp. 85–92.

Jonsson, I. G. (1966a). The friction factor for a current superimposed by waves. Tech. Univ. Denmark. Coastal Eng. Lab. Basic Research Prog. Rep. 11, pp. 2–12.

Jonsson, I. G. (1966b). Wave boundary layers and friction factors. *Proc. 10th Conf. Coastal Eng. Tokyo,* pp. 127–148.

Jonsson, I. G. (1980). A new approach to oscillatory rough turbulent boundary layers. *Ocean Eng.* **7**: 109–152.

Jonsson, I. G. and Carlsen, N. A. (1976). Experimental and theoretical investigations in an oscillatory turbulent boundary layer. *J. Hydraul. Res.* **14** (1): 45–60.

Kajiura, K. (1968). A model of the bottom boundary layer in water waves. *Bull. Earthquake Res. Inst.* **46**: 75–123.

Kamphuis, J. W. (1975). Friction factors under oscillatory waves. *Proc. A.S.C.E. J. Waterw. Harbors Coastal Eng. Div.* **101** (WW2): 135–144.

Karanfilian, S. K. and Kotas, T. J. (1978). Drag on a sphere in unsteady motion in a liquid at rest. *J. Fluid Mech.* **81**: 85–96.

Keulegan, G. H. (1948). Gradual damping of solitary waves. *J. Res. Nat. Bur. Standards.* **40**: 487–498.

Keulegan, G. H. (1959). Energy dissipation in standing waves in rectangular basins. *J. Fluid Mech.* **6**: 33–50.

Krishnaiyar, N. C. (1923). An experimental determination of the inertia of a sphere vibrating in a liquid. *Philos. Mag.* Ser. 6. **46**: 1049–1053.

Lamb, H. (1932). *Hydrodynamics,* 6th ed. Cambridge University Press, Cambridge.

Lau, J. and Travis, B. (1973). Slowly varying Stokes waves and submarine longshore bars. *J. Geophys. Res.* **78** (21): 4489–4497.

Lee, K. C. (1979). Aerodynamic interaction between two spheres at Reynolds numbers around 10^4. *Aero. Q.* **15**: 371–385.

Lhermitte, P. (1958). Contribution à l'étude de la couche limite des houles progressives. C.O.E.C. No 136. Imprimerie Nationale. Paris.

Lin, C. J., Lee, K. J., and Sather, N. F. (1970). Slow motion of two spheres in a shear field. *J. Fluid Mech.* **43**: 35–47.

Liu, P. L-F. (1973). Damping of water waves over porous bed. *Proc. A.S.C.E. J. Hydraul. Div.* **99** (HY12): 2263–2271.

Lofquist, K. E. B. (1980). Measurements of oscillatory drag on sand ripples. *Proc. 17th Conf. Coastal Eng. Sydney.*

Longuet-Higgins, M. S. (1981). Oscillating flow over steep sand ripples. *J. Fluid Mech.* **107**: 1–35.

Lukasik, S. J. Grosch, C. E. (1963). Discussion of "Laminar damping of oscillatory waves" (by P. S. Eagleson). *Proc. A.S.C.E. J. Hydraul. Div.* **89** (HY1): 231–239.

Macpherson, H. (1980). The attenuation of water waves over a non-rigid bed. *J. Fluid Mech.* **97**: 721–742.

Mallard, W. W. and Dalrymple, R. A. (1977). Water waves propagating over a deformable bottom. *Proc. 9th Offshore Tech. Conf. OTC 2895. Houston*, pp. 141–146.

Martin, H. (1925). Uber tonhohe und dampfung der schwingungen von saiten in verschiedenen flussigkeiten. *Ann. Phys. Lpz.* **77** (4): 627–657.

Maull, D. J. and Milliner, M. G. (1978). Forces on a circular cylinder having a complex periodic motion. In *Mechanics of wave-induced forces on cylinders*, T. L. Shaw, Ed. Fearon Pitman Publishers, Belmont, Calif., pp. 490–502.

Maull, D. J. and Norman, S. J. (1978). A horizontal circular cylinder under waves. In *Mechanics of wave-induced forces on cylinders*, T. L. Shaw, Ed. Fearon Pitman Publishers, Belmont, Calif., pp. 359–378.

Mercier, J. A. (1973). Large amplitude oscillations of a circular cylinder in a low-speed stream. Ph.D. Thesis. Stevens Inst. of Tech.

Milne Thomson, L. M. (1968). *Theoretical Hydrodynamics*, 5th ed. Macmillan, New York.

Morison, J. R., O'Brien, M. P., Johnson, J. W., and Schaaf, S. A. (1950). Forces exerted by surface waves on piles. *Pet. Trans.* **189**: 149–157, 193–212.

Murray, J. D. (1965). Viscous damping of gravity waves over a permeable bed. *J. Geophys. Res.* **70** (10): 2325–2331.

Naheer, E. (1977). Stability of bottom armoring under the attack of solitary waves. Calif. Inst. of Tech. W.M. Keck Lab. Report KH-R-34.

Nath, J. H. and Yamamoto, T. (1974). Forces from fluid flow around objects. *Proc. 14th Conf. Coastal Eng. Copenhagen*, pp. 1808–1827.

Nath, J. H., Yamamoto, T., and Wright, C. (1976). Wave forces on pipes near the ocean bottom. *Proc. 8th Ann. Offshore Tech. Conf. Houston*, pp. 741–748.

Odar, F. and Hamilton, W. S. (1964). Forces on a sphere accelerating in a viscous fluid. *J. Fluid Mech.* **18**: 302–314.

O'Neill, M. E. (1964). A slow motion of viscous liquid caused by a slowly moving solid sphere. *Mathematika* **11**: 65–74.

Poisson, S. D. (1832). Sur les mouvements simultanés d'un pendule et de l'air environnant. *Mem. Sci. Paris.* **11**: 521–582.

Prevost, J. H., Eide, O., and Anderson, K. H. (1975). Discussion of "Wave induced pressures in permeable seabeds" (by H. Moshagen and A. Torum). *Proc. A.S.C.E. J. Waterw. Harbors Coastal Eng. Div.* **101** (WW4): 464–465.

Putnam, J. A. (1949). Loss of wave energy due to percolation in a permeable sea bottom. *Trans. A.G.U.* **30** (3): 349–356.

Reid, R. O. and Kajiura, K. (1957). On the damping of gravity waves over a permeable sea bed. *Trans. A.G.U.* **38** (5): 662–666.

Richardson, J. F. and Jeronimo, M. A. D. S. (1979). Velocity-voidage relations for sedimentation and fluidisation. *Chem. Eng. Sci.* **34**: 1419–1422.

Riedel, H. P., Kamphuis, J. W., and Brebner, A. (1972). Measurement of bed shear stress under waves. *Proc. 13th Conf. Coastal Eng. Vancouver*, pp. 587–603.

Roshko, A., Steinolfson, A. and Chattoorgoon, V. (1975). Flow forces on a cylinder near a wall or near another cylinder. *Proc. 2nd Conf. Wind Eng. Res. Fort Collins.* Pap. IV-15.

Rubinow, S. I. and Keller, J. B. (1961). The transverse force on a spinning sphere moving in a viscous fluid. *J. Fluid Mech.* **11**: 447–459.

Saffman, P. G. (1965). The lift on a small sphere in a slow shear flow. *J. Fluid Mech.* **22**: 385–400.

Sarpkaya, T. (1975). Forces on cylinders and spheres in a sinusoidally oscillating fluid. *Trans. A.S.M.E. J. Appl. Mech.* **42**: 32–37.

Sarpkaya, T. (1976a). Forces on cylinders near a plane boundary in a sinusoidally oscillating fluid. *Trans. A.S.M.E. J. Fluid Eng.* **98**: 499–505.

Sarpkaya, T. (1976b). In-line and transverse forces on smooth and sand roughened cylinders in oscillatory flow at high Reynolds number. Naval Postgraduate School. Monterey, California. Rep. NPS-69SL76062.

Sarpkaya, T. (1977). Unidirectional periodic flow about bluff bodies. Naval Postgraduate School. Monterey. California. Rep. NPS-69SL77051.

Sarpkaya, T. and Isaacson, M. (1981). *Mechanics of Wave Forces on Offshore Structures.* Van Nostrand Reinhold, New York.

Savage, S. B. and McKeown, S. (1983). Shear stresses developed during rapid shear of concentrated suspensions of large spherical particles between concentric cylinders. *J. Fluid Mech.* **127**: 453–472.

Savage, R. P. (1953). Laboratory study of wave energy losses by bottom friction and percolation. Beach Erosion Board. Tech. Memo. 31.

Schoneborn, P. R. (1975). Bewegung einzelner partikeln im instationaren stromungsfeld. *Chem. Ing. Tech.* **47**: 305.

Shinohara, K. and Tsubaki, T. (1959). On the characteristics of sand waves formed upon the beds of the open channels and rivers. Rep. Res. Inst. Appl. Mech. Kyushu Univ. **7** (25).

Silvester, R. (1974). *Coastal Engineering.* Elsevier, Amsterdam.

Sleath, J. F. A. (1973). A numerical study of the influence of bottom roughness on mass transport by water waves. *Proc. Inter. Conf. Numer. Methods Fluid Dyn. Southampton.*

Sleath, J. F. A. (1976). Forces on a rough bed in oscillatory flow. *J. Hydraul. Res.* **14** (2): 155–164.

Sleath, J. F. A. (1982a). The effect of jet formation on the velocity distribution in oscillatory flow over flat beds of sand or gravel. *Coastal Eng.* **6**: 151–177.

Sleath, J. F. A. (1982b). Friction coefficients of rippled beds in oscillatory flow. *Cont. Shelf Res.* **1** (1): 33–47.

Smith, J. D. (1977). Modeling of sediment transport on continental shelves. In *The Sea*, Vol. 6. E. D. Goldberg, I. N. McCave, J. J. O'Brien, and J. H. Steele, Eds. Wiley, New York, pp. 538–578.

Sternberg, R. W. (1972). Predicting initial motion and bedload transport of sediment particles in the shallow marine environment. In *Shelf Sediment Transport*, D. J. P. Swift, D. S. Duane, and O. H. Pilkey, Eds. Dowden, Hutchinson and Ross, Stroudsburg, Pennsylvania, pp. 61–82.

Stokes, G. G. (1851). On the effect of the internal friction of fluids on the motion of pendulums. *Trans. Camb. Philos. Soc.* **9**: 20–21.

Stuart, J. T. and Woodgate, L. (1955). Experimental determination of the aerodynamic damping on a vibrating circular cylinder. *Philos. Mag.* **46** (7): 40–46.

Swanson, W. M. (1961). The magnus effect: a summary of investigations to date. *Trans. A.S.M.E. J. Basic Eng.* **83**: 461–470.

Swart, D. H. (1974). A schematization of onshore-offshore transport. *Proc. 14th Conf. Coastal Eng. Copenhagen*, pp. 884–900.

Swart, D. H. (1976). Coastal sediment transport. Computation of longshore transport. Delft Hydraulics Laboratory. Rep. R968, Part 1.

Takaisi, Y. (1955). The forces on a circular cylinder moving with low speeds in a semi-infinite viscous liquid bounded by a plane wall. *J. Phys. Soc. Jpn.* **10** (5): 407–415.

Tanaka, H. and Shuto, N. (1981). Friction coefficient for a wave-current coexistent system. *Coastal Eng. Jpn.* **24**: 105–128.

Teleki, P. G. (1972). Velocity and shear stress in wave boundary layers. *Proc. 13th Conf. Coastal Eng. Vancouver*, pp. 569–586.

Teleki, P. G. and Anderson, M. W. (1970). Bottom boundary shear stresses on a model beach. *Proc. 12th Conf. Coastal Eng. Washington*, pp. 269–288.

Thomschke, H. (1971). Experimtelle untersuchung der stationaren umstromung von kugel und zylinder in wandnahe. Doctoral thesis. Karlsruhe University.

Treloar, P. D. and Brebner, A. (1970). Energy losses under wave action. *Proc. 12th Conf. Coastal Eng. Washington*, pp. 257–267.

Tunstall, E. B. (1973). Experimental study of vortices generated by oscillatory flow over rippled surfaces. Ph.D. Thesis. Univ. Calif. San Diego.

Van Dorn, W. G. (1966). Boundary dissipation of oscillatory waves. *J. Fluid Mech.* **24**: 769–779.

Verley, R. L. P. and Moe, G. (1979). The forces on a cylinder oscillating in a current. River and Harbour Lab. Tech. Univ. Norway. Report STF60A79061.

Vitale, P. (1979). Sand bed friction factors for oscillatory flows. *Proc. A.S.C.E. J. Waterw. Port Coastal Ocean Div.* **105** (WW3): 229–245.

Watson, and Martin (1962). The emanation of shallow-water waves from a simulated point source. U.S. Navy Mine Def. Lab. Interim report. I-7.

Willetts, B. B. and Murray, C. G. (1981). Lift exerted on stationary spheres in turbulent flow. *J. Fluid Mech.* **105**: 487–505.

Willmarth, W. W. and Enlow, R. L. (1969). Aerodynamic lift and moment fluctuations of a sphere. *J. Fluid Mech.* **36**: 417–432.

Wilson, J. F. and Caldwell, H. M. (1970). Force and stability measurements on models of submerged pipelines. Offshore Tech. Conf. Paper 1224. Vol. 1.

Yamamoto, T. H., Koning, L., Sellmeijer, H., and Van Hijum, E. (1978). On the response of a poro-elastic bed to water waves. *J. Fluid Mech.* **87**: 193–206.

Young, D. F. (1960). Drag and lift on spheres within cylindrical tubes. *Proc. A.S.C.E. J. Hydraul. Div.* **86** (HY6): 47.

Zhukovets, A. M. (1963). The influence of bottom roughness on wave motion in a shallow body of water. Bull Acad. Sci. USSR. Geophys. Ser. 10, pp. 933–948.

Zick, A. A. and Homsy, G. M. (1982). Stokes flow through periodic arrays of spheres. *J. Fluid Mech.* **115**: 13–26.

Six

SEDIMENT TRANSPORT

Oscillatory Flow

Movement of sediment causes many problems for the coastal engineer; beaches may erode, coastal structures may be undermined, and navigation channels and ports may silt up.

6.1. INITIAL MOTION

If the fluid velocities are not high enough to move the sediment on the bed, there will not be any problem. A first step in any study is to determine the conditions in which sediment will first start to move.

Start with the simplest possible situation, an infinite flat bed of sediment acted upon by a steady train of small-amplitude waves of constant height. The fluid velocity just above the boundary layer at the bed will be approximately simple harmonic. Many problems of engineering importance are, of course, more complicated than this. However, once the solution is known for the case of a flat bed it is possible to estimate the answer for more complex situations. The link between initial motion for rippled beds and initial motion for flat beds is discussed in Section 4.5. In this section as well as most of the other sections in this chapter, the assumption is that the sediment is not cohesive. Results for cohesive sediments are given in Section 6.6.

6.1.1.   Some Formulas for Initial Motion

Because of the importance of this problem, there have been many attempted solutions. The following are some of the formulas which have been suggested:

Bagnold (1946):

$$\frac{U_\infty}{\left(\frac{\rho_s-\rho}{\rho}\right)^{2/3} D^{0.433} T^{1/3}} = 2.38 \quad \text{(S.I. units)} \tag{6.1}$$

Sato and Kishi (1954):

$$\frac{U_\infty}{\left(\left(\frac{\rho_s-\rho}{\rho}\right)gD\right)^{1/2}} = 5.06 \tag{6.2}$$

Manohar (1955):
  (a) Initial motion in laminar boundary layer:

$$\frac{U_\infty \nu^{1/2}}{\left(\frac{\rho_s-\rho}{\rho}\right)gDT^{1/2}\tan\phi} = 0.025 \tag{6.3}$$

  (b) Initial motion in turbulent boundary layer:

$$\frac{U_\infty}{\left(\frac{\rho_s-\rho}{\rho}\right)^{0.4} g^{0.4} \nu^{0.2} D^{0.2}} = 7.45 \tag{6.4}$$

Kurihara et al. (1956):

$$\frac{U_\infty}{\left(\frac{\rho_s-\rho}{\rho} gD \tan\phi\right)^{1/2}} = 1.95 \tag{6.5}$$

Larras (1956):

$$\frac{(U_\infty - W)T^{1/2}}{\left(\frac{\rho_s-\rho}{\rho}\right)^{1/3} \nu^{1/2}} = 95 \tag{6.6}$$

Vincent (1957):

$$\frac{U_\infty D}{W} = 0.0012 \qquad \text{(S.I. units)} \qquad (6.7)$$

Eagleson and Dean (1959):

$$\frac{U_\infty \nu^{1/2}}{\left(\dfrac{\rho_s - \rho}{\rho}\right) gDT^{1/2}} = 0.016 \qquad (6.8)$$

Goddet (1960):

$$\frac{U_\infty}{\left(\dfrac{\rho_s - \rho}{\rho}\right)^{2/3} g^{2/3} D^{1/4} T^{3/8} \nu^{1/24}} = 0.33 \qquad (6.9)$$

Ishihara and Sawaragi (1962), for $\left(\dfrac{\rho_s - \rho}{\rho}\dfrac{g}{\nu^2}\right)^{1/3} D \leqslant 35$:

$$\frac{U_\infty}{\left(\dfrac{\rho_s - \rho}{\rho}\right)^{3/4} g^{3/4} D^{1/4} T^{1/2}} = 0.054 \qquad (6.10)$$

Sato et al. (1962):

$$\frac{U_\infty}{\left(\dfrac{\rho_s - \rho}{\rho}\right)^{2/3} g^{2/3} D^{1/3} T^{1/3}} = 0.39 \qquad (6.11)$$

Bonnefille and Pernecker (1966), for $\left(\dfrac{\rho_s - \rho}{\rho}\dfrac{g}{\nu^2}\right)^{1/3} D \leqslant 18$:

$$\frac{U_\infty \nu^{1/6}}{\left(\dfrac{\rho_s - \rho}{\rho}\right)^{5/6} g^{5/6} D^{1/2} T^{1/2}} = 0.063 \qquad (6.12)$$

for $\left(\dfrac{\rho_s - \rho}{\rho}\dfrac{g}{\nu^2}\right)^{1/3} D > 18$:

$$\frac{U_\infty \nu^{19/30}}{\left(\dfrac{\rho_s - \rho}{\rho}\right)^{16/15} g^{16/15} D^{6/5} T^{1/2}} = 0.0087 \qquad (6.13)$$

Horikawa and Watanabe (1967), for initial movement:

$$\frac{U_\infty f_w^{1/2}}{\left(\dfrac{\rho_s - \rho}{\rho} gD \tan \phi\right)^{1/2}} = 0.39 \tag{6.14}$$

where f_w is given by Kajiura's theoretical solution.
Carstens et al. (1969):

$$\frac{U_c}{\left(\dfrac{\rho_s - \rho}{\rho} gD\right)^{1/2}} = 1.37 \tag{6.15}$$

where U_c is the amplitude of the velocity at $0.6D$ above the mean bed level.
Silvester and Mogridge (1970):

$$\frac{U_\infty v^{1/18}}{\left(\dfrac{\rho_s - \rho}{\rho}\right)^{7/9} g^{7/9} D^{1/3} T^{1/2}} = 0.034 \tag{6.16}$$

Chan et al. (1972):

$$\frac{U_\infty}{\left(\dfrac{\rho_s - \rho}{\rho}\right)^{3/4} g^{3/4} D^{1/4} T^{1/2}} = 0.148 \tag{6.17}$$

Komar and Miller (1973, 1974), for $\left(\dfrac{\rho_s - \rho}{\rho} \dfrac{g}{v^2}\right)^{1/3} D \leqslant 12.5$:

$$\frac{U_\infty}{\left(\dfrac{\rho_s - \rho}{\rho}\right)^{2/3} g^{2/3} D^{1/3} T^{1/3}} = 0.24 \tag{6.18}$$

for $\left(\dfrac{\rho_s - \rho}{\rho} \dfrac{g}{v^2}\right)^{1/3} D > 12.5$:

$$\frac{U_\infty}{\left(\dfrac{\rho_s - \rho}{\rho}\right)^{4/7} g^{4/7} D^{3/7} T^{1/7}} = 1.05 \tag{6.19}$$

Dingler (1975):

$$\frac{U_\infty \nu^{1/6}}{\left(\frac{\rho_s - \rho}{\rho}\right)^{5/6} g^{5/6} T^{1/2} D^{1/2}} = 0.052 \tag{6.20}$$

Hallermeier (1980), for $D \leqslant 0.7$ mm and $U_\infty < 0.35$ m/s:

$$\frac{U_\infty}{\left(\frac{\rho_s - \rho}{\rho}\right)^{3/4} g^{3/4} D^{1/4} T^{1/2}} = 0.14 \tag{6.21}$$

for $\varepsilon = \left(\frac{\rho_s - \rho}{\rho}\right)^{1/2} \dfrac{g^{1/2} D^{0.79} T^{0.355}}{180.9 \nu^{0.645}} \geqslant 1$:

$$\frac{U_\infty}{\left(\frac{\rho_s - \rho}{\rho}\right)^{1/2} g^{1/2} D^{1/2}} = 2.83 \tag{6.22}$$

for $\varepsilon < 1$ and either $D \geqslant 0.7$ mm or $U_\infty > 0.35$ m/s:

$$U_\infty = \frac{\varepsilon^2 U_{\infty 2} + \delta^2 U_{\infty 1}}{(\varepsilon^2 + \delta^2)} \tag{6.23}$$

where $U_{\infty 1}$ and $U_{\infty 2}$ are the values of U_∞ given by (6.21) and (6.22) and

$$\delta = 2 - \frac{U_{\infty 1}}{0.35} \quad \text{(S.I. units)} \tag{6.24}$$

Lenhoff (1982):

$$\frac{U_\infty D}{\nu} (f_w)^{1/2} = 0.859 D_*^{(1 + 0.092 \log D_*)} \tag{6.25}$$

where

$$D_* = \left(\frac{\rho_s - \rho}{\rho} \frac{g}{\nu^2}\right)^{1/3} D \tag{6.26}$$

In addition to these explicit formulas, essentially graphical criteria for initial motion have been proposed by Kajiura (1968), Rance and Warren (1968), Madsen and Grant (1976), and Sleath (1978). Sternberg and Larsen (1975) have shown that a slightly modified version of Komar and Miller's formula (6.18) for fine sediments gives good agreement with measurements on site.

6.1.2. Theoretical Background

Some of the formulas listed in Section 6.1.1 are purely empirical but others are based, at least in part, on theoretical considerations. To have some understanding of the limitations of the theoretical formulas it is helpful to outline some of the assumptions and general trends.

All theoretical formulas start from a consideration of the balance of forces on a grain of sediment which is just at the limit of equilibrium. The fluid forces tend to drag the grain from the bed, whereas gravity tends to pull it back. It was shown by Shields (1936) for steady flow that this limiting condition could be expressed as

$$\frac{\tau_c}{(\rho_s - \rho)gD} = f\left(\frac{u_* D}{v}\right) \tag{6.27}$$

This expression is derived as outlined in Section 6.7. In steady flow, τ_c is the critical value of the shear stress τ_0 on the bed at which the grains of sediment first begin to move but in oscillatory flow it ought to be taken as the total horizontal force per unit area acting on the bed rather than just the shear stress. The reason for this is that in oscillatory flow a major contribution to the force on the grains of sediment comes from the horizontal pressure gradient within the fluid, whereas in steady flow this pressure gradient is not usually important. When allowance is made for this, the same expression might be expected to apply in oscillatory flow if either the lift force on the grain of sediment were negligible or if there were a similar relationship between lift and drag as for steady flow. At the present time there is insufficient evidence to make it clear whether either of these assumptions is justified.

Since the shear velocity is given by

$$u_* = \left(\frac{\tau_c}{\rho}\right)^{1/2} \tag{6.28}$$

it follows that

$$\frac{u_* D}{v} = \left(\frac{\tau_c}{(\rho_s - \rho)gD} \times \frac{\rho_s - \rho}{\rho} \frac{gD^3}{v^2}\right)^{1/2} \tag{6.29}$$

Thus (6.27) could also be written as

$$\frac{\tau_c}{(\rho_s-\rho)gD}=f_2\left(\frac{\rho_s-\rho}{\rho}\frac{gD^3}{v^2}\right) \tag{6.30}$$

This form is more convenient than (6.27) in oscillatory flow since the variables on the right-hand side are independent of the fluid velocity and period.

To make use of (6.30) it is necessary to be able to calculate the maximum horizontal force $\hat{\tau}_0$ per unit area of bed and the function f_2.

It would seem from the measurements of Kamphuis discussed in Chapter 5 that the variation of $\hat{\tau}_0$ with Reynolds number R may be split up into three regimes as follows:

1. For sufficiently low values of R (see Fig. 5.5) the bed is effectively smooth and the flow laminar and hence, from (5.2),

$$\hat{\tau}_0=\mu U_\infty\beta 2^{1/2} \tag{6.31}$$

Substituting in (6.30) we obtain the condition for initial motion

$$\frac{U_\infty v^{1/2}}{\left(\dfrac{\rho_s-\rho}{\rho}\right)gDT^{1/2}}=\frac{1}{(2\pi)^{1/2}}\,f_2\left(\frac{\rho_s-\rho}{\rho}\frac{gD^3}{v^2}\right) \tag{6.32}$$

2. For sufficiently large values of R the flow near the bed is fully developed rough turbulent and the friction factor is given, to a reasonable approximation, by (5.49) and (5.50). Thus, for $a/k_s>1.57$

$$\hat{\tau}_0=\frac{\rho U_\infty^2}{2}\times 0.00251\,e^{5.21(k_s/a)^{0.19}} \tag{6.33}$$

From (6.30)

$$\frac{U_\infty\,e^{2.61(k_s/a)^{0.19}}}{\left(\dfrac{\rho_s-\rho}{\rho}gD\right)^{1/2}}=\left[797 f_2\left(\frac{\rho_s-\rho}{\rho}\frac{gD^3}{v^2}\right)\right]^{1/2} \tag{6.34}$$

3. Between these two extremes there is a smooth transition.

Figures 6.1 and 6.2 show the critical values of U_∞ predicted by (6.1) to (6.23) for two grades of sand in fresh water at 20°C. Where relevant, $\tan\phi$ has

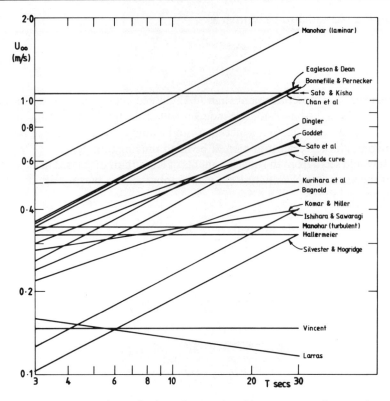

Figure 6.1. Comparison of critical values of U_∞ predicted by various initial motion formulae for 0.8 mm sand in fresh water at 20°C.

been taken equal to 1.0. For a given sediment and a given fluid, (6.32) would give U_∞ proportional to $T^{1/2}$, whereas, bearing in mind that a is equal to $U_\infty T/2\pi$, (6.34) suggests that U_∞ increases more slowly with T: for the conditions of Fig. 6.1, (6.34) predicts a rate of increase similar to that of Komar and Miller's curve.

Most of the curves in Fig. 6.1 and 6.2 show U_∞ increasing at a rate equal, or very close to $T^{1/2}$. The fact that·so many of the curves show the trend predicted for laminar flow is not entirely surprising. Some of the formulas, for example, that of Eagleson and Dean and also Manohar's "laminar" relationship, start off from the assumption of laminar flow. Many of the others are based on experiments with relatively fine sediments in laboratory channels for which the flow would probably have been laminar.

All of the curves in Fig. 6.1 and 6.2 are based, at least in part, on actual measurements. Thus there is some range of experimental conditions for which each one of these curves could be shown to give the best results. The

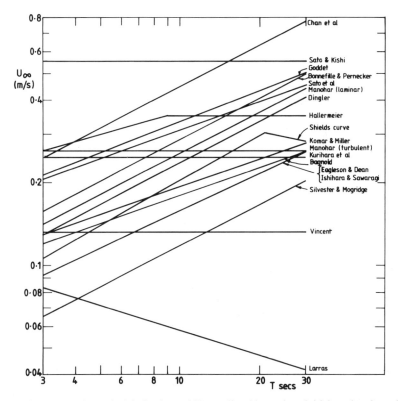

Figure 6.2.   Comparison of critical values of U_∞ predicted by various initial motion formulas for 0.2 mm sand in fresh water at 20°C.

very great difference between the predicted values of U_∞ shown in Fig. 6.1 and 6.2 illustrates the danger of extrapolating empirical curves beyond the experimental range for which they were established.

Why do these various curves diverge so much? One reason is the experimental difficulty of estimating the initial motion condition; different observers have different ideas about what constitutes initial motion. Another important source of error is that the function f_2 in (6.30) is not a constant. Komar and Miller (1974) and Madsen and Grant (1975) suggested, independently, that the function f in (6.27) and hence the function f_2 in (6.30) could be obtained from Shields' well-known curve for steady flow. Figure 6.3 shows a comparison between measurements of $\hat{\tau}_0/(\rho_s - \rho)gD$, using Kamphuis' design curves (see Fig. 5.5) to calculate $\hat{\tau}_0$, and Shields' curve. The agreement is remarkably good. Komar and Miller as well as Madsen and Grant suggested that $\hat{\tau}_0$ should be calculated from Jonsson's (1966) curves. However, Hallermeier (1980) showed that slightly better agreement between

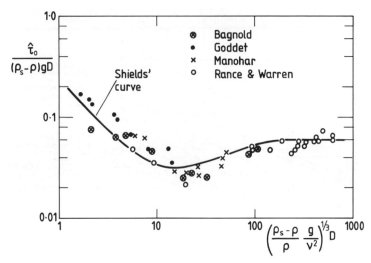

Figure 6.3. Comparison of experimental results for initial motion in oscillatory flow with Shields' steady flow curve.

theory and experiment is obtained if Kamphuis' curves are used instead. It should be mentioned that the experimental results shown in Fig. 6.3 represent the average value of $\hat{\tau}_0/(\rho_s - \rho)gD$ for each value of $[(\rho_s - \rho)g/\rho v^2]^{1/3}D$. To avoid confusion, error bands are not included. The scatter on either side of the mean is in all cases small.

Good agreement between oscillatory and steady flow results was found by Ishihara and Sawaragi (1962). On the other hand, Sleath (1978) suggested that unsteady and steady flows may be fundamentally different and that different curves ought to be used in the two cases. He also suggested that new curves could incorporate some of the effects of the lift L and moment M which are neglected if use is made of Kamphuis' or Jonsson's curves. Although this approach is superficially attractive, particularly in view of the results discussed in Chapter 5 showing that lift is not always negligible, it does add to the complication of any particular calculation and the overall results do not appear to be significantly better than those achieved using Kamphuis' and Shields' curve.

It is clear that no simple algebraic expression such as (6.1), (6.2), and so on, can adequately represent the complex variation of τ_c and f_2 in (6.30) over the whole range of experimental conditions. At the present time the best approach appears to be to use Shields' curve together with Kamphuis' curves for the friction factor. The curves labeled Shields curve in Fig. 6.1 and 6.2 were obtained in this way. An example of how the calculation is carried out is given in Section 6.14.

6.1.3. Effect of Bed Permeability

When the bed is permeable, the fluctuation in pressure induced by the waves will cause flow into and out of the bed, as discussed in Chapter 2. This seepage has two effects.

First, the seepage will modify the flow in the boundary layer above the bed, which will change the shear stress exerted by the flow on the bed. In general, seepage out of the bed reduces the shear stress while seepage into the bed increases it. However, these effects may be reversed if the boundary layer is near the laminar–turbulent transition since seepage into the bed may keep the flow laminar and vice versa. Several formulas are available for the bed shear stress τ_s in steady flow with seepage. For example, Oldenziel and Brink (1974) quote Turcotte's formula

$$\tau_s = \tau_0 - \rho v_0 (13.9 \bar{u}_*) \tag{6.35}$$

In addition, seepage exerts a vertical force on the grains of sediment. Martin and Aral (1971) show that the seepage force on a grain on the surface is only 50% of that on an embedded grain but, even allowing for this, it is clear that upward seepage will reduce the stability of surface grains, whereas downward seepage will increase it.

These two effects counteract each other. Martin (1970) and Watters and Rao (1971) carried out tests in steady flow and concluded that seepage did not significantly affect the initial motion condition for values of $(1/\rho g)\partial p/\partial y$ ranging from $+1$ down almost to the point at which fluidization of the bed occurred. The condition for bed fluidization is

$$\frac{1}{\rho g}\frac{\partial p}{\partial y} = -\left(\frac{\rho_1 - \rho}{\rho}\right) \tag{6.36}$$

where ρ_1 is the density of the saturated bed material. If the specific gravity of the dry sediment were 2.65 and the ratio of voids to total volume were 0.35, the critical condition would be

$$\frac{1}{\rho g}\frac{\partial p}{\partial y} = -1.07 \tag{6.37}$$

However, Oldenziel and Brink (1974) found, also for steady flow, that seepage into the bed decreased the rate of sediment transport while seepage out of the bed increased it. If the rate of sediment transport is affected, it would be expected that the initial motion criterion would also be changed. A result opposite to that of Oldenziel and Brink was obtained by Willetts and Drossos

(1975). This discrepancy may be caused by the somewhat coarser sediment used by Willetts and Drossos or possibly the limited area over which suction was applied in their experiments.

These results are all for steady flow. Kruijt (1976) carried out experiments in oscillatory flow and concluded that, for values of $(1/\rho g)\partial p/\partial y$ from $+1$ down almost to the point at which fluidization occurred, bed seepage had no observable effect on the initial motion condition. He was also unable to detect any significant effect of bed seepage on sediment transport within this range. Martin (1970) pointed out that pressure gradients outside this range are unlikely to be found with natural waves except in the immediate vicinity of solid structures placed in or on the bed.

Madsen (1974) showed that failure of the bed could also be caused by the horizontal pressure gradient becoming too large. The critical condition for this type of failure is

$$\frac{1}{\rho g}\frac{\partial p}{\partial x} = \left(\frac{\rho_1 - \rho}{\rho}\right)\tan\phi \tag{6.38}$$

For relatively loose sand in seawater the right-hand side of (6.38) would be about 0.6. This critical value could be surpassed under the steep forward slope of a near breaking wave.

6.2. SEDIMENT TRANSPORT AS BEDLOAD

The principal mechanisms of sediment transport in oscillatory flow are similar to those in steady flow. Sediment transported as "bedload" remains more or less continuously in rolling or sliding contact with the bed. In "suspension," the particles of sediment fall freely relative to the moving fluid. Of course, grains of sediment may be transported as bedload during part of the wave cycle and then lifted into suspension during another part. The mode of sediment transport described in steady flow as "saltation," in which particles of sediment are carried in successive leaps along the bed, has not yet been observed in oscillatory flow. This may be due to the relative scarcity of data available for oscillatory flows.

Once again, we restrict our attention at this stage to simple harmonic motions. Of course, waves usually generate a small steady current as well as the oscillatory motion, which clearly has a significant effect on the net sediment transport in any given direction. However, it is probably more logical to postpone consideration of this net drift to the last part of this chapter, where we examine the combined action of waves and currents. The effect of oscillatory motion which is not pure simple harmonic is considered in Section 6.4.

6.2.1. Experimental Results

Measurements of bedload in oscillatory flow with no net current have been made by Manohar (1955), Kalkanis (1964), Abou Seida (1965), and Sleath (1978). The measurements of Manohar, Kalkanis, and Abou Seida were all made with trays set into the bed and consequently only the total bedload transport during the course of one half-cycle could be measured. Manohar was interested only in the net sediment transport in a given direction and all of his tests were carried out with very asymmetric oscillations. Sleath used a photographic technique which was restricted to low sediment transport rates but did allow variation of sediment transport rates during the course of the cycle to be determined. This work shows two main results:

1. There is a well-defined critical value of the amplitude of the fluid velocity U_∞ outside the boundary layer below which movement of sediment does not occur if conditions have remained the same long enough for unstable grains to bed down. In this respect oscillatory flow is different from steady flow where the critical condition is less well defined because even at very low fluid velocities and after a prolonged period of stable flow some unstable grains continue to be carried into the test area from upstream.

2. Once the amplitude of the fluid velocity exceeds this critical value grains of sediment appear to move throughout the cycle. In other words, grains continue to move at fluid velocities below the critical value of U_∞ provided that at some point during the cycle the fluid velocity exceeds the critical value. The reason for this is that grains eroded when the fluid velocity exceeds the critical value require a much smaller velocity to keep them moving. When they eventually come to rest as the fluid velocity reverses some of them settle in such unstable positions that only a very small fluid velocity is necessary to set them in motion again.

These effects are illustrated in Fig. 6.4. The measurements were carried out with gravel of median diameter 4.24 mm in an oscillating tray rig at constant stroke. The critical value of U_∞ below which no movement of any sort occurred, once unstable grains had had a chance to bed down, was 0.4 m/s. The relative motion of the bed and the fluid outside the boundary layer was simple harmonic so it is clear from Fig. 6.4 that significant sediment motion occurred for relative velocities well below 0.4 m/s.

The measurements in Fig. 6.4 represent the mean sediment transport rates averaged for successive periods of one twentieth of a cycle over 20 cycles (except for the measurements with the lowest value of U_∞ for which only 11 cycles were averaged). The actual sediment transport rates during the course of a single cycle show significant fluctuations on either side of the mean curves.

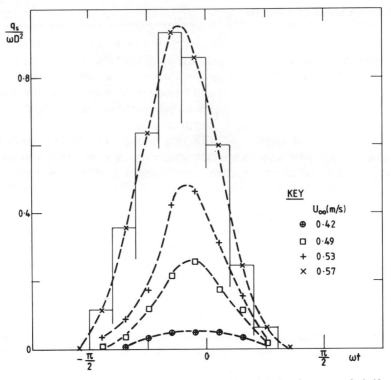

Figure 6.4. Variation in the sediment transport rate of gravel during the course of a half wave cycle (after Sleath, 1978).

Sleath (1978) suggested that the mean sediment transport rate varied with time as follows:

$$q_s = \frac{8}{3} Q_s \cos^3(\omega t + \phi)|\cos(\omega t + \phi)| \qquad (6.39)$$

where Q_s is the mean volumetric sediment transport rate, averaged over a half-cycle, and ϕ is the phase lead. In Sleath's tests, ϕ ranged between about 10 and 20°.

Various formulas have been proposed for Q_s. Madsen and Grant (1976) derived the following modified form of the Einstein-Brown equation suggested by Brown (1950):

$$\frac{Q_s}{WD} = C\psi^3 \qquad (6.40)$$

where ψ is the Shields function $\hat{\tau}_0/(\rho_s-\rho)gD$ and C is a coefficient which varies according to the value of ψ/ψ_c. For $\psi/\psi_c=1.03$, $C=4.3$ but as $\psi/\psi_c\to\infty$, $C\to12.5$.

Shibayama and Horikawa (1980) found that better agreement with experiment was obtained if C was taken equal to 19. They also suggested that during the acceleration phase the sediment transport rate varied like $\cos^6\omega t$, whereas during deceleration the sediment transport was proportional to $\cos\omega t$. However, more recently, Horikawa et al. (1982) found good agreement between experiments at very high sediment transport rates and (6.40) with $C=12.5$, as originally suggested by Madsen and Grant.

A somewhat different formula was proposed by Sleath (1978):

$$\frac{Q_s}{\omega D^2}=47(\psi-\psi_c)^{3/2} \tag{6.41}$$

Sleath (1982) suggested that (6.41) may apply only to relatively coarse sediments and that for finer grains the following formula may be more appropriate:

$$\frac{(q_s)_{\max}}{\left[\left(\frac{\rho_s-\rho}{\rho}\right)gD^3\right]^{1/2}}=5.2(\psi-\psi_c)^{3/2} \tag{6.42}$$

A similar expression was obtained by Vincent et al. (1981). If ψ is taken to be the instantaneous value of the Shields parameter, their relationship may be written

$$q_s\propto(\psi-\psi_c)\psi^{1/2} \tag{6.43}$$

These formulas should be treated with considerable caution since the data on which they are based are few. Also, although most of the experiments were carried out with flat beds of sediment it is possible that ripples occurred in some cases. This could clearly distort the data significantly.

6.2.2. Analytical Models

Probably the most serious attempt to develop an analytical model for bedload transport in oscillatory flow is that put forward by Kalkanis (1964) and extended by Abou Seida (1965). This model follows closely the model developed for steady flow by Einstein (1950). It is too lengthy to reproduce here but the main assumptions are as follows:

1. Erosion of a particle of sediment takes place when the lift exceeds the immersed weight. The in-line force on the particle is neglected.
2. The probability of particle erosion is assumed to have a Gaussian distribution.
3. Once eroded, particles move a fixed distance proportional to D before coming back to the bed.
4. The rate of erosion of particles from the bed is at all instants equal to the rate of deposition.

The result is the familiar Einstein bedload function with somewhat different coefficients to take account of the different circumstances in the present case.

All four assumptions are open to question in oscillatory flow. Lift is frequently small compared with the in-line force, particles clearly travel different distances at different phases in the cycle, rate of erosion is greater than deposition rate at the beginning of the half-cycle but less at the end. Finally, Sleath's (1978) measurements of the fluctuations in the sediment transport rate show poor agreement with the hypothesis that the probability of erosion has a Gaussian distribution. In particular, the measurements appeared to indicate that the probability of erosion is not statistically independent and that erosion of one particle may provoke the immediate erosion of surrounding particles. In view of these comments, it is perhaps not surprising that Abou Seida found that he could obtain agreement between his theory and the results of other investigators only if he introduced an empirical correction factor. He explained this correction factor as being due to acceleration effects not allowed for in Einstein's steady flow model.

More recently, Kobayashi (1982) derived an expression for sediment transport on a gentle slope. This is based on the formula suggested by Kalinske (1942) for steady flow together with the assumption that sediment transport responds instantaneously to change in flow conditions. Agreement with experimental data for average sediment transport rates is reasonable but the calculations for the way in which the transport rate varies during the course of the cycle are less satisfactory.

6.3. SEDIMENT SUSPENSION

A significant proportion of the sediment transported along a beach occurs in suspension. Once sediment has been lifted into suspension by the oscillatory flow even the weakest steady current can carry the sediment along.

6.3.1. Entrainment of Sediment from the Bed

The first question which has to be asked is how the sediment is carried up from the bed into suspension. Many investigators have been concerned with sediment suspension above rippled beds, but it should be remembered that high levels of turbulence, as in a breaking wave, can also entrain sediment from plane beds.

For rippled beds the process is indicated schematically in Fig. 6.5. In this figure the phase is that of the fluid outside the boundary layer which is assumed to have a velocity $U_\infty \cos \omega t$. Zero phase corresponds to the maximum velocity. During most of each half-cycle there is, as indicated in Fig. 6.5a a steady flow over the upstream face of the ripple and a vortex in the lee of the crest. The upstream flow carries sediment up and over the crest and then out over the lee vortex. Figure 6.6 gives an example of how the concentration varies with height close behind a crest in an oscillatory flow water tunnel. The jet of sediment entrained from the crest is clearly marked. Near its maximum the concentration is well described by

$$C = C_0 \exp -\left(\frac{y-\delta}{\sigma}\right)^2 \qquad (6.44)$$

where δ and σ are coefficients that do not vary with height and y is measured

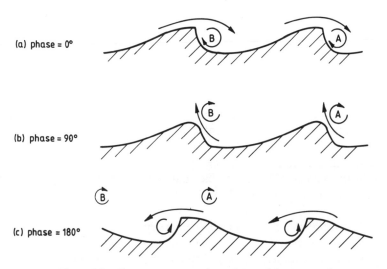

Figure 6.5.   Flow patterns at various phases of the wave cycle.

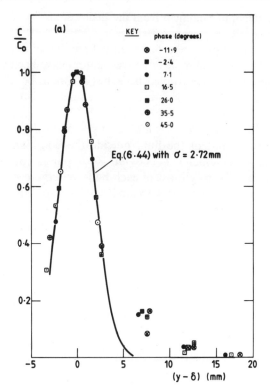

Figure 6.6. The variation in sediment concentration with height just downstream of a ripple crest.

up from the crest. For the measurements shown in Fig. 6.6, $\sigma = 2.72$ mm and δ varied from 0 down to about -7 mm depending on the phase. The measurements were made 23 mm behind the crest.

The jet of sediment entrained from the crest diffuses rapidly with distance downstream. Most of the sediment is trapped in the lee vortex and carried back toward the crest. A certain amount is carried over the lee vortex to join the sediment being dragged up the upstream face of the next ripple. At this stage in the wave cycle none of the sediment entrained from the bed rises significantly above the level of the ripple crests.

However, as the flow reverses the lee vortex appears to gain in strength and scoop more sediment from the bed. Then, as indicated in Fig. 6.5b, the reverse flow pushes the lee vortex back over the crest. As it goes, the vortex hurls its load of sediment up into the flow above. At this point the sediment can reach a height of several centimeters above the ripple crests. This plume of sediment is then carried around by the flow until the sand in it has settled back onto the bed or been absorbed by plumes thrown up at the end of subsequent half-cycles.

Why the vortex in the lee of the crest suddenly seems to grow in strength as the flow reverses is not entirely clear. It may be due to the greater instability of the flow at this point but it also appears to receive some help from the vortex pushed out into the flow at the end of the previous half-cycle. As seen in Fig. 6.5c the ejected vortex is carried along with the flow. Shortly before the next flow reversal the vortex passes over the adjacent crest giving an added impetus to the flow below and entraining more sediment into the lee vortex.

The basic mechanism for sediment suspension with rippled beds is thus the plume of sediment hurled up from the bed by the vortex in the lee of each ripple when the flow reverses at the end of each half-cycle.

6.3.2. Analytical Models

Early attempts to formulate analytical models were based on the assumption that the mechanisms of suspension were basically similar in oscillatory flows to those in steady flow. Thus it is the turbulence that allows sediment to remain in suspension: the sediment carried up from the bed by the turbulent eddies balances the tendency of the particles to settle toward the bed under the influence of gravity. In view of what was said in Section 6.3.1, this assumption is almost certainly not the whole story for suspension with rippled beds but is probably nearer the truth when suspension by breaking waves is being considered.

The equation of continuity for sediment motion in two dimensions is

$$\frac{\partial C}{\partial t} + \frac{\partial (uC)}{\partial x} + \frac{\partial}{\partial y}[(v - W)C] = 0 \qquad (6.45)$$

If, apart from random fluctuations due to turbulence, u and C do not vary in the horizontal direction the second term in this equation will be zero. In addition, the time-mean value of the vertical velocity v will also be zero. However, it does not follow that the vertical flux of sediment, vC, is zero because turbulence transports sediment from regions of high concentration to regions of low concentration even if there is no mean velocity. Under these circumstances the vertical flux of sediment may be written

$$vC = \varepsilon \frac{\partial C}{\partial y} \qquad (6.46)$$

where ε is a diffusion coefficient. Thus (6.45) becomes

$$\frac{\partial}{\partial y}\left(WC+\varepsilon\frac{\partial C}{\partial y}\right)=\frac{\partial C}{\partial t} \tag{6.47}$$

If the concentration does not vary with time we obtain

$$WC+\varepsilon\frac{\partial C}{\partial y}=0 \tag{6.48}$$

A different way of deriving this equation is outlined, for steady flows, in Section 6.8.

Much of the early work in this field was done by Homma and his colleagues. On the basis of mixing-length theory for steady flows Homma and Horikawa (1962) suggested

$$\varepsilon=Ab^2\left|\frac{\partial u}{\partial y}\right| \tag{6.49}$$

where A is an empirical constant and b is the vertical displacement of a fluid particle during a wave cycle. The reasoning behind the choice of (6.49) was that the elliptical motion of the fluid particles produced by wave action is similar to that of turbulent eddies. Thus the mixing length l may be taken as proportional to the orbital amplitude b of the fluid particles.

Subsequently Homma et al. (1965) suggested a somewhat different expression, still based on mixing-length theory:

$$\varepsilon=\frac{K^2|\partial u/\partial y|^3}{(\partial^2 u/\partial y^2)^2} \tag{6.50}$$

The solutions obtained when (6.49) or (6.50) is substituted into (6.48) do not show very good agreement with experiment. To some extent this is probably due to the assumption that the elliptical motions of fluid particles in water waves produce mixing similar to that of turbulent eddies. In reality, the potential flow solution for progressive waves shows no mixing of fluid particles from one layer to another, whereas turbulence produces vigorous mixing.

Bakker (1974) has also made use of mixing-length theory. By analogy with steady flow he took mixing length proportional to y so that

$$\varepsilon=K^2 y^2\left|\frac{\partial u}{\partial y}\right| \tag{6.51}$$

where K is the Karman constant. Assuming (6.47) and making use of his numerical solution for the fluid velocities in oscillatory turbulent flow, he obtained concentration profiles at various stages of the wave cycle.

A somewhat different approach has been adopted by Bhattacharya (1971) and Kennedy and Locher (1972), who suggest that suspension is caused by the combined influence of turbulence and a periodic entrainment associated with the wave-induced velocities of the fluid. This second effect is identical from one cycle to the next and consequently cannot be treated by means of mixing-length theory. This nonturbulent upward entrainment of sediment is attributed to the delay time t' between a change in fluid velocity and the corresponding change in that of the particles of sediment. This idea is analogous to that put forward by Hattori (1969) for standing waves. Thus, in terms of time-mean quantities averaged over a wave cycle, (6.48) is replaced by

$$W\bar{C} + \varepsilon\frac{\partial \bar{C}}{\partial y} = \overline{\left(v - t'\frac{\partial v}{\partial t}\right)C_p} \qquad (6.52)$$

Here C_p is the time-varying component, excluding turbulent fluctuations, of the instantaneous local concentration. It is assumed that variations in concentration other than those caused by turbulence result from vertical oscillation of the mean concentration profile, so that

$$\frac{\partial C_p}{\partial t} = -K_1 v \frac{\partial \bar{C}}{\partial y} \qquad (6.53)$$

where K_1 is a constant. The vertical velocity v is taken to be that given by linear shallow water wave theory.

This approach still leaves the problem of what assumption to make about the diffusion coefficient ε. Also, Nielsen (1979) suggested that it is illogical to assume a delay between fluid and particle motions in the derivation of (6.52) but not in (6.53). If the same delay is assumed in (6.53), the term on the right-hand side of (6.52) becomes zero. However, although the details of this model may be questioned the idea that upward entrainment of sediment is not just due to turbulence is certainly correct. Even brief observation of wave-induced sediment entrainment from rippled beds indicates that most of the sediment is lifted from the bed in a regular and repeatable fashion as described in Section 6.3.1.

This idea of a regular and repeatable entrainment of sediment into suspension has been developed further by Nielsen (1979). However, once again, in the absence of adequate experimental information, there is still the basic problem of what assumption to make about the entrainment process.

The current situation appears to be that most of the available models can produce reasonable agreement with experiment if empirical coefficients are suitably chosen but that quite different results can be obtained equally easily. In all cases significant assumptions are necessary. It would consequently be prudent to treat currently available formulas as essentially empirical and extrapolate them to nonlaboratory situations only with considerable caution.

So far we have discussed only progressive waves. Hattori (1969) developed a model for standing waves based on (6.45) and the hypothesis that there is a lag between fluid and sediment motions. In fact, Hattori assumed that the sediment particle always moves at the same velocity as the fluid a fixed distance behind it. He also assumed that the diffusion coefficients in the horizontal and vertical directions were constant. Making use of shallow water wave theory for the fluid velocities he found that the time-mean concentration was given by

$$\bar{C} = \bar{C}_0 \exp[A(1 - \cos bx) - By] \qquad (6.54)$$

where A and B are constants that depend on the values chosen for the diffusion coefficients and the delay distance. In this expression x is measured from a node of the wave profile, so (6.54) shows maximum concentration at the antinodes and minimum concentration at the nodes. This result may seem surprising since the fluid velocities near the bed are greatest at the nodes; nevertheless, it is what is actually observed. Nielsen (1979) showed that the reason for this was that the steady drifts of fluid discussed in Section 2.2.1 tend to carry suspended sediment toward the antinodes. It would seem that it is not the delay between fluid and sediment motions which is of major interest but the second-order fluid velocities (which are neglected in Hattori's model).

6.3.3. Measurements of Sediment in Suspension

In contrast with measurements of bedload there have been numerous investigations of sediment in suspension. Early studies, such as those of Shinohara et al. (1958), Fairchild (1959), and Homma and Horikawa (1962), were made with siphons or pumped samplers. More recently Fairchild (1977) and Nielsen (1979) used similar devices. With this type of sampler it is difficult to match the intake velocity to that of the surrounding fluid at the measuring point. In addition, it is difficult to obtain an accurate record of concentration variations during the course of the wave cycle. For these reasons, most recent studies, such as those of Homma and Horikawa (1963), Homma et al. (1965), Horikawa and Watanabe (1970), Das (1971), Bhattacharya (1971), Macdonald (1973), Nakato et al. (1977), and Sleath (1982), have been made with light absorption devices. Such instruments have a light source at one point in the fluid and a photoelectric cell or similar device at another point. The intensity of the light picked up by the photoelectric cell depends on the concentration of sediment in suspension. The more sediment there is, the less the light transmitted. The disadvantage of this sort of device is that it is inherently nonlinear and consequently requires careful calibration. It does, however, allow a continuous record of sediment concentration to be obtained. Measurements of sediment in suspension have also been carried out using a resistance gage by Hattori (1969).

Variation of Concentration with Time

Figure 6.7 shows a typical recording of the concentration of sediment measured at a fixed point above the crest of a ripple in oscillatory flow. The measurement was made with 0.4-mm sand in an oscillatory flow water tunnel at a height of 15 mm above the crest. The record seen in Fig. 6.7

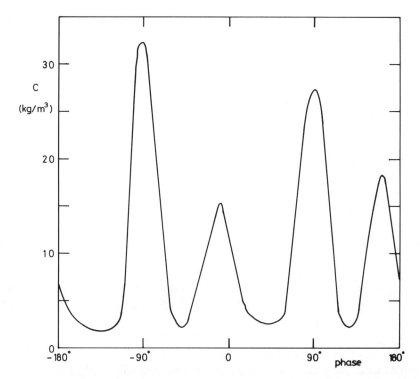

Figure 6.7.   Example of the way in which sediment concentration at a fixed point above a ripple crest varies with time.

represents the mean of 60 cycles, which is why turbulent fluctuations are not apparent. To interpret this record it is necessary to remember that a plume of sediment is thrown up from each ripple crest each time the flow reverses and that these plumes are subsequently carried around with the flow as the sediment settles back toward the bed. As before, phase in Fig. 6.7 is measured relative to that of the maximum velocity just outside the boundary layer. The velocity well away from the bed reverses at $-90°$ and $+90°$ and is maximum at $0°$ and $180°$. Thus the peaks in the concentration record in Fig. 6.7 at phases of $-90°$ and $+90°$ correspond to the plumes thrown up on flow reversal by the crest above which the probe is mounted. The weaker peaks at about $-10°$ and $170°$ represent the remains of plumes thrown up by adjacent crests at a previous flow reversal and subsequently carried by the flow past the measuring probe. Clearly a probe positioned above a crest will always record peaks at about $-90°$ and $+90°$. However, the number of smaller peaks recorded between these two phases will depend on the ratio of the orbital amplitude a of the fluid to ripple wavelength L. For small values of a/L the plumes thrown up by adjacent crests may not be carried a full wavelength. In that case no intermediate peak would be observed. For large values of a/L, plumes may be carried several wavelengths, in which case more than one subsidiary peak would be recorded by the probe.

A similar interpretation can be applied to the variation of concentration with time for other positions of the measuring device.

Variation of Concentration with Height

Most experimenters have attempted to fit their results for the time-mean concentration $\bar{C}$ to one of the following formulas:

$$\bar{C} = \bar{C}_1 y^{-m} \tag{6.55}$$

or

$$\bar{C} = \bar{C}_0 e^{-\alpha y} \tag{6.56}$$

where $\bar{C}_0$, $\bar{C}_1$, m, and α are coefficients that do not vary with height y above the bed. Equation (6.55) is obtained if the diffusion coefficient ε is assumed directly proportional to y in (6.48), whereas if ε is assumed to be constant we obtain (6.56).

Swart (1976) compared (6.55) and (6.56) with 86 sets of measurements and determined the root-mean-square error. He concluded that (6.55) gave a slightly better agreement with experiment than (6.56) but that the difference was not significant. This conclusion, that there is little to choose between the various empirical relationships for $\bar{C}$, was also reached by Kennedy and Locher (1972). Agreement with (6.56) is improved if measurements in the immediate vicinity of the bed, where the concentration rises sharply, are excluded.

The difficulty with both of these equations lies in the estimation of the empirical coefficients. The following empirical relationships have been suggested for α:

Macdonald (1971): for $0.06 < U_\infty < 0.34$ m/s; $a \geqslant 0.72$ m; $W = 0.011$ m/s:

$$\alpha = 60.5 - 124.1\, U_\infty \qquad \text{(S.I. units)} \tag{6.57}$$

Nielsen (1979):

$$\frac{W}{\alpha[h + 0.0288(a^3 k_s)^{1/4}]gT}$$
$$= 0.00146 \left(\frac{W}{U_\infty}\right)^{0.32} \exp\left[\frac{\ln(U_\infty/W) - 1.42}{1 + 5.75 \times 10^{-19}(U_\infty/W)^{14.5}}\right] \tag{6.58}$$

Sleath (1982):

$$\alpha = 0.2\beta \left(\frac{U_\infty h}{\nu}\right)^{-1/6} \tag{6.59}$$

Macdonald's tests were carried out with sediment sprinkled over a bed with fixed ripples. It is possible that the quantities of sediment available for entrainment were inadequate under certain conditions. Nielsen's measurements were made with siphons. This technique might introduce errors when the fall velocity of the sediment is not negligible compared with the velocity of the fluid. Sleath's expression is probably incomplete in that it makes no allowance for the properties of the sediment.

Equations (6.58) and (6.59) are for measurements above a ripple crest. Macdonald's tests were with an oscillating tray, so it is not possible to discriminate between measurements above crest and trough. Most investigators find some difference in the concentration profiles above crest and trough, but Nielsen showed that the actual values of α were not significantly different in the two cases.

On the other hand, the value of the reference concentration $\bar{C}_0$ at the level of the ripple crests does vary significantly according to the measuring point. Nielsen (1979) suggests the following:

Above ripple crest:

$$\bar{C}_0 = 0.028(\psi - 0.05)\frac{2}{\pi}\cos^{-1}\left(\frac{\psi_c}{\psi}\right) \tag{6.60}$$

Above ripple trough:

$$\bar{C}_0 = 0.015(\psi - 0.05)\frac{2}{\pi}\cos^{-1}\left(\frac{\psi_c}{\psi}\right) \tag{6.61}$$

In these expressions the Shields parameter ψ is for grain roughness only. In other words, $\hat{\tau}_0$ is to be evaluated using curves such as those of Kamphuis (Fig. 5.5). The concentration $\bar{C}_0$ is measured in cubic meters of sediment per cubic meter of water.

The results presented have all been for the time-mean concentration. Homma et al. (1965) found that the maximum and minimum concentrations, C_{max} and C_{min}, at a given point were related to the time-mean concentration $\bar{C}$ as follows:

$$C_{max} = 1.90\bar{C} \tag{6.62}$$

$$C_{min} = 0.59\bar{C} \tag{6.63}$$

On the other hand Bhattacharya (1971) found, for sloping beds, that

$$C_{max} \propto (\bar{C})^{0.80} \tag{6.64}$$

Breaking Waves

With nonbreaking waves sediment concentrations are usually insignificant at more than about three ripple heights above the bed. Breaking waves, however, lift sediment into suspension over the whole depth. When the waves break there is a dramatic increase in turbulence levels. Thus those analytical models which assume turbulence to be the dominant factor in sediment suspension are more likely to be correct under these conditions than when the waves do not break. As mentioned in Section 6.3.2, Bakker (1974) used his numerical model to calculate concentration profiles. Horikawa and Watanabe (1968) suggested that Kajiura's model might be used in a similar manner. Although these approaches are promising, a number of difficulties remain. For example, Wang and Hwang (1982) suggest that the fall velocity of the sediment is significantly modified under these conditions. It is also unclear what assumption should be made about the reference concentration C_0 at the bed.

There is at present insufficient quantitative data for breaking waves to enable us to resolve these questions with confidence. Nielsen found the following:

1. The time-mean value of the reference concentration $\bar{C}_0$ at the bed is the same for breaking and nonbreaking waves.
2. A rough approximation to the concentration profile is provided for breaking waves by assuming that the nonbreaking wave expressions apply over the bottom 20% of the water depth and that above that level the concentration is approximately constant.

Fairchild (1977) observed that plunging breakers lifted much more sediment into suspension than spilling breakers.

Standing Waves

Hattori (1969) obtained good agreement with his (6.54) provided the coefficients A and B were correctly chosen. In his tests he found

$$A = 0.66$$
$$B = 0.62d$$

(6.65)

6.4. EFFECTS OF WAVE ASYMMETRY

Thus far we have considered only pure simple harmonic motion of the fluid near the bed. The effect of superimposed steady currents will be examined later but it has to be remembered that asymmetry in the oscillatory flow will also affect the sediment transport. This is clearly shown in experiments carried out with an oscillating tray by Manohar (1955). Finite amplitude waves have a higher peak velocity in the direction of wave propagation than in the reverse direction. To simulate this effect Manohar arranged that the period of oscillation during the forward stroke of the tray should be less than that during the return stroke but that the motion should remain simple harmonic during the course of each separate half-cycle. This arrangement produced pronounced net transport of the sediment.

A simple model for this net transport would be to assume that the instantaneous sediment transport rate is proportional to some power of the relative velocity between the bed and the fluid outside the boundary layer.

For example,

$$q_s = A U_\infty \cos \omega t |U_\infty \cos \omega t|^n \qquad (6.66)$$

For Manohar's experimental situation in which the frequency was ω_1 during one half-cycle and ω_2 during the next this would give

$$(Q_s)_{net} = \frac{A}{T}\left[\int_{-\pi/2\omega_1}^{\pi/2\omega_1} (U_\infty \cos \omega_1 t)^{n+1} dt - \int_{\pi/2\omega_2}^{3\pi/2\omega_2} |U_\infty \cos \omega_2 t|^{n+1} dt \right] \qquad (6.67)$$

A variation on this method was adopted by Kamphuis (1973), who assumed that the sediment transport during each half-cycle was proportional to the cube of the time-mean velocity during the course of that half-cycle. The trouble with this approach is that the coefficients n and A in (6.66) probably vary during the course of the half-cycle and, in addition, the phase shift between sediment motion and fluid velocity mentioned in Section 6.2 would have a significant effect on the answer.

The method suggested by Madsen and Grant (1976) is to calculate the sediment transport for each half-cycle separately using (6.40). This produces good agreement with Manohar's results at low sediment transport rates but agrees less well at higher transport rates. It is not clear whether this discrepancy arises from shortcomings in the theory or the experiments.

Manohar's results have also been analyzed by Hallermeier (1982). He found reasonably good agreement, at higher sediment transport rates, with the following empirical expression for the mean transport during the forward half-cycle:

$$\frac{Q_s}{\omega D^2} = \left[\frac{\rho U_\infty^2}{10(\rho_s - \rho)gD} \right]^{3/2} \qquad (6.68)$$

6.5. SOLITARY WAVES

An extreme example of wave asymmetry is provided by solitary waves, for which there is a strong forward flow, under the crest, but no return flow. Naheer (1977) obtained the following empirical relationships for the initial motion condition:

For spheres:

$$\left(\frac{H}{d}\right)^2 = 4.13 \left[\frac{\rho_s - \rho}{\rho} \left(\frac{D}{d}\right)^{2/3} \tan \phi \right]^{1.43} \qquad (6.69)$$

For gravel:

$$\left(\frac{H}{d}\right)^2 = 3.81 \left[\frac{\rho_s - \rho}{\rho}\left(\frac{D}{d}\right)^{2/3} \tan \phi\right]^{1.47} \tag{6.70}$$

Naheer also derived a theoretical expression for the initial motion condition but this gave poor agreement with experiment. He suggests that this may have been because of the neglect of effects of fluid inertia.

The technique used by Naheer to determine the initial motion condition was photographic. This allowed him to measure the proportion P of the surface particles of gravel moved during each wave cycle:

$$1000P = -0.925 + 3.19 \log\left(\frac{H}{d}\right) - 2.35 \log\left[\frac{\rho_s - \rho}{\rho}\left(\frac{D}{d}\right)^{2/3} \tan \phi\right] \tag{6.71}$$

This expression gives some indication of the strength of the bedload transport although, for quantitative estimates, it would also be necessary to know the average distance through which the particles were displaced.

6.6.   COHESIVE SEDIMENTS

The results given in preceding sections of this chapter have all been for non-cohesive sediments. However, when the grain diameter is less than about 0.04 mm cohesion may significantly alter the way in which sediment is moved by wave action.

Cohesion is the tendency of particles of sediment to attract each other because of the electrostatic charges which they carry. Particles in suspension collect into flocs, which have a much higher fall velocity than that of the individual particles. Particles already on the bed resist erosion much more effectively than might have been expected from experiments with non-cohesive particles.

6.6.1.   Initial Motion

Because the particles of cohesive sediments are so small the critical shear stress for initial motion will be the same for wave-induced motion and steady flow: at such small Reynolds numbers acceleration effects are negligible. We may thus make use of formulas obtained in steady flows.

Unfortunately, even for steady flows there is no generally accepted formula for the initial motion of cohesive sediments. Migniot (1977) presents experimental results which, for values of the yield strength $\tau_y < 1 \text{ N/m}^2$, show the critical shear stress τ_c for initial motion to be

$$\tau_c = 0.256(\tau_y)^{0.46} \tag{6.72}$$

where both τ_c and τ_y are in newtons per square meter.

For values of $\tau_y > 1 \text{ N/m}^2$ Migniot suggests

$$\tau_c = 0.256\tau_y \tag{6.73}$$

This latter expression is, however, inconsistent with the results of other investigators. For example, Abdel-Rahmann (1964) found significant erosion for bed shear stresses as low as 2 N/m^2 for a value of $\tau_y = 12430 \text{ N/m}^2$. Of course, with these very fine particles the decision of a particular observer as to what constitutes initial motion is highly subjective so that some divergence between different investigators is only to be expected.

Dunn (1959) carried out experiments with sediments ranging from sand to silty clay. He suggested

$$\tau_c = 0.001(\tau_y + 8630) \tan (30 + 1.73 \, I_p) \tag{6.74}$$

in which τ_c and τ_y are in newtons per square meter, I_p is the plasticity index, and the argument of the tangent is in degrees.

Other experimental results and a useful discussion of the problem are given in the A.S.C.E. manual *Sedimentation Engineering* (1975). It is clear that the initial motion condition depends critically on the physical and chemical properties of the sediment as well as on the experimental conditions. At the present time no formula should be expected to give more than a rough estimate.

6.6.2. Transport in Suspension

Because of the very low fall velocities associated with cohesive sediments, it is usual to assume that, for steady flows, the concentration is more or less uniform over the whole depth of flow above the bed layer. Owen (1977) suggests the following formula for the concentration C of sediment in suspension at any time t:

$$C = C_0 \exp\left[-\frac{AW}{d}\left(1 - \frac{\tau_0}{\tau_d}\right)t \right] \tag{6.75}$$

Here C_0 is the concentration at time $t = 0$, A is a constant, and τ_d is the critical shear stress for deposition. It is usually accepted that the critical shear stress at which particles are deposited on the bed is less than that required for their erosion.

Owen recommends that the fall velocity W be measured on site. The main factors governing the flocculation of particles of mud or clay are fairly well understood but it is not yet possible to predict the size, density, or fall velocity of the flocs. Laboratory measurements of fall velocity are unsatisfactory because the size of the flocs is influenced by fluid shear, particularly that associated with turbulence, and it is very difficult to reproduce in the laboratory the turbulence found on site.

Little is known about this problem in oscillatory flows, such as those produced by wave action, but (6.75) is probably a reasonable first approximation if mean values, averaged over a wave cycle, are used for C and τ_0.

6.6.3. Bedload Transport

The term bedload is used here for the dense layer of mud, which is found to move under the action of waves or currents, even though the mechanisms are very different from those for noncohesive sediments with which the term is usually associated.

The passage of water waves tends to produce orbital motions in beds of mud similar to those in the water above. In addition to these orbital motions, waves also produce a steady drift in the mud layer which is similar to the mass transport current in the fluid above. Figure 6.8 shows how the steady drift velocity varies with distance below the surface in this bed layer.

For muds of viscosity ranging from 3×10^{-5} up to 7×10^{-5} m^2/s Lhermitte (1958) found the following relationship between the drift velocity $\bar{u}_s$ at the surface of the bed of mud and the theoretical maximum value $(\bar{u}_{mt})_{max}$ of the mass transport velocity in the laminar boundary layer above a smooth rigid bed:

$$\bar{u}_s = 0.25(\bar{u}_{mt})_{max} \tag{6.76}$$

It will be remembered from Chapter 2 that

$$(\bar{u}_{mt})_{max} = 1.391\left(\frac{U_\infty^2 b}{\omega}\right) \tag{6.77}$$

In fact, Lhermitte gave a different relationship for $(\bar{u}_{mt})_{max}$ but this is presumably due to the relatively small number of tests on which he based his empirical expression.

The actual quantities of sediment transported in the direction of wave

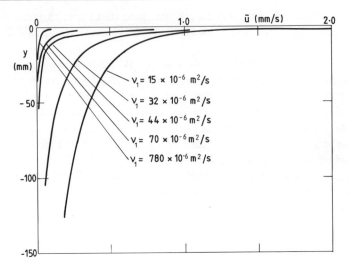

Figure 6.8. Examples of the way in which the steady drift velocity produced by wave action in beds of mud varies with depth and viscosity (after Lhermitte, 1958).

propagation depend on the experimental conditions. Migniot suggests

$$Q_s \propto \frac{1}{(v_1)} \tag{6.78}$$

Help in estimating the constant of proportionality may be obtained from the test results presented by Lhermitte (1958), some of which are reproduced by Migniot (1977).

Steady Flow

6.7. INITIAL MOTION

The forces acting on a particle of sediment on the surface of the bed are illustrated in Fig. 6.9. Using (5.73), we have

$$F \propto \tau_0 D^2 \tag{6.79}$$

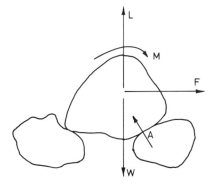

Figure 6.9.   Forces on a particle of sediment on the surface of the bed.

Also, since

$$F = C_D \times \tfrac{1}{2}\rho u^2 \times \frac{\pi D^2}{4} \qquad (6.80)$$

$$L = C_L \times \tfrac{1}{2}\rho u^2 \times \frac{\pi D^2}{4} \qquad (6.81)$$

where u is the local fluid velocity and C_D and C_L are drag and lift coefficients, it follows that

$$L = \frac{C_L}{C_D} \times F \qquad (6.82)$$

The coefficients C_L and C_D are both functions of the local Reynolds number $u_* D/\nu$. Thus, from (6.79) and (6.82),

$$L \propto \tau_0 D^2 f\left(\frac{u_* D}{\nu}\right) \qquad (6.83)$$

The immersed weight is

$$W \propto (\rho_s - \rho)g D^3 \qquad (6.84)$$

We take moments for the point A around which the particle is just about to rotate. The moment arm of W is proportional to D. For the sake of generality we assume that the moment arms of F and L about A are equal to D times some function of the Reynolds number $u_* D/v$. The moment arms of F and L depend on $u_* D/v$ as well as D because a change in Reynolds number may produce a changed pattern of flow round the particle.

When moments are taken about A, the moment M may be neglected provided an appropriate adjustment is made to the moment arm of the force F. This is another reason for adopting a rather general expression for this moment arm. Thus, at the limit of equilibrium,

$$F \times Df_1\left(\frac{u_* D}{v}\right) + L \times Df_2\left(\frac{u_* D}{v}\right) = \text{const} \times W \times D \qquad (6.85)$$

Substitution of (6.79), (6.83), and (6.84) leads to

$$\frac{\tau_c}{(\rho_s - \rho)gD} = f\left(\frac{u_* D}{v}\right) \qquad (6.86)$$

where τ_c is the critical value of τ_0 for which grains just begin to move. As stated in Section 6.1.2, this is the condition obtained by Shields (1936). The same result could be obtained directly by dimensional analysis.

Figure 6.10 shows Shields curve together with the experimental data he originally used. On the whole, the experimental points seem to follow a reasonably well-defined curve. However, other investigators have found less good agreement with this curve. By way of example, White's (1940)

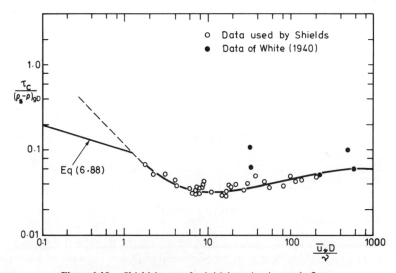

Figure 6.10.   Shields' curve for initial motion in steady flow.

measurements are also shown in Fig. 6.10. There are several possible reasons for discrepancies between different sets of data:

1. Different investigators have different ideas about what constitutes the initial motion condition. Should it be taken as the point at which only one or two grains are moved or should some other limit be adopted?

2. The results in Fig. 6.10 are expressed in terms of the time-mean shear velocity $\bar{u}_*$ and the time-mean value of the critical shear stress τ_c. No account has been taken of turbulence. Different turbulent intensities from one experimental installation to another could produce differing results.

3. For any given median grain size, different sediments may have differing resistance to erosion. The shape of the grain will clearly have some effect and so will the spread of particle sizes in any given sample and the way in which the bed was laid down in the first place.

An attempt to allow for the varying erodability of different sediments was made by White (1940). For a horizontal bed he suggested

$$\frac{\tau_c}{(\rho_s - \rho)gD} = 0.18 \tan \phi \qquad (6.87)$$

where ϕ is the angle of repose of the sediment. Although the idea of introducing the angle of repose is an attractive one the experimental results do not appear to be significantly better when it is allowed for than when it is neglected. This may be because the other factors listed above are more important than the relatively small differences in erodability of different sediments.

The lowest value of the Reynolds number $\bar{u}_* D/\nu$ in the data used by Shields was 1.9. Consequently, the shape of the curve which he originally proposed was purely speculative at lower values of $\bar{u}_* D/\nu$. More recently, Mantz (1977) showed that for $0.03 < \bar{u}_* D/\nu < 1.0$ the experimental results actually follow the curve

$$\frac{\tau_c}{(\rho_s - \rho)gD} = 0.1 \left(\frac{\bar{u}_* D}{\nu} \right)^{-0.3} \qquad (6.88)$$

In practice we are usually concerned with sand or silt in water. For any given temperature we may express the critical shear stress under these conditions directly in terms of the grain size. Figure 6.11 shows the result

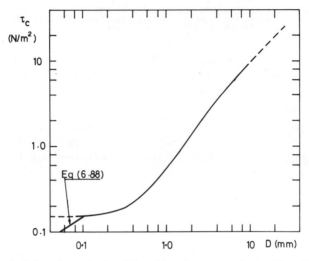

Figure 6.11. Variation with grain size of the critical shear stress obtained from Shields' curve for sand in fresh water at 20°C.

obtained from Shields' curve for sediment of specific gravity 2.65 in water at 20°C. This curve holds for values of D down to about 0.1 mm. Below that, Mantz' (6.88) should be used instead.

The foregoing results apply only to flat beds of noncohesive sediment. Results for initial motion of cohesive sediment are presented in Section 6.6.1. For nonflat beds the critical condition for initial motion is dependent on the bed profile. Menard (1950) observed that the critical velocity for duned beds was only 75–88% of that for flat beds for sediments with grain sizes ranging from 0.062 up to 0.7 mm. Rathbun and Goswami (1966) observed the critical velocity for a rippled bed of 0.3-mm sand to be only 46% of that for a flat bed. On the other hand the critical shear stresses in Rathbun and Goswami's experiments were 0.22 N/m² for the flat bed and 0.30 N/m² when the bed was rippled.

6.8. SUSPENSION

This section is concerned with the suspension of noncohesive sediments. Some results for suspension of cohesive sediments in steady flow are given in Section 6.6.2.

6.8.1.   The Variation of Concentration with Height

At first sight it is surprising that a steady flow of water can maintain a stable distribution of sand in suspension. Since sand is heavier than water it might be expected that the grains would eventually settle to the bed. The reason why stable suspensions are possible is that the turbulent eddies are constantly transporting sediment-laden fluid from one level to another. Since the concentration increases toward the bed the fluid carried up from below contains more sediment than that carried down from above. Thus turbulence produces a net upward flux of sediment which balances the tendency of the sediment to settle back toward the bed.

This process may be represented by the following model. Consider a horizontal plane of area A at height y above the bed. If the plane is large enough and the turbulence is isotropic the fluid will, on average, be carried up over half of the plane and down over the other half. Suppose that the mean upward velocity of the turbulent eddies is v'. Similarly, the mean downward velocity will also be v'. Since the sediment has a fall velocity W with respect to the surrounding fluid, the sediment being carried up has an absolute velocity $v' - W$ whereas that being carried down has a velocity $v' + W$.

Next assume that the typical length scale of the turbulent eddies is l so that, on average, the fluid is being carried up from the level $y - l$ and down from the level $y + l$. For a steady state to exist the quantity of sediment carried up must equal the quantity carried down. Thus

$$C_{y-l}(v' - W)\frac{A}{2} = C_{y+l}(v' + W)\frac{A}{2} \tag{6.89}$$

In this equation C_{y+l} and C_{y-l} represent the concentrations at the levels $y + l$ and $y - l$ from which the sediment is being entrained. By Taylor's theorem

$$C_{y+l} = C + l\frac{\partial C}{\partial y} + l^2\frac{\partial^2 C}{\partial y^2} + \cdots$$

$$C_{y-l} = C - l\frac{\partial C}{\partial y} + l^2\frac{\partial^2 C}{\partial y^2} - \cdots \tag{6.90}$$

Substituting in (6.89) and neglecting terms in l^2 and above we find

$$WC + \varepsilon\frac{\partial C}{\partial y} = 0 \tag{6.91}$$

where $\varepsilon = v'l$ may be thought of as a diffusion coefficient. This is the same as (6.48), which was derived in a different way in Section 6.3.2.

This model should not, of course, be interpreted too literally. In reality turbulent eddies have a wide range of differing length scales and sediment-laden fluid is not really transported a fixed distance l before it starts to mix with the surrounding fluid. Nevertheless, (6.91) is found to hold over a wide range of conditions provided ε is appropriately determined.

Since (6.91) was derived with the aid of mixing lengths it is natural to look to mixing length theory to supply an expression for the diffusion coefficient ε. In Section 1.16.4 we saw that the Reynolds stress was

$$\tau_1 = -\overline{\rho u' v'} \tag{6.92}$$

and that

$$u' = -l \frac{\partial \bar{u}}{\partial y} \tag{6.93}$$

Thus

$$v'l = \frac{\tau_1}{\rho(\partial \bar{u}/\partial y)} \tag{6.94}$$

The overbar has been dropped in (6.94) because (6.91) involves time-mean quantities. We see that if the value of $v'l$ for momentum exchange is assumed to be the same as that for sediment transport, (6.94) provides a means of evaluating ε.

In fully turbulent flow the Reynolds stress is very much larger than the viscous stress. Consequently, outside the viscous sublayer, τ_1 may be taken equal to the total shear stress τ. For free-surface flow

$$\tau = \tau_0 \left(\frac{d-y}{d} \right) \tag{6.95}$$

Thus

$$\varepsilon = \frac{\tau_0}{\rho(\partial \bar{u}/\partial y)} \left(\frac{d-y}{d} \right) \tag{6.96}$$

Substituting (6.96) into (6.91), making use of (1.94) for $\partial \bar{u}/\partial y$, and integrating leads to

$$\frac{C}{C_a} = \left(\frac{d-y}{d-y_a}\frac{y_a}{y}\right)^{W/Ku_*}$$

(6.97)

where C_a is the concentration at some reference height y_a above the bed.

Equation (6.97) was first derived by Rouse (1937). Figure 6.12 shows examples of measurements made by Vanoni (1946) in a laboratory channel. As predicted by (6.97), each set of measurements follows a reasonable straight line when plotted with logarithmic axes. Similar results were observed in Vanoni's other tests. However, the slope of the experimental curves was not always the same as that given by (6.97). When the concentration of sediment

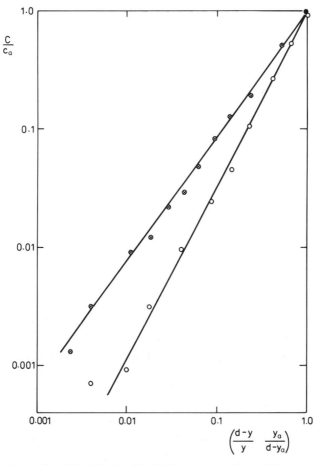

Figure 6.12. Examples of the variation in sediment concentration with height in steady flow (after Vanoni, 1946).

in suspension was low, agreement between theory and experiment was close but, at higher concentrations, agreement could be obtained only if a value of the Karman constant K less than 0.4 was adopted. Recently, Coleman (1981) pointed out that since (1.94) does not hold over the whole depth of flow, (6.97) cannot be expected to apply over the whole depth either. Thus the earlier measurements, which appeared to indicate a changing value of K, in fact only confirm that (6.97) is not valid outside the overlap layer (see Section 1.16.1).

There have been many attempts to improve on (6.97). For example, Itakura and Kishi (1980) used their revised expression for the velocity distribution (1.103) to obtain

$$\frac{C}{C_a} = \left[\left(\frac{d-y}{d-y_a}\right)^\phi \frac{y_a}{y}\right]^{W/K\bar{u}_*} \tag{6.98}$$

where

$$\phi = 7Kg\left(\frac{\rho_s - \rho}{\rho}\right)\frac{W\bar{C}d}{\bar{u}_*^3} \tag{6.99}$$

and $\bar{C}$ is here the mean volumetric concentration averaged over the whole cross section.

6.8.2.   Transport Rate of Sediment in Suspension

The sediment transport rate is given by

$$Q_{ss} = \int_a^d \bar{u}C\,dy \tag{6.100}$$

where a is the value of y at which suspended load gives way to bedload. Clearly (6.97) cannot be valid right down to $y=0$ since this would make the concentration infinite. Because of the voids between grains the volumetric concentration cannot exceed about 0.6 even when the sediment is tightly packed together. Einstein (1950) suggested that the lower limit for suspension should be taken as

$$a = 2D \tag{6.101}$$

To make use of (6.97) to calculate the sediment transport rate, it is necessary to know the concentration at some reference height. The most satisfactory solution is to make a measurement of concentration for the flow concerned. However, in many situations this may not be possible. Einstein suggested that under these circumstances the concentration at the reference height a could be calculated from

$$C_a = \frac{11.6 Q_s}{2\bar{u}_* D} \qquad (6.102)$$

where Q_s is the bedload transport rate. Various other expressions have been suggested for the reference concentration (Yalin, 1963; Smith, 1977; Itakura and Kishi, 1980) but none is wholly satisfactory.

6.9. BEDLOAD, SALTATION, AND TOTAL LOAD

6.9.1. Terminology

In the immediate vicinity of the bed, the moving grain is supported by collisions with adjacent grains and the reaction of the bed rather than the turbulent eddies which were seen in the preceding section to be important for suspension. Typically, particles in the bed layer tend to move by rolling or sliding. This form of sediment transport is referred to as bedload. Einstein (1950) suggested that the bed layer was two grain diameters thick but most other researchers prefer a somewhat larger thickness.

Grains moving as bedload tend to remain in close contact with the bed. Occasionally, however, it is possible to observe a mode of transport in which a grain is hurled up from the bed, temporarily supported by the fluid above, and then crashes back to the bed hurling up more grains to repeat the process. This is called saltation. It is a particularly common mode of transport for wind-blown sediments. In water it seems to be less important and is usually ignored.

The term total load is used for the sum of bedload and that part of the suspended load which consists of sediment also to be found in the bed. Steady flows also transport in suspension significant quantities of very fine sediment which is not found in the bed. This is called washload. The quantities of this washload in suspension are determined by events occurring well upstream, such as the caving in of banks. Washload remains in suspension despite the fact that it is not constantly resupplied from the bed because its fall velocity is so small. However, because it is not supplied from the bed it is not possible to estimate the quantity of washload with the aid of formulas based on local flow conditions.

6.9.2.   Formulas for Bedload and Total Load

Table 6.1 lists some of the formulas proposed for bedload and total load. This is not a complete list but is intended to give an indication of the large number of formulas available and of their general similarity when expressed in terms of the same variables. Of the formulas not included in Table 6.1, mention should be made of the methods of Colby and Hembree (1955) and Toffaletti (1969), both of which are extensions of Einstein's (1950) model; the Ackers and White (1973) formula, which will be considered in more detail below; and a similar formula due to Yang (1979). In addition, a number of "regime" formulas, such as those of Blench (1966) and Inglis (1968), have proved useful in open channel flows although their application to marine hydraulics seems dubious. In some of the formulas shown in Table 6.1 the

TABLE 6.1.   SOME FORMULAS FOR BED LOAD AND TOTAL LOAD

Investigator	Formula	Comments
Du Boys (1879)	$Q_s = A\tau_0(\tau_0 - \tau_c)$	Bedload
Donat (1929)	$Q_s = A\bar{U}^2(\bar{U}^2 - \bar{U}_c^2)$	Bedload
Rubey (1933)	$Q_s = AS^{1.4}Q^{0.6}(Q^{0.6} - Q_c^{0.6})$	Bedload
O'Brien and Rindlaub (1934)	$Q_s = A(\tau_0 - \tau_c)^m$	Bedload
MacDougall (1933)	$Q_s = AS^B(Q - Q_c)$	Bedload
Schoklitsch (1934)	$Q_s = A\dfrac{S^{3/2}}{D^{1/2}}(Q - Q_c)$	Bedload
Waterways Experimental Station	$Q_s = \dfrac{A}{n}(\tau_0 - \tau_c)^m$	Bedload
Shields (1936)	$Q_s = AQS\dfrac{(\tau_0 - \tau_c)}{(\rho_s - \rho)gD}$	Bedload
Kalinske (1942)	$Q_s = \bar{u}_* Df\left(\dfrac{\tau_0}{\tau_c}\right)$	Bedload
Meyer-Peter and Muller (1948)	$Q_s = A\left(\dfrac{\tau_0 - \tau_c}{(\rho_s - \rho)gD}\right)^{3/2}$	Bedload
Brown (1950) (Einstein-Brown formula)	$Q_s = AD^{3/2}\left(\dfrac{\tau_0}{(\rho_s - \rho)gD}\right)^3$	Bedload

TABLE 6.1. *(continued)*

Investigator	Formula	Comments
Einstein (1950)	$Q_s = AD^{3/2} f\left(\dfrac{\tau_0}{(\rho_s - \rho)gD}\right)$	Bedload. (Total load obtained as sum of bedload and suspended load)
Laursen (1958)	$Q_s = Q\left(\dfrac{D}{d}\right)^{7/6}\left(\dfrac{\tau_0 - \tau_c}{\tau_0}\right) f\left(\dfrac{\bar{u}_*}{W}\right)$	Total load
Garde and Albertson (1958)	$Q_s = Q\dfrac{D}{d}\left(\dfrac{\bar{u}_* d}{v}\right)^{2/3} f(D)$	Total load
Barekyan (1962)	$Q_s = AQS\left(\dfrac{\bar{U} - \bar{U}_c}{\bar{U}_c}\right)$	Bedload
Bishop et al. (1965)	$Q_s = AD^{3/2} f\left(\dfrac{\tau_0}{(\rho_s - \rho)gD}\right)$	Bedload
Bogardi (1965)	$Q_s = Q\left(\dfrac{D}{d}\right)^{7/6}\left(\dfrac{\tau_0 - \tau_c}{\tau_0}\right) f\left(\dfrac{gD}{\bar{u}_*^2}, D\right)$	Total load
Bagnold (1966)	$Q_s = A\bar{U}f\left(\bar{U}, \dfrac{\tau_0}{(\rho_s - \rho)gD}\right)$	Total load
Chang et al. (1967)	$Q_s = A\bar{U}(\tau_0 - \tau_c)$	Total load
Engelund and Hansen (1967)	$Q_s = A\dfrac{\bar{U}^2 D}{\bar{u}_*}\left(\dfrac{\tau_0}{(\rho_s - \rho)gD}\right)^2$	Total load

coefficient A is a constant, whereas in others it depends on the characteristics of the sediment.

All of the formulas listed in Table 6.1 are for noncohesive sediments. In steady flow, particles fine enough to exhibit cohesion are principally transported in suspension.

Although many of the formulas are similar in form it will be seen that some involve a critical flow condition, below which no transport of sediment takes place, whereas others do not. This is an important difference for those working with scale models where the flow may be close to the critical condition. On site, the constantly changing conditions make the possible existence of a critical value of τ_0, $\bar{U}$, or Q relatively unimportant.

Faced with the embarrassingly large number of available formulas the most sensible course is to choose one or more which appear to give good results for conditions similar to those of interest. Although some of the formulas are derived from theoretical considerations it is probably better to regard them all as basically empirical since all involve empirical coefficients or correction factors.

Comparisons of various formulas are presented by the A.S.C.E. in the manual *Sedimentation Engineering* (1975), by White et al. (1975), and by Yang and Molinas (1982). The A.S.C.E. compares 13 formulas with a series of measurements of sediment discharge in two rivers in the United States. White et al. compare 8 formulas with 1020 measurements in laboratory channels and 260 measurements in natural water courses. The data used by Yang and Molinas consisted of 1093 laboratory measurements and 166 river measurements. Seven formulas were investigated. Of the formulas tested, that due to Engelund and Hansen (1967) showed good performance in all three comparisons. A slightly better performance in the White et al. comparison was achieved by the Ackers-White (1973) formula (which was not included in the A.S.C.E. comparison). This formula also performed well in Yang and Molinas' comparison. It should be pointed out that "good" performance in the context of sediment transport does not have quite the same meaning as in some other branches of engineering. In the White et al. comparison even the Ackers-White formula predicted sediment transport rates within a factor of two of the measured rate in only 68% of the cases.

Because of their relatively good performance in the above comparisons and because they are increasingly widely used in practice the Engelund-Hansen and Ackers-White formulas are now outlined in more detail. Bagnold's model is also described because it is so widely referred to in recent oceanographic literature.

Engelund-Hansen Formula

This total load formula was put forward by Engelund and Hansen in 1967:

$$\frac{Q_s}{\left(\dfrac{\rho_s - \rho}{\rho}\, gD^3\right)^{1/2}} = \frac{0.1}{C_f}\left(\frac{\tau_0}{(\rho_s - \rho)gD}\right)^{5/2} \qquad (6.103)$$

More recently, Engelund and Fredsoe (1982) suggested that the coefficient 0.1 on the right-hand side of this equation should be reduced to 0.08.

This formula was derived with the aid of a number of hypotheses about the way in which the sediment is moved. One of these was that the particles move at a speed proportional to the shear velocity $\bar{u}_*$.

Ackers-White Formula

Once again, this is a total load formula. It was proposed by Ackers and White in 1973 and is based on dimensional analysis with exponents determined empirically. It may be written as follows:

$$\frac{Q_s}{\bar{U}d} = \frac{D_{35}}{d}\left(\frac{\bar{U}}{\bar{u}_*}\right)^n C_1 \left(\frac{F-A}{A}\right)^m \tag{6.104}$$

In this equation

$$F = \left(\frac{\bar{U}}{2.46\ln\left(\frac{10d}{D_{35}}\right)}\right)^{1-n} \frac{\bar{u}_*^n}{\left(\frac{\rho_s-\rho}{\rho}gD_{35}\right)^{1/2}} \tag{6.105}$$

In addition, if

$$D_* = \left(\frac{\rho_s-\rho}{\rho}\frac{g}{v^2}\right)^{1/3} D_{35} \tag{6.106}$$

for $D_* > 60$

$$\begin{aligned} n &= 0 \\ A &= 0.17 \\ m &= 1.5 \\ C_1 &= 0.025 \end{aligned} \tag{6.107}$$

for $1 < D_* \leqslant 60$

$$\begin{aligned} n &= 1 - 0.243\ln D_* \\ A &= \frac{0.23}{D_*^{1/2}} + 0.14 \\ m &= \frac{9.66}{D_*} + 1.34 \\ C_1 &= \exp[2.86\ln D_* - 0.434(\ln D_*)^2 - 8.13] \end{aligned} \tag{6.108}$$

The equation is not recommended for use when $D_* < 1$ since this corresponds to cohesive sediment.

The form presented above assumes that the mean volumetric transport rate may be obtained from a single calculation based on the grain size D_{35}, which is exceeded by 65% by weight of the sediment. An alternative would be to split the sediment into size fractions and carry out the calculation for each fraction separately.

Bagnold's Model

The most recent version of this model is that given by Bagnold (1966). The basic idea behind the model is that sediment transport requires work to be done by the flow. The stream power is $\tau_0 \bar{U}$ but because of the limited efficiency of the transport process only a fraction e_b of this power is available to carry the sediment along.

On the other hand, the work rate required to transport the bedload is equal to the product of bedload transport rate and $\tan \alpha$, where $\tan \alpha$ is the coefficient of dynamic solid friction. Equating the required work to the available work gives the following expression for the bedload transport rate Q_s:

$$\left(\frac{\rho_s - \rho}{\rho}\right) Q_s \ \tan \alpha = \tau_0 \bar{U} e_b \tag{6.109}$$

Similar arguments lead to an expression for the suspended load transport rate Q_{ss}:

$$\left(\frac{\rho_s - \rho}{\rho}\right) Q_{ss} \frac{W}{\bar{U}} = \tau_0 \bar{U}(1 - e_b)e_s \tag{6.110}$$

where e_s is the efficiency of the suspended load transport process and W is the fall velocity. Bagnold (1966) gives empirical curves for e_b and $\tan \alpha$ and suggests that $(1 - e_b)e_s$ should be taken equal to 0.01.

One possible reason Bagnold's model did not perform as well as the Ackers-White and Engelund-Hansen methods in the various comparisons mentioned above is that sediment transport rate is not generally a single-valued function of shear stress. Also, the curves for e_b and $\tan \alpha$ and the expression for $(1 - e_b)e_s$ are based on relatively few data.

Combined Steady Plus Oscillatory Flows

6.10.   INITIAL MOTION

6.10.1.   Wave Propagation in the Direction of the Current

There have been very few studies of the initial motion condition in combined steady and oscillatory flow. Figure 6.13 shows an example of results obtained by Hammond and Collins (1979) for flat beds of sediment oscillated with simple harmonic motion in a steady flow. In Fig. 6.13 the velocity $\bar{u}$ is the time-mean velocity measured at 0.02 m above the bed.

To understand these results it is helpful to consider two extreme situations.

1.   If the frequency of the oscillation is very low the oscillatory flow may, at each instant, be treated as if it were steady. Acceleration effects are negli-

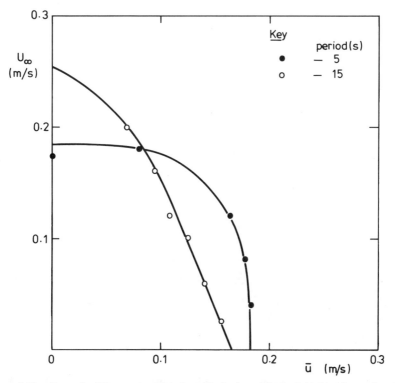

Figure 6.13.   Example of the way in which the critical value of U_∞ for initial motion varies with $\bar{u}$ in combined steady and oscillatory flow (after Hammond and Collins, 1979).

gible. Thus motion of the sediment takes place when the sum of the steady and oscillatory components of velocity in the vicinity of the grains reaches the critical value for a steady current alone. This condition would correspond to a straight line on Fig. 6.13 between the value of U_∞ at which $\bar{u}=0$ and the value of $\bar{u}$ for $U_\infty=0$. Hammond and Collins' measurements suggest that for periods of oscillation equal to 15 s the results are approaching this straight line condition but have not quite reached it.

Vincent (1957) also suggested that the effective velocity for initial motion should be taken as the sum of the oscillatory and steady velocities for the case of very weak currents, such as the mass transport current produced by wave action.

2. If the frequency of the oscillatory flow is high, the wave-induced boundary layer will be very thin compared with that of the steady flow and the wave and steady motions will be uncoupled. In the extreme case, the condition for initial motion would be for either U_∞ or $\bar{u}$ to exceed the critical values corresponding, respectively, to no mean current and no oscillatory flow. As shown by Fig. 6.13 the results for a period of 5 s appear to be approaching this extreme. Experiments carried out by Natarajan (1969) showed little effect of mean current on the initial motion condition for periods less than 1.8 s and $\bar{U}/U_\infty < 0.26$.

6.10.2.   Wave Propagation Direction Not Collinear with the Current

In light of Hammond and Collins' results discussed in the preceding section, it is to be expected that at low frequencies the initial motion condition would be given by the vector sum of the oscillatory and steady velocities, whereas at high frequencies the wave and current motions are probably uncoupled so that initial motion would take place when either the current or the waves exceed their respective limiting conditions. Natarajan (1969) also carried out experiments with mean currents at right angles to the direction of oscillation. Periods of oscillation did not exceed about 1.7 s and $\bar{U}/U_\infty$ was less than 0.28. Under these conditions the steady current appeared to have little effect on the initial motion limit.

6.11.   ONSHORE–OFFSHORE TRANSPORT AND EQUILIBRIUM GRAIN SIZE DISTRIBUTION

6.11.1.   Sediment Transport Rate

One of the most important factors determining whether a beach will build up or erode is the transport of sediment in the onshore–offshore direction.

Because the mass transport velocity offshore of the breakers is in the direction of wave propagation in the immediate vicinity of the bed, at any rate if the bed is not too rough, this current tends to carry sediment in toward the shore. This tendency is opposed by rip and turbidity currents and by the component of gravity acting back down the slope. In a closed system with the wave conditions held constant the bed would eventually reach an equilibrium profile for which these various factors would exactly balance. In real life, however, conditions are constantly changing and a beach is rarely in equilibrium with the existing wave field.

Because of the practical importance of onshore–offshore transport there have been many attempts to predict its magnitude and direction. The following mechanisms have been put forward:

1. Winds acting on the water surface (King and Williams, 1949).
2. Tidal variations (Shephard, 1950).
3. Rip currents (e.g., Cook and Gorsline, 1972).
4. Variations in wave steepness (Dean, 1973), height (Hashimoto and Uda, 1979), power (Short, 1978), asymmetry (Wells, 1967).

Seymour and King (1982) reviewed the various approaches and compared eight different models with site measurements in California. They found that none of the existing models was entirely successful but that the best correlation with measured beach changes was obtained for models that assume wave steepness to be the most important variable. In particular, Dean's (1973) parameter

$$\frac{0.6 H_0 g T}{\pi \lambda_0 W}$$

appeared to predict not only the direction but also, to some extent, the magnitude of the onshore–offshore transport. According to Dean, onshore transport occurs when this parameter is less than unity and offshore transport when it is greater. A modified version of Dean's parameter due to Hattori and Kawamata (1980) was found to be less successful than the original formulation unless the suggested numerical limits were altered.

The basis of Dean's model is as follows. Sand grains are lifted into suspension as the wave crest passes. If they fall back to the bed during the first half of the wave cycle they will be transported onshore. If they fall back during the second half they will be carried offshore.

Dean's model is based on a consideration of sediment transported in suspension. Several investigators have derived models based on equations for bedload and total load transport. Bailard and Inman (1980), Bowen (1980), and Bailard (1981) used Bagnold's formulas for sediment transport, and Shibayama and Horikawa (1980) used a modified version of Madsen and Grant's equation. Only the first of these models was examined by Seymour and King. Taking the bedload transport "efficiency" to be 12% they found poor agreement between the model and site measurements. [More recently Bailard (1982) suggested bedload efficiency equal to 10% and, for his total load model, suspended load efficiency equal to 2%.] The main reason suggested by Seymour and King for the disappointing performance of Bailard and Inman's model was that the calculated net transport was the small difference between large onshore and offshore transport rates so that small errors in the original formula became large errors in the final answer. This difficulty also affects the other models mentioned above. The problem is made more severe by the fact that empirical coefficients in the various formulas usually are based on laboratory data so that extrapolation to site conditions is risky.

6.11.2.   Variation in Grain Size in the Offshore Direction

Beaches frequently show a regular variation in grain size with distance from the shore (see, e.g., Inman, 1955). Offshore of the breakers the grain size tends to decrease with increasing depth. The grain size also tends to decrease onshore of the breaker line as far as the midtide level on the beach. However, coarser sediments frequently are found further up the beach, particularly on top of the summer berm.

Eagleson et al. (1958) suggested that offshore of the breakers this sorting is a result of the opposing effects of gravity tending to pull sediment down the slope into deeper water and the mass transport current, which tends to carry particles on the bed in the direction of wave propagation. For waves coming in at right angles to a beach sloping at an angle θ to the horizontal these forces will exactly balance for a particle of mass m and diameter D if

$$mg \sin \theta = C_D \rho \frac{\pi D^2}{8} \bar{u}^2 \qquad (6.111)$$

The left-hand side of this equation represents the component of the gravity force acting down the slope and the right-hand side is the force resulting from the wave-induced mass transport current.

Making use of a modified version of the expression for C_D given by Carty (see Section 5.7.1) and an approximate form of Longuet-Higgins' solution for the mass transport velocity, Eagleson and Dean (1959) obtained an expression for the size of grains which are just in equilibrium between the two forces:

$$D = \left[\frac{\rho}{(\rho_s - \rho)\, gT\lambda \sin\theta \sinh^2 bd} \, \frac{131 H^2 v}{} \right]^{7/6} \left(\frac{\pi}{vT} \right)^{2/3} \qquad (6.112)$$

Equation (6.112) gives qualitative but not quantitative agreement with experiment. One possible reason for the discrepancy is the use of a smooth bed laminar flow expression for the mass transport velocity. Natural beds are certainly rough and usually turbulent when the wave action is strong enough to move the sediment.

Another possibility is that the dynamic equilibrium which is the basis of (6.112) is not stable. Eagleson et al. did observe that for steady waves in a laboratory channel there was a position on a sloping beach for which a given size of particle would move neither onshore nor offshore. But if the particle were displaced from this position, it would then be carried away in one direction or another. On site the waves are never steady so that particles would be constantly displaced from their equilibrium positions. It may be that no moving grain can be stable. If so, the beach slope may be determined by the grains which are at the initial motion limit but not actually moving. Using a similar approach to that outlined above, that is, equating the fluid drag to the restraining force due to gravity, Eagleson and Dean arrived at an expression for the limiting grain size. If beach slope is assumed small, this expression may be reduced to

$$D = \frac{\rho}{(\rho_s - \rho)\, gT^{3/2} \sinh bd(1.3 + \sin\theta)} \, 260 v^{1/2} H \qquad (6.113)$$

In this case it is the oscillatory component of velocity rather than the mass transport velocity which tends to move the particle. Once again the smooth bed laminar flow expression is adopted for the fluid velocity distribution. On the whole the agreement between (6.113) and experiment is less good than for (6.112).

It will be seen that when $\theta = 0$ (for a horizontal bed) (6.113) is the same as (6.8).

Sato and Kishi (1954) also suggested that the grain size distribution is determined by the initial motion condition. Assuming bed shear stress proportional to U_∞^2 and water depth d small compared with the length of the waves, they obtained

$$D = \text{const} \times d^{-3/2} \qquad (6.114)$$

However, this relationship does not show particularly good agreement with experiment.

6.12.   LONGSHORE TRANSPORT (LITTORAL DRIFT)

The transport of sand parallel to the coast has two main components. In the immediate vicinity of the beach the sawtooth motion of the fluid produces a significant net transport: when waves approach the beach at an angle the uprush is also at an angle, whereas the downrush is much more nearly directly down the beach. Second, the steady currents parallel to the shore also produce significant sediment transport, particularly in the vicinity of the breaking waves, which entrain large quantities of sediment into suspension. Figure 6.14 shows some measurements reported by Zenkovitch (1960). Two of the peaks in the record of concentration of sediment in suspension are associated with wave breaking over the offshore bars but there is also a very pronounced peak at the shoreline. This is caused by the sawtooth motion of the fluid already mentioned. Zenkovitch also measured the longshore transport rate of sediment, shown by the bar chart in Fig. 6.14. The height of each block has been obtained by dividing the total transport rate for that block, given by Zenkovitch in cubic meters per hour, by the width of the block perpendicular to the shoreline. Even outside the immediate vicinity

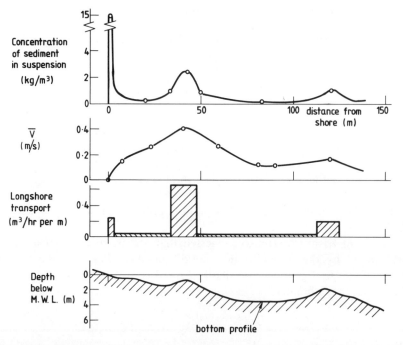

Figure 6.14.   Variation of sediment concentration, longshore current, longshore transport, and bed profile with distance from the shore (after Zenkovitch, 1960).

of the breakers and the shoreline there is some net longshore transport since grains set in motion by the oscillatory wave velocities will be carried along parallel to the coast by the longshore current. In the breaker zone most of the sediment transport occurs as suspension, but away from the breakers bedload predominates.

This longshore transport of sediment causes considerable problems for those trying to prevent siltation of ports, erosion of beaches, and so on. Consequently, prediction of the longshore transport in any given situation is very important. This is usually done by one of the following methods (in order of merit):

1. If the longshore transport is known at a nearby site, the transport at the point of interest can be estimated by making allowance for local conditions.
2. Charts or surveys showing the changes in bed level over a period of years, combined with dredging records, may give some indication. This method is particularly appropriate if there is some structure in the vicinity which traps all or most of the longshore drift.
3. Empirical formulas based on local wave conditions may be used to provide a rough estimate.

Table 6.2 shows some of the empirical formulas that have been proposed. The quantity P_l is the component of the energy flux parallel to the coast at the breakers:

$$P_l = \frac{\rho g}{16} (H^2 c_g)_b \sin 2\alpha_b \qquad (6.115)$$

If it is assumed that when the waves break the water is sufficiently shallow for the group velocity c_g to equal the phase velocity c, then

$$P_l = \frac{\rho g}{16} \left(\frac{H_b^2 \lambda_b}{T} \right) \sin 2\alpha_b \qquad (6.116)$$

The fact that almost all of the formulas consist of a relationship between Q_s and P_l is an indication that only wave-induced transport is being considered. The additional transport due, for example, to tidal currents would have to be determined separately. This question will be discussed in the next section. The only exception is the second formula of Komar and Inman (1970), which may also hold when steady currents other than those induced by waves are present.

TABLE 6.2. SOME FORMULAS FOR LONGSHORE TRANSPORT (Q_s in m³/day; P_l in tonnes-m/day/m; D in m)

Author	Formula	Data base
Caldwell (1956)	$Q_s = 1.20 P_l^{0.8}$	Field measurements in Florida and California
Savage (1959)	$Q_s = 0.219 P_l$	Model tests and field data of Watts and Caldwell. Laboratory data of Krumbein, Saville, Sauvage and Vincent
Ijima, Sato, Aono, Ishii (1960)	$Q_s = 0.130 P_l^{0.54}$	Field measurements in Japan
Ichikawa, Ochiai, Tomita, Murobuse (1961)	$Q_s = 0.131 P_l^{0.8}$	Field measurements in Japan
Manohar (1962)	$Q_s = 55.7 D^{0.59} \left(\dfrac{\rho_s - \rho}{\rho} \right)^{-0.41} P_l^{0.91}$	Field data of Watts, Caldwell. Laboratory data of Krumbein, Saville, Shay and Johnson, Sauvage and Vincent and Savage
Ijima, Sato, Tanaka (1964)	$Q_s = 0.060 P_l$	Field measurements in Japan
Sato (1966)	$Q_s = 0.120 P_l$	Same data as above
Komar, Inman (1970)	$Q_s = 0.778 P_l$	Field measurements in California and field data of Watts and Caldwell
Komar, Inman (1970)	$Q_s = 0.283 \dfrac{\bar{V} P_l}{(U_\infty \sin \alpha)_b}$	Same data as above
Das (1972)	$Q_s = 0.325 P_l$	Field data of Watts, Caldwell, Moore and Cole, Komar, Thornton and Johnson. Laboratory data of Krumbein, Saville, Shay and Johnson, Sauvage and Vincent and Savage and Fairchild
CERC (1977)	$Q_s = 0.401 P_l$	As above, plus light weight sediment data of Sauvage and Vincent and Price and Tomlinson

The parameter Q_s is the volumetric longshore transport rate. The gravimetric rate I_s may be calculated (see, e.g., Das, 1972) from the relation

$$I_s = 0.6(\rho_s - \rho)gQ_s \qquad (6.117)$$

Table 6.2 gives the impression that there is considerable agreement between the various investigators about the form of the longshore transport equation. However, agreement on the general form of the equation conceals very significant disagreement on the actual values of the numerical constants, as shown by Fig. 6.15. One reason for the discrepancies is that not all of the formulas are based on the same data. Figure 6.16 shows the data collected by Das (1971) together with Das' (1972) curve and the C.E.R.C. (1977) curve for purposes of comparison. It is clear that widely different relationships could be obtained if only a limited amount of data was considered. The enormous scatter in Fig. 6.16 draws attention to one of the principal problems in this field, which is that reliable data are difficult to obtain. This is probably

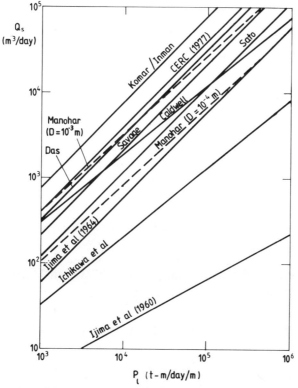

Figure 6.15. Comparison of formulas for longshore transport.

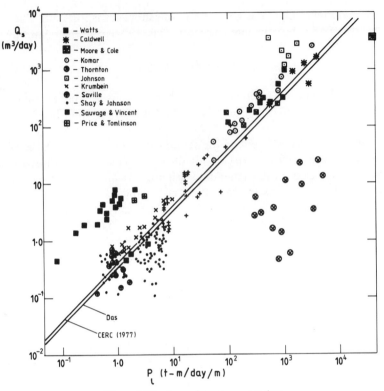

Figure 6.16.   Longshore transport data.

why most investigators have restricted themselves to a relation between Q_s and P_l. Other quantities such as the grain size of the sediment must be important but the scatter of the available data is too great to allow these secondary effects to be investigated. Manohar's formula suggests that a change in grain size from 0.1 to 1.0 mm increases the longshore transport by a factor of 3.9. In comparison with the scatter in the available data this is a small change.

It should be mentioned that the formula recommended by the C.E.R.C. (1977) is the same as the one obtained by Das (1972) when data for lightweight sediments were not excluded.

6.13. SEDIMENT TRANSPORT IN OTHER WAVE PLUS CURRENT FLOWS

Most of the formulas discussed in Sections 6.11 and 6.12 relate to sediment transport by waves alone. Combinations of waves with nonwave-induced currents require separate consideration.

6.13.1. Suspension

The transport rate of sediment in suspension is equal to the integral from
the bed to the free surface of the concentration at a given height times the
fluid velocity at that height. If the steady current is very weak, it is probably
reasonable to assume that the concentration is given by one of the formulas
outlined in Section 6.3 for waves alone. Alternatively, if the waves are very
weak, the steady flow expressions for sediment transport in suspension given
in Section 6.8 provide a first approximation.

However, in many situations it is not acceptable to neglect the nonlinear
interactions between the waves and the steady current. A method for obtaining the concentration profile under these circumstances, and hence the
sediment transport rate, has been put forward by Smith (1977). The assumptions are:

1. The basic equation determining the concentration is (6.47).
2. In that equation

$$\varepsilon = K_0 y \qquad (6.118)$$

where K_0 is a constant which Smith takes equal to the Karman constant
times the shear velocity. This expression for ε follows from the assumption
that eddy viscosity is proportional to distance from the bed and ε is proportional to eddy viscosity.

If ε is independent of time and the concentration is expressed as a Fourier
series in $\cos \omega t, \ldots$, each term in the series may be treated separately. For
example, suppose the concentration has a time-mean component and a
component that varies in time like the real part of $\exp(i\omega t)$. Substitution of
(6.118) into (6.47) and integration gives the solution for the concentration
profile as

$$C = \bar{C}_a \left(\frac{a}{y}\right)^{2p} + C_a \left(\frac{a}{y}\right)^p \left[\left(\frac{\ker_p \xi \ker_p \xi_a + \kei_p \xi + \kei_p \xi_a}{\ker_p^2 \xi_a + \kei_p^2 \xi_a}\right) \cos \omega t \right.$$

$$\left. + \left(\frac{\ker_p \xi \kei_p \xi_a - \kei_p \xi \ker_p \xi_a}{\ker_p^2 \xi_a + \kei_p^2 \xi_a}\right) \sin \omega t \right]$$

$$(6.119)$$

where $p = W/K_0$, $\xi = 2(\omega y/K_0)^{1/2}$, $\xi_a = 2(\omega a/K_0)^{1/2}$, $\bar{C}_a$ is the time-mean concentration at some reference height a, C_a is the fluctuating component of the
concentration at that height and $\ker_p$, $\kei_p$ are Kelvin functions of order p.
Knowing the concentration, the suspended load transport rate may be
calculated with the aid of the formulas for fluid velocity outlined in Chapters
1 and 2.

Equation (6.119) has not been verified experimentally. One of the principal uncertainties about this expression is the assumption that the diffusion coefficient does not vary with time. Clearly if ε does vary during the course of the wave cycle it will not be permissible to treat each time-varying component of the concentration record separately. A model in which ε is not assumed constant was put forward by Bakker (1974). Once again, the equation used as a starting point is (6.47). However, in this case the expression used to calculate ε is

$$\frac{\tau}{\rho}=\varepsilon\frac{\partial\bar{u}}{\partial y} \tag{6.120}$$

This follows from Bakker's assumption that the diffusion coefficient ε is equal to the eddy viscosity. The shear stress τ and the velocity $\bar{u}$ are given by his numerical model for the velocity distribution, discussed in Chapter 2; consequently, the solution for the concentration profile may be obtained numerically from (6.47). Bakker (1974) presents examples of the computed solutions but does not attempt any comparison with experiment. Although the form assumed for ε in Bakker's model is somewhat more realistic than in Smith's model some of the mixing-length expressions used by Bakker to obtain the velocity distribution are questionable.

Swart (1976) studied this problem by adopting a basically empirical approach. He arrived at a similar expression to that of Smith for the variation of the time-mean component of concentration with height. According to Swart, the exponent $2p$ in (6.119) is given by

$$2p=1.05\left(\frac{W}{K\bar{u}_{*WC}}\right)^{0.96}\left(\frac{k_s}{d}\right)^{0.013W/K\bar{u}_{*WC}} \tag{6.121}$$

Here the shear velocity $\bar{u}_{*WC}$ is the value for combined waves and currents given by (6.130) below.

To specify the concentration profile completely, Smith's, Bakkers, and Swart's models require knowledge of the way in which the concentration varies in time at some reference level. In his sample computations Bakker took the concentration at the bed to be equal to the probability that the lift force on a particle of sediment on the bed is larger than its immersed weight, using the expression for this probability given by Einstein (1950). This is clearly a very crude approximation and was adopted by Bakker for illustration only.

Smith (1977) offers two possible expressions for the concentration at the lower limit of suspension which, like Einstein (1950), he takes to be

$a = 2D$. The first expression is a modified version of that suggested by Yalin (1963):

$$C_a = \frac{0.0113C_0(\tau - \tau_c)}{\tau_c + 0.0113\tau}$$ (6.122)

where C_0 is the concentration of sediment in the bed itself.

The other alternative is the expression suggested by Einstein (1950),

$$C_a = \frac{11.6Q_s}{2\bar{u}_* D}$$ (6.123)

where Q_s is the bed load transport rate.

Since (6.122) and (6.123) were derived for steady flows, their use in combined steady plus oscillatory flow requires experimental confirmation. A few laboratory tests were carried out by Abou Seida (1965), who suggested that (6.123) should be modified to

$$C_a = \frac{0.62Q_s}{2u_D D}$$ (6.124)

where u_D is the fluid velocity at a distance D above the bed

6.13.2.   Bedload

In this section the term bedload is taken to include all sediment transport within a distance from the bed equal to two or three times the Nikuradse roughness k_s. When the bed is rippled the oscillatory motion causes plumes of sediment-laden fluid to be hurled up at the end of each half-cycle. However, these plumes of sediment seldom reach more than a few ripple heights above the bed and consequently remain, according to our present definition, as bedload. Clearly the boundary between bedload and suspended load is arbitrary.

Bagnold (1963) extended his steady flow bedload theory to the case of waves plus currents. His modified relationship may be written

$$\left(\frac{\rho_s - \rho}{\rho}\right)Q_s = \frac{e_b}{\tan \alpha - \tan \theta}\tau_0 \bar{u}$$ (6.125)

where the efficiency e_b and the coefficient of dynamic solid friction $\tan \alpha$ are given by empirical curves. In the sea, bed slope $\tan \theta$ may not be negligible, which is why it appears in this equation but not in (6.109). Bagnold (1963) suggested that $\bar{u}$ and τ_0 should be taken as the mean fluid velocity near the bed and the shear stress on the bed respectively.

A somewhat similar approach was adopted by Madsen and Grant (1976), who suggested that their formula for the mean sediment transport rate in pure oscillatory flow might be extended to the case of waves plus currents. At each instant in the wave cycle the Shields parameter ψ is calculated from the expression

$$\psi = \frac{\rho f_{wc} u|u|}{2(\rho_s - \rho)gD} \tag{6.126}$$

Here f_{wc} is Jonsson's friction factor for combined waves plus currents, given by (5.120), and u is the resultant of the depth-averaged mean velocity and the oscillatory component of velocity just outside the boundary layer at the bed. Making use of this expression for ψ, (6.40) is integrated over a complete wave cycle to obtain the net sediment transport as bedload.

Neither Bagnold nor Grant and Madsen compared their calculated sediment transport rates with experimental measurements for combined wave and current flows. It has been observed by several experimenters (e.g., Inman and Bowen, 1962; Natarajan, 1969) that net sediment transport in the direction of the current does not increase steadily with increasing mean current. If the steady current exceeds a certain limit, the net sediment transport starts to decrease in magnitude and may even reverse altogether. This surprising result was attributed by Inman and Bowen to the asymmetry in vortex formation generated by the asymmetry of the flow near the bed: the stronger combined flow in the direction of the mean current generates stronger vortices in the lee of the ripples, which then hurl out more sediment as the flow turns against the mean current. Of course, if the steady current became so strong that no reversal took place at any stage of the wave cycle, sediment transport could only be in the direction of the mean current. Thus any reversal in the direction of net sediment transport as the current is increased can only be temporary. It is clear that this rather complicated sequence of events will not be reproduced by either Bagnold's or Madsen and Grant's models.

In addition to the experiments of Inman and Bowen and Natarajan, laboratory measurements of sediment transport with combined currents and waves have been made by Abou Seida (1965) and Bliven et al. (1977). On the basis of these measurements Hallermeier (1982) suggested the following empirical formula for the sediment transport rate during each half-cycle:

$$Q_s = a\omega^2 \left[\frac{\rho}{10(\rho_s - \rho)g} \right]^{3/2} u^2 D^{1/2} \qquad (6.127)$$

Here u is the resultant of the depth-averaged time-mean velocity and the oscillatory velocity U_∞ just outside the boundary layer and a and ω are the orbital amplitude of the fluid and the frequency of oscillation.

Bliven et al. suggested two possible empirical expressions for the net sediment transport

$$\frac{Q_s g}{\rho W^3} = 0.32 \left(\frac{U_\infty}{\bar{U}} \right)^{0.98} \qquad (6.128)$$

and

$$\frac{Q_s g}{\rho W^3} = 0.03 \left(\frac{\bar{U}}{W} \right)^{1.12} \qquad (6.129)$$

Equation (6.128) gave slightly less scatter.

6.13.3. Total Load

The extension of steady flow formulas to combined steady plus oscillatory flow has been carried out for several total load formulas. For example, this approach has been applied by Swart (1976) to the Ackers-White and Engelund-Hansen formulas described in Section 6.9 and a modified version of the Frijlink formula suggested by Bijker (1967). Swart assumed that these steady flow formulas could be corrected for wave effects by substituting the mean shear velocity $\bar{u}_{*wc}$ for the combined flow for that for steady flow $\bar{u}_*$ alone. The expression he used for $\bar{u}_{*wc}$ was a modification of a formula suggested by Bijker (1967). After some manipulation Swart obtained

$$\frac{\bar{u}_{*wc}}{\bar{u}_*} = \left(1 + 8.28 f_w \log^2 \left(\frac{12d}{k_s} \right) \frac{U_\infty^2}{\bar{U}^2} \right)^{1/2} \qquad (6.130)$$

where f_w is given by (5.49) and (5.50). In addition, Swart replaces the F in (6.104) by F_{wc} where

$$F_{wc} = \left(\frac{\bar{u}_{*wc}}{\bar{u}_*} \right)^n F \qquad (6.131)$$

Swart compared the three modified formulas with measurements of sediment transport made by Bijker (1967) in a wave tank. Tests were carried out with waves both normal and at an oblique angle to the direction of the mean current. The bed of sediment was horizontal. Figures 6.17, 6.18, and 6.19 show how the computed total load compares with the measured transport rate. It was pointed out by Swart that the measured transport rates were not entirely reliable. Two bed materials were used: both were sand, one had a median diameter 0.25 mm, and the other had a diameter 0.34 mm. Sediment was collected in a trap 0.15 m wide. Subsequent experiments with a much wider trap suggested that the actual total load of sediment being transported might be as much as three times the value obtained with the 0.15-m-wide trap. However, even allowing for this uncertainty in the measurements, it is clear from Fig. 6.17, 6.18, and 6.19 that the Ackers-White method is very much more satisfactory than the other two methods.

More recently, Swart (1977) suggested that when $U_\infty/\bar{u}_*$ is greater than 10 (i.e., for relatively weak currents) the expression for A in (6.108) should be replaced by

$$A = 2.29 \left[\frac{\rho f_w}{(\rho_s - \rho)g} \right]^{1/2} \frac{T^{0.043}}{D^{0.12}} \tag{6.132}$$

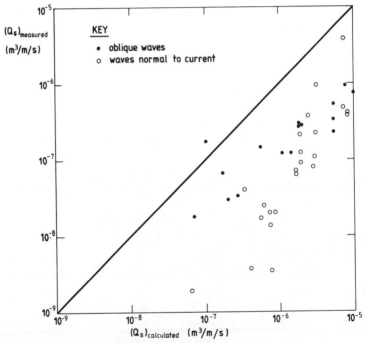

Figure 6.17. Comparison of measured sediment transport rates with the values calculated using the Bijker-Frijlink formula (after Swart, 1976).

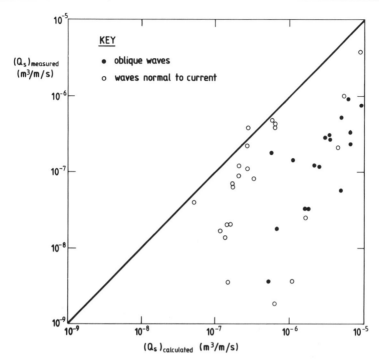

Figure 6.18. Comparison of measured sediment transport rates with the values calculated using the Engelund-Hansen formula (after Swart, 1976).

where the variables are all in S.I. units. The value of f_w is that for a flat bed of the same sediment under the same wave conditions. He also suggests that, for values of $U_\infty/\bar{u}_*$ between 10 and 3, A should be assumed to vary linearly from the value given by (6.132) to that given by (6.108). For values of $U_\infty/\bar{u}_*$ less than 3, A is given by (6.108) as before.

The conclusion that the modified Ackers-White formula gives the best results is supported by Willis (1978). Willis' approach is basically similar to that of Swart, although he suggests that in (6.130) the coefficient 8.28 should be replaced by 5.0.

Van de Graaff and Van Overeem (1979) used the various formulas discussed to calculate the longshore transport due to waves alone and compared this with the predictions of the formula recommended by the C.E.R.C. Shore Protection Manual (see Table 6.2). None of the formulas discussed in this section gave close agreement with the C.E.R.C. formula, although Van de Graaff and Van Overeem suggested that overall trends were somewhat better represented by the Frijlink-Bijker formula. However, to make a comparison of this sort it is necessary to adopt some expression for the

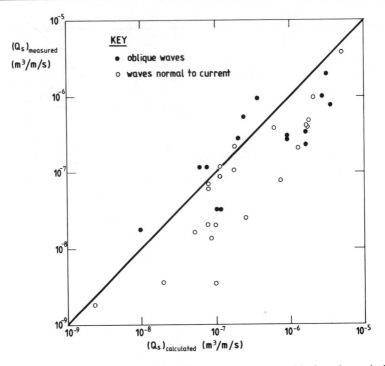

Figure 6.19. Comparison of measured sediment transport rates with the values calculated using the Ackers-White formula (after Swart, 1976).

longshore drift current set up by the waves. There is little agreement on the correct form of the longshore drift and, as pointed out by Van de Graaff and Van Overeem, the results obtained from their comparisons are very sensitive to the distribution assumed for the current. They also point out that the C.E.R.C. formula is itself subject to doubt so that comparisons based on it should be treated with caution.

As previously mentioned, Bagnold's model has also been applied to the calculation of total load in situations involving waves and currents. For example, Inman and Bagnold (1963) used it to develop an expression for longshore transport which Komar and Inman (1970) showed to give reasonable agreement with site measurements. More recently, Bailard (1981) applied Bagnold's total load model to the problem of onshore–offshore transport. In this case the comparison with site measurements (Bailard, 1982) was less good. The correct conclusion to be drawn from these and other studies is probably that reached by Kachel and Sternberg (1971) in connection with Bagnold's bedload model: the model can be applied successfully in the marine environment but only if the empirical coefficients are considerably modified.

6.14. EXAMPLES

1. Progressive waves of height 3 m and period 15 s are advancing toward a coast. There is no steady current. When the depth of water is 20 m what is the minimum grain size of sand or gravel which will just not be moved by wave action? Take $v = 10^{-6}$ m²/s.

Following the method outlined in Example 1a of Section 2.18, the amplitude of the velocity just outside the boundary layer at the bed is

$$U_\infty = 0.924 \text{ m/s}$$

Thus

$$R = \frac{U_\infty^2}{\omega v} = 2.04 \times 10^6$$

Section 6.1 indicates that use of Shields curve and Kamphuis' Fig. 5.5 for the friction factor gives satisfactory results over a wide range of conditions. Since this method is less straightforward than the explicit formulas listed in Section 6.1.1, its use is illustrated here. The first difficulty is that, with the problem in its present form, it is necessary to iterate. As an initial estimate we use the result given by Bagnold's (6.1). This is

$$D = 0.00646 \text{ m}$$

Thus

$$\frac{a}{D} = 341$$

$$\left(\frac{\rho_s - \rho}{\rho} \frac{g}{v^2} \right)^{1/3} D = 163.4$$

From Fig. 5.5

$$f_w = 0.013$$

Since this calculation is at best only approximate, the difference between the median grain diameter D and the value D_{90} used in Fig. 5.5 has been ignored. Hence

$$\frac{\hat{\tau}_0}{(\rho_s - \rho)gD} = \frac{\rho U_\infty^2 f_w/2}{(\rho_s - \rho)gD} = 0.053$$

For the calculated value of $\{[(\rho_s-\rho)/\rho](g/v^2)\}^{1/3}D$, Fig. 6.3 suggests that the Shields parameter is equal to 0.06. The estimated grain size is thus too large. Repeating the procedure outlined above we obtain, successively

D	a/D	$\left(\dfrac{\rho_s-\rho}{\rho}\dfrac{g}{v^2}\right)^{1/3}D$	f_w	$\dfrac{\hat{\tau}_0}{(\rho_s-\rho)gD}$	Required Value from Fig. 6.3
0.005	441	126	0.010	0.053	0.056
0.0048	460	121	0.010	0.055	0.055

Thus the minimum grain size for stability is 4.8 mm.

Clearly the rate at which the iteration converges may be improved by plotting estimates against grain size and interpolating.

2.   Waves of height 3 m and period 15 s are propagating over a horizontal bed in water of depth 20 m. The sediment consists of sand of median diameter 0.8 mm. The steady current is in a direction at right angles to that of wave propagation and has a surface velocity of 0.4 m/s. Obtain estimates of suspended load and total load.

(a)   Suspended load. In this case the steady current is relatively weak. It is thus reasonable to assume that it has little effect on the distribution of sediment in suspension. Consequently, an estimate of suspended load is

$$\int_{y=2D}^{\infty} \bar{C}\bar{u}\, dy$$

where $\bar{C}$ is the time-mean concentration for waves alone, given by (6.56), and $\bar{u}$ is the time-mean velocity at that height.

To make use of (6.56) for $\bar{C}$ we need the coefficients α and $\bar{C}_0$. For a flat bed of 0.8-mm sand with these waves, Fig. 5.5 gives (assuming $D_{90}=0.8$ mm and $v=10^{-6}$ m^2/s)

$$f_w=0.006$$

Hence

$$\frac{\hat{\tau}_0}{(\rho_s-\rho)gD}=0.198$$

This is the Shields parameter for a flat bed as required by Nielsen's

(6.60). For this sand

$$\left(\frac{\rho_s-\rho}{\rho}\frac{g}{v^2}\right)^{1/3}D=20.2$$

Figure 6.3 gives the critical value of the Shields parameter as

$$\psi_c=0.032$$

Thus from (6.60) the reference concentration above a ripple crest is

$$\bar{C}_0=0.0037$$

Using the ripple height of 0.16 m obtained in Example 1 of Section 4.18, (6.59) gives

$$\alpha=12.6\,\text{m}^{-1}$$

For a weak steady current such as that in the present example the bed roughness will be dominated by the wave-induced vortex ripples which were found in Section 4.18 to be of height 0.16 m and length 1.6 m. From (1.106)

$$k_s=0.4\,\text{m}$$

Thus if the roughness length is assumed the same for a current at right angles to the wave direction, (1.99) and (1.100) give

$$\bar{u}_*=0.022\,\text{m/s}$$
$$\bar{U}=0.34\,\text{m/s}$$

Since the calculation is at best only approximate we will assume, for the integration of $\bar{C}\bar{u}$, a mean bed level above which $\bar{u}$ is given by (1.99) and $\bar{C}$ is given by (6.56) with the values of $\bar{C}_0$ and α shown above. Although (6.61) gives a lower value of $\bar{C}_0$ above a ripple trough, it should be remembered that this is the value at the crest level. Near the bed the concentration would be higher. The origin of (1.99) is chosen to make $\bar{u}$ equal to zero at the mean bed level. The final result is

$$\text{suspended load}=0.00003\,\text{m}^3\text{ of sediment/m·s}$$

(b)   Total load. Swart found that the Ackers-White formula gave reasonable agreement with experiment in combined flows of this sort provided the shear velocity was calculated from (6.130):

$$\bar{u}_{*wc} = 0.022 \left[1 + 8.28 \times 0.11 \log^2 \left(\frac{12 \times 20}{0.4} \right) \times \left(\frac{0.924}{0.34} \right)^2 \right]^{1/2}$$

$$= 0.16 \text{ m/s}$$

We assume that D_{35} in the Ackers-White formula is 0.8 mm. Then, in (6.104) we have

$$D_* = 20.2$$
$$n = 0.27$$
$$m = 1.82$$
$$C_1 = 0.032$$
$$F = 0.117$$
$$F_{wc} = 0.20$$

Since $U_\infty / \bar{u}_* > 10$, we use (6.132) for A. This gives

$$A = 0.12$$

Thus

$$Q_s = 0.000005 \text{ m}^3/\text{m} \cdot \text{s}$$

It should be emphasized that in a situation such as this it would be desirable to make calculations with several formulas.

REFERENCES

Abdel-Rahmann, N. M. (1964). The effect of flowing water on cohesive beds. *Versuchsanst. Wasserbau Erdbau Eidg. Tech. Hochsch.*, Contrib. 56. Zurich, pp. 1–114.

Abou Seida, M. M. (1965). Bed load function due to wave action. *Univ. Calif. Hydraul. Eng. Lab. Rep.* HEL-2-11.

Ackers, P. and White, W. R. (1973). Sediment transport: new approach and analysis. *Proc. A.S.C.E. J. Hydraul. Div.* **99** (HY11): 2041–2060.

A.S.C.E. (1975). *Sedimentation Engineering.* A.S.C.E., New York.

Bagnold, R. A. (1946). Motion of waves in shallow water. Interaction of waves and sand bottoms. *Proc. Roy. Soc.* Ser. A. **187**: 1–15.

Bagnold, R. A. (1963). Mechanics of marine sedimentation. In *The Sea*, Vol. 3, M. N. Hill, Ed. Wiley-Interscience, New York, pp. 507–528.

Bagnold, R. A. (1966). An approach to the sediment transport problem from general physics. U.S. Geol. Survey. Prof. Pap. 422-J.

Bailard, J. A. (1981). An energetics total load sediment transport model for a plane sloping beach. *J. Geophys. Res.* **86** (C11): 10938–10954.

Bailard, J. A. (1982). Modeling on-offshore transport in the surfzone. *Proc. 18th Conf. Coastal Eng., Cape Town.*

Bailard, J. A. and Inman, D. L. (1980). An energetics bedload model for a plane sloping beach, local transport. *J. Geophys. Res.* **86** (C3): 2035–2043.

Bakker, W. T. (1974). Sand concentration in oscillatory flow. *Proc. 14th Conf. Coastal Eng., Copenhagen*, pp. 1129–1148.

Barekyan, A. S. (1962). Discharge of channel forming sediments and elements of sand waves. *Sov. Hydrol.* (A.G.U.) No. 2.

Bhattacharya, P. K. (1971). Sediment suspension in shoaling waves. Ph.D. Thesis. Univ. Iowa.

Bijker, E. W. (1967). Some considerations about scales for coastal models with movable bed. Delft Hydraulics Lab. Pùb. No. 50.

Bishop, A. A., Simons, D. B. and Richardson, E. V. (1965). Total bed material transport. *Proc. A.S.C.E. J. Hydraul. Div.* **91** (HY2): 175–191.

Blench, T. (1966). *Mobile Bed Fluviology*, T. Blench, Alberta, Canada.

Bliven, L., Huang, N. E., and Janowitz, G. S. (1977). An experimental investigation of some combined flow sediment transport phenomena. Center for Marine and Coastal Studies. North Carolina State University, Rep. 77-3.

Bogardi, J. L. (1965). European concepts of sediment transportation. *Proc. A.S.C.E. J. Hydraul. Div.* **91** (HY1): 29–54.

Bonnefille, R. and Pernecker, L. (1966). Le début d'entraînement des sédiments sous l'action de la houle. *Bull. CREC.* **15**: 27–32.

Bowen, A. J. (1980). Simple models of nearshore sedimentation; beach profiles and longshore bars. In *The Coastline of Canada*, S. B. McCann, Ed. Geological Survey of Canada. Paper 80-10: 1–11.

Brown, C. B. (1950). Sediment transportation. In *Engineering Hydraulics*, H. Rouse, Ed. Wiley, New York.

Caldwell, J. M. (1956). Wave action and sand movement near Anaheim Bay, California. Beach Erosion Board. Tech. Memo 68.

Carstens, M. R., Neilson, F. M., and Altinbilek, H. D. (1969). Bed forms generated in the laboratory under an oscillatory flow: analytical and experimental study. U.S. Army C.E.R.C. Tech. Memo 28.

Chan, K. W., Baird, M. H. I., and Round, G. F. (1972). Behaviour of dense particles in a horizontally oscillating liquid. *Proc. Roy. Soc.* Ser. A. **330**: 537–559.

Chang, F. M., Simons, D. B., and Richardson, E. V. (1967). Total bed-material discharge in alluvial channels. *Proc. 12th Cong. IAHR. Fort Collins, Colorado.*

Coastal Engineering Research Center. (1977). Shore protection manual. *U.S. Army Corps of Engineers.* 3rd ed.

Colby, B. R. and Hembree, C. H. (1955). Computations of total sediment discharge, Niobrara river near Cody, Nebraska. U.S. Geol. Surv. Water Supply Paper 1357.

Coleman, N. L. (1981). Velocity profiles with suspended sediment. *J. Hydraul. Res.* **19** (3): 211–229.

Cook, D. O. and Gorsline, D. S. (1972). Field observations of sand transport by shoaling waves. *Mar. Geol.* **13**: 31–55.

Das, M. M. (1971). Mechanics of sediment suspension due to oscillatory water waves. Univ. Calif. Hydraul. Eng. Lab. Tech. Rep. HEL-2-32.

Das, M. M. (1972). Suspended sediment and longshore sediment transport data review. *Proc. 13th Conf. Coastal Eng., Vancouver*, pp. 1027–1048.

Dean, R. G. (1973). Heuristic models of sand transport in the surf zone. *Proc. Conf. Eng. Dyn. Surf Zone, Sydney, Australia.*

Dingler, J. R. (1975). Wave formed ripples in nearshore sands Ph.D. Thesis. Univ. Calif. San Diego.

Donat, J. (1929). Uber sohlangriff und geschiebetrieb. *Wasserwirtschaft* **26, 27**.

Du Boys, M. P. (1879). le Rhône et les rivières à lit affouillable. *Mem. Doc. Ann. Ponts Chaussées.* Ser. 5. **18**: 141–195.

Dunn, I. S. (1959). Tractive resistance of cohesive channels. *Proc. A.S.C.E. J. Soil Mech. Found. Div.* **SM3**: 1–24.

Eagleson, P. S. and Dean, R. G. (1959). Wave-induced motion of bottom sediment particles. *Proc. A.S.C.E. J. Hydraul. Div.* **85** (HY10): 53–79.

Eagleson, P. S., Dean, R. G., and Peralta, L. A. (1958). The mechanics of the motion of discrete spherical and bottom sediment particles due to shoaling waves. Beach Erosion Board. Tech. Memo 104.

Einstein, H. A. (1950). The bed-load function for sediment transport in open channel flows. U.S. Dept. Agriculture. Soil Conservation Service. Tech. Bull. 1026.

Engelund, F. and Hansen, E. (1967). A monograph on sediment transport in alluvial streams. *Teknisk Forlag, Copenhagen.*

Engelund, F. and Fredsoe, J. (1982). Sediment ripples and dunes. *Ann. Rev. Fluid Mech.* **14**: 13–37.

Fairchild, J. C. (1959). Suspended sediment sampling in laboratory wave action. Beach Erosion Board. Tech. Memo 115.

Fairchild, J. C. (1977). Suspended sediment in the littoral zone at Ventnor, New Jersey, and Nags Head, North Carolina. C.E.R.C. Tech. Pap. 77-5.

Garde, R. J. and Albertson, M. L. (1958). Discussion of "The total sediment load of streams" by E. M. Laursen. *Proc. A.S.C.E. J. Hydraul. Div.* **84** (HY6): 1856–59–64.

Goddet, J. (1960). Etude du début d'entraînement des matériaux mobiles sous l'action de la houle. *La Houille Blanche* **15**: 122–135.

Hallermeier, R. J. (1980). Sand motion initiation by water waves: two asymptotes. *Proc. A.S.C.E. J. Watrw. Port Coastal Ocean Div.* **106** (WW3): 299–318.

Hallermeier, R. J. (1982). Oscillatory bedload transport: data review and simple formulation. *Cont. Shelf Res.* **1** (2): 159–190.

Hammond, T. M. and Collins, M. B. (1979). On the threshold of transport of sand-sized sediment under the combined influence of unidirectional and oscillatory flow. *Sedimentology* **26**: 795–812.

Hashimoto, H. and Uda, T. (1979). Analysis of beach profile changes at Ajigaura by empirical eigenfunctions. *Coastal Eng. Jpn.* **22**: 47–57.

Hattori, M. (1969). The mechanics of suspended sediment due to wave action. *Proc. 13th Conf. IAHR Kyoto*, pp. 399–406.

Hattori, M. and Kawamata, R. (1980). Onshore-offshore transport and beach profile change. *Proc. 17th Conf. Coastal Eng. Sydney*, pp. 1175–1194.

Homma, M. and Horikawa, K. (1962). Suspended sediment due to wave action. *Proc. 8th Conf. Coastal Eng. Mexico*, pp. 168–193.

Homma, M. and Horikawa, K. (1963). A laboratory study on suspended sediment due to wave action. *Proc. 10th Cong. IAHR. London*, pp. 213–220.

Homma, M., Horikawa, K. and Kajima, R. (1965). A study on suspended sediment due to wave action. *Coastal Eng. Jpn.* **8**: 85–103.

Horikawa, K. and Watanabe, A. (1967). A study on sand movement due to wave action. *Coastal Eng. Jpn.* **10**: 39–57.

Horikawa, K. and Watanabe, A. (1970). Turbulence and sediment concentration due to wave. *Coastal Eng. Jpn.* **13**: 15–24.

Horikawa, K. and Watanabe, A. (1968). Laboratory study on oscillatory boundary layer flow. *Coastal Eng. Jpn.* **11**: 13–28.

Horikawa, K., Watanabe, A., and Katori, S. (1982). Sediment transport under sheet flow condition. *Proc. 18th Conf. Coastal Eng. Cape Town*.

Ichikawa, T., Ochiai, O., Tomita, K., and Murobuse, K. (1961). Waves and coastal sediment characteristics at Tagono-ura coast, Suruga Bay. *Proc. 8th Conf. Coastal Eng. Jpn.*, pp. 161–167. (in Japanese)

Ijima, T., Sato, S., Aono, H., and Ishii, K. (1960). Wave and coastal sediment characteristics at Fukue coast, Atsumi Bay. *Proc. 7th Conf. Coastal Eng. Jpn.*, pp. 69–79. (in Japanese)

Ijima, T., Sato, S. and Tanaka, N. (1964). On the coastal sediment at Kashima Harbour coast. *Proc. 11th Conf. Coastal Eng. Jpn.*, pp. 175–180. (in Japanese)

Inglis, C. C. (1968). Discussion of "Systematic evaluation of river regime," by C. R. Neill and V. J. Galey. *Proc. A.S.C.E. J. Waterw. Harbors Div.* **94** (WW1): 109–114.

Inman, D. L. (1955). Areal and seasonal variations in beach and nearshore sediments at La Jolla, California. Beach Erosion Board. Tech. Memo 39.

Inman, D. L. and Bagnold, R. A. (1963). Littoral processes. In *The Sea*, Vol. 3, M. N. Hill, Ed. Wiley-Interscience, New York, pp. 529–533.

Inman, D. L. and Bowen, A. J. (1962). Flume experiments on sand transport by waves and currents. *Proc. 8th Conf. Coastal Eng. Mexico*, pp. 137–150.

Ishihara, T. and Sawaragi, T. (1962). Laboratory studies on sand drift the critical velocity and the critical water depth for sand movement and the rate of transport under wave action. Fundamental studies on dynamics of sand drifts- Report 3. *Coastal Eng. Jpn.* **5**: 59–65.

Itakura, T. and Kishi, T. (1980). Open channel flow with suspended sediments. *Proc. A.S.C.E. J. Hydraul. Div.* **106** (HY8): 1325–1343.

Jonsson, I. G. (1966). Wave boundary layers and friction factors. *Proc. 10th Conf. Coastal Eng. Tokyo*, pp. 127–148.

Kachel, N. B. and Sternberg, R. W. (1971). Transport of bedload as ripples during an ebb current. *Mar. Geol.* **19**: 229–244.

Kajiura, K. (1968). A model of the bottom boundary layer in water waves. *Bull. Earthquake Res. Inst.* **16**: 75–123.

Kalinske, A. A. (1942). Criteria for determining sand transportation by surface creep and saltation. *Trans. A.G.U.*: 639–643.

Kalkanis, G. (1964). Transportation of bed material due to wave action. U.S. Army C.E.R.C. Tech. Memo 2.

Kamphuis, J. W. (1973). Sediment transport by waves over a flat bed. *Eng. Dyn. Coastal Zone, Sydney, Australia.*

Kamphuis, J. W. (1975). Friction factors under oscillatory waves. *Proc. A.S.C.E. J. Waterw. Harbors Coastal Eng. Div.* **101** (WW2): 135–144.

Kennedy, J. F. and Locher, F. A. (1972). Sediment suspension by water waves. In *Waves on Beaches*, R. E. Meyer, Ed. Academic Press, New York.

King, C. A. M. and Williams, W. W. (1949). The formation and movement of sand bars by wave action. *Geog. J.*: 70–85.

Kobayashi, N. (1982). Sediment transport on a gentle slope due to waves. *Proc. A.S.C.E. J. Waterw. Port Coastal Ocean Div.* **108** (WW3): 254–271.

Komar, P. D. and Inman, D. L. (1970). Longshore sand transport on beaches. *J. Geophys. Res.* **75** (30): 5914–5927.

Komar, P. D. and Miller, M. C. (1973). The threshold of sediment movement under oscillatory water waves. *J. Sed. Petrol.* **43**: 1101–1110.

Komar, P. D. and Miller, M. C. (1974). Sediment threshold under oscillatory waves. *Proc. 14th Conf. Coastal Eng. Copenhagen*, pp. 756–775.

Kruijt, J. A. (1976). On the influence of seepage on incipient motion and sand transport. Tech. Univ. Norway River Harbour Lab. Rep. STF 60.A76046.

Kurihara, M., Shinohara, K., Tsubaki, T. and Yoshioka, M. (1956). Sand movement on a sandy beach by wave action. *Proc. 3rd Conf. Coastal Eng. Jpn.* (in Japanese)

Larras, J. (1956). Effets de la houle et du clapotis sur les fonds de sable. IV Journ. Hydraul. Rep. 9. Paris.

Laursen, E. M. (1958). The total sediment load of streams. *Proc. A.S.C.E. J. Hydraul. Div.* **54** (HY1): 1–36.

Lenhoff, L. (1982). Incipient motion of sediment particles. *Proc. 18th Conf. Coastal Eng. Cape Town.*

Lhermitte, P. (1958). Contribution à l'étude de la couche limite des houles progressives. C.O.E.C. No. 136 Ministère de la Défense Nationale. Paris.

Macdonald, T. C. (1973). Sediment transport due to oscillatory waves. Univ. Calif. Hydraul. Eng. Lab. Tech. Rep. HEL-2-39.

MacDougall, C. H. (1933). Bed-sediment transportation in open channels. *Trans. A.G.U.* **14**: 491–495.

Madsen, O. S. (1974). Stability of a sand bed under breaking waves. *Proc. 14th Conf. Coastal Eng. Copenhagen*, pp. 776–794.

Madsen, O. S. and Grant, W. D. (1975). The threshold of sediment movement under oscillatory waves: a discussion. *J. Sed. Petrol.* **45**: 360–361.

Madsen, O. S. and Grant, W. D. (1976). Sediment transport in the coastal environment. M.I.T. Ralph M. Parsons Lab. Report 209.

Manohar, M. (1955). Mechanics of bottom sediment movement due to wave action. Beach Erosion Board. Tech. Memo 75.

Manohar, M. (1962). Discussion of "Laboratory determination of litteral transport rates," by R. P. Savage. *Proc. A.S.C.E. J. Waterw. Harbors Div.* **85** (WW4): 144–147.

Mantz, P. A. (1977). Incipient transport of fine grains and flakes by fluids: extended Shields diagram. *Proc. A.S.C.E. J. Hydraul. Div.* **103** (HY6): 601–615.

Martin, C. S. (1970). Effect of a porous sand bed on incipient sediment motion. *J. Water Resour.* **6** (4): 1162–1174.

Martin, C. S. and Aral, M. M. (1971). Seepage forces on interfacial bed particles. *Proc. A.S.C.E. J. Hydraul. Div.* **97** (HY7): 1081–1100.

Menard, H. W. (1950). Sediment movement in relation to current velocity. *J. Sed. Petrol.* **20** (3): 148–160.

Meyer-Peter, E. and Muller, R. (1948). Formulas for bed-load transport. *Proc. 2nd Cong. IAHR. Stockholm*, pp. 39–64.

Migniot, C. (1977). Action des courants, de la houle et du vent sur les sediments. *La Houille Blanche* **32** (1): 9–47.

Naheer, E. (1977). Stability of bottom armoring under the attack of solitary waves. Cal. Inst. Tech. W.M. Keck Lab. Rep. KH-R-34.

Nakato, T., Locher, F. A., Glover, J. R., and Kennedy, J. F. (1977). Wave entrainment of sediment from rippled beds. *Proc. A.S.C.E. J. Waterw. Port Coastal Ocean Div.* **103** (WW1): 83–99.

Natarajan, P. (1969). Sand movement by combined action of waves and currents. Ph.D. Thesis. University of London.

Nielsen, P. (1979). Some basic concepts of wave sediment transport. Inst. Of Hydrodynamics and Hydraulic Eng. Tech. Univ. Of Denmark. Series Paper 20.

O'Brien, M. P. and Rindlaub, B. D. (1934). The transportation of bed-load by streams. *Trans. A.G.U.* **15**: 593–603.

Oldenziel, D. M. and Brink, W. E. (1974). Influence of suction and blowing on entrainment of sand particles. *Proc. A.S.C.E. J. Hydraul. Div.* **100** (HY7): 935–950.

Owen, M. W. (1977). Problems in the modeling of transport, erosion, and deposition of cohesive sediments. In *The Sea*, Vol. 6, E. D. Goldberg, I. N. McCave, J. J. O'Brien, and J. H. Steele, Eds. Wiley, New York, pp. 515–537.

Rance, P. J. and Warren, N. F. (1968). The threshold of movement of coarse material in oscillatory flow. *Proc. 11th Conf. Coastal Eng. London*, pp. 487–491.

Rathbun, R. E. and Goswami, A. (1966). Discussion of "Sediment transportation mechanics: initiation of motion." Task committee on preparation of sedimentation manual. *Proc. A.S.C.E. J. Hydraul. Div.* **92** (HY6): 251–253.

Rouse, H. (1937). Modern conceptions of the mechanics of fluid turbulence. *Trans. A.S.C.E.* **102**: 463–543.

Rubey, W. W. (1933). Settling velocities of gravel sand and silt particles. *Am. J. Sci.* **25** (148): 325–338.

Sato, S. (1966). Coastal sediment. Summer seminar on Hydraulic Eng. *Jpn. Soc. Civil Eng.*: 19.1–19.29.

Sato, S., Ijima, T., and Tanaka, N. (1962). A study of critical depth and mode of sand movement using radioactive glass sand. *Proc. 8th Conf. Coastal Eng. Mexico*, pp. 304–323.

Sato, S. and Kishi, T. (1954). Shearing force on sea bed and movement of bed material due to wave motion. *J. Res. Public Works Res. Inst.* **1** (3): 1–11.

Savage, R. P. (1959). Laboratory study of the effect of groins on the rate of littoral transport: equipment development and initial tests. Beach Erosion Board. Tech. Memo 114.

Schoklitsch, A. (1934). Geschiebetrieb und die geschiebefracht. *Wasserkr. Wasserwirtsch.* **39** (4).

Seymour, R. J. and King, D. B. (1982). Field comparisons of cross-shore transport models. *Proc. A.S.C.E. J. Waterw. Port Coastal Ocean Div.* **108** (WW2): 163–179.

Shephard, F. P. (1950). Beach cycles in Southern California. Beach Erosion Board. Tech. Memo 20.

Shibayama, T. and Horikawa, K. (1980). Bed load measurements and prediction of two-dimensional beach transformation due to waves. *Coastal Eng. Jpn.* **23**: 179–190.

Shields, A. (1936). Anwendung der aehnlichkeitsmechanik und der turbulenz forschung auf die geschiebebewegung. *Mitt. Preuss. Versuchsanstalt Wasserbau Schiffbau. Berlin,* **26**.

Shinohara, K., Tsubaki, T., Yoshitaka, M., and Agemori, C. (1958). Sand transport along a model sandy beach by wave action. *Coastal Engineering Jpn.* **1**: 111–130.

Short, A. D. (1978). Wave power and beach stages: a global model. *Proc. 16th Conf. Coastal Eng. Hamburg,* pp. 1145–1162.

Silvester, R. and Mogridge, G. R. (1970). Reach of waves to the bed of the continental shelf. *Proc. 12th Conf. Coastal Eng. Washington,* pp. 487–491.

Sleath, J. F. A. (1978). Measurements of bed load in oscillatory flow. *Proc. A.S.C.E. J. Waterw. Port Coastal Ocean Eng. Div.* **104** (WW3): 291–307.

Sleath, J. F. A. (1982). The suspension of sand by waves. *J. Hydraul. Res.* **20**: 439–452.

Smith, J. D. (1977). Modeling of sediment transport on continental shelves. In *The Sea,* Vol. 6. E. D. Goldberg, I. N. McCave, J. J. O'Brien, and J. H. Steele, Eds. Wiley, New York, pp. 539–578.

Sternberg, R. W. and Larsen, L. H. (1975). Threshold of sediment movement by open ocean waves: observations. *Deep Sea Res.* **122**: 299–309.

Swart, D. H. (1976). Coastal sediment transport. Computation of longshore transport. Delft Hydraulics Lab. Report R968 (1).

Swart, D. H. (1977). Weighted value of depth of initiation of movement. Report NR10. Stellenbosch. South Africa.

Toffaletti, F. B. (1969). Definitive computation of sand discharge in rivers. *Proc. A.S.C.E. J. Hydraul. Div.* **95** (HY1): 225–248.

U.S. Waterways Experimental Station. (1935). Studies of river bed materials and their movement with special reference to the lower Mississippi river. USWES. Vicksburg. Paper 17.

Van de Graaff, J. and Van Overeem, J. (1979). Evaluation of sediment transport formulae in Coastal Engineering practice. *Coastal Eng.* **3**: 1–32.

Vanoni, V. A. (1946). Transportation of suspended sediment by water. *Trans. A.S.C.E.* **111**: 67–133.

Vincent, C. E., Young, R. A., and Swift, D. J. P. (1981). Bed-load transport under waves and currents. *Mar. Geol.* **39**: 71–80.

Vincent, G. E. (1957). Contribution to the study of sediment transport on a horizontal bed due to wave action. *Proc. 6th Conf. Coastal Eng. Miami,* pp. 326–355.

Wang, H. and Hwang, P. A. (1982). Suspended sediment in surf zone. *Proc. 18th Conf. Coastal Eng. Cape Town.*

Watters, G. Z. and Rao, M. V. P. (1971). Hydrodynamic effects of seepage on bed particles. *Proc. A.S.C.E. J. Hydraul. Div.* **97** (HY3): 421–439.

Wells, D. R. (1967). Beach equilibrium and second-order wave theory. *J. Geophys. Res.* **72** (2): 497–504.

White, C. M. (1940). The equilibrium of grains on the bed of a stream. *Proc. Roy. Soc. Ser. A.* **174** (958): 322–338.

White, W. R., Milli, H., and Crabbe, A. D. (1975). Sediment transport theories: a review. *Proc. Inst. Civil Eng.* **59** (2): 265–292.

Willetts, B. B. and Drossos, M. E. (1975). Local erosion caused by rapid forced infiltration. *Proc. A.S.C.E. J. Hydraul. Div.* **101** (HY12): 1477–1488.

Willis, D. H. (1978). Sediment load under waves and currents. *Proc. 16th Conf. Coastal Eng. Hamburg*, pp. 1626–1637.

Yalin, M. S. (1963). An expression for bed load transportation. *Proc. A.S.C.E. J. Hydraul. Div.* **89** (HY3): 221–250.

Yang, C. T. (1979). Unit stream power equations for total load. *J. Hydrol.* **40**: 123–138.

Yang, C. T. and Molinas, A. (1982). Sediment transport and unit stream power function. *Proc. A.S.C.E. J. Hydraul. Div.* **108** (HY6): 774–793.

Zenkovitch, V. P. (1960). Fluorescent substances as tracers for studying the movement of sand on the sea bed. *Dock and Harbour Auth.* **40**: 280–283.

AUTHOR INDEX

SUBJECT INDEX